THE HEIDELBERG DIARY

DAILY DEVOTIONS ON THE
HEIDELBERG CATECHISM

THE HEIDELBERG DIARY

DAILY DEVOTIONS ON THE HEIDELBERG CATECHISM

WILLEM J. OUWENEEL

PAIDEIA PRESS
2016

ISBN 978-0-88815-190-2

A Publication of the
Reformational Publishing Project
www.refpubproject.com

DEDICATION

For advancing the international

and intergenerational

blessing of

The Heidelberg Catechism

for the faith-life of God's people,

The Heidelberg Diary

is dedicated

to the nurturing of believers and their children

today and in coming generations

Prof. Dr. Willem J. Ouweneel (1944) has Ph.D. degrees in the natural sciences (Utrecht University, Netherlands, 1970), in philosophy (Free University Amsterdam, Netherlands, 1986), and in theology (University of the Orange Free State, Bloemfontein, South Africa, 1993). He was professor of dogmatic theology from 1995 to 2004 (Evangelical Theological Faculty, Leuven, Belgium). He has written numerous books in the fields of the Bible, science, and theology, mostly in Dutch. In English he has published, among other books, *What Then Is Theology?*, *The Ninth King*, and his Eternity trilogy about Reformed theology: *The Eternal Torah*, *The Eternal Covenant*, and *Eternal Righteousness* (forthcoming).

WHAT MUST BE SAID FIRST

In this book we will embark upon a very special adventure. I will introduce to you one of the most influential guides on Christian doctrine that Protestant Christianity has ever seen. It is called the Heidelberg Catechism (HC), because it was drafted in the city of Heidelberg, and officially adopted on January 19, 1563. This German city, on the banks of the Neckar River, was once the capital of one of the most important of the many independent regions into which the German ("Holy Roman") Empire was divided at the time. The Germans call this region the Pfalz; English-speaking people call it the Palatinate. (The name comes from the Latin *Palatinum*, an adjective derived from *palatium*, from which the English word *palace* was derived.) The land was so important because it was one of only seven lands whose rulers elected the Holy Roman Emperor. Therefore, these rulers were called prince-electors (German: Kurfürsten).

At the time, the land was ruled by elector Count Frederick III of the Palatinate (1515–1576), whose nickname was "the Pious." He was a convinced adherent of the Reformation, which Martin Luther had started in Wittenberg, two years after Frederick's birth, and promoted Protestantism in his land as much as possible. Unfortunately, Protestantism had already been divided into Lutherans (who followed Luther) and Calvinists (who followed John Calvin, the Reformer of Geneva), who disagreed on some important issues, such as the Lord's Supper.

The Calvinists were usually referred to as "Reformed." (So you see, the Lutherans were Reformational, but not Reformed.) Frederick chose the side of the Reformed. But please remember that on all the principal issues of the Christian faith, the Lutherans and the Reformed wholeheartedly agreed! In order to help his subjects to understand the Christian faith as Protestants interpreted it, Frederick made a plan. Heidelberg had a university, which of course had a theological faculty. This was now in the hands of the Protestants. Frederick asked the professors, especially one named Zacharias Ursinus, to develop a kind of course in which the main elements of the Christian faith were to be explained. Such a doctrinal summary was called a catechism, from a Greek verb meaning "to teach orally." Cathechesis was the age-old term for religious teaching of children and of adult converts. A catechism usually has the form of a series of questions on religious subjects, followed by the answers. Often, the pupils were required to learn both the questions and the answers by heart.

It is fascinating to see how young the professors were whom Count Frederick asked to draft a new catechism. At the time of the request, Zacharias Ursinus (1534–1583) was only about 27. His main co-worker, Caspar Olevianus (1536–1587), preacher to Frederick's court, was at the time only 25. Imagine! Today, a theologian is only just beginning his academic career at such an age. As a comparison, remember that John Calvin wrote the first version of his *Institutes of the Christian Religion* when he was only 26! Well, you know, these people died much earlier on average than we do (Luther was only 62 when he died, Calvin 54, Olevianus 50, and Ursinus only 48). So I suppose God gave them the grace to make early starts!

The HC was not the first Protestant Catechism. Luther's Large Catechism dates from 1529, and Calvin's Genevan Catechism (first version) from 1541. As I said, we should not exaggerate the differences between the two traditions. After all, the Reformed Ursinus was a pupil and friend of Luther's most influential colleague and fellow-thinker, Philipp Melanchthon (1497–1560). However, in drafting the HC, Ursinus and Olevianus relied more on the Genevan Catechism, and also on the simple catechism written by the Polish Reformer John à Lasco (1499–1560).

The well-known Westminster Larger and Shorter Catechisms date from a much later time (about 1647), and are much more extensive, including a number of theological ideas that at the time of the HC had hardly been developed. In my opinion, the HC therefore stands closer to scriptural language than the Westminster Catechisms; it is also simpler and more concise. At any rate, I would hardly know a catechism that I would recommend more to Evangelical readers than the HC. (I mention this because I prefer to call myself an Evangelical, having decended from about fifteen thousand Dutch Reformed ancestors.)

As far as my own country is concerned, the HC was brought from Heidelberg to the Netherlands by pastor Peter Dathenus (c. 1531–1588), who was one of the leading theologians in the Dutch-speaking world at the time. The Provincial Synod of the Dutch city of Alkmaar (1573) required that, in all churches in the afternoon service, a sermon on a subject from the HC was to be preached, an example that was followed by the other Dutch provinces. In 1586, the HC was accepted by the National Synod of The Hague. The famous Synod of Dort (i.e., Dordrecht, the Netherlands) of 1618–19 reviewed the HC, and prescribed it for all professors, pastors, elders, and deacons in the Dutch Reformed Church. Dutch Reformed immigrants took the HC with them to the English-speaking world.

Of course, the HC is not inspired like the Bible is. It is a piece of fallible human writing — and yet, one is amazed at what a masterpiece it is! Written so shortly after the Reformation! I know of hardly any academic theological expert who would agree with every single detail of it, but what does that matter? Of course, we miss certain elements that, if the Catechism were written today, would probably be included, such as the place of Israel, more details on the work of the Holy Spirit in the believer, and more details on the meaning of the Kingdom of God in believers' practical life. But remember, this is a "student textbook." It was drafted to teach children and newly converted Christians. If we would have more details about this or that, the textbook could easily become too long.

The HC contains three parts (Misery, Deliverance, and Gratitude); I discern sixteen subjects in it, varying from the *Introduction* to *The Lord's Prayer*. The subject matter is divided into fifty-two Lord's Days (Lord's Day 1 to Lord's Day 52), so that the pastor can preach on the Catechism for a whole year, and then start again if he so wishes. And there are a total of one hundred twenty-nine questions and answers (Q&A 1 to Q&A 129). I have distributed the entire contents over three hundred and sixty-five days, so that the reader can use the book as a devotional and go through it for an entire year. On some Q&As I will dwell for just one day, on others for as many as five days. I wish my readers God's richest blessing as they move from Day 1 to Day 365. How great it would be if parents would study this book with their children! After all, the HC was intended for the youngsters in Christian families in the first place.

Remember: my aim is not (teaching) the HC as such, but my aim is the same as that of the HC itself: to bring the reader closer to Scripture. And even that is not my final aim (or that of the HC, for that matter): my desire is that the reader may be brought closer to the God of Scripture, and to his only Son: Jesus Christ.

I thank Dr. Nelson D. Kloosterman very warmly for his expert editorial work on the manuscript of this book. And I am deeply thankful to my publisher, John Hultink, for encouraging me to undertake this project.

Willem J. Ouweneel
Completed in Cwm Cywarch (Dinas Mawddwy, Wales, UK)
July 18, 2015

※ ※ ※

P.S. In this book, I use the ESV (English Standard Version), unless I indicate differently. For the HC, I use the version of the Christian Reformed Church of North America (www.crcna.org/welcome/beliefs/confessions/heidelberg-catechism). For an older, and more literal translation of the HC see www.reformed.org/documents/index.html?mainframe=http://www.reformed.org/documents/heidelberg.html.

P.P.S. If the text of this devotional is read aloud, I recommend not reading aloud the Scripture references that are mentioned within parentheses. It is cumbersome to listen to them. They are intended for private further study only.

P.P.P.S. If you love languages, this is how Q&A 1 read in the original languages: Latin and (old) German (followed by the oldest Dutch edition and an older English edition):

Quaestio 1. Quae est unica tua consolatio in vita et in morte?
Responsio. Quod animo pariter et corpore, sive vivam, sive moriar, non meus, sed fidissimi Domini et servatoris mei Iesu Christo sum proprius, qui pretioso sanguine suo, pro omnibus peccatis plenissime satisfaciens, me ab omni potestate diaboli liberavit . . .

1. Frage. Was ist dein einiger trost in leben vnd in sterben?
Antwort. Das ich mit Leib vnd Seel, beyde in leben vnd in sterben nicht mein, sonder meines getrewen Heilands Jesu Christi eigen bin, der mit seinem thewren blut, für alle meine sünden volkomlich bezalet, vnd mich auß allem gewalt des Teuffels erlöset hat . . .

1. Vraag. Welke is uw eenige troost, beide in het leven en sterven?
Antwoord. Dat ik met lichaam en ziel, beide in het leven en sterven, niet mijn, maar mijns getrouwen Zaligmakers Jezus Christus eigen ben, die met zijn dierbaar bloed voor al mijne zonden volkomen betaald en mij uit alle heerschappij des duivels verlost heeft . . .

Question 1. What is thy only comfort in life and death?

Answer. That I with body and soul, both in life and death, am not my own, but belong unto my faithful Savior Jesus Christ; who, with his precious blood, has fully satisfied for all my sins, and delivered me from all the power of the devil. . . .

Abbreviations of Bible Versions Used

AMP   Amplified Bible
ASV   American Standard Version
BRG   BRG Bible
CEB   Common English Bible
CEV   Contemporary English Version
CJB   Complete Jewish Bible
DLNT Disciples' Literal New Testament
ERV   Easy-to-Read Version
ESV   English Standard Version
EXB   Expanded Bible
ISV   International Standard Version
GNV   1599 Geneva Bible
GW   God's Word translation
JUB   Jubilee Bible 2000
LEB   Lexham English Bible
MSG   The Message
NIV   New International Version
NKJV New King James Version
NLT   New Living Translation
NLV   New Life Version
NOG   Names of God Bible
TLB   Living Bible
WYC   Wycliffe Bible
YLT   Young's Literal Translation

DAY 1 – MY ONLY COMFORT
(Lord's Day 1, Q&A 1, part 1)

Q. What is your only comfort in life and in death?
A. That I am not my own, but belong—body and soul, in life and in death—to my faithful Savior, Jesus Christ.

What a tremendous start for the Catechism! We do not plunge into all kinds of complicated theological subjects right away, but first we are asked a very personal and very practical question. "Your" is not plural here, but singular. You, man or woman, boy or girl, what is your comfort? Whatever your circumstances are, whatever your sins may be, but also whatever your health condition, or your social or economic circumstances, may be, where do you find any comfort, the consolation that keeps you going? We need comfort when we are mourning, when we feel miserable, when we are crying. No human being can go through life without crying once in a while. When you do, you need comfort. You may have good people around you who offer words of consolation. But where do you find a comfort that is really effective, not only in this life, but also in death—and even beyond?

The answer is striking. I am not on my own. Or more strongly: I am *not my own*. I belong to someone who is the greatest possible blessing, not only for my soul but even for my body; not only when I am going to die but also during my entire life here on earth.

Notice that the "I" who answers here speaks as a believer. This is almost always the case in the Catechism. This is not a gospel book to attract outsiders (although they *may* be attracted by it when reading it) but to instruct believers, especially young believers. The Catechism takes for granted that the children of believers who faithfully serve the Lord are believers themselves. At the youngest possible age, they may learn what it is to belong not to oneself, nor to one's parents, but to Jesus Christ.

Also notice that the text does not say something like "Jesus is mine," although that is certainly true. It says instead, "I belong to *Jesus*." I am his servant. He is my Savior, that is, he saved me first, and now I serve him. The bride in the Song of Solomon begins by saying, "My beloved is mine, and I am his" (2:16; cf. 6:2), but later she says, "I am my beloved's, and his desire is for me" (7:10). What is greater for a believer than to say this?

❖   ✦   ❖

DAY 2 – HE DELIVERED ME FROM SIN AND DEVIL
(LORD'S DAY 1, Q&A 1, PART 2)

A. . . . He has fully paid for all my sins with his precious blood, and has set me free from the tyranny of the devil.

After the believer has said that he belongs to his faithful Savior Jesus Christ, he tells us how he came to belong to him. By nature, none of us has such a relationship with Jesus Christ. Originally, we were all his enemies. What has happened that we now do belong to him, that we are his servants and followers? What did we do in order to enter into such a relationship? The answer is: Nothing. The only thing we contributed—if you can say it that way—was our sins, and then—thank God—our faith. Jesus himself did everything. This was already alluded to in his title "Savior," that is, the One who saved us.

The next questions follow logically from this: from what did he save us, and how did he save us from these evils? Of course, later in the Catechism, all such questions are dealt with extensively. But already here, the answers are neatly summarized. Jesus saved us from two powers: sin and the devil. As a third power, death could also have been mentioned. The text alludes to 1 Peter 1:18–19, "[Y]ou were ransomed . . . with the precious blood of Christ, like that of a lamb without blemish or spot." A costly price was paid so that our sins could be blotted out forever (cf. 1 Cor. 6:20; Rev. 5:9).

Moreover, Jesus has set me free from the tyranny of the devil. John says, "[T]he Son of God appeared . . . to destroy the works of the devil" (1 John 3:8). It is God's plan that people "may turn from darkness to light and from the power of Satan to God" (Acts 26:18). Through his death, Jesus destroyed "one who has the power of death, that is, the devil" (Heb. 2:14). In this last verse, death is mentioned as well: Jesus is "our Savior, . . . who abolished death and brought life and immortality to light through the gospel" (2 Tim. 1:10).

What a terrific start for this Catechism! It presents to us right away the surpassingly important Man who is described in it, Jesus Christ, the Son of God, as well as his wonderful work of redemption. He gave his blood, that is, his life, and in this way, he set me free from sin and the devil. By dying he delivered me from death! No wonder I feel comforted.

✦   ✦   ✦

DAY 3 – HE WATCHES OVER ME
(LORD'S DAY 1, Q&A 1, PART 3)

A. . . . He also watches over me in such a way that not a hair can fall from my head without the will of my Father in heaven; in fact, all things must work together for my salvation.

Jesus not only delivered me from the power of sin, the devil, and death. Jesus not only makes sure that one day, I will enter into everlasting blessedness. He also watches over me as long as I am still on this earth. He keeps me and guides me in every way. The text illustrates this by comparing two sayings that Jesus himself has spoken. One is from Matthew 10:29, "Are not two sparrows sold for a penny? And not one of them will fall to the ground apart from your Father." The other saying is from Luke 21:18, "[N]ot a hair of your head will perish." Here, God the Father is introduced for the first time in the Catechism. Jesus the Son watches over me, the Father protects me, and we may add, the Holy Spirit guides me (John 16:13). The Triune God is on my side!

Not a hair can fall from my head "without the will of my Father." The text in Matthew is a bit more careful by saying, "without your Father" (KJV). That is, I am not always sure whether a certain evil befalls me because my Father wants it. But I am definitely sure that no evil can befall me apart from my Father. In some way or another, he is always involved. I am not always sure whether it is he who causes me to go through a dark valley, but the least I can say is that he is always at my side in such a valley (Ps. 23:4).

The difficult things in my life—even if they are sometimes caused by the devil (Mark 1:13; Luke 13:16; 22:31; 2 Cor. 12:7)—are always part of God's ways with me here on earth. The text alludes to the following saying of the apostle Paul: "[W]e know that for those who love God all things work together for good, for those who are called according to his purpose" (Rom. 8:28). Whatever things happen to us in life, they can never come as a surprise to God. On the contrary, he uses them to reach the great goal of our earthly life, namely, to worship God and to become more and more conformed to the image of Christ (v. 29). Nothing in my life is in vain, nothing is fortuitous. That, too, is a terrific comfort: I am always in the hands of him who guides and steers my entire life!

✦   ✦   ✦

DAY 4 – HE GIVES ME ASSURANCE
(Lord's Day 1, Q&A 1, part 4)

A. . . . Because I belong to him, Christ, by his Holy Spirit, assures me of eternal life.

With a view to the future, the Catechism tells us that Christ by his Holy Spirit assures us of eternal life. The Word of God tells us that whoever believes in his Son will not perish but have eternal life (John 3:15–16). That is a general promise. By the Holy Spirit Jesus assures me that I have eternal life on account of faith in him: "The Spirit himself bears witness with our spirit that we are children of God" (Rom. 8:16). When he was still on earth, Jesus himself made this firm promise: "My sheep hear my voice . . . I give them eternal life, and they will never perish, and no one will snatch them out of my hand . . . no one is able to snatch them out of the Father's hand" (John 10:27–29). This makes our comfort even greater: Jesus gives his followers eternal life, and no power in the universe can snatch them out of his hand, or out of the Father's hand.

John likes to speak of eternal life as a present possession: when you believe, you already have it. This is because John emphasizes that Jesus himself is our life: "God gave us eternal life, and this life is in his Son. Whoever has the Son has life" (1 John 5:11–12). Paul rather speaks of eternal life as something to look forward to: "[N]ow that you have been set free from sin . . . the fruit you get leads to sanctification and its end, eternal life" (Rom. 6:22). At the same time, to him eternal life is something we can in faith claim already now: "Take hold of the eternal life to which you were called" (1 Tim. 6:12). It is something that lies ahead of us, but to some extent we can already enjoy it now. It is the future bliss that lies ahead of us, not just in heaven but in connection with the Kingdom of God (cf. Dan. 12:2; Matt. 19:16, 29; 25:46).

Notice the word "assure": what power can take from us what the Son of God himself assures to us? "I am sure that neither death nor life, nor angels nor rulers, nor things present nor things to come, nor powers, nor height nor depth, nor anything else in all creation, will be able to separate us from the love of God in Christ Jesus our Lord" (Rom. 8:38–39).

✳ ✳ ✳

DAY 5 – I WISH TO LIVE FOR HIM
(LORD'S DAY 1, Q&A 1, PART 5)

A. . . . *and makes me wholeheartedly willing and ready from now on to live for him.*

The first answer given in the Catechism ends with a note about our devotion and consecration to Christ. Too many Christians are too much occupied with their final destination: heaven. This means they are too little focused on the purpose that God has for their present life on earth, already now. Christianity is not just about heaven or hell. It is first and foremost about the question: For whom are you living—here on earth? Later in the Catechism we will see that we do not believe in Jesus just as Savior, but also as Lord. These two titles of his are inseparable. You have a Savior to take you to heaven; you have a Lord to take you through this world. He is in charge. As the apostle Paul says, Christ "died for all, that those who live might no longer live for themselves but for him who for their sake died and was raised" (2 Cor. 5:15). And elsewhere: "For if we live, we live to the Lord, and if we die, we die to the Lord. So then, whether we live or whether we die, we are the Lord's" (Rom. 14:8).

To be sure, serving the Lord is a divine obligation. We have been placed under the "law of Christ" (1 Cor. 9:21; Gal. 6:2). But it is much more than that: we serve him not simply because we must, but because—as the text says—we have been made "wholeheartedly willing and ready" to serve him. Believers have a renewed heart, which *loves* to serve the Lord because it loves *him*. As Jesus said himself: "If you love me, you will keep my commandments. . . . Whoever has my commandments and keeps them, he it is who loves me" (John 14:15, 21). So, Jesus' commandments are kept because of love for him. Therefore, the law of Christ is a "law of liberty" (James 1:25; 2:12) because we obey this law out of our own free will. It does not conflict with our liberty at all. On the contrary, this law demands of us precisely what our renewed hearts by the Holy Spirit desire most of all: serving our Lord, living for him. Perhaps this is a nice way of describing all subsequent questions and answers in the Catechism: they aim at helping us to (better) learn how to worship God and how to live for Christ.

✳   ✳   ✳

DAY 6 – WHAT MUST WE KNOW?
(Lord's Day 1, Q&A 2, part 1)

Q. What must you know to live and die in the joy of this comfort?
A. Three things.

Some Christians know very much about God, about Christ, and about their salvation, and others know very little. Perhaps some know as little as this: "One thing I do know, that though I was blind, now I see" (John 9:26). Some people misunderstand the apostle Paul and say, "I know nothing except Jesus Christ and him crucified" (cf. 1 Cor. 2:2)—as if Paul did not know much more than that! He only knew this little when he addressed the Corinthian pagans. Others think of another word by Paul: "[I]f you confess with your mouth that Jesus is Lord and believe in your heart that God raised him from the dead, you will be saved" (Rom. 10:9). So that's enough; what more do we need to be saved?

Now I don't think that it is okay when some people almost seem to be proud that they know only a minimal part of God's gospel. If they would really love the Lord, they would also love his Word, and have an eager desire to know him and his Word in an ever deeper way. Yet, it is fair to ask the question: What *is* this minimum that we need to know to live and die in the joy of the gospel's comfort? This "knowing" is not just knowing with your brains but knowing with your heart. It is the knowledge of *faith* that the Catechism is speaking about.

Notice how beautiful it is that the text speaks of the *joy* of this comfort. We not only need to know *that* we are saved, but we desire to live and die in the *joy* of this knowledge. After David had sinned terribly, this was one of the things that he missed and that he prayed for: "Restore to me the *joy* of your salvation" (Ps. 51:12), that is, the joy of the salvation you gave me.

The Catechism tells us that, whether you know much or little about God and his Word, this is the very minimum you have to know in order to be saved. First, you have to realize that you *need* to be saved because you are a prisoner of the power of sin, death, and the devil. Second, you have to know the *way out* of this spiritual captivity. Third, you have to learn how to live once you have received your salvation. That's what the Catechism will work out in all the following answers!

✢   ✢   ✢

DAY 7 – MY MISERY AND MY DELIVERANCE

(Lord's Day 1, Q&A 2, part 2)

A. . . . first, how great my sin and misery are; second, how I am set free from all my sins and misery.

If a person flatly denies that he has a health problem, you can hardly convince him to see a doctor. If a person flatly denies that he is a sinner, you can hardly convince him that he needs deliverance from sin. Most people will readily admit that they do wrong things once in a while, but that is not enough. Apparently, they have not the slightest idea "how great their sin and misery are." We do not just do wrong things—we *are* wrong from head to toe.

To be sure, in the literal sense none us really knows how *great* his or her sin and misery are. Only at the judgment seat of Christ we will fully realize how much we have been forgiven (cf. 1 Cor. 13:12b), and we will never love the Lord more for it than at that moment (cf. Luke 7:47). However, already now we need to realize to some extent what it is to experience by nature the misery of sin. We know this from the Bible, but also from our own practical experience.

Please note that the Catechism does not say that we have to learn these three things (misery, deliverance, gratitude) in this very order. Peter was a disciple of Jesus almost from the start (John 1:35–42). I suppose he was simply attracted by the greatness of Jesus. It was only some time later that he exclaimed to Jesus: "Depart from me, for I am a sinful man, O Lord" (Luke 5:8). Sooner or later you have to find out that your sins cause a separation between you and Jesus (cf. Isa. 59:2). You love him as your Master, but you discover soon that you also need him as your Savior. If you want to share Jesus' eternal bliss, you cannot get around the need of forgiveness and deliverance. In many encounters that Jesus had with so many different people, the problem of sin came up pretty soon (e.g., Matt. 9:1–2; John 3:6a; 4:16–18; 5:14; 8:11; also see Luke 15:18, 21; 18:13).

This is the conclusion: you cannot live and die in the joy of the comfort of belonging to Jesus if you do not see that you are a sinner, and that you cannot be saved without confessing your sins to God and accepting Jesus as your Savior. The Catechism will have much more to say on this!

✳   ✳   ✳

DAY 8 – TRUE GRATITUDE
(Lord's Day 1, Q&A 2, part 3)

A. . . . third, how I am to thank God for such deliverance.

If you look at the matter in a superficial way, you might argue that, if you acknowledge that you are a sinner, and you confess your sins to God, that will be quite enough: "If we confess our sins, [God] is faithful and just to forgive us our sins and to cleanse us from all unrighteousness" (1 John 1:9). However, the Catechism adds an important point: if you want to live and die in the *joy* of the comfort of belonging to Jesus you must learn to become a "thanksgiver," a worshipper. After Jesus had healed ten lepers, he complained: "Were not ten cleansed? Where are the nine? Was no one found to return and give praise to God except this foreigner?" (Luke 17:17–18). This foreigner was a Samaritan. He understood better that many Jews in those days—and many Christians in our day—what gratitude is.

In the rest of the Catechism, it will become clear that this gratitude does not entail just saying "Thank you" to God. True Christian gratitude encompasses our entire Christian life. For instance, you cannot ask God for forgiveness, and then keep living in sin as if nothing has happened. "[H]e who confesses [his transgressions] *and forsakes them* will obtain mercy" (Prov. 28:13). Therefore Paul says, "Do not present your members to sin as instruments for unrighteousness, but present yourselves to God as those who have been brought from death to life, and your members to God as instruments for righteousness" (Rom. 6:13). Living in gratitude is living no longer under the power of sin but under the authority of the Lord Jesus and of the Holy Spirit (cf. Matt. 5:16; Eph. 5:8–10).

Please note that this is not just a life of continually trying to avoid sin. That would be negative. No, Christian living is very positive: it is living in an attitude of praise and worship, of dedication to God, of consecrating our lives to Jesus. The *joy* of our comfort involves not just the joy of our forgiveness and deliverance—it involves the joy for serving *this* wonderful God and Father, and following *this* wonderful Lord and Master. The Catechism will come back to this extensively.

✦ ✦ ✦

DAY 9 – KNOWING YOUR MISERY
(Lord's Day 2, Q&A 3, part 1)

Q. How do you come to know your misery?
A. The law of God tells me.

The Catechism now comes to its first great subject: the misery that people experience by nature as a consequence of sin. The question is asked: How do you know your misery; that is, How do you know that you are a miserable sinner? The answer is: The law of God tells me. Of course that is not the *entire* answer. We should never forget that the Catechism is very concise and does not tell us everything about a subject. On the one hand, there are people who have never heard of the Sinaitic law, and yet do realize that they are sinners: "For all who have sinned without the law will also perish without the law, and all who have sinned under the law will be judged by the law. . . . For when Gentiles, who do not have the law, by nature do what the law requires, they are a law to themselves" (Rom. 2:12, 14).

On the other hand, there are people who do know the Sinaitic law, and yet do not at all understand from it that they are sinners. This is because they deceive themselves, or they are hypocrites, or they simply are very decent people. Think of what the apostle Paul could write, years after his conversion: "If anyone else thinks he has reason for confidence in the flesh, I have more: . . . as to righteousness under the law, [I was] blameless" (Phil. 3:4, 6b). You know that the law is compared to a mirror (James 1:23–25). Looking into this mirror, Paul could say, somewhat like the Wicked Queen in *Snow White*: "Magic mirror on the wall, who is the most righteous one of all?" And the mirror would answer: "You are the most righteous of them all!" Inspired by God's Spirit, he said of himself: I was blameless!

So how *did* Paul come to know his misery after all? By meeting Jesus Christ on the road to Damascus! In the eyes of Jesus he saw his own misery. *Then* he began to realize that he was the foremost of all sinners (1 Tim. 1:15). And *then* he took a second look at the law of God—and discovered that all his misery in fact had been described there already! Later, he could write: "[T]hrough the law comes knowledge of sin" (Rom. 3:20; cf. 7:7).

❖   ❖   ❖

DAY 10 – THE LAW OF GOD (I)
(Lord's Day 2, Q&A 3, part 2)

A. The law of God tells me.

Yesterday we learned that, if the Holy Spirit does not come to open our eyes to the truth, even the law of God will never be able to show us what and who we really are. Blessed are we if the Spirit has come to us! It's all there in God's law—but we need eyes to see it! Many Pharisees were hypocrites. They had the audacity to ask Jesus: "Are we also blind?" Jesus said to them, "If you were blind, you would have no guilt; but now that you say, 'We see,' your guilt remains" (John 9:40–41). These people could not be helped. How do you get someone to an ophthalmologist if he firmly believes that he has no eye problem? As the Lord said at another occasion: "Those who are well have no need of a physician, but those who are sick" (Matt. 9:12).

In fact, the law of God has two very different purposes, which are both dealt with in the Catechism. First, there is the negative purpose, and this is to show to sinners that they *are* indeed sinners. As Paul puts it: "[I]f it had not been for the law, I would not have known sin. For I would not have known what it is to covet if the law had not said, 'You shall not covet.' But sin, seizing an opportunity through the commandment, produced in me all kinds of covetousness" (Rom. 7:7–8). In two days, we will look at the very positive purpose of the law.

You always have to pay attention whether in a certain passage the positive or the negative purpose of the law is meant. For instance, look at this passage: "[W]e know that the law is good, if one uses it lawfully, understanding this, that the law is not laid down for the just but for the lawless and disobedient, for the ungodly and sinners, for the unholy and profane, for those who strike their fathers and mothers, for murderers, the sexually immoral, men who practice homosexuality, enslavers, liars, perjurers" (1 Tim. 1:8–11). Here, Paul speaks as if the law has *only* a negative purpose: the law is not for the just, but for the wicked! *This* is the meaning the Catechism refers to at present: the law as a mirror in which the lawless, the ungodly, and the unholy can see who they really are.

✦   ✦   ✦

DAY 11 – THE LAW OF GOD (II)
(Lord's Day 2, Q&A 3, part 3)

A. The law of God tells me.

Yesterday we saw that the law of God has two very different purposes, which are both dealt with in the Catechism. First, there is the negative purpose, and this is to show to sinners that indeed they *are* sinners. However, there is also a very positive purpose of the law, which is worked out extensively in Lord's Days 34–44 of the Catechism. It is good to consider already now these two sides of God's law. Scripture makes very clear that New Testament believers are under the law of Christ (1 Cor. 9:21; Gal. 6:2). Paul said, "Owe no one anything, except to love each other, for the one who loves another has fulfilled the law. For the commandments . . . are summed up in this word: 'You shall love your neighbor as yourself.' Love does no wrong to a neighbor; therefore love is the fulfilling of the law" (Rom. 13:8–10). Jesus said, "If you love me, you will keep my commandments. . . . Whoever has my commandments and keeps them, he it is who loves me" (John 14:15, 21; cf. 15:10–17).

We will come back to this later; now we will limit our attention to the first purpose of the law: it is a mirror to show us our sinfulness. Please remember that God is the Judge of all people. In the end, it does not matter how people feel about themselves but how God feels about them. We are sinners not only because we experience we are. No, it is *his* criteria that count. Therefore God gave mankind his law. God says, "You shall not do this"—and we realize that this is exactly what our sinful nature would love to do. God says, "You shall do that"—and we realize that our sinful nature does not at all like to do that. This is what God's law shows us. And the better you see it, the better you will realize how blessed we are that God has delivered us from the power of this sinful nature through the person and the work of the Lord Jesus!

James knows the law in a very positive sense: as the "law of liberty" (1:25; 2:12) and the "royal law" (2:8). But he also knows the law as that which convicts us as transgressors (2:9; cf. v. 11; 4:11–12). The law is a stick to support those who walk with it—but it is also a stick to smite sinners.

✤ ✤ ✤

DAY 12 – GOD'S REQUIREMENTS
(Lord's Day 2, Q&A 4, part 1)

Q. What does God's law require of us?
A. Christ teaches us this in summary in Matthew 22:37–40.

God is the Creator, and we are his creatures. As such, there will always be commandments standing between the Master and his servants. Even in eternity, we will still be called God's servants (literally, slaves) (Rev. 22:3). If Paul says that we are not "under law but under grace" (Rom. 6:14), the context makes clear that he means we are not under legalism, a system under which you have to earn heaven by your own merit. The same Paul tells us that believers are under the law of Christ (1 Cor. 9:21; Gal. 6:2), under the commandments of God (Rom. 13:8–10; 1 Cor. 7:19).

These commandments are like the manual that you get when you purchase some technical apparatus. It tells you what is the most profitable way to use this apparatus. God's law is like such a manual, telling you what is the best way to function as a creature in this world. If you look at the matter from this perspective, you will understand that God's law is actually a gift of love. God's law is "your very life," says Moses (Deut. 32:47). Even in eternity, God will keep requiring from us, but it will always be out of love.

The content of God's law is precisely the same: it is the principle of love. God does not so much require of us that we *do* this or that, or *not do* this or that. No, first and foremost he is interested in the attitude of our *hearts*. The father tells his child, "My son [or daughter], give me your heart" (Prov. 23:26). Of course it is important what we do or don't do. But more important than that is the true inclination of our hearts, the mentality with which we do or don't do certain things. That attitude, that inclination, that mentality is summarized in this one word: love. We humans have been created in such a way that we are able to receive God's love, and to return love to God, and also love our fellow humans. I know, sin has come in, and has spoiled everything. Hatred almost seems to be more common than love. But that does not alter God's requirements. He keeps telling us: May your heart be opened to my love, and return that love to me, and pass it on to others.

✳   ✳   ✳

DAY 13 – LOVE GOD!
(LORD'S DAY 2, Q&A 4, PART 2)

A. . . . "'You shall love the Lord your God with all your heart, and with all your soul, and with all your mind.' This is the greatest and first commandment.

If you were asked to summarize the entire law of God, would you have answered that love is its essence? In fact, it is quite surprising to see how Jesus did summarize the law in Matthew 22. Yet, it was not altogether new: some Jewish rabbis had done the same. One Jewish tradition says, "All that you do, do only out of love." In this love, there is, so to speak, a vertical and a horizontal dimension. Love God—that is vertical. Love your neighbor—that is horizontal. Love toward God comes first, of course. All the love that you may have for your fellow humans is worthless if you do not love God. And if you do love God, you do this with everything you are and have: heart, soul, and mind (cf. Deut. 6:5). In Luke, the Lord is even quoted as having mentioned four aspects of your being: "You shall love the Lord your God with all your heart and with all your soul and with all your strength and with all your mind" (10:27). This involves your thinking, your will, your feelings, your faith, your hopes. If you truly love someone, your entire being and your entire life are involved.

You can easily check for yourself if you really love God. Do you love to be in his presence? We call this prayer. Do you love reading what he has to say to you through his Word? Is your heart so full of him that you cannot keep silent about him? We call this witnessing. Do you love to tell him about his greatness and goodness? We call this worship. Do you love to do things for him, just to please him? These are the usual symptoms when you are in love with someone. Actually, these are the features of all true love, and it is no different when it comes to your love for God. Jesus is our great example in this regard. He spent hours in the Father's presence, he knew his Word by heart, he worshipped him, he spoke about him to other people all the time, and he could say, "My food is to do the will of him who sent me" (John 4:34).

It is a commandment to love God; it is your duty as his child. But if you do not do it voluntarily and wholeheartedly, it is of little meaning to God, and of little benefit to yourself.

✴   ✴   ✴

DAY 14 – LOVE YOUR NEIGHBOR!
(Lord's Day 2, Q&A 4, part 3)

A. . . . "And a second [commandment] is like it: 'You shall love your neighbor as yourself.' On these two commandments hang all the law and the prophets."

Besides loving God, we are also commanded to love our neighbor; as Leviticus 19:18 says, "You shall love your neighbor as yourself." Not only Jesus quoted this verse, but also Paul: "For the commandments . . . are summed up in this word: 'You shall love your neighbor as yourself'" (Rom. 13:9); "the whole law is fulfilled in one word: 'You shall love your neighbor as yourself'" (Gal. 5:14). And James wrote, "If you really fulfill the royal law according to the Scripture, 'You shall love your neighbor as yourself,' you are doing well" (2:8). The emphasis on love as the essence of God's law was not new. Rabbi Hillel reportedly said, "What is hateful to you, do not to your neighbor: that is the whole law, while the rest is the commentary thereof; go and learn it." Jesus said something very similar but in a more positive way: "[W]hatever you wish that others would do to you, do also to them, for this is the Law and the Prophets" (Matt. 7:12). Likewise, the Catechism says of the two commandments: "On these two commandments hang all the law and the prophets."

If you hear some of the Ten Commandments ("Honor your father and your mother. . . . You shall not murder. You shall not commit adultery. You shall not steal. You shall not bear false witness against your neighbor," Exod. 20:12–16), then remember that behind them is always the great principle of love (cf. Rom. 13:8–10). That is, you ought to honor your parents out of love. You ought to protect your neighbor's life and possessions out of love. You ought to avoid adultery out of love for your own spouse, and the other's spouse. You serve the neighbor with the truth out of love.

Your love for God and your love for your neighbor are always closely linked. As John wrote, "If anyone says, 'I love God,' and hates his brother, he is a liar; for he who does not love his brother whom he has seen cannot love God whom he has not seen" (1 John 4:20). But also: "Everyone who loves the Father loves whoever has been born of him. By this we know that we love the children of God, when we love God and obey his commandments" (5:1–2).

✦   ✦   ✦

DAY 15 – NO LIVING UP TO THE LAW
(Lord's Day 2, Q&A 5, part 1)

Q. Can you live up to all this perfectly?
A. No. I have a natural tendency to hate God and my neighbor.

It seems quite strange that God gave humans a law that in fact they could not, and cannot, keep at all. Humans cannot live up to the law in a perfect way, and not even in an imperfect way. There *are* humans who have no relationship with God, and yet admit that the Ten Commandments are reasonable and fair. They sometimes even exclaim that, if all people would live according to this law, the world would be a better place to live in. Yet, even these "noble" people do not live up to the Ten Commandments at all, especially if you take the law according to the deep meaning that Jesus attached to it. You may never have killed a fellow human—but how often did you *wish* someone dead? You may never have committed adultery—but how often did you covet your neighbor's spouse (cf. Matt. 5:27–28)? You may never have stolen (although such people are rare)—but how often did you fail to share with your needy neighbor what you have (cf. Eph. 4:28; 1 John 3:17)? On top of this, we have this word from James: "[W]hoever keeps the whole law but fails in one point has become accountable for all of it" (2:10). So how could anyone maintain that he lives up to the law, even imperfectly?

Now what is the use of a law, no matter how beautiful, if no humans can keep it? Whatever may be the answer, don't blame the law! Paul says, "[T]he law is holy, and the commandment is holy and righteous and good" (Rom. 7:12). The law that says we should stop at a red traffic light is a good and useful law, even if some drivers ignore it. This tells us something about reckless drivers, not about this law as such. The law is okay—some drivers are not okay. God's law is not just okay, it is perfect, because it is God's own word. We would be perfectly happy if we all would perfectly keep it, and the world would be a perfect place. But unfortunately we do not keep it. Deep down in our hearts we know how good and wise it would be if we would all keep God's law. But by nature, we have a double problem. We *cannot* keep it, and actually we do not *want* to either, because usually this does not serve our self-interest.

❧   ❧   ❧

DAY 16 – HATING GOD AND YOUR NEIGHBOR

(LORD'S DAY 2, Q&A 5, PART 2)

A. . . . I have a natural tendency to hate God and my neighbor.

We have seen that the essence of God's law is love. If we cannot live up to the law of love, it is no wonder that the Catechism describes our natural behavior as one characterized by hatred. Notice the word "natural" here. The text says that we have a "natural" tendency to sin. We will see that this does not refer to the nature of humanity as it was created by God, but to the nature of *fallen* humanity. Originally we were intended for love. Since the fall into sin, we cannot but hate. Instead of loving God we hate him. Instead of loving our neighbor we hate him or her.

Now is this not a bit exaggerated? Do unbelieving people know nothing about love? Do many of them not love their spouses and their children? Are there not quite a few non-Christians who are great examples of altruism to quite a few not-so-altruistic Christians? This is correct. But take a closer look. In many—if not all—of these forms of love, is there not a lot of self-interest? Do we not love ourselves most of all? If we do show signs of love, is it not because in all cases we expect a lot of compensation in return? How much *unselfish* love is there?

The Bible puts it even more strongly: "[T]he intention of man's heart is evil from his youth" (Gen. 8:21). "The heart is deceitful above all things, and desperately sick" (Jer. 17:9). "[T]he mind that is set on the flesh is hostile to God, for it does not submit to God's law; indeed, it cannot" (Rom. 8:7). And notice especially this statement of Paul: we "were once foolish, disobedient, led astray, slaves to various passions and pleasures, passing our days in malice and envy, *hated* by others and *hating one another*" (Titus 3:3).

Do not deceive yourself. When you were still without God, the only person you *really* loved was you. In comparison to that, all so-called love for others was nothing but non-love—hatred. We were *enemies* of God (Rom. 5:10), hostile to him and to each other (cf. Eph. 2:14, 16; Col. 1:21). How bad we were was proven by the fact that we were even hostile toward the noblest person the world has ever seen—Jesus Christ (Heb. 12:3).

✦   ✦   ✦

DAY 17 – GOD'S GOOD CREATION
(Lord's Day 3, Q&A 6, part 1)

Q. Did God create people so wicked and perverse?
A. No. God created them good and in his own image, that is, in true righteousness and holiness.

Because of their belief in a general evolution, many Christians today do not believe in a historical fall into sin anymore. They seem to believe that people's sinfulness is just their evolutionary imperfection. However, in the Bible it is basic that we understand that God created humans in a perfect way, and that afterward people fell into sin at a certain moment in time and space. We *were* good, and we *became* bad. Originally, God's law was intended for good people, because good people would be able to keep it, and even *love* to keep it. Since the Fall, it is the reverse: bad people are not able to keep God's law, and even *hate* to keep it. That is because their nature has become "wicked and perverse," as our text puts it.

What a great statement this is: God created people "good and in his own image." In contrast with even the highest animals, humanity originally exhibited the mental and moral image of God (Gen. 1:26–27; 9:6). This does not mean that expressions such as "true righteousness and holiness" would have made much sense to Adam and Eve themselves. (The expression is quoted from Eph. 4:24, but there it refers to *renewed* humanity.) *We* have learned what is holy and righteous the hard way—by having been thoroughly familiar with *un*righteousness and *un*holiness. Remember the name of that peculiar tree in the Garden of Eden: tree of the knowledge of both *good* and evil (Gen. 2:9–10). The first humans did not yet know what was evil—but in fact, neither did they know what was good. They learned it the hard way; by their fall into sin, they fell into evil, and from then on could do nothing else but evil. Now they also began to understand what is good, but they were no longer able to *do* good, until through redemption it was granted to them to *know* the good, *and to do it* through the power of the Holy Spirit. Redemption does not just entail a restoration of the old world of Genesis 1–2. On the contrary, by God's grace it leads to a world that is far better than the world that Adam and Eve lost! A world in which we will have a nature that cannot sin anymore.

✢   ✢   ✢

DAY 18 – GOD'S PURPOSE: KNOWING HIM

(Lord's Day 3, Q&A 6, part 2)

A. . . . God created [people] good . . . so that they might truly know God their creator.

It was God's creational purpose that humans would "know" him. This is a beautiful way to put it. "Knowing" often has a special meaning in the Bible. Genesis 4:1 says, "Adam knew his wife," that is, had intercourse with her. Joseph "took his wife [Mary], but knew her not" (Matt. 1:24–25), that is, had no intercourse with her until Jesus was born. "Knowing" in such cases involves relationship, fellowship, intimacy. Jesus said to his Father, "[T]his is eternal life, that they know you the only true God, and Jesus Christ whom you have sent" (John 17:3). Here, "knowing" basically means the same thing: relationship, fellowship, intimacy with God. The apostles preached "the eternal life, which was with the Father and was made manifest to us . . . so that you too may have fellowship with us; and indeed our fellowship is with the Father and with his Son Jesus Christ" (1 John 1:2–3). This is eternal life: knowing God, having fellowship with the Father and the Son in the power of the Holy Spirit.

This is a tremendous thought: God created humans in order to enter into an intimate relationship with them. As soon as he had created the first human couple, he began speaking to them, communication being an important aspect of fellowship (Gen. 1:28; cf. v. 22). He appointed them to function as viceroys over his creation (vv. 26, 28), which could be successful only if there would be close contact between the King of kings and his vassals. Even after the first humans had fallen into sin, God immediately came to stretch out his hand to them, saying, "Where are you?" (3:9). Adam and Eve had hidden themselves from God. Sin had made a separation between God and them (cf. Isa. 59:2). Yet, God intervened to restore the bond between fallen humanity and himself. For his creational purpose remained: repentant and redeemed humanity was destined to know God, not just as their Creator, but in his triune being: Father, Son, and Holy Spirit. David said, "The friendship [intimate fellowship] of the LORD is for those who fear him, and he makes known to them his covenant" (Ps. 25:14).

✦   ✦   ✦

DAY 19 – LOVING HIM, LIVING WITH HIM

(LORD'S DAY 3, Q&A 6, PART 3)

A. . . . God created [people] good . . . so that they might love [God] with all their heart, and live with God in eternal happiness.

Protestant Christians love to put a lot of emphasis on the principle of faith. But the two other principles are of equal importance: hope and love (cf. 1 Cor. 13:13). Christians are described not only as those who believe in God but also as those who love God: "[W]e know that for those who love God all things work together for good" (Rom. 8:28). "What no eye has seen, nor ear heard, nor the heart of man imagined, what God has prepared for those who love him" (1 Cor. 2:9). And James speaks of the "crown of life" as well as the "kingdom," "which God has promised to those who love him" (1:12; 2:5). You see, this is very characteristic of Christians: they believe in God, they hope in God, and above all: they *love* God.

This is not just a beautiful side effect of being a Christian. No, it is essential. We were created for this purpose: to love God, and to live with God forever, that is, in an eternal atmosphere of mutual love. This is why the first of the two commandments in which Jesus summarized God's law was about loving God. In his first letter, John gives immature believers five characteristics by which they could recognize a real Christian. One of these is that a true Christian loves God, and that he proves this by loving God's children and keeping God's commandments: "Everyone who believes that Jesus is the Christ has been born of God, and everyone who loves the Father loves whoever has been born of him. By this we know that we love the children of God, when we love God and obey his commandments. For this is the love of God, that we keep his commandments" (5:1–3). John is very straightforward about this: if you do not love God's people, and if you consistently do your own thing, you cannot be a real Christian. We may make mistakes—and in fact we often do—but basically this is what should characterize us: loving our fellow Christians and keeping God's law.

God has predestined us for living with him in eternal happiness. Imagine how hard it would be to spend eternity with God and with your fellow Christians if they did not love you, and if you did not love *them*.

✢ ✢ ✢

DAY 20 – PRAISING AND GLORIFYING HIM

(Lord's Day 3, Q&A 6, part 4)

A. . . . God created [people] good . . . to praise and glorify him.

The Catechism mentions four purposes for which God created humans: first, to know him; second, to love him; third, to live with him forever; and fourth, to praise and glorify him. Not only to worship him when we will be with him in eternal happiness, but to worship him already now. This entails leading a life of thanksgiving and praise: "[G]ive thanks in all circumstances" (1 Thess. 5:18); "be filled with the Spirit, addressing one another in psalms and hymns and spiritual songs, singing and making melody to the Lord with your heart, giving thanks always and for everything to God the Father in the name of our Lord Jesus Christ" (Eph. 5:18–20).

Perhaps you know that the word "Jew" could be rendered as "one who praises." "Jew" comes from "Judean," and this word comes from "Judah," which means "praise" (cf. what Judah's mother said at his birth: "This time I will praise the LORD," Gen. 29:35). Similarly, it is the essence of the Christian's existence that he praises and worships God. We do not read anywhere that the Father is "seeking" servants—he "seeks" (i.e., he longs for) *worshipers* (John 4:23). Worship is telling God how much we love him, appreciate him, admire him. Worshiping is telling God how great he is, how magnificent, beautiful, splendid, glorious, lustrous, and also how loving, kind, gracious, merciful, good, and patient.

Notice this difference: we *thank* God for what he gives to us. When we *praise* him, the emphasis is shifted from the gift to the giver. But when we *worship* him, we do not think of the gift at all anymore, but only of God's greatness. The verb "to glorify" literally means "to make glorious," but of course we cannot add anything to God's glory. Glorifying God means *proclaiming* his glories, describing his excellences in an admiring, praising way. The crowds "glorified God" because of God's wondrous acts in Jesus (Luke 7:16; 13:13; Acts 11:18; 21:20; Gal. 1:24). Even of Jesus we read, "He rejoiced greatly in the Holy Spirit, and said, 'I praise You, O Father'" (Luke 10:21 NASB). Never forget to worship God, not even one day!

✢ ✢ ✢

DAY 21 – IT IS ALL DUE TO THE FALL

(LORD'S DAY 3, Q&A 7, PART 1)

Q. Then where does this corrupt human nature come from?
A. The fall and disobedience of our first parents, Adam and Eve, in Paradise.

If God creates something, it can only be good, for he is a good God: he "saw everything that he had made, and behold, it was very good" (Gen. 1:31). By nature, however, present-day humans are very bad. Already in Genesis 6:5 we read, "The LORD saw that the wickedness of man was great in the earth, and that every intention of the thoughts of his heart was only evil continually." What happened that such good people turned into such bad people? The answer is found in Genesis 3; we call it humanity's fall into sin. Adam and Eve fell, and in them we all fell.

The effect of this fall was tremendous. The apostle Paul says of it, "[S]in came into the world through one man, and death through sin, and so death spread to all men because all sinned . . . one trespass led to condemnation for all men . . . by the one man's disobedience the many were made sinners" (Rom. 5:12, 18–19). What happened was not just a mistake; it was a "trespass," it was "disobedience" to God's commandments. Jesus called the devil "a murderer from the beginning" (John 8:44) because he caused the spiritual death of Adam and Eve. God had said that in the day they would eat of the forbidden tree they would surely die (Gen. 2:17). And indeed, Eve was cunningly deceived by the devil (2 Cor. 11:3), she ate, and also gave her husband to eat from the forbidden fruit—and they "died" in the spiritual sense. God's test had been a simple test of obedience: Obey me, and I will bless you. However, Adam and Eve fell for the enticing words of the devil: "You will be like God" (Gen. 3:5). Thus, the sin of the first humans was an act of pure rebellion. They had received everything from God, and they spoiled everything. Until this very day, we are dealing with the terrible consequences of what they did.

Solomon said, "If the serpent bites before it is charmed, there is no advantage to the charmer" (Eccl. 10:11)—but when the serpent "bit" Adam and Eve, the "charm" had already taken place: God prepared a Lamb even before the foundation of the world (1 Pet. 1:19–20). What the serpent corrupted, the Lamb will restore.

❖　　❖　　❖

DAY 22 – A POISONED NATURE
(Lord's Day 3, Q&A 7, part 2)

A. The fall and disobedience of our first parents . . . has so poisoned our nature that we are all conceived and born in a sinful condition.

With the term "poisoned" we still remain in the sphere of Genesis 3. When the serpent "bit" Adam and Eve, so to speak, he injected his deadly poison into them. As a consequence, they died a spiritual death, from which only God could revive them (as in fact he did). Because we all descend from the first human couple, our nature is thoroughly sinful. Jesus explained to Nicodemus (in my words) that, even if we were born from our natural mothers a thousand times, we would still be sinful because our origin is sinful: "That which is born of the flesh is flesh," that is, has the characteristics of the flesh; and by way of contrast: "That which is born of the Spirit is spirit," that is, has the characteristics of the Holy Spirit (John 3:6). We have all been fathered by sinful fathers, and have been given birth by sinful mothers, just as *they* had sinful parents.

Notice that the Catechism does *not* say that we have "inherited" the *guilt* of Adam and Eve, as it has sometimes been asserted. Adam and Eve were responsible for their own guilt, just as we are for ours. The Bible says very clearly that the "son shall not suffer for the iniquity of the father" (Ezek. 18:20). Sons may suffer from the *effects* of their fathers' sins (cf. Exod. 20:5; Num. 14:18; Deut. 5:9), but that is something very different. No, we do not inherit Adam's *guilt*, but we definitely inherit the sinful *condition* that Adam entered into through his fall. The Bible never says that sinners are condemned because of Adam's sin. No, sinners are condemned because of their own sins (cf. 2 Cor. 5:10; Rev. 20:12). We are not responsible for the fact that we have inherited Adam's nature—but we are definitely responsible for the sins that this nature produces. We will not have to account for our sinful origin, but certainly for the results of it: "For we will all stand before the judgment seat of God" (Rom. 14:10). "[E]ach one's work will become manifest, for the Day will disclose it, because it will be revealed by fire, and the fire will test what sort of work each one has done" (1 Cor. 3:13).

✦ ✦ ✦

DAY 23 – CONCEIVED AND BORN AS SINNERS

(Lord's Day 3, Q&A 7, part 3)

A. The fall . . . has so poisoned our nature that we are all conceived and born in a sinful condition.

There are plenty of biblical references to this undeniable fact that we are all "conceived and born in a sinful condition," as the Catechism puts it. This expression is almost a direct quotation from Psalm 51:5, where repentant David says, "Behold, I was brought forth in iniquity, and in sin did my mother conceive me" (v. 5). Some people think that David was born out of wedlock, for instance because his father left him aside in 1 Samuel 16, when the prophet Samuel came to see the family. In that case, Psalm 51 would refer to his mother's sinful behavior. But actually, there is no proof for this idea; moreover, it would hardly fit into the psalm. David was not speaking of his mother's sins, but of his own sins. He confessed that he not only had done sinful things, but that he was sinful even down to his very roots. He was a sinner by birth, just as we all are. We are not sinners because we sin, but we sin because we are sinners. The tree is bad; no wonder the fruits are bad (Matt. 7:17–19; 12:33). *By nature* we are "children of wrath, like the rest of mankind" (Eph. 2:3).

There are more biblical proofs that we are sinners by birth: "[T]he intention of man's heart is evil from his youth" (Gen. 8:21). "Who can bring a clean thing out of an unclean? There is not one" (Job 14:4). "What is man, that he can be pure? Or he who is born of a woman, that he can be righteous?" (15:14). "The wicked are estranged from the womb; they go astray from birth, speaking lies" (Ps. 58:3). Humans are conceived and born as sinful beings. This does not mean that people *sin* from the moment of their conception, but that their *nature* is corrupt from the start, and this will lead them to sin.

By the way, the disciples apparently believed that a person can sin even in his mother's womb (John 9:2)! And the rabbis concluded from Genesis 25:22 that Esau had sinned already in his mother's womb. However this may be, let this be the final conclusion: "[T]here is no one who does not sin" (1 Kings 8:46). "[T]here is none who does good, not even one" (Ps. 14:3). This is hard, but it is the truth.

✦   ✦   ✦

DAY 24 – UNABLE TO DO ANY GOOD
(LORD'S DAY 3, Q&A 8, PART 1)

Q. But are we so corrupt that we are totally unable to do any good and inclined toward all evil?
A. Yes, unless we are born again by the Spirit of God.

To understand this Q&A, we must remember that the word "we" does not refer here to believers, but to humans in their natural sinful condition. Many times in the Catechism, the "I" or the "we" are believers, but not here. From the answer it is clear that a contrast is made between these "we" *and* those who are born again. The new nature of the believer, in the power of the Holy Spirit, *is* definitely able to do good, and is definitely *not* inclined toward all evil. On the contrary, Paul says that "God shows his love for us in that while we *were* still sinners, Christ died for us" (Rom. 5:8). A sinner is someone who is in the *power* of sin. Believers may still sin, but they are no longer in the *power* of sin; this is what Paul means when he says that we have been "set free from sin" (6:7, 18, 20, 22). Therefore, Paul can say that we are no more "sinners," that is, people who are "totally unable to do any good and inclined toward all evil."

But there is another question we have to ask here. Can we really say that unbelievers are "totally unable to do any good"? Are there not many non-Christians who are more altruistic than some Christians? Each one of us knows non-Christians who are far nicer people than some Christians we know. Yes, that may be true. But please, remember, it is not we who formulate what is good and nice, but God. The Bible speaks of "dead works" (Heb. 6:1; 9:14); I take these to be nice works, acts of altruism and the like, which, however, have no value for eternity because they have not been done out of love for God, by the Spirit of God. *This* is the decisive point. If you love the Lord, you will do what he expects of you (John 14:15). But if you do nice things without this love they are worthless. In fact, they are even evil. Only in this way can we understand what the Catechism is saying here. What counts is not *your* ideas about good and evil, but *God's*. Things are never just good in themselves. They can be good only if they have been done out of *love* for God, and out of *obedience* to him. The rest has only very limited value—at any rate, never eternal value.

✦   ✦   ✦

DAY 25 – LOST, UNLESS BORN AGAIN
(Lord's Day 3, Q&A 8, part 2)

A. Yes, unless we are born again by the Spirit of God.

Notice this emphatic "Yes": yes, we are totally unable to do any good, and we are inclined toward all evil. It's a total loss, no repair possible. The redemption of the penitent sinner does not entail a kind of restoration or improvement, because that won't work. Jeremiah asks, "Can the Ethiopian change his skin or the leopard his spots? Then also you can do good who are accustomed to do evil" (Jer. 13:23). That's a beautiful way to tell us that evil persons as such cannot be turned into good people.

The transformation of the sinner into a child of God is so radical that it is described in radical terms. The apostle Paul expresses this in terms of the "old self" and the "new self" (literally, "old man" and "new man"; Rom. 6:6; Eph. 2:15; 4:22; Col. 3:9), and the term "new creation": "[I]f anyone is in Christ, he is a new creation. The old has passed away; behold, the new has come" (2 Cor. 5:17; cf. Gal. 6:15).

Jesus describes the transformation of the sinner in terms of a "new birth," and this is what the Catechism refers to. He tells Nicodemus: "Unless [a person] is born again he cannot see the kingdom of God" (John 3:3). "Again" does not mean: a second time from the same mother (v. 4). That would not help us one bit. No, it means being born in a totally new way: "unless [a person] is born of water and the Spirit, he cannot enter the kingdom of God" (v. 5). The "water" that Jesus refers to has been explained in several different ways, but at least the reference to the Spirit is clear. If you are born again from the "flesh" of your mother, you will always remain "flesh." But if you are "born of the Spirit," you will become as spiritual as the Spirit is (v. 6).

Moreover, notice that no one can cause himself to be born. It is the Spirit who does it. This is similar to another important metaphor: by nature we are dead in our trespasses (Eph. 2:1, 5; Col. 2:13). Nothing can help us, unless someone comes along who will raise us from death: "God, . . . when we were dead in our trespasses, made us alive together with Christ—by grace you have been saved" (Eph. 2:4–5).

✳ ✳ ✳

DAY 26 – IS GOD UNJUST?

(LORD'S DAY 4, Q&A 9, PART 1)

Q. But doesn't God do us an injustice by requiring in his law what we are unable to do?
A. No, God created human beings with the ability to keep the law.

The question that the Catechism asks here is quite understandable. Is it fair if a ruler imposes on his subjects a law that he knows they will never be able to keep? Imagine the government would invent a law demanding all citizens every week to run a marathon, and the penalty for breaking it is death. I suppose those citizens would soon begin to revolt! Likewise, is it fair if God demands that sinners do things they *cannot* possibly do? To be sure, sinners do not *want* to do these things either. But even if they wanted, they would not be able to. You remember the previous Q&A in the Catechism: humans are by nature "unable to do any good and inclined toward all evil." There you have it: *unable*. So what use is it if God demands of sinners things that they cannot possibly do?

The answer is, I think, threefold. First, it remains totally fair if God demands of people, for instance, not to kill, rob, or cheat each other. People would all be far better off if they would stop doing such things. Apart from dishonoring God, killing, robbing, and cheating are detrimental to human relationships. People do not only offend God, they ruin *themselves*. That is stupid. They could better listen to God's commandments, because this would be for their own benefit.

Second, don't forget that when God gave his first regulations to the first humans, they were definitely able to keep them. This is the answer that the Catechism gives. It was these humans themselves who were so stupid that they voluntarily entered into a condition in which they were no longer able to obey God. This was their own choice. You cannot blame God for giving laws to people who themselves chose to give up their capacity for keeping them.

Third, this situation of God giving fair laws and humans being unable to keep them, is not God's last word on the matter. The Catechism will explain in great detail how God, through the work of Jesus Christ, opened a way for people to *regain* both their willingness and their capacity for keeping Gods laws: through rebirth and through the power of the Holy Spirit.

✤　✤　✤

DAY 27 – PROVOKED BY THE DEVIL
(Lord's Day 4, Q&A 9, part 2)

A. . . . human beings . . . [were] provoked by the devil.

In the biblical account of the fall of the first humans into sin, the devil played an important role. You may say that the devil is not mentioned at all in Genesis 3; it is only the serpent that is referred to. But who *is* "the" serpent? John gives the answer; he speaks of "that ancient serpent, who is called the devil and Satan, the deceiver of the whole world" (Rev. 12:9; cf. 20:2). This is why Jesus called the devil "a murderer from the beginning" (John 8:44). Paul says, "[T]he serpent deceived Eve by his cunning" (2 Cor. 11:3), and just a little later speaks of Satan who "disguises himself as an angel of light" (v. 14). John adds, "[T]he devil has been sinning from the beginning" (1 John 3:8). So the Catechism is perfectly right in saying that the first humans were "provoked," not just by the serpent, but by the devil. They were incited, roused, challenged, enticed, seduced into sin.

Interestingly, Paul says that an overseer should not be "a recent convert, or he may become puffed up with conceit and fall into the condemnation of the devil" (1 Tim. 3:6). This can mean that such a person should not "fall under the devil's spell" (CEB), as Adam and Eve once did. Or it can mean that such a person "would be condemned for his pride the same as the devil was" (ERV). In the latter case, apparently both the devil and the first humans fell into the sin of pride. Some expositors point to Isaiah 14:13–14, "I will ascend to heaven . . . I will make myself like the Most High," and apply this to the devil. At any rate, conceit did definitely play a role in the fall of the first humans. The devil said to Eve, "You will not surely die. For God knows that when you eat of it your eyes will be opened, and you will be like God, knowing good and evil" (Gen. 3:4–5).

You see what this means? It amounts to claiming: God is jealous about you, he does not want you to be like him, knowing good and evil. He withholds from you something you are entitled to: that tree through which you can get that knowledge that God wants to keep to himself! And Adam and Eve believed the devil.

✳   ✳   ✳

DAY 28 – WILLFUL DISOBEDIENCE
(Lord's Day 4, Q&A 9, part 3)

A. . . . human beings . . . [acted] in willful disobedience . . .

In the answer that the Catechism gives there is an interesting tension. You might think that, if Adam and Eve were "provoked" by the devil, they were only victims, and the devil was the main culprit. But no, the text adds immediately that Adam and Eve acted "in willful disobedience." So don't try to excuse them! If someone "provokes" you, you do not have to accept the challenge; that's your own choice. The first two humans sinned because they *wanted* to sin. Of course, they could have only a vague idea of what their disobedience was going to bring about. But that does not eliminate their responsibility. The devil was guilty as hell—literally—but Adam and Eve were too.

Yet, perhaps we can make a little distinction after all. There is an extraordinary statement by the apostle Paul. He says, "Adam was not deceived, but the woman was deceived and became a transgressor" (1 Tim. 2:14). Elsewhere he says that "the serpent deceived Eve [not Adam] by his cunning" (2 Cor. 11:3). Eve herself had said to the Lord, "The serpent deceived me, and I ate" (Gen. 3:13). If you read this in a superficial way, you might think that Eve was more blameworthy than Adam because she was seduced, and Adam was not. If you think this, you forget that Adam sinned too. If he was not seduced, the only conclusion can be that he *deliberately* sinned; the expression "willful disobedience" applies more to him than to Eve. To be sure, he tried to blame Eve: *she* gave him to eat. However, if Adam was not seduced, it means that he could and should have refused.

In church history, Eve has often been blamed by church leaders (who were all men!) for being the main cause of the misery of sin and death. In fact, I believe Paul makes clear that it is the other way round. Eve was seduced; she fell into the trap that Satan presented to her. That is bad enough—but Adam was worse. He was not seduced; he deliberately followed his wife into apostasy. He was the more "willfully disobedient" of the two. After all these centuries in which Eve has been blamed, let's finally face it: the man was the guiltier of the two.

✦   ✦   ✦

DAY 29 – HUMANS ROBBING THEMSELVES
(LORD'S DAY 4, Q&A 9, PART 4)

A. . . . human beings . . . robbed themselves and all their descendants of these gifts.

The last thing the Catechism tells us in this Q&A is that Adam and Eve by their fall into sin not only "robbed themselves" but also "all their descendants of these gifts." If you want to know what "these gifts" are you have to go back all the way to Q&A 6: "knowing God their creator, loving him with all their heart, living with God in eternal happiness, praising and glorifying him." When the first human couple fell, the intimate bond with God was severed for a while, until they were restored by the grace of God. They did not really love him anymore—for could you call it love if you begin to believe that God begrudged them certain benefits that God allegedly wished to keep for himself? They did not live with God in happiness anymore, for mistrust and suspicion destroy happiness. And they certainly did not praise God anymore; their act of disobedience was rather a complaint against God.

They hardly realized what terrible effects their act would have for their descendants. When daddy smokes and drinks, and beats up mom, he hardly realizes what lasting effect this will have on his kids. There was a man sitting next to a boiling hot lava stream. Thoughtlessly, he threw his stick into the stream. His dog, trained to do so, jumped after the stick, and was burnt alive. Without thinking about it, we may have a tremendous impact on others through things we carelessly do, or words we say. Adam and Eve were scarcely aware of the fact that for thousands of years the billions of their future children would suffer from the sinful nature that would be inherent in them because of their first parents' trespass.

Noah's getting drunk caused a rift among his sons and brought a curse upon Ham, especially on his son Canaan. Abraham's taking Hagar, and fathering Ishmael, caused havoc that lasted until this very day (the tension between Muslims and Israelis). David's taking Bathsheba and having Uriah killed led to his paying dearly: it cost him four of his sons (cf. 2 Sam. 12:6). Yet, Adam's sin had the largest consequences: none of his descendants was ever born without a sinful nature—except Jesus.

✦ ✦ ✦

DAY 30 – GOD IS ANGRY
(LORD'S DAY 4, Q&A 10, PART 1)

Q. Does God permit such disobedience and rebellion to go unpunished?
A. Certainly not. God is terribly angry with the sin we are born with as well as the sins we personally commit.

There are at least two things that are quite surprising about God. The first is that God cannot do something that we humans are quite capable of doing. We are often quite able to turn a blind eye to certain bad things people have done to us. We often easily forgive such bad things, or we decide to ignore them even if the sinner did not confess his sins to us. It may even seem as if we are more forgiving than God is, because God can *never* overlook any sin. In reality, God is far more forgiving than we are, because *he* never refuses to forgive repentant sinners and *he* never keeps a grudge or any resentment toward those who confess their sins to him. But the point is this: we may turn our backs to what people do to us, but God can never let any sin simply go. There is no sin in the world, not even the smallest, that is not either punished forever, or forgiven forever. For the latter option, God needs a holy *foundation*: he needs a holy *substitute* that is able as well as willing to blot those sins out. There are, then, two conditions for God's forgiveness: objectively, God's needs a sacrifice; subjectively, God demands our true repentance and confession.

But there is a second thing that is quite surprising about God. The text says that God is "terribly angry with the sin we are born with as well as the sins we personally commit"; he is angry with both our sinful *condition* and with the *fruits* that this condition produces. But the text does not say that God is angry with the *sinner*. I don't think it would be wrong to say such a thing, for John says, "[W]hoever does not obey the Son shall not see life, but the wrath of God remains on him" (John 3:36). But Paul specifies: "[T]he wrath of God is revealed from heaven against all ungodliness and unrighteousness of men" (Rom. 1:18). God is angry with sin, but he loved the world so much that he gave his only Son (John 3:16). God can do something that *we* hardly manage to do: he is "terribly angry" with sin, more than anyone of us is, but he loves sinners, more than anyone of us does. That's really amazing!

✶ ✶ ✶

DAY 31 – GOD IS A JUST JUDGE
(Lord's Day 4, Q&A 10, part 2)

A. . . . As a just judge, God will punish them both now and in eternity.

Because God created human beings, he has every right to them. He rewards them when they serve him, and punishes them when they turn away from him. He does so as a perfectly just Judge. He is in charge. In the end, all will have to recognize that he fairly rewards the righteous, and fairly punishes the wicked. God will "be justified in his words and blameless in his judgment" (cf. Ps. 51:4). "Just are you, O Holy One, who is and who was, for you brought these judgments. . . . Yes, Lord God the Almighty, true and just are your judgments!" (Rev. 16:5, 7). God is the One "who will by no means clear the guilty" (Exod. 34:7). "For you are not a God who delights in wickedness; evil may not dwell with you. The boastful shall not stand before your eyes" (Ps. 5:4–5). If a person does not wish to have anything to do with God all his life, who could complain that God is unfair if he assigns such a person to a place where this person will be eternally without God?

Now you may say, Is it really fair, if a person has been sinning for, say, eighty or ninety years, to punish this person not only now but with an eternal punishment? What is ninety years compared to eternity? But wait a moment. Is this not what we experience in everyday life? Suppose you get distracted for a second, you get into a terrible accident, and you go through the rest of your life as a cripple. What is that single second compared to a lifetime? You get angry, and in your rage you kill a person. It may be over in a minute, but you might get a life sentence for it. Again, what is that minute compared to decades of years in a prison? Yet, no one will complain that such a punishment is not fair.

We have been created as eternal beings, and we decide during our lives whether we wish to repent and convert to God, or to continue in our rebellion toward God. "[I]t is appointed for man to die once, and after that comes judgment" (Heb. 9:27). We ought to be aware of the fact that decisions may have eternal consequences. If you say all your life, I want it my way, don't complain, that God in the end will say: You can have it your way.

✣   ✣   ✣

DAY 32 – CURSED IS THE TRESPASSER

(Lord's Day 4, Q&A 10, part 3)

A. . . . "Cursed is everyone who does not observe and obey all the things written in the book of the law."

It is quite a solemn thought that there is no sin in the entire universe that will go unpunished forever. A just Judge could not, and would not, do otherwise. Any specific sin will be blotted out *either* by sending the one who committed it to hell, *or* by Christ having borne the punishment for that sin on the cross for all those who believe in him. God definitely can *forgive* sins, but only if there is an adequate substitute that can undergo the punishment, and if the sinner is truly repentant and receives this substitute in faith. This latter point will be worked out later in the Catechism, of course.

For the present, the text dwells on this important subject: the just Judge will bring a curse on those who remain unrepentant and in the end die in their sins. God cannot turn a blind eye to any sin whatsoever. Most people, perhaps we all, can hardly imagine how righteous and holy God is. The prophet Habakkuk called God the One who is "of purer eyes than to see evil and cannot look at wrong" (Hab. 1:13). God simply cannot *stand* it. The clearest and most solemn proof of this is that, at the moment Jesus Christ was "made sin" for us (2 Cor. 5:21), a holy and righteous God had to turn his face away from him, so that Jesus had to cry: "My God, my God, why have you forsaken me?" (Matt. 27:46; cf. Ps. 22:1). Only these two are ever truly forsaken by God: in the past it was Jesus on the cross, in the future it will be the unrepentant sinner in hell.

The Catechism quotes Moses saying, "Cursed be anyone who does not confirm the words of this law by doing them" (Deut. 27:26). A "curse" is mischief that is proclaimed upon someone. As the prophet Nahum said, "The Lord is a jealous and avenging God; the Lord is avenging and wrathful; the Lord takes vengeance on his adversaries and keeps wrath for his enemies" (1:2). There are temporary curses, and there is an eternal curse. Whatever Moses meant, the application is that every sinner who remains unrepentant should know that an eternal curse is awaiting him. If you are such a person, hasten to come to the Lord and confess your sins!

✤　　✤　　✤

DAY 33 – IS GOD MERCIFUL?
(Lord's Day 4, Q&A 11, part 1)

Q. *But isn't God also merciful?*
A. *God is certainly merciful, but also just. . . .*

G*race* is for those who do not merit anything. *Mercy* is for those who are in misery and need help. The sinner needs both from God, for he does not deserve anything, and he is in deep need. The two, grace and mercy, go together quite often in the Old Testament, at the first occasion even in God's own words: "The LORD, the LORD, a God merciful and gracious, slow to anger, and abounding in steadfast love and faithfulness, keeping steadfast love for thousands, forgiving iniquity and transgression and sin" (Exod. 34:6–7; cf. Num. 14:18; Neh. 9:17; Ps. 86:15; 103:8; 145:8; Joel 2:13; Jonah 4:2). Yes, says the Catechism, God is merciful. But don't forget, he is also just. And we may add, Yes, he is just. But don't forget, he is also merciful.

There is always a tension in such statements: God is this, but he is also that. Attributes such as merciful and just seem in some way opposed to each other: the word "merciful" implies showing mercy to the sinner, the word "just" implies punishing the sinner. However, we should take care not to assume any tension within God himself. *We* may sometimes feel divided between our conflicting moods and character traits, but God is not like that. God is not "partly" merciful and "partly" just, as if once in a while a conflict between the various "parts" might arise. No, God is always *completely* merciful, also in his justice. And God is always *completely* just, also in his mercy. There is never any tension, any conflict, within him. God is so wise that he always acts mercifully and justly at the same time. He shows mercy to sinners in such a way that his justice is not hurt a bit. And I believe that, even when he acts justly to unrepentant sinners, this is never without mercy. Is it not both justice and mercy that God takes the trouble to show even to the greatest sinners why they have deserved his judgment by carefully pointing out their evil deeds to them (Rev. 20:12–13)? In every act of God both his mercy and his justice come to light in a perfect way. Amazing God! He is to be eternally adored for both his justice and his mercy!

✤　　✤　　✤

DAY 34 – THE SUPREME PENALTY
(LORD'S DAY 4, Q&A 11, PART 2)

A. . . . God's justice demands that sin, committed against his supreme majesty, be punished with the supreme penalty.

The Catechism does not give in easily! We would think that this is a wonderful moment to tell us more about God's mercy. The Catechism will do this in due time, but not now. Sometimes, in preaching the gospel, we start too soon with the mercy of God before people are sufficiently impressed with the seriousness of sin and of God's judgment. This may lead to superficial conversions. They are like "the one who hears the word and immediately receives it with joy, yet he has no root in himself, but endures for a while, and when tribulation or persecution arises on account of the word, immediately he falls away" (Matt. 13:20–21). The deeper you learn your misery, the deeper will be your spiritual life as a believer, and the greater will be your gratitude (cf. Luke 7:47).

Notice here the important fact that indeed *every* sin is a sin against God. If you lie to a person, or steal from him, or hurt him, you sin against him. But at the same time you also sin against God, because falsehood, theft, and violence are in blatant contrast with the holiness that characterizes God himself and for which he created us. God intended you to be truthful; by acting deceitfully, you dishonor him. God intended you to be a giver, not a taker; by stealing you dishonor him. God intended you to protect your neighbor, or even put your life at risk for him; by acting violently, you dishonor God. Therefore, if you lie, or steal, or hurt a person, you have to confess this to that person, but also to God. You dishonored that person, but it is far more important that you dishonored God.

If you are good to others, you honor God, even if you do not realize it (cf. Matt. 25:40). If you are bad to others, you dishonor God, even if you do not realize it (cf. v. 45). The slightest sin against your neighbor is an affront to God's "supreme majesty." Remember, it is not important how you and I feel about this. Our own moral views are not the standard. The only thing that matters is how God feels about it. *His* commandments are the standard. They are his prerogative, for he is our Creator and our Judge.

✳   ✳   ✳

DAY 35 – ETERNAL PUNISHMENT
(Lord's Day 4, Q&A 11, part 3)

A. ... God's justice demands that sin, committed against his supreme majesty, be punished with the supreme penalty—eternal punishment of body and soul.

In our human legislation, small crimes are punished with light sentences, and large crimes are punished with heavy sentences. In God's ways with humanity, it is not very different. If his people commit small sins, his chastisement may be light; if they commit great sins, his chastisement may be severe. But in the light of eternity, things are different. Even the smallest sin is an affront to God's supreme majesty, and deserves the supreme penalty, that is, eternal punishment of body and soul. James says, "[W]hoever keeps the whole law but fails in one point has become accountable for all of it" (2:10). That is, whether you break one single commandment, or you break all the commandments, may make a big difference in God's providential ways with you on earth. But in the end, in the light of eternity, you deserve the supreme penalty just the same. The smallest leak makes a hydraulic system worthless. The smallest stain on a dress—and the shopkeeper cannot sell it anymore. The smallest sin makes you ripe for eternal judgment.

The Catechism rightly tells us that eternal punishment is one of "body and soul." Strictly speaking, hell is not what the wicked enter into when they die, but what they enter into at their resurrection, when body and soul will be reunited. Jesus said, "Do not fear those who kill the body but cannot kill the soul. Rather fear him who can destroy both soul and body in hell" (Matt. 10:28). For the righteous, resurrection will mean life, for the wicked it will mean judgment (John 5:29). First, the wicked were spiritually dead in the sense of Ephesians 2:1 ("dead in their trespasses and sins"). Second, they undergo physical death at the moment they die. Third, when they will be raised, they will still be called "dead" (Rev. 20:12), and after having been condemned at the "great white throne" they will enter into what is called "the second death" (vv. 6, 14), that is, eternal death, also called "the eternal fire" and "eternal punishment" (Matt. 25:41, 46). Blessed are those who will take part in the resurrection of life (cf. Rev. 20:6)!

✤ ✤ ✤

DAY 36 – SATISFIED JUSTICE
(LORD'S DAY 5, Q&A 12, PART 1)

Q. According to God's righteous judgment we deserve punishment both now and in eternity: how then can we escape this punishment and return to God's favor?
A. God requires that his justice be satisfied.

This Q&A opens the second of the three major parts of the Catechism, namely, the one on Deliverance. This part begins with an introduction of several Q&As, then we have a long treatment of the Apostles' Creed; then the doctrine of justification by faith; then the doctrine of the sacraments: baptism and the Lord's Supper; and finally the doctrine of the Kingdom of God. You can easily see that this is the central part of the Catechism!

It starts with a kind of introduction in Q&As 12 through 20, in which Jesus Christ is introduced. Christianity is about Christ, so it is high time that the Catechism begins speaking about him. But it does so in a careful way. It began with human misery because, if we do not acknowledge our sick condition, we will not seek a physician. What use is it to introduce the doctor if I do not yet know I am terribly ill?

But now the question comes up as to *what kind* of physician we need. There are good and bad physicians. There are real physicians and quacks. Christians believe that, although folks like Buddha, Confucius, and Muhammad may be interesting, they cannot heal you. They may recommend to you a certain lifestyle, but that will not do anything for your miserable condition. We need true *medicine*. We do not need good examples—assuming that Buddha, Confucius, and Muhammad can supply us with that—we need a medicine so powerful that it can snatch us away from the gates of hell. Good examples and new lifestyles will not do; we need *salvation*. Buddha, Confucius, and Muhammad cannot save us; they did not die for us, they did not bear our sins. Nor can I save myself by even the best of lifestyles, and by even the deepest remorse. By nature, we are like the man in the parable who owed his king millions of dollars, and possessed nothing (Matt. 18:23–25). I need someone to pay that price for me. Buddha, Confucius, and Muhammad claim they can help me earn a few bucks. But that will not do. I need someone to pay off my enormous debt. Where do I find such a person? That is perhaps the most important question of your entire life.

✦ ✦ ✦

DAY 37 – FULL PAYMENT DEMANDED
(Lord's Day 5, Q&A 12, part 2)

A. God requires that his justice be satisfied. Therefore the claims of this justice must be paid in full, either by ourselves or by another.

There are many different metaphors that help us to realize our misery and the way God delivers us from it. If the metaphor of a prison is used, you need to be set free. In the metaphor of death you need to be made alive. If you are drowning, you need a lifeline. If you are on the way to hell, you have to be turned around; we call this "conversion." If you are deadly ill, you need the appropriate medicine. If you fell into a pit, you need someone to help you out. Etc.

In the present Q&A, another metaphor is used, namely, one of debt and payment. You can escape God's punishment and return to his favor only if the enormous debt of your sins is paid. We find this metaphor several times in the New Testament. Jesus said, "[T]he Son of Man came not to be served but to serve, and to give his life as a ransom for many" (Matt. 20:28). You know what it is to ransom a person: you pay a price to set him free. "For there is one God, and there is one mediator between God and men, the man Christ Jesus, who gave himself as a ransom for all" (1 Tim. 2:5–6). "[Y]ou were ransomed from the futile ways inherited from your forefathers . . . with the precious blood of Christ, like that of a lamb without blemish or spot" (1 Pet. 1:18–19). "You are not your own, for you were bought with a price. So glorify God in your body" (1 Cor. 6:19–20; cf. 7:23).

God's justice must be satisfied. His honor must be restored, which was stained by humans. A price has to be paid. Either you pay for your sins yourself, or—if you cannot pay—somebody else has to pay it for you. God said to Israel, "I will not acquit the wicked" (Exod. 23:7). Now compare this with Paul's statement that God is the One "who justifies the ungodly" (Rom. 4:5)! Isn't this a wonderful contrast? The wicked has to *pay*; he will not be acquitted—unless (and this is what Paul refers to) some other person pays the price. The price must be paid one way or another. If you cannot do it yourself, you need someone to do it for you. The big question is this: Where do you find such a person? See the next Q&As!

✢   ✢   ✢

DAY 38 – CAN WE PAY?
(Lord's Day 5, Q&A 13)

Q. *Can we make this payment ourselves?*
A. *Certainly not. Actually, we increase our debt every day.*

Imagine that you had a huge debt, really enormous. Imagine you decided to pay off one percent every month because that's about all you can afford. Then you can calculate that in one hundred months you will have paid off your entire debt. Let's assume that your life depends on you paying off this colossal debt. If you do not pay it off in ten years, you'll be dead. But you think you'll be fine. In less than nine years your guilt will be gone. But now imagine that, to your dismay, you find out that your debt is not decreasing at all, but steadily increasing. Let's say it increases by ten percent every month. So instead of paying off one percent, in reality your debt is increasing by nine percent every month. All your paying off is simply worthless. You will never manage to pay off your debt; on the contrary you keep increasing it every month, every day. What could be more discouraging than that? You begin to realize that you will never be able to save your life. The death sentence hangs over you; in ten years you'll be finished.

This is precisely the situation with the sinner. Even when he comes to faith, he will still have to pray every day: "Forgive us our debts" (Matt. 6:12). You see that in this case the "we" in the Catechism is comprehensive: it refers to both the wicked and the righteous. For both groups, the same rule is valid: they increase their debt every day. There is this enormous difference, however: even though it is sad that the believer also daily adds to his sins ("we all stumble in many ways," or "many times," James 3:2), he knows that his debts have been *covered*. The Catechism does not yet bring this in, but I cannot avoid emphasizing this point. Even believers increase their debt every day—but at the same time, Paul can say: "Who shall bring any charge against God's elect? It is God who justifies" (Rom. 8:33), and: God has "forgiven us all our trespasses, by canceling the record of debt that stood against us with its legal demands. This he set aside, nailing it to the cross" (Col. 2:13–14). What a blessing!

✠　　✠　　✠

DAY 39 – WHO ELSE CAN PAY?
(Lord's Day 5, Q&A 14, part 1)

Q. Can another creature—any at all—pay this debt for us?
A. No.

No creature can ever pay for the debt of another creature. No ordinary human being nor any angel is capable of doing this. You might think that animals can do it, because animals were sacrificed in the Old Testament at God's command. Do we not read, "[W]ithout the shedding of blood there is no forgiveness of sins" (Heb. 9:22), and does this not refer to the animal sacrifices? It does. But we have to realize that this animal blood had not the slightest value *in itself.* "[I]t is impossible for the blood of bulls and goats to take away sins" (10:4). This blood had value only by pointing forward to the true and only sacrifice of Christ. Therefore, Hebrews 10 continues, ". . . Consequently, when Christ came into the world, he said, 'Sacrifices and offerings you have not desired, but a body have you prepared for me; in burnt offerings and sin offerings you have taken no pleasure. Then I said, Behold, I have come to do your will, O God. . . .' . . . [B]y that will we have been sanctified through the offering of the body of Jesus Christ once for all" (vv. 5–10; cf. Ps. 40:6–8). So no, animal blood as such cannot take away our sins either.

Now you may argue, We are saved by faith, through the blood of Jesus—but isn't Jesus also a "creature" after all? He is God, but he is also a Man, and therefore a creature. Well, I think that the Catechism implies that Jesus is *not* a creature, and that the Catechism is right. When Jesus became Man, when the Word became flesh (John 1:14), the Son of God took part in his own creation. That's correct. But it is hard to say that the One through whom God created all things (John 1:3; Heb. 1:2) became a "creature." Colossians 1 also emphasizes that God created all things through him (v. 16), and does so after having said, "He is the image of the invisible God, the firstborn [i.e., first in rank] of all creation" (v. 15). When the Son took part in his own creation, he was necessarily the number one among all creatures, for here God's creational Instrument himself had become human. He was more than a creature; he was God and Man in one person.

✦   ✦   ✦

DAY 40 – EACH HAS TO BEAR HIS OWN LOAD

(Lord's Day 5, Q&A 14, part 2)

A. . . . To begin with, God will not punish any other creature for what a human is guilty of.

It is an important principle in the Bible that one creature cannot be punished for the guilt of another creature. As the Lord says, "The soul who sins shall die. The son shall not suffer for the iniquity of the father, nor the father suffer for the iniquity of the son. The righteousness of the righteous shall be upon himself, and the wickedness of the wicked shall be upon himself" (Ezek. 18:20). The second half of the Catechism's answer deals with the fact that no other creature is *able* to undergo the punishment for someone else; we will see this tomorrow. But first, the Catechism emphasizes that, even if it *were* possible, it would not be *fair* to let one human being die for the sins of another human being. "Let each one test his own work, and then his reason to boast will be in himself alone and not in his neighbor. For each will have to bear his own load" (Gal. 6:4–5).

Don't think that Exodus 20:4 speaks otherwise; it says that God visits "the iniquity of the fathers on the children to the third and the fourth generation of those who hate me" (cf. Deut. 5:9). First, I think that this text rather speaks of the consequences of the fathers' sins for the children. But even if the text is speaking of real punishment, remember those last four words: "those who hate me." You see, the point is not that a man's poor grandchildren and great-grandchildren have to suffer from his sins. No, these descendants *themselves* are hating God. (I know, these words are lacking in Exod. 34:7 and Num. 14:18, but please read these verses in the light of Exod. 20:4.)

Don't excuse these people! Hatred is a heinous thing, which sometimes seems to be transferred from one generation to the next one. But this does not change the fact that each generation is and remains fully responsible for its own hatred. Never blame your ancestors. No generation is punished for the sins of a previous generation; it is only punished for its own sins. Don't blame God either! His judgment is always fair. Never think you are being punished for your parents' sins; they will have to bear their own load.

✢ ✢ ✢

DAY 41 – WHO CAN DELIVER OTHERS?
(Lord's Day 5, Q&A 14, part 3)

A. . . . Furthermore, no mere creature can bear the weight of God's eternal wrath against sin and deliver others from it.

In the previous Q&A, it was established that it would not be fair and just to punish one human being for what another human being is guilty of: "the wickedness of the wicked shall be upon himself"; "each will have to bear his own load." A new argument follows now: by nature we are all sinners; how would we ever be able to deliver others from the power of sin if by nature we are ourselves under this power? Even the most righteous person in the world could not do that. What person in biblical times was closer to God than Moses? "[T]he LORD used to speak to Moses face to face, as a man speaks to his friend" (Exod. 33:11). "[W]hen Moses went into the tent of meeting to speak with the LORD, he heard the voice speaking to him from above the mercy seat" (Num. 7:89). God said, "If there is a prophet among you, I the LORD make myself known to him in a vision; I speak with him in a dream. Not so with my servant Moses. He is faithful in all my house. With him I speak mouth to mouth, clearly, and not in riddles, and he beholds the form of the LORD" (12:6–8).

What greater man of God can you imagine? But even this great man of God could not take the guilt of the people upon himself. After Israel's sin with the golden calf, Moses said to the LORD, "Alas, this people has sinned a great sin. They have made for themselves gods of gold. But now, if you will forgive their sin—but if not, please blot me out of your book that you have written." But the LORD said to Moses, "Whoever has sinned against me, I will blot out of my book" (Exod. 32:31–33). Psalm 49 gives this as a general rule: "Truly no man can ransom another, or give to God the price of his life, for the ransom of their life is costly and can never suffice, that he should live on forever and never see the pit" (vv. 7–9).

Here you see the enormous problem of humanity. Humans cannot ransom themselves, and they cannot ransom other humans. The only possible person left is God himself. But how could the immortal God die for our sins? Think about it! What can be the only solution to this greatest question of all times?

✦   ✦   ✦

41

DAY 42 – WORTHY AND ABLE
(LORD'S DAY 5, Q&A 15, PART 1)

Q. What kind of mediator and deliverer should we look for then?
A. One who is a true and righteous human. . . .

The Catechism steadily and consistently works toward a certain and inescapable conclusion. Someone who is just a human cannot deliver another human from his guilt. This is first, because he has his own guilt; second, because humans are not great enough to deliver other humans; and third, because God does not accept such replacements: "each will have to bear his own load." So it seems that only God can deliver humans from their guilt. But how can God die for us? How can God himself bear the weight of his own eternal wrath against sin? That is, how can God take his own wrath upon himself? God is the Judge; how can he, at the same time, be our Mediator, that is, the One who can bridge the gap between sinful humanity and a wrathful God?

The question hangs in the air. It is like the question in Revelation 5: "Who is worthy to open the scroll and break its seals?" John comments: "No one in heaven or on earth or under the earth was able to open the scroll or to look into it" (vv. 2–3). You see, no one was *worthy*, and no one was *able*. You need both: some may be worthy but not able. Some may be able but not worthy. A wicked world needs someone who is both.

It is like that in the Catechism's question: first, who is worthy to accomplish the work of deliverance? No human is great enough! Second, who is able to accomplish this work? Not God as such; he cannot mediate between himself and the humanity he is angry with. According to the Bible, there can only be one answer: the mediator must be someone who is both human and God. He must be a person that is one hundred percent human as well as one hundred percent God, and yet be one person. Sometimes Jesus' humanity is underlined: "[T]here is one God, and there is one mediator between God and men, the *man* Christ Jesus, who gave himself as a ransom for all" (1 Tim. 2:5–6). Sometimes his divinity is emphasized: ". . . our great *God* and Savior Jesus Christ, who gave himself for us to redeem us from all lawlessness and to purify for himself a people for his own possession who are zealous for good works" (Titus 2:13–14). We need both: One who is both God and Man.

✤ ✤ ✤

DAY 43 – ONE PERSON, TWO NATURES
(Lord's Day 5, Q&A 15, part 2)

A. One who is a true and righteous human, yet more powerful than all creatures, that is, one who is also true God.

Of course, the Catechism does not reach its conclusion on the nature of the true Mediator by pure logic only. Through the New Testament, it knows already beforehand what the conclusion is going to be. That is, within a few Q&As it is going to introduce Jesus Christ to us, who is truly God and truly Man in one person. But the teacher does not do so right away; he creates some tension and anticipation first. He wishes to make the pupil ripe for the final conclusion: think first about the question what kind of Deliverer we need! What conditions does he have to satisfy? It will not do if he is just Man. But he cannot be just God either. The crucial point is this: he must be both!

What the pupil will have derived by him- or herself, by means of these persistent Q&As, will be of far greater value to him or her than if the teacher would have revealed the answer right away. Think, pupil! What kind of Mediator do we need?

In reality, it took the Christian church several centuries before it had worked this all out for herself. It had to get rid of a lot of erroneous teachings. First, there was so-called docetism, which denied the true humanity of Christ. It claimed that God had taken upon himself just the outer appearance of a Man, and only for a while. Second, there were those who denied the true deity of Christ; they claimed that he was only the first and the greatest of God's creatures (Arianism). Third, some said that Christ was actually two persons: a human person and a divine person. Fourth, some claimed that Christ had only one nature: his human nature had merged into his divine nature. Fifth, some asserted that Christ was a divine spirit in a human body.

Finally, in the year 451, the church came to a conclusion that since then has been accepted by almost all Christian churches: Christ is one person with two natures, the divine nature and the human nature. He is truly God and truly Man in one person. And because he is not only human but also divine, his human nature is spotless, sinless, true, and righteous, more powerful than all creatures.

✤　✤　✤

DAY 44 – THE TRUE MEDIATOR
(Lord's Day 6, Q&A 16, part 1)

Q. Why must the mediator be a true and righteous human?
A. God's justice demands that human nature, which has sinned,
must pay for sin.

The biblical notion of the "mediator" is quite important; it is the person who builds a bridge between God, humanity's Creator and holy Judge, on the one hand, and fallen, sinful humanity, on the other hand. Such a mediator was the person that Job was looking for; he said, God "is not a man, as I am, that I might answer him, that we should come to trial together. There is no arbiter between us, who might lay his hand on us both" (9:32–33). The gulf remained; Job was not aware of any possible bridge. In the same book, Elihu speaks of the "mediator, one of the thousand, to declare to man what is right for him" (33:23). He presented him to Job, but naturally he could do so only in the vaguest possible way. Elsewhere it was God himself who looked for a mediator: "I sought for a man among them [i.e. the Israelites] who should build up the wall and stand in the breach before me for the land, that I should not destroy it, but I found none" (Ezek. 22:30).

In the New Testament, the fog is finally lifted, and we begin to recognize the one and only true mediator between God and humanity: "[T]here is one God, and there is one mediator between God and men, the man Christ Jesus, who gave himself as a ransom for all" (1 Tim. 2:5–6). He paid the price, and thus led, and leads, repentant sinners back to God. "Christ has obtained a ministry that is as much more excellent than the old [covenant] as the [new] covenant he mediates is better" (Heb. 8:6). Christ "is the mediator of a new covenant, so that those who are called may receive the promised eternal inheritance, since a death has occurred that redeems them from the transgressions committed under the first covenant" (9:15; cf. 12:24).

Perhaps the most beautiful way to describe the task he has accomplished is this: "Christ suffered once for sins, the righteous for the unrighteous, that he might bring us to God" (1 Pet. 3:18). Not just take us to heaven, or to the new earth, but back into the arms of God, just like the prodigal son landed in the arms of his Father (Luke 15:20). Our goal is not heaven, but God himself.

✤ ✤ ✤

DAY 45 – TRUE AND RIGHTEOUS
(LORD'S DAY 6, Q&A 16, PART 2)

A. God's justice demands that human nature, which has sinned, must pay for sin; but a sinful human could never pay for others.

The mediator must be a human, but not just any human. He must be "a true and righteous human" (Q&A 15). We realize immediately that such a person, in the true sense of the word, since the Fall has never lived in this world except One. This is the One called "Faithful and True," who "in righteousness judges" (Rev. 19:11). He is "the holy one, the true one" (3:7). He was as truly a human as you and I: "Since . . . the children share in flesh and blood, he himself likewise partook of the same things" (Heb. 2:14). He was "born in the likeness of men" (Phil. 2:7). And at the same time he was totally different, even as a Man. God sent "his own Son in the likeness of sinful flesh" (Rom. 8:3), but the difference was this: it is *in us* that the flesh is sinful. But in his case, his flesh, though being like our flesh, was *without sin*. We have a fourfold testimony for this: he "committed no sin" (1 Pet. 2:22), he "knew no sin" (2 Cor. 5:21), "in him there is no sin" (1 John 3:5), "in every respect [he] has been tempted . . . yet without sin" (Heb. 4:15).

Have you ever tried to imagine a human being who was really totally without sin? Even Pilate had to say, "I find no guilt in him" (John 18:38; 19:4). Jesus was the truly righteous One. Pilate's wife called him "that righteous man" (Matt. 27:19). Peter called him "the Holy and Righteous One" (Acts 3:14; cf. 1 Pet. 3:18). Stephen and Ananias called him "the Righteous One" (7:52; 22:14). Paul called him "the righteous judge" (2 Tim. 4:8). John called him "Jesus Christ the righteous" (1 John 2:1). Throughout the centuries, people have blurted out all kinds of nonsense about Jesus. But not many have ever dared to doubt the fact that he was "a true and righteous human." To be sure, some great men of God have been called "righteous and holy" as well, such as John the Baptist (Mark 6:20). But they were such by the redeeming grace of God. Jesus was such all by himself. He was the only human in all of history who did not need redemption—and therefore he was the only human in all of history who could *bring about* redemption.

✦ ✦ ✦

DAY 46 – TRUE GOD AND MAN
(Lord's Day 6, Q&A 17, part 1)

Q. Why must the mediator also be true God?
A. So that the mediator, by the power of his divinity, might bear the weight of God's wrath in his humanity.

Jesus Christ was *worthy* to be our deliverer because he was a true and righteous human; he was without sin (see previous Q&A). Jesus was also *able* to be our deliverer because he was God. This is a far-reaching statement. Many people who call themselves Christians are not happy with it. They suggest it is okay if we call him "divine," or the "Son of God" as a kind of honorary title—but not God. At best, they are prepared to ascribe "divinity" to him but not "deity," if you can appreciate the difference. Yet, the Catechism says he is "true God." And it is in good company, for the Bible does so too, sometimes even explicitly and directly. John says, "In the beginning was the Word, and the Word was with God, and the Word was God. . . . And the Word became flesh" (John 1:1, 14), and speaks of God's "Son Jesus Christ," who "is the true God and eternal life" (1 John 5:20). Paul speaks of "Christ, who is God over all" (Rom. 9:5) and of "our great God and Savior Jesus Christ" (Titus 2:13); Peter does similarly (2 Pet. 1:1). We could draw many more proofs from the New Testament. His enemies even accused him of "making himself God" (John 10:33).

Now notice the tension in the Catechism's answer: because Christ is *God* he is able to "bear the weight of *God's* wrath *in his humanity.*" When we speak of bearing God's wrath, we indeed think of Jesus "in his humanity," that is, as the Man who had to say on the cross, "My *God*, my *God*, why have you forsaken me?" (Matt. 27:46). Only a Man who is intimate with God can speak in such a way. And yet, at this very moment he was also God—if you wish, God the Son. We should never separate the two natures of Christ, the human one and the divine one. But we should certainly distinguish between the two. It was a *Man* who spoke to his *God* on the cross. But only because this Man *was* God was he able to bear God's wrath. We have to fully maintain the tension in the Catechism's answer. That is, we can never fully unravel the mystery of Christ's person: truly God, truly Man. But what we cannot unravel we can certainly admire and worship!

✦   ✦   ✦

DAY 47 – RESTORING RIGHTEOUSNESS
(Lord's Day 6, Q&A 17, part 2)

A. . . . the mediator . . .[was to] earn for us and restore to us righteousness and life.

What was the goal of our mediator Jesus Christ? He restored the bridge between God and us for a negative and a positive purpose. The negative one was to remove the iniquities that had made a separation between God and us (cf. Isa. 59:2). He saved us from the power of sin, the devil, and death. The positive purpose was to restore to us righteousness and life. Through the word "restore" the Catechism reminds us of what we lost in the Garden of Eden. Adam was without sin, and through redemption we receive a new nature, which is again without sin (cf. 1 John 3:6, 9). At the same time, there is a huge difference: Adam was not supposed to fall into sin, but he *could* fall, and he did. However, our new nature can never fall into sin again. As long as we are still here on earth, *we* can sin, that is, the "flesh" (the sinful nature that is still in us) can sin—but not the new self (cf. Eph. 4:24; Col. 3:10).

This is what many men of God have always told us: through Christ's redemption *we gain much more than Adam ever lost.* Of course we do. Could you imagine the first humans ruining everything in five minutes, and God needing thousands of years just to bring us back to where it began? No, this is why some church fathers spoke of the "happy fall" or our "happy guilt," because they realized that through fall and redemption God is working toward a new world of "righteousness and life" that without the Fall would not have been possible. He is not just repairing the old world, nor is he replacing it—he is *elevating* it through the redemptive work of Christ.

World history is not a circle but an upward spiral: one day we will reach a far better world than Adam lost. This was God's wonderful plan right from the start. Adam could not even *tell* what "righteousness" and "life" meant because he did not know what *un*righteousness and death meant. He did not yet know good or evil (cf. Gen. 2:9, 17). *We* know righteousness and life after a world history of so much unrighteousness and death. We *know* good and evil—and by Christ's work are destined for the good. Thank God for it!

❈   ❈   ❈

DAY 48 – CHRIST OUR REDEMPTION
(Lord's Day 6, Q&A 18, part 1)

Q. Then who is this mediator—true God and at the same time a true and righteous human?
A. Our Lord Jesus Christ, who was given to us to completely deliver us and make us right with God.

I don't know why this answer was changed in the CRC version of 2011; the original version said, "Our Lord Jesus Christ: 'who of God is made unto us wisdom, and righteousness, and sanctification, and redemption.'" Of course, this is almost a direct quotation from 1 Corinthians 1:30, "[B]ecause of [God] [or, from God] you are in Christ Jesus, who became to us wisdom from God, righteousness and sanctification and redemption." This is Paul's splendid way to describe the results of the work of Christ here. Apparently he wants to say that these results can never be separated from the person of Christ. It is in *him* that we have these great things: wisdom, righteousness, sanctification, and redemption. We will never possess them apart from him. They are not gifts that are handed to us and become our own irrespective of, and separated from, the giver.

In eternity we will have these four blessings "in him," and we will never forget this. They are "from" (or "because of") God, that is, he made the plan and he sent his Son, but we have these blessings "in" (or "through") Jesus. In Christ's redemptive work, first, all the wisdom of God's counsels has been revealed, even far more than in creation (cf. Eph. 3:10, "so that through the church the manifold wisdom of God might now be made known"). Second, Christ became our "righteousness," that is, by faith in him we have been justified (i.e., made righteous). He who was righteous became sin, so that we, who were sin, became the righteousness of God (cf. 2 Cor. 5:21).

Third, Christ became our "sanctification" or "holiness," that is, by faith in him we have been sanctified (i.e., made holy). You might say (cf. 2 Cor. 5:21 again), he who was holy became sin, so that we, who were sin, became the holiness of God. And fourth, Christ became to us "redemption," that is, in and through him we have been redeemed from the power of sin, the devil, and death. He embodies this redemption as it were, in his person and work. Never enjoy your righteousness, holiness, and redemption without remembering through whom you received it, and in whom you possess it!

✣ ✣ ✣

DAY 49 – CHRIST OUR DELIVERER
(LORD'S DAY 6, Q&A 18, PART 2)

A. Our Lord Jesus Christ . . . was given to us to completely deliver us.

We have seen that, now and then, the word "we" in the Catechism seemed to refer to unbelievers in particular. But here, the "we" is clearly believers again. He is *our* Lord Jesus Christ, as the New Testament says many times (from Acts 15:26 to Jude 1:25). It is wonderful if someone can even sincerely say that Jesus is "*my* Lord," as did Elizabeth, Mary Magdalene, Thomas, and Paul (Luke 1:43; John 20:13, 28; Phil. 3:8).

This version of the Catechism even adds: "he was given to *us*." We are familiar with the thought that he gave himself "*for* us" (Titus 2:14; cf. Gal. 1:4; Eph. 5:2). Perhaps the most conspicuous passage where it is actually said that he was given *to* us is this: "And [God] put all things under [Christ's] feet and gave him as head over all things to the church, which is his body, the fullness of him who fills all in all" (Eph. 1:22–23). Christ is described here as the One who was "raised from the dead and seated" by God "at his right hand in the heavenly places, far above all rule and authority and power and dominion, and above every name that is named" (vv. 20–21). Imagine the greatness and majesty of the risen and glorified Christ! And *as such* God gave him to the church, the body of Christ, to be its "head over all things." The church is so precious and important to God that he gave to her the best gift he could imagine to be her head: the glorified Christ! The same One who was "given to us to completely deliver us," has now become the head of the church, and the Lord of every individual believer.

The term "deliverance" indicates that by nature we were in captivity, in the hands of heinous enemies: sin, the devil, and death. Let me mention two biblical examples: "through death" Christ did "destroy the one who has the power of death, that is, the devil," and did "deliver all those who through fear of death were subject to lifelong slavery" (Heb. 2:14–15). The Lord Jesus Christ "gave himself for our sins to deliver us from the present evil age, according to the will of our God and Father" (Gal. 1:3–4). What a great deliverer he is!

✦ ✦ ✦

DAY 50 – CHRIST OUR RESTORER
(Lord's Day 6, Q&A 18, part 3)

A. Our Lord Jesus Christ . . . was given to us to . . . make us right with God.

This version of the Catechism says that Christ was given to us "to make us right with God." An interesting expression! It suggests the great New Testament truth of justification, which literally means "making right(eous)." But perhaps the expression even more strongly suggests the idea of reconciliation. If you make right with someone, it means you have hurt that person, and now you put the situation right by making a confession of what you did wrong, and by extending again the hand of friendship. Actually, the text does not say that *we* "make *it* right with God" but that *Christ* "makes *us* right with God." There was someone who put us straight, who intervened for us, and reconciled us with God.

In a certain sense, Jesus confessed our sins to God as if they were his, in order to make us right with God as our representative. We see this foreshadowed in the high priest at Atonement Day: "Aaron shall lay both his hands on the head of the live goat, and confess over it all the iniquities of the people of Israel, and all their transgressions, all their sins" (Lev. 16:21). This is what Jesus did on the cross by bearing our sins (1 Pet. 2:24). Thus he reconciled us with God: "[W]hile we were enemies we were reconciled to God by the death of his Son" (Rom. 5:10–11). God "through Christ reconciled us to himself" (2 Cor. 5:18–20); "you, who once were alienated and hostile in mind, doing evil deeds, he has now reconciled in his body of flesh by his death, in order to present you holy and blameless and above reproach before [God]" (Col. 1:21–22).

The Bible never says that God had to be reconciled with *us*, or that he had to make it right with us. He never behaved as our enemy; "his hand is stretched out still" (Isa. 9:17, 21; 10:4). *We* were enemies, *we* were hostile, *we* needed to be made right with God, not the other way around. On the contrary, it is God who makes his "appeal" through his "ambassadors," who say: "We *implore* you on behalf of Christ, be reconciled to God" (2 Cor. 5:20). God in his love begging the sinner—what a humiliating but also glorious thought!

✢　✢　✢

DAY 51 – THE HOLY GOSPEL
(LORD'S DAY 6, Q&A 19, PART 1)

Q. How do you come to know this?
A. The holy gospel tells me.

How do we know about Jesus Christ as the only true mediator between God and humanity, and the only true deliverer from the power of sin, the devil, and death? The Catechism's answer is simple: the holy gospel tells me. Actually, one might answer: the holy Bible tells me. But the core message of the Bible is here described as "gospel." You will probably know that the English word "gospel" comes from "good spell," and that means "good message." This is also precisely the meaning of the Greek word *euangelion* or *evangelion*, of which "gospel" is the translation. We still know this Greek term from words like "evangelist" (gospel preacher) and "evangelizing" (preaching the gospel). Outside the Bible, and independent from the Bible, we hear very little about Jesus, and even less about the gospel. But the Bible itself is full of the gospel, from beginning to end.

This is almost literally true. Almost the first words of the Bible are these: "[T]he Spirit of God was hovering over the face of the waters. And God said, 'Let there be light,' and there was light" (Gen. 1:2–3). According to the apostle Paul, we may read the gospel already in these words, for he speaks of "the light of the gospel of the glory of Christ, who is the image of God. . . . For God, who said, 'Let light shine out of darkness,' has shone in our hearts to give the light of the knowledge of the glory of God in the face of Jesus Christ" (2 Cor. 4:4, 6). Similarly, if the Bible almost begins with telling us about the "tree of life" (Gen. 2:9), it almost ends with saying: "Blessed are those who wash their robes, so that they may have the right to the tree of life and that they may enter the city by the gates" (Rev. 22:14).

In between, there are announcements of judgment for those who refuse to love and obey God; but the preponderant message is the one of redemption, hope, and blessing, anchored in the person of Jesus Christ, the Son of God. Hearing the gospel is hearing the "gospel of Jesus (Christ)" (Mark 1:1; Rom. 16:25; 2 Thess. 1:8); it is the "gospel of the Son of God" (Rom. 1:9).

❊   ❊   ❊

DAY 52 – THE GOSPEL IN PARADISE
(LORD'S DAY 6, Q&A 19, PART 2)

A. . . . God began to reveal the gospel already in Paradise.

Of course, the Catechism refers here to the well-known word of God after humanity's fall: "I will put enmity between you and the woman, and between your offspring and her offspring; he shall bruise your head, and you shall bruise his heel" (Gen. 3:15). This statement by God is often called the *prot(o)evangelium*, the "first gospel" announced by God to fallen Adam and Eve. Actually, this is not a very accurate description. First, these words are not addressed to the first humans at all but to the devil. Second, these words do not form a promise but rather a threat. They do not announce the redemption of God's people but rather God's judgment on the devil. Third, they do not even literally refer to Christ but very generally to "the woman's" (i.e., Eve's) offspring, that is, all those that would be born of Eve.

Yet, this is not all; there is more to it. Already in Genesis 4, we could say that Cain represents the devil's offspring (cf. John 8:44; 1 John 3:10), and Abel represents the woman's offspring: the offspring of "life" (cf. Gen. 3:20). Cain killed Abel, that is, in the language of Genesis 3:15, the devil's offspring "bruised the heel" of Eve's offspring, and this has gone on for thousands of years, the devil persecuting the children of God.

I am not impressed with the argument that "seed" (offspring) is a collective noun. God told Abraham, "[I]n your offspring shall all the nations of the earth be blessed" (Gen. 22:18), and Paul comments: "It does not say, 'And to offsprings,' referring to many, but referring to one, 'And to your offspring,' who is Christ" (Gal. 3:16). He could have said the same of Genesis 3:15; in the end, and indirectly, the verse *is* a promise and a piece of "gospel" insofar as it does announce that one day the woman's "offspring," that is, Christ, would bruise the devil's head (the "serpent" is the devil, Rev. 12:9; 20:2). "The reason the Son of God appeared was to destroy the works of the devil" (1 John 3:8). If Paul says, "The God of peace will soon crush Satan under your feet" (Rom. 16:20), we may assume he was thinking of Genesis 3:15.

✤　　✤　　✤

DAY 53 – THE GOSPEL OF PATRIARCHS AND PROPHETS

(Lord's Day 6, Q&A 19, part 3)

A. . . . later God proclaimed [the gospel] by the holy patriarchs and prophets.

The gospel is the "good message" about redemption and hope, which pervades the entire Bible. It was first preached by God in the Garden of Eden, and then in the time of the "holy patriarchs": Abraham, Isaac, and Jacob. God told Abraham, "[I]n your offspring shall all the nations of the earth be blessed" (Gen. 22:18), and Paul says he was referring to Christ: in Christ shall all the nations of the earth be blessed (Gal. 3:16). Jacob blessing his sons said, "The scepter shall not depart from Judah, nor a lawgiver from between his feet, until Shiloh comes; and to Him shall be the obedience of the people" (Gen. 49:10 NKJV). Both Jews and Christians have seen in this verse a reference to the Messiah.

And then the prophets! Should we even begin quoting from them? Peter said, "To him [i.e., Christ] all the prophets bear witness that everyone who believes in him receives forgiveness of sins through his name" (Acts 10:43). Paul writes of "the gospel of God, which he promised beforehand through his prophets in the holy Scriptures, concerning his Son" (Rom. 1:1–3). If we limit ourselves to passages speaking of redemption and forgiveness, we will always think of Isaiah 53 first: "[H]e was pierced for our transgressions; he was crushed for our iniquities; upon him was the chastisement that brought us peace, and with his wounds we are healed. . . . [I]t was the will of the Lord to crush him; he has put him to grief; when his soul makes an offering for guilt, he shall see his offspring" (vv. 5, 10).

Micah says, "[God] will again have compassion on us; he will tread our iniquities underfoot. You will cast all our sins into the depths of the sea" (7:19). And God says through Zechariah, "I will pour out on [God's people] a spirit of grace and pleas for mercy, so that, when they look on me, on him whom they have pierced, they shall mourn for him, as one mourns for an only child . . . On that day there shall be a fountain opened for the house of David and the inhabitants of Jerusalem, to cleanse them from sin and uncleanness" (12:10; 13:1). The pierced One turns out to be the great Purifier!

✢   ✢   ✢

DAY 54 – THE GOSPEL IN THE SACRIFICES

(Lord's Day 6, Q&A 19, part 4)

A. . . .God foreshadowed [the gospel] by the sacrifices and other ceremonies of the law.

It is wonderful to ponder the way Christ and his redemptive work are presented in the Levitical laws of the sacrifices (Lev. 1–7) and other ceremonies! These "other ceremonies of the law," such as the Passover (Exod. 12) and other Jewish festivals (Lev. 23; Num. 28–29; Deut. 16), as well as rituals like the one for healed lepers (Lev. 14), all contain certain animal sacrifices. Each and every type of animal sacrifice in the Sinaitic laws points in its own specific way to the work of Christ on the cross. The two most basic types of sacrifice are the burnt offering (Lev. 1; always coupled with the grain offering in Lev. 2) and the sin offering (Lev. 4; the guilt offering of Lev. 5 is a special example of this). Of both types we read that they have been prescribed by God to make atonement for the sinner (Lev. 1:4; 4:20, 26, 31, 35). A third type of animal sacrifice is the peace offering (Lev. 3; 7:11–36). Nowhere is the peace offering said to make atonement, but Ezekiel 45:17 speaks in a general way of "the sin offerings, grain offerings, burnt offerings, and peace offerings, to make atonement on behalf of the house of Israel."

"Atonement" is a typical English term, first used in Tyndale's English Bible translation and derived from being "at one," "in accord" (with each other). As such it covers two different New Testament expressions: "propitiation" and "reconciliation." Propitiation involves the blotting out of sins: "Jesus Christ . . . is the propitiation for our sins" (1 John 2:1–2; cf. 4:10; Heb. 2:17). Christ Jesus was put forward by God "as a propitiation by his blood, to be received by faith" (Rom. 3:25). The language of the Levitical sacrifices is here directly applied to the work of Christ (see extensively Heb. 10:1–10). The other important term is "reconciliation," which involves the work by which God and his enemies—insofar as they repent and come to faith—are put "at one" (Rom. 5:11; 2 Cor. 5:18–20; Col. 1:20–22). Both aspects of the work of Christ are clearly represented by the Levitical sacrifices; already in them, the light of the gospel brightly shines!

✣ ✣ ✣

DAY 55 – THE GOSPEL OF GOD'S SON
(Lord's Day 6, Q&A 19, part 5)

A. . . . finally God fulfilled [the gospel] through his own beloved Son.

Finally! All the loose threads of the Old Testament come together, all the Old Testament images are brought to fulfillment, all the foreshadowing becomes reality. "Christ is the end [or, goal, or fulfillment, or culmination] of the law for righteousness to everyone who believes" (Rom. 10:4). "[W]hen the fullness of time had come, God sent forth his Son" (Gal. 4:4). Festivals, sacrifices, rituals, these "are a shadow of the things to come, but the substance belongs to Christ" (Col. 2:16–17). "Long ago, at many times and in many ways, God spoke to our fathers by the prophets, but in these last days he has spoken to us by his Son" (Heb. 1:1–2). "In this the love of God was made manifest among us, that God sent his only Son into the world, so that we might live through him" (1 John 4:9).

Precisely at the coming of Christ into this world, we realize that the gospel of which these Q&As speak is wider than God's redemptive gospel for poor sinners. When John the Baptist and Jesus Christ himself began their preaching, it was another aspect they emphasized: "Repent, for the kingdom of heaven is at hand" (Matt. 3:2; 4:17); Jesus proclaimed the "gospel of the kingdom" (4:23). This involves not only saving individual sinners but reclaiming the world for God. Not only the Deliverer but the *King* has arrived. And this too was foreshadowed in the Old Testament: he is the "son" of Isaiah 9:6–7: "For to us a child is born, to us a son is given; and the government shall be upon his shoulder, and his name shall be called Wonderful Counselor, Mighty God, Everlasting Father, Prince of Peace. Of the increase of his government and of peace there will be no end, on the throne of David and over his kingdom, to establish it and to uphold it with justice and with righteousness."

"Behold, your king is coming to you; righteous and having salvation is he, humble and mounted on a donkey, on a colt, the foal of a donkey . . . and he shall speak peace to the nations; his rule shall be from sea to sea, and from the River to the ends of the earth" (Zech. 9:9–10). What a prospect!

❖   ❖   ❖

DAY 56 – ARE ALL SAVED?
(LORD'S DAY 7, Q&A 20, PART 1)

Q. Are all people then saved through Christ just as they were lost through Adam?
A. No.

In some sense many of us would wish that the answer would be: "Yes, all people are saved through Christ." Many people indeed believe in such a universal atonement because they cannot imagine how a loving God can let certain people get lost forever. They even have Bible verses for this belief: "God our Savior . . . desires all people to be saved" (1 Tim. 2:3–4). This is true—but the problem is that many people *themselves* do not desire to be saved. God does not force them against their will. Yes, God is "patient . . . not wishing that any should perish, but that all should reach repentance" (2 Pet. 3:9). But the problem is that many people *themselves* do not wish to reach repentance, and so they do perish. It is not primarily God who brings destruction on them; they are "bringing upon *themselves* swift destruction" (2 Pet. 2:1). "[T]he grace of God has appeared, bringing salvation for all people" (Titus 2:11), and "one act of righteousness [i.e., the work of Christ] leads to justification and life for all men" (Rom. 5:18). But the problem is that many people do not wish to *accept* this salvation. It is *for* them, but they flatly refuse it.

Was it God's fault that the first humans fell into sin? No. They themselves were responsible for it, and for all the consequences it brought. Is it God's fault that certain people will be lost forever? No. These people are responsible for not desiring to know God, to repent and to be saved, and have to bear all the consequences of it. People *chose* to abandon God, and they *choose* to stay away from him. The fact that, nevertheless, a number of people will be saved forever through faith in Christ is an act of God's pure grace. And even this does not leave out people's own responsibility: "Cast away from you all the transgressions that you have committed, and make yourselves a new heart and a new spirit! Why will you die, O house of Israel?" (Ezek. 18:31). "I have no pleasure in the death of the wicked, but that the wicked turn from his way and live; turn back, turn back from your evil ways, for why will you die, O house of Israel?" (33:11).

✣   ✣   ✣

DAY 57 – ONLY THOSE WHO BELIEVE
(Lord's Day 7, Q&A 20, part 2)

Q. Are all people then saved through Christ just as they were lost through Adam?
A. No. Only those are saved who through true faith are grafted into Christ and accept all his benefits.

We can quite easily understand the parallel that the Catechism's question suggests. It is the parallel between Adam as head of *his* family, and Christ (the "last Adam," 1 Cor. 15:45) as head of *his* family, so to speak. This is the message of Romans 5:18–19: "As one trespass led to condemnation for all men, so one act of righteousness leads to justification and life for all men. For as by the one man's disobedience the many were made sinners, so by the one man's obedience the many will be made righteous." There is here a big difference between the two verses. Verse 18 is about the *effect* of someone's act. The effect of Adam's one trespass was that all of humanity—for they are all descendants of Adam—came under God's condemnation. Similarly, the effect of Christ's "one act of righteousness," that is, his work on the cross, is "justification and life" offered to all of humanity. *All* have fallen in Adam, and in principle *all* can be saved in Christ. The work of Christ is vast enough to offer salvation to everyone.

However, verse 19 describes what actually happens. There are two groups here that are described as "the many." You have "the many" of Adam—they are his family so to speak—who are all sinners because of his fall. And you have "the many" of Christ—they are *his* family—who, by faith and by the grace of God (cf. 3:22–25) have been made righteous. The fall had consequences for *all*: it turned all people into sinners. And those who remain in the "family" of Adam will remain sinners in eternity, and suffer the consequences of it. Christ's work on the cross also had consequences for *all* because now God's ambassadors can offer God's salvation to *all* people. But only those who, through faith, move, so to speak, from the family of Adam to the family of Christ, will be factually saved. Only these effectively share in the results of Christ's work.

In conclusion we can say that to become a sinner, it is enough to be born of sinners. But to become a member of the family of faith you need to be born again, this time by the Holy Spirit (John 3:5–6).

❖   ❖   ❖

DAY 58 – GRAFTED INTO CHRIST
(Lord's Day 7, Q&A 20, part 3)

A. . . . Only those are saved who through true faith are grafted into Christ and accept all his benefits.

This is a beautiful expression: through true faith we are "grafted into Christ." You will not find it literally in the Bible. At best we can say that the expression is inspired by Romans 11:17–24, where Paul says that Gentile believers have been "grafted into" the olive tree. This olive tree is not Christ in person, but the analogy is quite acceptable: we have been "grafted into" Christ. The parallel with John 15 supports this: "As the branch cannot bear fruit by itself, unless it abides in the vine, neither can you, unless you abide in me. I am the vine; you are the branches. Whoever abides in me and I in him, he it is that bears much fruit, for apart from me you can do nothing. . . . By this my Father is glorified, that you bear much fruit and so prove to be my disciples" (vv. 4–8).

Of course, you need a "true faith" for this—not a "dead faith" (cf. James 2:17, 20, 26), which is no faith at all. "Whoever believes in the Son has eternal life; whoever does not obey the Son shall not see life, but the wrath of God remains on him" (John 3:36). Without the "obedience of faith" (cf. Rom. 1:5) you will never share in Christ's benefits, that is, all the beneficial results of his redemptive work (cf. Heb. 4:2). "[W]ithout faith it is impossible to please him, for whoever would draw near to God must believe that he exists and that he rewards those who seek him" (Heb. 11:6).

The believers are those who "*accept* all Christ's benefits." There must be an act of acceptance: stretch out your hands, and receive! I know, "by grace you have been saved through faith. And this is not your own doing; it is the gift of God" (Eph. 2:8). But this does not exclude your own responsibility. The Bible is very clear on this point: "[T]o all who did receive [or, accept] him, who believed in his name, he gave the right to become children of God" (John 1:12). "[Y]ou received [or, accepted] the word in much affliction, with the joy of the Holy Spirit" (1 Thess. 1:6). In order to get lost you have to do nothing. In order to be saved you have to accept the gospel, and rejoice in the grace that *made* you accept it!

✷　　✷　　✷

DAY 59 – TRUE FAITH
(Lord's Day 7, Q&A 21, part 1)

Q. What is true faith?
A. True faith is not only a sure knowledge by which I hold as true all that God has revealed to us in Scripture; it is also a wholehearted trust.

There are all kinds of faith. You have faith without works—it is dead (James 2:17, 26). There is faith that is not "working through love" (Gal. 5:6)—it *is* no genuine faith. There may be a "believer" who has "no root in himself, but ... when tribulation or persecution arises ... immediately he falls away" (Matt. 13:21). There are those who "believe" when they see signs and wonders—but their "faith" has no value to God (John 2:23–25). And then there are those whose faith involves "a sure knowledge by which they hold as true all that God has revealed to us in Scripture," but it is not "a wholehearted trust."

To be sure, seeing signs and wonders may certainly *help* faith. And "a sure knowledge" is even more valuable. Imagine someone who confessed the Christian faith but had no idea what he was talking about. He could not tell you anything about God or Christ, or about the contents of the Bible. That would be strange. If faith is a "wholehearted trust," you must have *some* idea *what* it is you put your trust in. However, the opposite is not necessarily true. You may have a lot of knowledge of Christianity, knowledge you may even be sure of, and yet not be a believer in the biblical sense. "Even the demons believe—and shudder" (James 2:19). There are Christians who really think that if you accept everything the Bible (or the Catechism, or the Apostles' Creed) says you are a Christian. Therefore, the Catechism adds that true faith is also a wholehearted *trust*. You do not only believe what God says in his Word, you *confide* in God, you *entrust* yourself to God.

True faith is commitment. It is surrender. It is entering into an eternal bond with God. *This* leads to not just intellectual knowledge of Christianity, but knowledge in the sense of relationship, intimacy, fellowship: "[T]his is eternal life, that they *know* you the only true God, and Jesus Christ whom you have sent" (John 17:3). It also leads to confidence, as Abraham had, who was "fully convinced that God was able to do what he had promised" (Rom. 4:21). "Let us then with confidence draw near to the throne of grace" (Heb. 4:16).

✳   ✳   ✳

DAY 60 – A WHOLEHEARTED TRUST
(Lord's Day 7, Q&A 21, part 2)

A. *True faith is . . . a wholehearted trust, which the Holy Spirit creates in me by the gospel.*

If faith is "a wholehearted trust," how is this trust born in your heart? Where does it come from? To be sure, it is we who have to believe. It is not the Holy Spirit believing for us, in our stead. *We* have to do it. God even *orders* us to believe; the opposite of "believing" is "disobeying" (John 3:36). There is "the command of the eternal God, to bring about the obedience of faith" (Rom. 16:26). God "commands all people everywhere to repent" (Acts 17:30). It is God imploring us, through his ambassadors, to be reconciled with him (2 Cor. 5:20). So if you do not believe God, you have a big problem: you disobey him. "[W]hoever does not believe will be condemned" (Mark 16:16). "Whoever does not believe God has made him a liar" (1 John 5:10). "[W]hoever believes in him is not condemned, but whoever does not believe is condemned already, because he has not believed in the name of the only Son of God" (John 3:18).

At the same time, however, it is perfectly true that, were it not for the Holy Spirit, none of us would ever have come to faith. Believing is one hundred percent our responsibility, but it is also one hundred percent true that it is the Holy Spirit who works this faith in our heart. Nobody can be born again without the work of the Holy Spirit within him (John 3:5–6). It was not just Lydia herself, but *the Lord* who opened her heart to the gospel (Acts 16:14). It is "the Lord your God" who "will circumcise your heart and the heart of your offspring, so that you will love the Lord your God with all your heart and with all your soul, that you may live" (Deut. 30:6).

God once told his people, "I will give you a new heart, and a new spirit I will put within you. And I will remove the heart of stone from your flesh and give you a heart of flesh. And I will put my Spirit within you, and cause you to walk in my statutes and be careful to obey my rules" (Ezek. 36:26–27). It is no different today. *You* must believe; that's an order. But after you *have* believed, you begin to realize that it was God who in his grace, through his Spirit, worked in your heart.

✤ ✤ ✤

DAY 61 – TO ME ALSO
(Lord's Day 7, Q&A 21, part 3)

A. True faith is . . . a wholehearted trust . . . that God has freely granted, not only to others but to me also.

This is one of those very personal moments in the Catechism: "not only to others but to me also." It reminds us of the Catechism's very first Q&A: "What is your only comfort in life and in death? That I am not my own, but belong—body and soul, in life and in death— to my faithful Savior, Jesus Christ. . . ." It does not say: What is the *Christian's* only comfort? It does not even say, What is *our* only comfort? It does not say, That *we* are not our own, etc. The Catechism is about the very personal faith of the individual believer. It is great to know that God has freely granted faith to millions of believers throughout history. But to know that would not help me a bit as long as that faith would not have been given to *me*.

Of course, it is important to realize that the content of my faith is basically identical to that of all those other believers. Together we are the church. But I am not just a tiny grain in a huge lump. *My* faith is *my* personal relationship to God and to the Lord Jesus Christ. Paul could say that he is "the Son of God, who loved *me* and gave himself for *me*" (Gal. 2:20). It is wonderful to know that Christ loved millions of people and gave himself for them. But that knowledge would not give me any assurance of salvation. I have to know that he died for *me*. "I am my beloved's, and his desire is for *me*" (Song 7:10). I want to be able to speak of "the surpassing worth of knowing Christ Jesus *my* Lord" (Phil. 3:8), and be able to say, "*my* God will supply every need of yours according to his riches in glory in Christ Jesus" (4:19). David could say, "The LORD is *my* rock and *my* fortress and *my* deliverer, *my* God, *my* rock, in whom I take refuge, *my* shield, and the horn of *my* salvation, *my* stronghold and *my* refuge, *my* savior" (2 Sam. 22:2–3), and Mary said, "my spirit rejoices in God *my* Savior" (Luke 1:47).

You know, it is great to be able to say with the Apostles' Creed, together with millions of other Christians, "I believe in the forgiveness of sins." But it is far greater to be able to say, by the grace of God, "I believe that my sins have been forgiven."

❖   ❖   ❖

DAY 62 – SHEER GRACE
(LORD'S DAY 7, Q&A 21, PART 4)

A. True faith is . . . a wholehearted trust . . . that God has freely granted . . . to me . . . forgiveness of sins, eternal righteousness, and salvation. These are gifts of sheer grace granted solely by Christ's merit.

Finally, this Q&A tells us *what* it is that God has "freely granted to me": God has forgiven me my sins; they do not stand between him and me anymore because they have been blotted out by the blood of Christ. Next, he has granted me eternal righteousness, which is the same as saying that he has justified me: as being forever united with the risen and glorified Christ I am perfectly righteous in his eyes, just as righteous as Christ is himself. I may not always *live* as a righteous person, but as far as my position in Christ is concerned, there is nothing that anyone could hold against me. "Who shall bring any charge against God's elect? It is God who justifies. Who is to condemn?" (Rom. 8:33–34).

Next, the text tells us we have been granted "salvation." That is, we have been saved from all the powers that had imprisoned us: sin, the devil, death, my old self, the law as a legalistic system. We will still have to be saved from the "flesh," that is, our old sinful nature, and from this mortal body with all its ailments. Christians still have to be saved from all their enemies, their persecutors and torturers. But in Christ we have it all, already now. He embodies for us all "wisdom from God, righteousness and sanctification and redemption" (1 Cor. 1:30).

The Catechism adds that these "are gifts of sheer grace, granted solely by Christ's merit." Paul says, "[B]y grace you have been saved through faith. And this is not your own doing; it is the gift of God, not a result of works, so that no one may boast" (Eph. 2:8–9). And elsewhere he summarizes it for us as follows: first, we have been "justified by [God's] grace as a gift." Second, we have it "through the redemption that is in Christ Jesus, whom God put forward as a propitiation by his blood." And third, we receive it "by faith" (Rom. 3:24–25). So you see, it is all due to *God's* "sheer grace," granted solely by *Christ's* merit. The only thing *we* have to do is to confidentially throw ourselves into God's arms. This is called faith—and even this is a gift of God, worked in us by his Holy Spirit.

✣ ✣ ✣

DAY 63 – PROMISED IN THE GOSPEL
(LORD'S DAY 7, Q&A 22, PART 1)

Q. What then must a Christian believe?
A. All that is promised us in the gospel.

This is an interesting way to put it: what we must believe is given to us in the "gospel" (say, in the Word of God) in the form of "promises." You could hardly mention any Christian blessing that does not have the element of a promise in it: something that still has to be fulfilled. The forgiveness of sins is a clear exception. At the moment we came to faith in Christ, we received the forgiveness of our sins, not only the sins we had committed until that point, but also the sins we unfortunately would still commit during the rest of our earthly life. In eternity, we will better see how much we have been forgiven, but we will not possess any more forgiveness than we, by God's grace, possess already now.

Another gift of God that has been fully granted us is the Holy Spirit. Jesus promised his disciples: "I will ask the Father, and he will give you another Helper, to be with you forever, even the Spirit of truth. . . . You know him, for he dwells with you and will be in you" (John 14:16–17). We have the Spirit dwelling in us already now. We may not always be *filled* with the Spirit (Eph. 5:18), we may not always *walk* by the Spirit (Gal. 5:16–18); yet, already our present mortal body is a temple of the Holy Spirit (1 Cor. 6:19).

For the rest, there is always the promise element. Spiritually, you have already been "made alive" (Eph. 2:5), but you still have to wait until God "will also give life to your mortal bodies through his Spirit who dwells in you" (Rom. 8:11); "we wait eagerly for . . . the redemption of our bodies" (v. 23). That will also involve being delivered from our sinful nature. All this waiting is connected with Christ's coming again: we are "waiting for our blessed hope, the appearing of the glory of our great God and Savior Jesus Christ, who gave himself for us to redeem us from all lawlessness and to purify for himself a people for his own possession who are zealous for good works" (Titus 2:13–14). "[W]hat sort of people ought you to be in lives of holiness and godliness, waiting for and hastening the coming of the day of God" (2 Pet. 3:11–12).

❖   ❖   ❖

DAY 64 – THE ARTICLES OF FAITH
(Lord's Day 7, Q&A 22, part 2)

A. All that is promised us in the gospel, a summary of which is taught us in the articles of our universal and undisputed Christian faith.

It is incredible to see how much, throughout church history, every detail of the Christian faith has been disputed. There is hardly any element over which there have been no fights, even violence, even religious wars. What a shame! At the same time, we can be thankful that, from a very early time, there has been a Christian document that almost all Christian denominations seem to agree upon. (I am not talking of borderline groups such as Jehovah's Witnesses and Mormons.) In this sense, this document is truly "universal" and "undisputed." It is a human document, not divinely inspired, not perfect; for instance, it fails a bit in properly describing Christ's work of redemption, and it does not explicitly state the deity of the Son and of the Holy Spirit. But we do not have any better document. Of course, we have the Nicene Creed, but this is far more extensive, and therefore also a little more open to criticism. But with the Apostles' Creed almost all Christians seem to be happy. Imagine, no matter how many differences there may be between Eastern Orthodox, Roman Catholic, and Protestant Christians, they agree upon the Apostles' Creed!

The Catechism speaks of the "articles of our Christian faith," but the common term is Apostles' Creed, although we can say with certainty that the twelve apostles did not write it. The Creed goes back to an older and shorter form, called the Old Roman Creed, which probably dates from the second century and runs as follows: "I believe in God the Father almighty; and in Christ Jesus his only Son, our Lord, who was born from the Holy Spirit and the Virgin Mary, who under Pontius Pilate was crucified and buried, on the third day rose again from the dead, ascended to heaven, sits at the right hand of the Father, whence he will come to judge the living and the dead; and in the Holy Spirit, the holy Church, the remission of sins, the resurrection of the flesh, (the life everlasting)" (these last words are lacking in the Greek version of this Creed). The core of our faith is all here, and we wholeheartedly say Amen to it.

✤   ✤   ✤

DAY 65 – A BAPTISMAL FORMULA
(LORD'S DAY 7, Q&A 23, PART 1)

Q. What are these articles?
A. I believe in God, the Father almighty, creator of heaven and earth.

Decisive for the origin of the Apostles' Creed was certainly the Great Commission that the risen Christ gave his twelve apostles: "Go therefore and make disciples of all nations, baptizing them in the name of the Father and of the Son and of the Holy Spirit" (Matt. 28:19). Nothing was more characteristic of young Christendom than this belief in the triune God, and no verse in the New Testament describes this more clearly, in one sentence, than this verse. You may think of a similar verse: "The grace of the Lord Jesus Christ and the love of God and the fellowship of the Holy Spirit . . ." (2 Cor. 13:14), or, ". . . the same Spirit . . . the same Lord . . . the same God" (1 Cor. 12:4–6). But in these verses it says "God," not "Father." From such verses alone you would never conclude that the Lord Jesus and the Holy Spirit are also God. But Matthew 28:19 is the most conspicuous: here for the first time, Father, Son, and Spirit are placed in juxtaposition, as equal partners.

If the apostles had to baptize in the name of Father, Son, and Spirit, it is obvious that these words were also *pronounced* at baptism. And it is equally obvious that, before someone was baptized, this person was asked whether he or she indeed believed in the three persons of the Godhead. Some even assume that people were immersed three times. The bishop asked a person, "Do you believe in God, the Father almighty, creator of heaven and earth?" The person answered, "I do believe," and was immersed a first time. Then the bishop asked, "Do you believe in Jesus Christ, his only begotten Son, our Lord?" The person answered, "I do believe," and was immersed a second time. Finally the question came, "Do you believe in the Holy Spirit, the holy church, the forgiveness of sins, the resurrection of the body?" After a third "I do believe," the person was immersed a third time.

We can easily understand that baptism—the formal transition from the pagan or Jewish world to the Christian church—played a great role in early Christianity, and that the oldest Christian Creed developed from a baptismal formula.

✤   ✤   ✤

DAY 66 – THREE PERSONS

(Lord's Day 7, Q&A 23, part 2)

A. *I believe in God, the Father . . . I believe in Jesus Christ, his only begotten Son . . . I believe in the Holy Spirit . . .*

In later Q&As we will enter extensively into all the details of the Apostles' Creed. At present, we limit ourselves to more general introductory remarks because the matter is important enough. Yesterday, we saw that the doctrine of the Trinity—the triune God, that is, Father, Son, and Holy Spirit—is the basis of the Apostles' Creed. It has been remarked that the Apostles' Creed as such does not explicitly declare the deity of the Son or of the Holy Spirit. That is correct. The text speaks of *God* the Father, but not of *God* the Son and of *God* the Holy Spirit. Yet, the tripartition of the Creed is quite suggestive: in its first part it speaks of the Father, in its second part of the Son, and in its third part of the Holy Spirit, just as in the baptismal formula of Matthew 28:19.

What was felt to be not explicit enough in the Apostles' Creed was richly supplied by the Creed of Nicaea-Constantinople (AD 381), at least as far as the Son was concerned: "We believe . . . in one Lord Jesus Christ, the only-begotten Son of God, begotten of the Father before all worlds (or, ages), Light of Light, very God of very God, begotten, not made, being of one substance with the Father." Some people have asserted that these additions involved *newer* ideas, which were born in later ages, and which were not yet in the minds at all of those who first formulated the Apostles' Creed (second, or even first century). But of course, this cannot be proven. On the contrary, if we believe—as we do—that these ideas are already contained in the New Testament, they were also in the minds of those who wrote the Apostles' Creed. They only had to be made more explicit in the fourth century because of various heresies that came up, especially Arianism. (Arius taught that the Son was the first and highest creature of God.)

Christians believe in the Trinity not because this is taught in the Nicene Creed but because it is in the New Testament. Therefore, they also believe that it lies on the surface of the Apostles' Creed: I believe in *God* the Father, *God* the Son, and *God* the Holy Spirit.

✤   ✤   ✤

DAY 67 – GOD THE SON
(Lord's Day 7, Q&A 23, part 3)

*A. . . . I believe in Jesus Christ . . . who was conceived . . . suffered
. . . was crucified, died, and was buried . . . rose again . . . ascended
to heaven and is seated at the right hand of God . . . he will come to
judge the living and the dead.*

By far the largest part of the Apostles' Creed is taken up with the second
person of the Godhead, "Jesus Christ, his only begotten Son, our Lord."
This is quite conspicuous. Christianity is about Christ. Don't think this is
self-evident! Strictly speaking, Buddhism is not about the person of the
Buddha, but about the teaching of Buddha. Islam is not about the person of
Muhammad, but about what Muhammad claimed he could tell about God.
In both cases, the messenger hid himself behind his message. Jesus was also
a messenger of God; the gospel is literally the "good message" from God,
and Jesus preached it. However, the message is not just about God—it is just
as much about Jesus himself. His redemptive work is the center of it, and
even his own person is the center of it.

In fact, it does not really matter who Buddha and Muhammad were. Their
biography is basically irrelevant; it is their message that counts: they point to
something or someone beyond themselves. But in Christianity, it is of vital
importance that we see that the Christian message is about Jesus himself, and
his work. His biography is so important that, in a summarized form, it makes
up the core of the Apostles' Creed. It tells us who he *is* (God's only begotten
Son, our Lord), and what *happened* to him: his miraculous conception, his
sufferings, his death, his burial, his resurrection, his ascension, and what he
will do: he will come again, this time to judge the living and the dead.

Jesus was a prophet, a messenger of God. But he was much more. He was
God himself as the Word that was made flesh (John 1:14), as the One who was
manifested in the flesh (1 Tim. 3:16). He did not just have a message to preach;
he also had a work to accomplish. This work was the vital core of the message.
And the person who accomplished it was essential to the work. And though it
is clear that Jesus' work is a little underrated in the Apostles' Creed—although
there are references to his sufferings and to the forgiveness of sins—the Nicene
Creed fills the gap: Jesus came down "for our salvation."

❋   ❋   ❋

DAY 68 – GOD THE SPIRIT

(LORD'S DAY 7, Q&A 23, PART 4)

A. . . . I believe in the Holy Spirit, the holy catholic church, the communion of saints, the forgiveness of sins, the resurrection of the body, and the life everlasting. Amen.

The third person of the Godhead receives remarkably little attention in the Creed. The Christian confesses that he believes in the Holy Spirit, and that's it. No wonder. Almost from the start, the church fathers described the Holy Spirit as the "unknown God," or in similar terms. Yet, the Nicene Creed has much more to tell us: we believe "in the Holy Spirit, the Lord [2 Cor. 3:17–18], the Giver of life [John 6:63; 2 Cor. 3:6], who proceeds from the Father [John 15:26], who together with the Father and Son is worshipped and glorified, and who spoke from the prophets [Zech. 7:12; 1 Pet. 1:10–11]."

If you read the Creed carefully, it might strike you that, after mentioning the Holy Spirit, the text does not repeat the term "I believe." This may suggest that everything that follows must be viewed as linked with the Holy Spirit. This is certainly true for the very first thing mentioned: the "holy catholic [i.e., universal] church." Paul calls the church the temple of the Holy Spirit (1 Cor. 3:16; 2 Cor. 6:16; Eph. 2:20–22). We might say that the spiritual glory of God the Father is manifested in the physical creation he made, and that similarly the spiritual glory of the Son is manifested in the Man Jesus Christ. Likewise, we may say that the spiritual glory of the Holy Spirit is manifested in the church of God. It has even been said that the church is a kind of "incarnation" of the Spirit, but that seems rather far-fetched. Nevertheless, there is a parallel with the incarnation of the Son: the latter's body, too, was a temple of the Holy Spirit (cf. Luke 1:35; John 2:19–21).

The matters that follow in the text are clearly linked with the Spirit as well: what is "the fellowship of the Holy Spirit" (2 Cor. 13:14) other than the communion of the saints? Peter links the forgiveness of sins with the gift of the Spirit (Acts 2:38). Paul says that the resurrection of the body is through the Spirit (Rom. 8:11). And as to life everlasting: Paul says that "the one who sows to the Spirit will from the Spirit reap eternal life" (Gal. 6:8). We see how important the Holy Spirit is!

✤   ✤   ✤

DAY 69 – CREATION
(Lord's Day 8, Q&A 24, part 1)

Q. How are these articles divided?
A. Into three parts: God the Father and our creation . . .

It is interesting to see that the Apostles' Creed links each of the three persons of the Godhead with a specific divine work: the Father is linked with the work of creation, the Son with the work of deliverance, and the Holy Spirit with the work of sanctification. Of course, this specialization does not involve three separate compartments, as if the two other persons have nothing to do with a specific work. In every work of God, all three persons of the Godhead are always involved; it is impossible that any one of the three would ever work independently of the other two. This is because they are not just three, but *one*, far more one than, for instance, husband and wife are one.

Paul speaks of the "one God, the Father, *from* whom are all things and for whom we exist, and one Lord, Jesus Christ, *through* whom are all things and through whom we exist" (1 Cor. 8:6). Notice the difference between "from" (the Father) and "through" (the Son). There is no doubt that the work of creation is "from" the Father, but there is no doubt either that this work was accomplished "through" the Son, and, as always, in the power of the Holy Spirit. John says, "All things were made through him" (John 1:3), that is, through the Word, the Son of God. And Paul says that all things were created "in" him, through him and for him (Col. 1:16); and Hebrews 1 says it was through the Son that God created the world (v. 2). The Holy Spirit, too, was involved in the work of creation, right from the start (Gen. 1:2; Ps. 104:30).

Paul says about God, "[F]rom him and through him and to him are all things" (Rom. 11:36). This is the triune God, Father, Son, and Holy Spirit. If you would like to distinguish between the two, you may say that all the divine works are *from* the Father, all works are *through* the Son, and they are accomplished *in* the Holy Spirit, that is, in the power of the Spirit. And finally, all things are also *to* God, or *for* (the triune) God, for his glory and honor. Father, Son, and Spirit are one just as soul, body, and spirit are one; none can act without the others being involved.

✢   ✢   ✢

DAY 70 – DELIVERANCE
(Lord's Day 8, Q&A 24, part 2)

A. . . . *God the Son and our deliverance* . . .

We have seen that the Apostles' Creed associates each of the three persons of the Godhead with a specific divine work: the Father is linked with the work of creation, the Son is coupled with the work of deliverance, and the Holy Spirit is associated with the work of sanctification. At the same time, we have emphasized that in every work of God, all three persons of the Godhead are always involved. Everybody understands that Jesus is specifically our Redeemer, but also understands that this fact cannot be separated from the role of the Father and the Spirit. In the book of Isaiah (e.g., 45:14–15, 21), and in the pastoral epistles (e.g., 1 Tim. 1:1), God is often called "the Savior God," or "God our Savior," and basically this is the triune God.

The three persons in the Godhead always participate in each divine work, and thus also in the work of redemption. To give a few examples: if "the Lord Jesus Christ . . . gave *himself* for our sins" (Gal. 1:3–4; cf. 2:20; Eph. 5:2, 25; 1 Tim. 2:6; Titus 2:14), it is just as true that the *Father* gave his only Son for us (John 3:16; cf. Rom. 8:32). And if Christ "offered himself without blemish to God," it was "through the eternal Spirit" (Heb. 9:14).

When Jesus began his final journey to the cross, he could say, "Behold, the hour is coming, indeed it has come, when you will be scattered, each to his own home, and will leave me alone. Yet I am not alone, *for the Father is with me*" (John 16:32). This is wonderfully depicted in the story of Abraham and Isaac climbing Mount Moriah, where at God's command the son was to be sacrificed by the father: "And Abraham took the wood of the burnt offering and laid it on Isaac his son. And he took in his hand the fire and the knife. *So they went both of them together.* . . . Abraham said, 'God will provide for himself the lamb for a burnt offering, my son.' *So they went both of them together*" (Gen. 22:6–8). On the cross, the *Man Christ Jesus* was forsaken by a holy and righteous God—but we may wonder whether the fellowship between God the Father and God the Son was ever interrupted.

✤　✤　✤

DAY 71 – SANCTIFICATION
(LORD'S DAY 8, Q&A 24, PART 3)

A. . . . *and God the Holy Spirit and our sanctification.*

One day, humanity was created by God. One other day, humanity fell into sin. This was our life until the day of our deliverance: the life of fallen humans, of sinners. This life was finished when we, by faith, received Jesus Christ as our deliverer, and we became a "new creation." Subsequently, there is a life *after* the day of our deliverance, here on earth, until the moment we enter into eternity, that is, at our death, or at the Second Coming of Christ. In this Q&A, this life is summarized in one single word: "sanctification." It is a life lived in holiness, in dedication and consecration. Actually, these words have specific and limited meanings, but here, the term "sanctification" is used as a description of our entire Christian life. And if we are serious about it, this is indeed a life lived under the guidance and in the power of the Holy Spirit. It was God's plan "that the righteous requirement of the law might be fulfilled in us, who walk not according to the flesh but according to the Spirit. . . . [T]hose who live according to the Spirit set their minds on the things of the Spirit . . . . [A]ll who are led by the Spirit of God are sons of God. For you did not receive the spirit of slavery to fall back into fear, but you have received the Spirit of adoption as sons, by whom we cry, 'Abba! Father!'" (Rom. 8:4–5, 14–15).

Please remember that all three persons of the Godhead are involved in this. It is especially the Holy Spirit that is characteristic of our Christian life, but at the end of the quotation just given we are viewed as sons of the Father, and we cry "Abba, Father!" How could we understand our Christian life if we did not realize that we are children and sons of the Father? And as far as the Son of God is concerned, would we not have a very limited view of the Christian life if we did not realize what it is to be disciples of Christ, followers of him, serving him? If we are truly guided by the Holy Spirit, we will recognize Jesus as our Lord (1 Cor. 12:3; cf. 1 Pet. 3:15), and through the "Spirit of the Lord" we will be transformed into the image of Christ (2 Cor. 3:17–18).

✳ ✳ ✳

DAY 72 – THE TRINITY
(LORD'S DAY 8, Q&A 25, PART 1)

Q. Since there is only one divine being, why do you speak of three:
Father, Son, and Holy Spirit?
A. Because that is how God has revealed himself in his Word.

This is a highly fascinating answer! If the professor asks the theology student why we believe in the Trinity, and the student answers, "Because the Bible teaches it," the professor will not be satisfied. He will demand that the student give a long argument explaining how and why the Christian church has come to believe in the doctrine of the Trinity. However, the Catechism is not a theological document—it is a church confession of faith. And as simple believers, we must sometimes have the courage to simply say, "It is written." This is what Jesus did in response to the devil (Matt. 4:4, 6, 10). He did not enter into a long dispute with the devil, but simply quoted Scripture.

In their own times, both the church father Augustine and the Reformer Martin Luther wrote something to this effect: We believe that the Father is God, we believe that the Son is God, and we believe that the Holy Spirit is God, and yet we believe there is only one God. And they added, How wonderful it would be if we could just leave it there. However, because of the heretics we have to *explain* at length what we believe and why we believe it. And then Augustine went on and wrote fourteen books on the subject!

Fortunately, we do not always have to give account to the heretics. Sometimes we love to stick to this confession: "It is written, and that's it." The *term* Trinity may not be in the Bible, but the *substance* of the matter is there. The Bible makes clear that the Father is God, that the Son is God, and that the Holy Spirit is God, and that, yet, there is only one God. We do definitely not believe in three "gods." With great liberty, we confess with our Jewish friends the *Shema*: "Hear, O Israel: The LORD our God, the LORD is one (or, The LORD our God is one LORD)." We are *monotheists*, just like Jews and Muslims. And at the same time, we believe that God is three: Father, Son, and Holy Spirit. Why? Because the Bible tells us so. We leave it to the theologians to work it out; at the present point, we are just *confessing*—deeply conscious of the vital significance of this confession.

✤   ✤   ✤

DAY 73 – THREE DISTINCT PERSONS
(Lord's Day 8, Q&A 25, part 2)

A. . . . these three distinct persons are one, true, eternal God.

Although the Catechism makes a "simple" confession here—one God, three persons—it does realize, and we as well, that this is not a simple subject at all. Take the word "person." In the sixteenth century, when the Catechism was written, it did not yet have the meaning that it has today. Since the Enlightenment, and with the rise of modern psychology, a "person" has become an independent individual, with one's own characteristics and one's own options and choices. Husband and wife are two persons, who are bound together by marriage; yet they have their own characters, their own preferences, their own choices, their own work; in many ways, they act independently of each other. However, the three persons within the Godhead *never* act independently of each other. Their activities are always interwoven, their wills and preferences are always identical. If we would stress the word "person" in the modern sense, we would end up with three "gods," and indeed this has happened in the past. It is precisely what Jews and Muslims accuse us of, and sometimes rightly so.

Others have made the opposite error by speaking of Father, Son, and Spirit as just three "faces" or "modes" of the one Godhead. They avoid terms like "persons" or "subsistencies," and emphasize the oneness of the Godhead. He is a God who reveals himself in three ways. But if we talk like this, we blur the differences between the three. Father, Son, and Spirit are not independent, but they are not identical either.

It is impossible to formulate this complicated matter in such a way that all possible misunderstandings are excluded in advance, once and for all. It is like tightrope walking: you very easily fall either to the right side or to the left side. Here fools rush in where angels fear to tread! Theologians love working all the problems out; that's their job. We are happy to *have* theologians; if they properly do their work, they can be a great help. But common believers are happy just to confess: Father, Son, and Holy Spirit are one, true, eternal God. We eat the fish, and leave the bones to the theologians!

✤ ✤ ✤

DAY 74 – ONE GOD

(Lord's Day 8, Q&A 25, part 3)

A. Because that is how God has revealed himself in his Word: these three distinct persons are one, true, eternal God.

In order to prove the great Christian truth of the Trinity, we have to prove only that the Father is God, the Son is God, the Spirit is God, and yet there is only one God. To begin with, we confess that the Lord is the one God and the only God (Deut. 6:4; cf. 1 Cor. 8:4, 6). The New Testament gives us many proofs that Jesus is God, sometimes in explicit statements: "the Word was God (John 1:1). Paul speaks of "Christ, who is God over all" (Rom. 9:5), and of "our great God and Savior Jesus Christ" (Titus 2:13; cf. 2 Pet. 1:1). And John speaks of God's "Son Jesus Christ," who "is the true God and eternal life" (1 John 5:20). The New Testament shows that the Holy Spirit is not only divine (no orthodox Jew would deny that), but also a distinct individuality, who is sent by the Son from the Father, who dwells in believers, teaches them, brings things to their remembrance, guides them, declares things to them, glorifies the Son (John 14:17, 26; 15:26; 16:13–15), prays (Rom. 8:26), can be lied to (Acts 5:3) and grieved (Eph. 4:30), etc.

It is striking to see how often the three are mentioned together. The Spirit descends on Christ from the Father (Matt. 3:16–17), people are baptized in the name of the Father, the Son, and the Holy Spirit (28:18–19). The Spirit, the Lord, and God (the Father) grant together the gifts and ministries (1 Cor. 12:4–6). Christians are blessed with "the grace of the Lord Jesus Christ and the love of God and the fellowship of the Holy Spirit" (2 Cor. 13:14). God sends the Holy Spirit, called the "Spirit of his Son," into believers' hearts (Gal. 4:6). The "God of our Lord Jesus Christ" gives them the "Spirit of wisdom" (Eph. 1:17). Through Christ we have access in one Spirit to the Father (2:18). The Father strengthens his people through his Spirit so that Christ dwells in their hearts (3:14–17). There is one Spirit, one Lord, one God and Father (4:4–6). God pours out his Spirit on his people through Jesus Christ (Titus 3:4–6).

The truth of the Trinity is everywhere in the New Testament—if you are just prepared to see it.

DAY 75 – MY GOD AND FATHER
(Lord's Day 9, Q&A 26, part 1)

Q. What do you believe when you say, "I believe in God, the Father almighty, creator of heaven and earth"?
A. That the eternal Father of our Lord Jesus Christ . . . is my God and Father because of Christ the Son.

This is a tremendous statement. In the Old Testament, God is the Father of Israel as a nation because he created them (Isa. 63:16; 64:8; Mal. 2:10). In Isaiah 9:6 it is the Messiah who is called "everlasting Father," but that is a very different thought. The idea of an "eternal Father," who from eternity was the Father of the "eternal Son," was totally unknown in the Old Testament. When Jesus came into this world, one of his great mandates was to make known the name of the Father—the eternal Father of the eternal Son—to his followers (John 17:6, 26). This is a great privilege: through the Holy Spirit, we now know God as the eternal Father of the eternal Son. But it is getting even better: *this* Father has become "*my* God and Father because of Christ the Son," says the Catechism.

The first time that this truth could possibly be expressed was after the resurrection of Christ. Then, Jesus said to Mary Magdalene: "I am ascending to my Father *and your Father*, to my God and your God" (John 20:17). In the Lord's Prayer, Jesus had spoken of "Our Father" (Matt. 6:9), but never before his resurrection did he say that *his* Father—the eternal Father of the eternal Son—had become the Father of his disciples as well. The Son's life first had to pass through death and resurrection before it could be shared with his followers. After his resurrection this became a spiritual reality: because the Son has become my life, the eternal Father of the eternal Son has become *my* Father: "[T]his is the testimony, that God gave us eternal life, and this life is in his Son. Whoever has the Son has life; whoever does not have the Son of God does not have life. . . . [W]e are in him who is true [i.e., God the Father], in his Son Jesus Christ. He is the true God [i.e., God the Son] and eternal life" (1 John 5:11–12, 20).

Jesus said "Abba, Father" in Gethsemane (Mark 14:36). And now *we* say "Abba, Father" to this same person (Rom. 8:15; Gal. 4:6) because we were born of him as his children (John 1:12–13), and adopted by him as his sons (Rom. 8:14–15, 23; Gal. 4:5; Eph. 1:5). What a privilege!

✤　✤　✤

DAY 76 – CREATION AND PROVIDENCE
(Lord's Day 9, Q&A 26, part 2)

A. . . . the eternal Father of our Lord Jesus Christ . . . out of nothing created heaven and earth and everything in them, who still upholds and rules them by his eternal counsel and providence.

We have seen before that the Son and the Spirit, too, were involved in the work of creation. But it is clear that the work "went out from" God the Father (cf. 1 Cor. 8:6). He created it out of nothing. And if you feel that wherever God is, there cannot be nothing, you could also say that he created "out of himself": out of "his eternal power and divine nature" (cf. Rom. 1:20). The Catechism uses the words of the law: "[I]n six days the LORD made heaven and earth, the sea, and all that is in them" (Exod. 20:11; cf. Acts 4:24; 14:15). He did it by his word and by the breath of his mouth (Ps. 33:6). He is the God who "calls those things which do not exist as though they did" (Rom. 4:17 NKJV). "By faith we understand that the universe was created by the word of God, so that what is seen was not made out of things that are visible" (Heb. 11:3).

This God is not the God envisioned by the deists: a God who, after having created the world, gave up on it and let it run by itself. No, there is not only the divine work of *creation* but also the ongoing divine work of *providence*: God's Son is the One "through whom also [God] created the world . . . and he [i.e., the Son] upholds the universe by the word of his power" (Heb. 1:2–3). It is God who does "good by giving you rains from heaven and fruitful seasons, satisfying your hearts with food and gladness" (Acts 14:17). "In him we live and move and have our being" (17:28). Psalm 104 is a wonderful description of the way God created his creation, and still looks after it.

The way God rules the universe is based upon his "eternal counsel," that is, the plans that he made before the foundation of the world (cf. Eph. 1:4–5, 9, 11). What the Catechism calls here God's "providence" are the various ways through which God realizes his eternal counsel within time and history. His ways may vary according to circumstances, but God's eternal counsel has been established once and for all: throughout history, he will work toward the goal that had been determined even before creation; this goal is the Kingdom of God.

✵   ✵   ✵

DAY 77 – PROVISION
(Lord's Day 9, Q&A 26, part 3)

A. ... I trust God so much that I do not doubt he will provide whatever I need for body and soul.

I need faith in God, my Savior, to inherit eternal salvation. But I also need faith (trust, confidence) in God, my Keeper, to get through the present world. I trust him when it comes to my eternal destination, but I trust him also for my daily circumstances. Whatever I need for body and soul, my Father in heaven will take care of it. "He who walks righteously ... his bread will be given him; his water will be sure" (Isa. 33:15–16). "I have been young, and now am old, yet I have not seen the righteous forsaken or his children begging for bread" (Ps. 37:25). "Cast your burden on the LORD, and he will sustain you; he will never permit the righteous to be moved" (55:22).

These are not easy verses, because there *have* been believers in history who starved to death—and it would be cheap to say that this always happened because, in fact, they were not righteous (enough). Yet, apparently these are the exceptions. The general rule has been proclaimed by Jesus himself: "Therefore I tell you, do not be anxious about your life, what you will eat or what you will drink, nor about your body, what you will put on. Is not life more than food, and the body more than clothing? Look at the birds of the air: they neither sow nor reap nor gather into barns, and yet your heavenly Father feeds them. Are you not of more value than they?" (Matt. 6:25–26; cf. Luke 12:22–31).

Of course, the way we experience this is also dependent upon our own claims and wishes. The apostle Paul said, "[G]odliness with contentment is great gain, for we brought nothing into the world, and we cannot take anything out of the world. But if we have food and clothing, with these we will be content" (1 Tim. 6:6–8). The same apostle, in the bad circumstances of prison, could say, "Not that I am speaking of being in need, for I have learned in whatever situation I am to be content. I know how to be brought low, and I know how to abound. In any and every circumstance, I have learned the secret of facing plenty and hunger, abundance and need. I can do all things through him who strengthens me" (Phil. 4:11–13). What a faith he had!

* * *

DAY 78 – TURN TO MY GOOD
(Lord's Day 9, Q&A 26, part 4)

A. . . . God . . . will turn to my good whatever adversity he sends upon me in this sad world.

What has happened to the "valley of tears" that was mentioned in the original text of the Catechism!? The expression comes from Psalm 84:6, where many translations have "Valley of Baca," while other translations render this as the "Valley of Weeping" (WYC: "valley of tears"). A valley of tears is not an easy or pleasant place to go through, but, as the psalm says, God's people "make it a place of springs; the early rain also covers it with pools. They go from strength to strength; each one appears before God in Zion" (vv. 6–7). This is because they have *faith* in God, and *hope* for a bright end of their journey. There is weeping, but there is also the strength of God to carry on.

So far, we have heard about God's creation and God's providence. Now the moment has come to realize again that this good world of God has been spoiled by sin and death. Travelling through the valley of tears, we come across all kinds of adversities—this is precisely why we sometimes have to weep. The Catechism tells us that it is God who sends these adversities upon us (cf. Isa. 45:7; Amos 3:6b), but usually the sense is more that of allowing or permitting such mischief. This is because we know that it is sometimes the devil who sends evils (cf. 1 Chron. 21:1; Job 1:12; 2:6–7; Matt. 13:39; Luke 22:31; John 13:2; Acts 5:3; 10:38; 1 Cor. 5:5; 2 Cor. 12:7; 1 Thess. 2:18; 2 Thess. 2:9; 1 Pet. 5:8). However, even in such cases things can never happen apart from God. He can even use Satan as an instrument in his ways with humanity.

This is summarized in a well-known verse to which the Catechism is clearly alluding here: "[W]e know that for those who love God all things work together for good, for those who are called according to his purpose" (Rom. 8:28). Whether we call God the direct cause of a certain mischief, or Satan, practically does not make much difference for us: we accept all things from God's hand, knowing that he uses them all in such a way that he turns them to our good. And that is a tremendous comfort in the midst of all our troubles and tears.

✻　　✻　　✻

DAY 79 – ALMIGHTY AND FAITHFUL
(LORD'S DAY 9, Q&A 26, PART 5)

A. . . . *God is able to do this because he is almighty God and desires to do this because he is a faithful Father.*

Notice the two key words here: God is *able* to help us through, and he is *willing* to help us through. He is able because he is almighty, and he is willing because he is faithful. Both elements are necessary. If God were able, but not willing—for instance, because he does not truly love us—his ability would be of no help to us. And if he were willing, but not able, he might weep with us, seek to comfort us, but in the end he would not be able to help us. But thank God, he is both almighty and faithful.

Some people do not understand this. They argue, If God is almighty, and yet does not stop all mischief right away, then he cannot be love. And if God is a loving God, and yet does not stop all mischief right away, then apparently he is not powerful enough. You cannot have it both ways, they argue. But they are wrong. They do not see that God may certainly allow a certain mischief *for a time*, if in this way, in the end, a greater good is reached than would have been possible without this mischief. The pain you endure at the dentist leads to a higher goal—better teeth—than otherwise would have been possible. Muscle aches and sweat during heavy training will lead to better sports results. Pain may be a necessary step to reach a greater goal. God *will* realize his purpose with us because he is powerful enough to do it. And he *loves* to realize his purpose because he loves *us*.

"What then shall we say to these things? If God is for us, who can be against us? He who did not spare his own Son but gave him up for us all, how will he not also with him graciously give us all things? . . . Who shall separate us from the love of Christ? Shall tribulation, or distress, or persecution, or famine, or nakedness, or danger, or sword? . . . [I]n all these things we are more than conquerors through him who loved us. For I am sure that neither death nor life, nor angels nor rulers, nor things present nor things to come, nor powers, nor height nor depth, nor anything else in all creation, will be able to separate us from the love of God in Christ Jesus our Lord" (Rom. 8:31–39).

✳   ✳   ✳

DAY 80 – THE POWER OF GOD
(LORD'S DAY 10, Q&A 27, PART 1)

Q. What do you understand by the providence of God?
A. The almighty and ever present power of God by which God up-
holds, as with his hand, heaven and earth and all creatures.

We now move a little further into the subject of divine providence. God has not only created the world, but he constantly cares about it and looks after it. He keeps it *in his hand*, as it were. God is "almighty," that is, he can do anything he wants; we call this his omnipotence. And his power is "ever present," wherever you go; we call this his omnipresence. As David said, "If I ascend to heaven, you are there! If I make my bed in Sheol, you are there! If I take the wings of the morning and dwell in the uttermost parts of the sea, even there your hand shall lead me, and *your right hand shall hold me*" (Ps. 139:8–10). The Lord said through Jeremiah, "Can a man hide himself in secret places so that I cannot see him? . . . Do I not fill heaven and earth?" (Jer. 23:24). "In his hand are the depths of the earth; the heights of the mountains are his also" (Ps. 95:4).

God is *everywhere*, and he has *all things* in his hand; nothing can escape from his eyes. Daniel spoke to king Belshazzar about "the God in whose *hand* is your breath, and whose are all your ways" (Dan. 5:23). "The king's heart is a stream of water in the *hand* of the LORD; he turns it wherever he will" (Prov. 21:1). "He's got the whole world in his hand," but he's also "got the little tiny baby in his hand," as well as the breath and the heart of any mighty king.

For the unbeliever, this is a threatening thought, that if God takes his hand away, a man's life comes to an end: the wicked "are cut off from your hand" (Ps. 88:5). But for the believer, God's providence is a very comforting thought. Whatever enemy may be against us, we are in God's hands. Even when God's discipline has to strike us, we will argue, as David did, "Let us fall into the hand of the LORD, for his mercy is great; but let me not fall into the hand of man" (2 Sam. 24:14). "Into your hand I commit my spirit . . . my times are in your hand" (Ps. 31:5, 15; cf. Luke 23:46). Jesus said, "No one will snatch [my sheep] out of my hand . . . no one is able to snatch them out of the Father's hand" (John 10:28–29). What a wonderful assurance!

✤   ✤   ✤

DAY 81 – RAIN AND DROUGHT
(LORD'S DAY 10, Q&A 27, PART 2)

A. . . . leaf and blade, rain and drought, fruitful and lean years, food and
drink.

God so rules the world that rain and drought, fruitful and lean years,
come to us by his fatherly hand. God "gives the rain in its season, the
autumn rain and the spring rain" (Jer. 5:24). And Paul said that God "did
good by giving you rains from heaven and fruitful seasons, satisfying your
hearts with food and gladness" (Acts 14:17). Moses said, "[Y]ou shall eat
and be full, and you shall bless the LORD your God for the good land he has
given you" (Deut. 8:10). However, he attached a condition to it: Israel had
to keep God's law. If God blessed them, they thanked him for it. But if he
withheld his blessing, they had to wonder why. It could be a test from God,
but it could also be a disciplinary measure. God sometimes gives rain, but
at other times he gives drought. He gives fruitful years, but sometimes the
years are lean, that is, the harvests are poor. And sometimes this is simply
the farmer's own fault: "The sluggard does not plow in the autumn; he will
seek at harvest and have nothing" (Prov. 20:4; cf. 24:30–31).

Remember that the Catechism is dealing here with God's providence,
not with *all* causes behind every event. Sometimes the misery that comes
over people has been caused by themselves, or by other people. It is true,
"[t]he rich and the poor meet together; the LORD is the maker of them
all" (Prov. 22:2). But it is also true that some people have made *themselves*
poor; or other people, who oppress and exploit them, have done this. God
allows this to happen; in this sense he is always involved. But that does not
take anything away from human responsibility.

Certain regions of the Netherlands were very godly because, throughout the centuries, they were flooded every few decades. People learned
to be dependent on the God who holds "the waters in the hollow of his
hand" (Isa. 40:12). Today, the Dutch are so clever in protecting the land
that flooding is virtually eliminated. Nowadays these regions are much
less godly, perhaps because they do not need God so desperately anymore!
You see how intricate is the relationship between God's sovereignty and
human responsibility.

�֍   ✤   ✤

DAY 82 – HEALTH AND SICKNESS
(Lord's Day 10, Q&A 27, part 3)

A. . . . health and sickness, prosperity and poverty.

Apart from biological causes, where does sickness come from? The Catechism says, From God. Charismatic Christians say, From Satan. And I would add, sometimes humans are themselves to be blamed because of their unhealthy lifestyle (smoking, drinking, obesity, stress, lack of movement and of rest). Who is right? It is obvious that you can make *yourself* very sick. It is also clear that the Bible ascribes certain diseases directly to Satan, as in the cases of Job (2:6–7), the woman who was bent over (Luke 13:10–17), and—if the "thorn in the flesh" was indeed an illness—the apostle Paul (2 Cor. 12:7–9). Jesus healed "all who were oppressed by the devil" (Acts 10:38), and of some sick we are told: "their diseases left them and the evil spirits came out of them" (19:12). Not *all* sickness comes directly from the devil, but he is sometimes definitely involved.

In some other cases of mischief, we may say with equal certainty, "An enemy [i.e., the devil] has done this" (Matt. 13:28, 39). Paul knew exactly at what times he was hindered by the Spirit of Jesus (Acts 16:7), and at what times he was hindered by Satan (1 Thess. 2:18). But at this moment the Catechism is not interested in such distinctions, and this for a very good reason: *believers always accept mischief from God's hand.* That is the point. Job did not know whether God or Satan was the direct cause of his misery; but he rightly said, "The LORD gave and the LORD has taken away" (1:21), and: "Shall we receive good from God, and shall we not receive evil?" (2:10). Satan may definitely be involved, as in the case of David: "*Satan* incited David" (1 Chron. 21:1). But God was behind it, for the parallel text says, "the LORD incited David" (2 Sam. 24:1).

God may not always be the direct cause of certain misery. But always remember two things. First, he is always involved in it; nothing can befall us apart from him, so that believers accept it from *his* hand. And second, *in* the misery he is always our refuge, our strength, and our help (Ps. 46:1); he is *with us* in it (23:4), in the waters and in the fire (Isa. 43:2).

❉   ❉   ❉

DAY 83 – NOT BY CHANCE
(Lord's Day 10, Q&A 27, part 4)

A. . . . God upholds, as with his hand, heaven and earth and all creatures, and so rules them that . . . all things, in fact, come to us not by chance . . .

The topic of chance is an interesting subject; many Christians have had ardent disputes about it. Does chance exist, or does it not? Let's be honest about it: if, in the streets of Buenos Aires, I would bump into my friend from Indonesia, we would certainly speak of a "remarkable coincidence," especially if we cannot discern any special divine purpose in this encounter. The Bible seems to speak in a similar way. It tells us that Ruth "happened to come to the" field of Boaz (Ruth 2:3; CEB and LEB say, "by chance"). In the parable of the good Samaritan, Jesus tells us: "Now by chance a priest was going down that road" (Luke 10:31). He had no difficulty using the word "chance"! Solomon wrote of people at large: "[T]ime and chance happen to them all" (Eccl. 9:11).

In fact we do see coincidences everywhere. And yet, especially in the case of Ruth we see God's wonderful guidance behind her actions. To the ordinary public it may seem to be a matter of chance, but the believer sees God's fatherly hand in what happened to her and Boaz. Whatever things come to us, they are never there purely by chance. We may not see it right away, but often, after a while, we look back and say, God was in the course of those events all along!

Some Christians refuse to play games in which dice are involved because of Proverbs 16:33, "The lot is cast into the lap, but its every decision is from the LORD." They feel throwing dice is tempting God. Now in the case of innocent children's games, I do not see much danger in it. But indeed, the Bible is full of cases in which the lot was cast, and God's hand was wonderfully seen in the results, as in the case of Achan (Josh. 7:14–15), Saul (1 Sam. 10:20–21), and Matthias (Acts 1:26). The word "Purim" means "lots"; the feast of Purim was given that name because the lot had been cast to exterminate Israel (Esther 3:7; 9:24). But the date that was determined was so far away that Israel had time enough to put up a defense of herself. God's hand was in the matter, even though God's name is never mentioned in the book of Esther! He was there all along.

❖ ❖ ❖

DAY 84 – GOD'S FATHERLY HAND
(Lord's Day 10, Q&A 27, part 5)

A. . . . God . . . so rules [all things] that . . . all things, in fact, come to us . . . by his fatherly hand.

At first glance, this statement seems to be one of resignation or acquiescence. It may sound to our ears like the hypocritical response of the priest Eli: "It is the Lord. Let him do what seems good to him" (1 Sam. 3:18). Or like the bitter answer of Naomi: "[T]he Lord has testified against me and the Almighty has brought calamity upon me" (Ruth 1:21). Both responses betrayed a wrong attitude. Notice that the Catechism does not, in some detached way, speak of the Lord, or of the Almighty, but of God's "fatherly hand." There is *love* in this expression, and the believer is aware of this. He or she never falls outside God's love; no matter how hard the circumstances are, the Father's hand is in it *for the believer's good.* "Are not two sparrows sold for a penny? And not one of them will fall to the ground apart from your Father" (Matt. 10:29).

Resignation can be an attitude of fatalism (like in the Islamic "It is Allah's will"), which is totally unbiblical. Eli was fatalistic, but the real men of God are not. They freely cried out to God with their "why?" (Ps. 44:23–24 is a striking example). The men of God often argued with him, such as Abraham did (Gen. 18:22–33), Moses (Exod. 32:11–14; 33:12–17), Elijah (1 Kings 19:4–18), and Jeremiah (Jer. 20). In an intimate relationship with God such arguing is even natural—precisely *because* the believer is convinced of the Father's love and care. Abraham and Moses were called "friends of God" (Exod. 33:11; 2 Chron. 20:7; Isa. 41:8; James 2:23). And Moses and Elijah belonged to the greatest men of God in the Old Testament (Mal. 4:4–6; Matt. 17:3; cf. Rev. 11:6).

Perhaps Job is the greatest Old Testament example of someone who hurled his "why's" to heaven but remained attached to God. He never got the answer he was looking for; in Job 38–41 God mainly emphasized his own majesty and wisdom. Yet, Job kept trusting God. This word of his says it all: "Though he slay me, I will hope in him; yet I will argue my ways to his face" (13:15). That is, I will protest, but at the same time I will cling to my heavenly Father, whatever happens to me.

✢   ✢   ✢

DAY 85 – PATIENCE
(Lord's Day 10, Q&A 28, part 1)

Q. How does the knowledge of God's creation and providence help us?
A. We can be patient when things go against us.

Patience is a tremendous gift of God. It is part of the fruit of the Spirit (Gal. 5:22; cf. Luke 8:15; 2 Cor. 6:6; Eph. 4:2; Col. 1:11; 3:12). Hebrews 6:12 and 15 speak of those who "through faith and patience" inherited what God had promised. And James wrote, "Be patient, therefore, brothers, until the coming of the Lord. See how the farmer waits for the precious fruit of the earth, being patient about it, until it receives the early and the late rains. . . . As an example of suffering and patience, brothers, take the prophets who spoke in the name of the Lord" (5:7, 10). "Be still before the Lord and wait patiently for him" (Ps. 37:7). "Rejoice in hope, be patient in tribulation, be constant in prayer" (Rom. 12:12; cf. 2 Cor. 1:6).

Patience is the quality you need when circumstances are against you, when the troubles last longer than you think you can bear, when you see no light at the end of the tunnel. Paul could say, "[W]e rejoice in our sufferings, knowing that suffering produces endurance" (Rom. 5:3). And James wrote, "[Y]ou know that the testing of your faith produces steadfastness. And let steadfastness have its full effect, that you may be perfect and complete, lacking in nothing" (James 1:3–4). Endurance and steadfastness are words that are equivalent to patience.

If we realize how vast God's creation is, and how intricate his government of this world—in fact, this the message of Job 38–41—we will understand that our individual lives are just tiny parts of a huge divine plan. We are certainly convinced of the Father's love and care, and of the fact that Father makes all things work together for our good (Rom. 8:28). But we also realize that God works with a different schedule. He promised Abram a son, but the man had to wait for 25 years. He promised Israel the exodus, but the people had to wait for 430 years. He promised his church the return of Christ, but we are waiting already for 2,000 years. The mills of God grind slowly but surely. None of his promises will ever fall to the ground, sure—but they may test our patience to the utmost.

✳ ✳ ✳

DAY 86 – THANKFULNESS
(Lord's Day 10, Q&A 28, part 2)

A. We can be . . . thankful when things go well.

Thankfulness is another tremendous gift of God. The entire third part of the Catechism is called "gratitude," which means the same. Paul says, "[B]e thankful. Let the word of Christ dwell in you richly, teaching and admonishing one another in all wisdom, singing psalms and hymns and spiritual songs, with thankfulness in your hearts to God. And whatever you do, in word or deed, do everything in the name of the Lord Jesus, giving thanks to God the Father through him" (Col. 3:15–17). "Rejoice always, pray without ceasing, give thanks in all circumstances; for this is the will of God in Christ Jesus for you" (1 Thess. 5:16–18). Sometimes you can even be thankful in advance: "[I]n everything by prayer and supplication *with thanksgiving* let your requests be made known to God" (Phil. 4:6). That is, you tell God your needs, and you express your thankfulness that he will answer your prayers—no matter in what way he will do this.

If we look at the content of our prayers, we often find that the time we spend in asking God far exceeds the time we spend in thanking and praising him. We may complain and sigh when circumstances are against us, but we often forget to thank him when things go well. God is happy with all those who pray to him—but what he *seeks* is worshipers (John 4:23), people who thank, praise, glorify, and honor him for all that he gives, and especially for all that he *is*. He is so much greater than our needs. Look beyond them and see *him*. He is so highly worthy of our thankfulness and praise. "I will give thanks to the Lord with my whole heart; I will recount all of your wonderful deeds" (Ps. 9:1; cf. 75:1). "The Lord is my strength and my shield; in him my heart trusts, and I am helped; my heart exults, and with my song I give thanks to him" (28:7). "I thank you that you have answered me and have become my salvation" (118:21).

Before you ask him for anything in the morning, don't forget to thank him first. The Levites "were to stand every morning, thanking and praising the Lord, and likewise at evening" (1 Chron. 23:30). That is a great example for us.

✢　　✢　　✢

DAY 87 – CONFIDENCE
(Lord's Day 10, Q&A 28, part 3)

*A. . . . for the future we can have good confidence in our
faithful God and Father that nothing in creation will separate
us from his love.*

The terms "confidence" and "trust" are in fact nothing but other words for "faith." We need faith to get to heaven, but we also need faith to get through this world. We have to trust God for our eternal salvation, but we also have to trust him for all our daily circumstances. God is "our faithful God and Father," and we need to have the faith *that* he indeed is faithful, with regard both to our eternal life and to our daily life. *Everything* is in God's hands—*you* only have to trust him.

It is obvious that the Catechism thinks here of Romans 8: "I am sure that neither death nor life, nor angels nor rulers, nor things present nor things to come, nor powers, nor height nor depth, nor anything else in all creation, will be able to separate us from the love of God in Christ Jesus our Lord" (vv. 38–39). This important chapter is full of things that are expected of *us*, like walking in the Spirit to fulfill the righteous requirement of God's law (vv. 4–6), killing the deeds of the "flesh" (vv. 12–13), living as sons and children of God (vv. 14–16), looking forward to a bright future beyond death and resurrection (vv. 18–30).

Although these things can be accomplished only in the power of the Holy Spirit, they belong to the domain of our *human* responsibility: *we* have to do them. However, the last verses of Romans 8 speak of *God's* side, of what *he* does: his sovereign, preserving love and care in the midst of all kinds of powers that may threaten us. Even the believer's own doubts, his or her own uncertainties and hesitations, can blur his or her bright prospect. But he or she should not allow this to happen. Don't look at your enemies, either those outside you or those still hiding within you. Look to him as the sole and only guarantee of your eternal salvation! Listen to his promises! "[W]e rejoice in our sufferings, knowing that suffering produces endurance, and endurance produces character, and character produces hope, and hope does not put us to shame, because God's love has been poured into our hearts through the Holy Spirit who has been given to us" (Rom. 5:3–5).

✤   ✤   ✤

DAY 88 – UNMOVABLE
(Lord's Day 10, Q&A 28, part 4)

A. . . . For all creatures are so completely in God's hand that without his will they can neither move nor be moved.

This sounds quite absolute! Is no creature capable of moving, or not moving, without the will of God? If we restrict ourselves to human beings, how can God order humans to move, and punish them if they refuse to move the way he wants them to God told Jonah, "Arise, go to Nineveh." Jonah did indeed arise, but only to flee to Tarshish, which lay in the opposite direction (Jonah 1:1–3). It was God's will that Jonah would move east, and he moved west. Apparently, this was not God's will, yet Jonah did it, and God had to stop him. So what about God's "will" without which no creature can move?

Theologians have made a distinction between the "resistible" and the "irresistible" will of God, which is quite helpful. Paul says that God our Savior "wants all people to be saved" (1 Tim. 2:4 NIV), and yet we know that not all people *will* be saved. This is the resistible will of God. Jonah also had to do with the resistible will of God, that is, the will that can be disobeyed. But there is also that other will, of which Paul speaks: "[W]ho can resist his will?" (Rom. 9:19). This is the will of God's counsel, of which the Lord says, "My counsel shall stand, and I will accomplish all my purpose" (Isa. 46:10), namely, through the "man of his counsel" (cf. v. 11), that is, Christ. Paul speaks of God "who works all things according to the counsel of his will" (Eph. 1:11). *This* is the will of God of which the Catechism is speaking: the will that cannot be resisted. This is the will by which God realizes his plans, whatever his creatures might undertake.

I think this is the meaning of the "two mountains of bronze" in Zechariah 6:1. The prophet sees four chariots, which are the four world empires of ancient times. They seem to be moving around freely. But in reality they can only move within the boundaries set by those two mountains. Daniel spoke to king Belshazzar about "the God in whose hand is your breath, and whose are all your ways" (Dan. 5:23). And Solomon said, "The king's heart is a stream of water in the hand of the Lord; he turns it wherever he will" (Prov. 21:1).

✤ ✤ ✤

DAY 89 – SAVIOR
(LORD'S DAY 11, Q&A 29, PART 1)

Q. Why is the Son of God called "Jesus," meaning "savior"?
A. Because he saves us from our sins.

We now start with the second and largest part of the Apostles' Creed: the one about Jesus. The first Q&A is about his name. In one Gospel, it is Joseph who receives the command to call the divine child that was to be born "Jesus" (Matt. 1:21), in another Gospel it is Mary who receives this command (Luke 1:31). The name "Jesus" comes from the Greek word *Yesous*, which itself comes from the Hebrew name *Yeshua*. This form comes from the verb *yasha*, which means "to save." So the entire name means as much as "he saves," namely, the Son saves. This explanation of the name is supported by the one given by the angel to Joseph: "She [i.e., Mary] will bear a son, and you shall call his name Jesus, for he will save his people from their sins" (Matt. 1:21). Jesus is the *Savior*, the One who brings salvation from sins. You could also say that he is the Deliverer or Redeemer, which all amounts to the same thing. He delivers his people from the powers of sin, the devil, and death.

In Matthew, the phrase "his people" clearly refers to Israel. But gradually, as this Gospel develops, the circle is widened, especially starting with chapter 13: " The field is the *world*" (v. 38). If Jesus says, "[T]he Son of Man came not to be served but to serve, and to give his life as a ransom for *many*" (20:28), these "many" definitely include all those who would come to faith in Jesus, from whatever nation they were. Similarly, at the institution of the Lord's Supper: "[T]his is my blood of the covenant, which is poured out for many for the forgiveness of sins" (26:28). Compare Jesus' earlier word, "[T]his gospel of the kingdom will be proclaimed throughout the whole world as a testimony to *all nations*" (24:14). And his later word, "Go . . . and make disciples of *all nations*" (28:19). Jesus saved not only believers among Israel from their sins, but also those from all the nations, to the end of the earth. This is why the Catechism can say, "he saves *us* from our sins." There is no limitation anymore, except this one: you have to *confess* your sins (1 John 1:9), and *believe* in the Lord Jesus (Gal. 3:22).

✳ ✳ ✳

DAY 90 – NO OTHER SAVIOR
(Lord's Day 11, Q&A 29, part 2)

A. Because . . . salvation should not be sought and cannot be found in anyone else.

There is no other Savior than God; as he said through the prophet: "Besides me there is no savior" (Isa. 43:11). Since the coming of Jesus Christ, we can further specify this in the words of the apostle Peter, to which the Catechism is clearly alluding: "Jesus is the stone that was rejected by you, the builders, which has become the cornerstone [cf. Ps. 118:22]. And there is salvation in no one else, for there is no other name under heaven given among men by which we must be saved" (Acts 4:11–12). And Paul wrote, "[T]here is [but] one God, and there is [only] one mediator between God and men, the man Christ Jesus, who gave himself as a ransom for all" (1 Tim. 2:5–6).

Do you know that, in the time of the apostles, there were literally hundreds of religions in the Roman Empire? *All* of them have died out, except two: Judaism and Christianity. One of the interesting reasons for this was their claim of exclusivity. Christians claimed that there was only one way to God, and that was Jesus. As Jesus himself had said, "I am the way, and the truth, and the life. No one comes to the Father except through me" (John 14:6). Now, this was either the most arrogant claim ever made, or it was a pitiful example of self-deceit—or it was the truth.

If it were just a question of pronouncing the most truthful message, Hinduism, Buddhism, Islam, etc., could easily claim *they* have it. They can all give you a recipe for serving the true God, or gods, or for reaching eternal bliss. But when it is a question of *sins* standing between you and God (cf. Isa. 59:2), who can really help you? Did Confucius die for you? Or Socrates? Or Buddha? Or Muhammad? Of course not. They pointed to a way you should go—they did not have the power of taking away your sins, nor could they grant you the power to go the way they pointed out (apart from the question whether it was the *right* way they pointed out). Jesus Christ did and does both: he died for the sins of all those who believe in him, and he gives us the power of the Holy Spirit to travel the way *he* points out to us: the way to the Father through him.

✣　✣　✣

DAY 91 – THE ONLY SAVIOR

(Lord's Day 11, Q&A 30, part 1)

Q. Do those who look for their salvation in saints, in themselves, or elsewhere really believe in the only savior Jesus?
A. No. Although they boast of being his, by their actions they deny the only savior, Jesus.

If you would ask a Roman Catholic or an Eastern Orthodox theologian whether there is any salvation through saints—that is, through human beings who after their death have been canonized—he would answer, Of course not; salvation is through Christ alone. Rightly so. But whether simple believers in the countryside of thoroughly Catholic or Orthodox countries feel the same way is another matter. You often see in churches in such countries how especially women go directly to the statue of the Virgin Mary, and tell her about all their needs, as if she were the one who could really help them. Some Catholics even call her "co-redemptrix," referring to her alleged role in the work of redemption. This is a great mistake. Salvation is only in her Son, Jesus Christ. We think here of Paul's words: "[E]ach one of you says, 'I follow Paul,' or 'I follow Apollos,' or 'I follow Cephas,' or 'I follow Christ.' Is Christ divided? Was Paul crucified for you? Or were you baptized in the name of Paul?" (1 Cor. 1:12–13). Don't think that those who said, "I follow Christ," were the best ones! They had turned Christ into the head of a partisan group, just as others did with Paul, Apollos, or Cephas (i.e., Peter). In a sense, they were perhaps the worst ones.

Others look for their salvation "in themselves." These are the people who think that by keeping God's commandments, that is, by doing good works, they can please God and earn heaven. But Paul says, "You are severed from Christ, you who would be justified [or, counted righteous] by the law; you have fallen away from grace" (Gal. 5:4). You have no power in yourself to please God through your deeds. You depend on *grace*; you need a *Savior.* You cannot save yourself.

A third group looks "elsewhere" for their salvation. They may call themselves Christians (they "boast of being his"), they may have high regard for Jesus, but they claim that it is arrogant to call Christianity the only way of salvation. They forget that Christianity is not at all a way of salvation—*Christ* is! Who can be compared with him? Mary? Muhammad? Morals? You need a *Savior,* and there is only One!

❖   ❖   ❖

DAY 92 – PERFECT OR NOT?
(LORD'S DAY 11, Q&A 30, PART 2)

A. . . . *Either Jesus is not a perfect savior, or those who in true faith accept this savior have in him all they need for their salvation.*

Basically, there are only two alternatives: Jesus is the perfect Savior, or he is not. If you claim that there is salvation also through the saints, or through your own good works, or through other great spiritual leaders in history, then Jesus is not a "perfect savior." He may have made his own interesting contribution to the blessing of humanity, but no more than that. There are many ways that lead to heaven, according to this idea. As a Freemason once said to me, "I believe God is on the top of the mountain, and on all sides of the mountain there are many ways that lead to the top. People think their roads are very different, or that their road is the only correct one. But when they arrive at the top, they find out that all these various people have reached the same goal." My answer was this: "I do not believe in ways leading to the top. I believe that God has *come down* from the top in the person of his Son, Jesus Christ, because I myself *did not have the power to reach God*. So God sent his Son in order to set me free from all powers that held me captive."

All alleged roads to the top in reality bump into the same wall: the wall of our sins that make a separation between God and us (Isa. 59:2). We needed someone to break down that wall. We did not simply need a "spiritual guide" to the top—we needed a *Savior* to *take* us to the top by dying for our sins, and by showing us the way to the Father.

There is only one alternative to such an idea of many roads leading to the same goal: Jesus is the one and only Savior. You cannot share him with anyone or anything else. Only he bore my sins on the cross, only he gives me the power of the Holy Spirit to lead a life that is pleasing to God. The rest is a mass of pitiful mistakes—pitiful because they are *deceptive*. People *think* they are on their way to the top, only to find out, when it is too late, that they are on their way to the bottom. "For in him *all the fullness of God* was pleased to dwell, and through him to reconcile to himself all things, whether on earth or in heaven, making peace by the blood of his cross" (Col. 1:19–20; cf. 2:10).

✣   ✣   ✣

DAY 93 – THE ANOINTED

(Lord's Day 12, Q&A 31, part 1)

Q. Why is he called "Christ," meaning "anointed"?
A. Because he has been ordained by God the Father and has been anointed with the Holy Spirit.

The name "Christ" comes from the Greek word *christos*, derived from the verb *chrio*, "to anoint." It is the equivalent of "Messiah," which comes from the Hebrew *Mashiah*, derived from the verb *mashah*, "to anoint." Christ is the Anointed One. In general, in the Old Testament the "anointed one" was the king of Israel: first Saul, then David, then the king from the house of David. The book of Psalms often speaks of "the anointed," which basically refers to the Davidic king, but at a deeper level to the Messiah, the promised perfect King of Israel, who would restore the people, and rule the nations (2:2; 18:50; 20:6; 28:8; 45:7; 84:9; 89:38, 51; 132:10, 17). The term "Messiah" refers first and foremost to the end-time King of Israel, "ordained" by God (cf. Ps. 2:6).

I once heard a rabbi say, "Jesus could not be the Messiah because he was never anointed with oil." There are two answers to this. First, what higher authority should have done this anointing? Moses was never anointed either; again, what higher authority could have done this? Second, if Jesus was not anointed with oil, he nonetheless did receive a higher anointing: the *Father* anointed him with the *Holy Spirit*. Peter explained this to Cornelius: "God anointed Jesus of Nazareth with the Holy Spirit and with power. He went about doing good and healing all who were oppressed by the devil, for God was with him" (Acts 10:38). This anointing took place at Jesus' baptism by John the Baptist: "[W]hen Jesus . . . had been baptized and was praying, the heavens were opened, and the Holy Spirit descended on him in bodily form, like a dove" (Luke 3:21–22). Shortly afterward, Jesus explained to the people in the synagogue of Nazareth: "The Spirit of the Lord is upon me, because he has anointed me" (4:18; cf. Isa. 61:1). And in Hebrews 1:9, it is said to God's Son: "God, your God, has anointed you with the oil of gladness beyond your companions" (cf. Ps. 45:7).

So Jesus *was* indeed the Anointed One—however, not anointed by a man, but by God; anointed not with oil, but with the Holy Spirit, as the prophets had foretold.

❖　❖　❖

DAY 94 – OUR CHIEF PROPHET
(LORD'S DAY 12, Q&A 31, PART 2)

A. . . . *anointed with the Holy Spirit to be our chief prophet and teacher who fully reveals to us the secret counsel and will of God concerning our deliverance.*

Christians of old have spoken of the threefold office of Christ: Prophet, Priest, and King. Similarly, the followers of Jesus are prophets, priests, and kings, as we will see. The Catechism starts with describing the prophetic office of Christ. The apostle Peter told the Jews, "Moses said, 'The Lord God will raise up for you a prophet like me from your brothers. You shall listen to him in whatever he tells you. And it shall be that every soul who does not listen to that prophet shall be destroyed from the people'" (Acts 3:22–23; cf. Deut. 18:15–19). Peter applied these words to Christ.

A prophet is someone who is near to God, and speaks God's words to the people "for their upbuilding and encouragement and consolation" (1 Cor. 14:3). The prophet needs God's anointing for this because it is through the Holy Spirit that he speaks; he is the "man with God's Spirit" (Hos. 9:7 ERV). Paul explains that "no one comprehends the thoughts of God except the Spirit of God," but that God, through this same Spirit, reveals his thoughts to his servants (1 Cor. 2:10–11). As the prophet of old said, "[T]he LORD God does nothing without revealing his secret to his servants the prophets" (Amos 3:7).

Of course, because Jesus is the Son of God, he is a prophet of a very special kind; as the Catechism says, he "fully reveals to us the secret counsel and will of God concerning our deliverance." Even more than that, he revealed to us who God really was: "No one has ever seen God; the only God [or, the only Son] who is at the Father's side, he has made him known" (John 1:18). Jesus said himself, "[N]o one knows the Father except the Son and anyone to whom the Son chooses to reveal him" (Matt. 11:27). He told his disciples, "I have called you friends, for all that I have heard from my Father I have made known to you" (15:15), and said to his Father, "I have manifested your name to the people whom you gave me out of the world" (17:6; cf. v. 26). No one has ever known the mind of the Father as the Son did—and, as the Anointed, he revealed it to his followers through the Holy Spirit.

✤　✤　✤

DAY 95 – OUR ONLY HIGH PRIEST
(Lord's Day 12, Q&A 31, part 3)

A. . . . anointed with the Holy Spirit to be . . . our only high priest who has delivered us by the one sacrifice of his body, and who continually pleads our cause with the Father.

Jesus is not only Prophet but also Priest. The book of Hebrews explains extensively that Jesus, though not descended from the tribe of Levi, is yet a priest, but then according to a different order: that of Melchizedek, who was king and priest of Salem (Heb. 5:6, 10; 6:20; 7:11, 17; see Gen. 14:18–20 and Ps. 110:4). However, although Jesus was not of Aaron's family, his priestly ministry is entirely according to the model of Aaron's ministry. Aaron had one special task on Atonement Day, for which he had his white clothes (Lev. 16). For all his other tasks throughout the year, he had his special, colorful clothes. Jesus, too, had and has two priestly tasks. He fulfilled the Day of Atonement on the cross, once and for all: he became "a merciful and faithful high priest in the service of God, to make propitiation for the sins of the people" (Heb. 2:17); "he entered once for all into the holy places [as Aaron did on Atonement Day], not by means of the blood of goats and calves but by means of his own blood, thus securing an eternal redemption . . . he has appeared once for all at the end of the ages to put away sin by the sacrifice of himself" (9:12, 26; cf. 10:11–14).

The second task of Jesus as our great Priest is the one that he carries out every day for us since he took his place at the right hand of God. Aaron interceded for the people by carrying their names on his shoulders and his chest before God in the sanctuary. Likewise, Jesus is now "in the presence of God *on our behalf*" (Heb. 9:24). "For we do not have a high priest who is unable to sympathize with our weaknesses, but one who in every respect has been tempted as we are, yet without sin. Let us then with confidence draw near to the throne of grace, that we may receive mercy and find grace to help in time of need" (4:15–16). As our high priest, Jesus "is able to save to the uttermost those who draw near to God through him, since he always lives to make intercession for them" (7:25). Paul, too, says that Christ is always interceding for us at the right hand of God (Rom. 8:34). What a wonderful priest we have!

✤　✤　✤

DAY 96 – OUR ETERNAL KING
(Lord's Day 12, Q&A 31, part 4)

A. . . . anointed with the Holy Spirit to be . . . our eternal king who governs us by his Word and Spirit.

We find the expression "eternal king" in 1 Timothy 1:17 (KJV), where the ESV reads, "To the King of the ages, immortal, invisible, the only God, be honor and glory forever and ever." However, this refers to the triune God, not specifically to Christ, as in 2 Peter 1:11, "the eternal kingdom of our Lord and Savior Jesus Christ." Even of Jesus' followers it is said, "[T]hey will reign forever and ever" (Rev. 22:5). It is the eternal Kingdom of God in Christ (cf. Rev. 12:10), together with his saints.

The Catechism speaks here of the Kingdom of Christ in its present meaning, just as it did with respect to Christ as Prophet and Priest. Christ is our Lord, who "governs us by his Word and Spirit." Too many Christians, when referring to the Kingdom of Christ, refer only to the future, either to what is called the Millennial Kingdom, or the new heavens and the new earth. But already today, Jesus is the One who can say, "All authority in heaven and on earth has been given to me" (Matt. 28:18). We may "not yet *see* everything in subjection to him" (Heb. 2:8), but at least we see the Kingdom of God wherever Jesus' followers submit to his government and guidance, that is, acknowledge him as their Lord and show this through their deeds. God the Father "has delivered us from the domain of darkness and transferred us to the kingdom of his beloved Son" (Col. 1:12–13).

When there is dissension among believers, Paul can refer them to the Kingdom of God in a very practical way: "For the kingdom of God is not a matter of eating and drinking [or whatever triviality may cause discord among Christians] but of righteousness and peace and joy in the Holy Spirit. Whoever thus serves Christ is acceptable to God and approved by men" (Rom. 14:17–18).

Already today, the Kingdom of God is a Kingdom not of (idle) words but of power (1 Cor. 4:20) because Christ is ruling in his Kingdom through his Word and in the power of the Holy Spirit. Wherever the Spirit is working, there is Christ's Kingdom. Wherever people lovingly serve and obey him, there is Christ's Kingdom.

✳ ✳ ✳

DAY 97 – FREEDOM
(Lord's Day 12, Q&A 31, part 5)

A. . . . anointed with the Holy Spirit to be . . . our eternal king . . . who guards us and keeps us in the freedom he has won for us.

One might think that the rule of a King who has all authority and power over his subjects is the opposite of true freedom. However, the Catechism emphasizes that this is a mistake. If the subjects of a certain king wholeheartedly love him, and love to serve him, and if this king issues laws that are for the benefit of, and are pleasing to, his subjects, they would never view themselves as not free—on the contrary. *We* have been placed into the Kingdom of the Father's beloved Son (Col. 1:13). It is all love there, and where there is true love, there is freedom: "[I]f the Son sets you free, you will be free indeed" (John 8:36). "For freedom Christ has set us free" (Gal. 5:1). In the Kingdom of God, it is the "royal law" that rules (James 2:8). A law oppresses, you might think; but *this* law is called the "law of liberty" (1:25; 2:12). It is not a paradox to say that those who have been "set free of sin" have become "slaves of righteousness" and "slaves of God" (Rom. 6:18, 22). In the Kingdom of God, all are totally subject to the will of the King (cf. Matt. 28:18–19)—and this is the very summit of true Christian liberty.

It is freedom to be in the hands of the King, out of which no power can snatch us (John 10:28). In the Kingdom of Christ the devil is a conquered enemy (Rev. 12:10–11). Outside this Kingdom is slavery, because there the dark powers reign: sin, the devil, and death. Within the Kingdom there is freedom, because here we find those who have been set free by the King, and who are guarded and kept in this freedom. Outside is darkness, the devil, and death; within is light, love, and life. The two worlds never meet, never merge. Outside we are a powerless prey in the hands of the powers, within we are empowered servants of the King of kings. Outside there is fear, within there is rest and assurance. "By this is love perfected with us, so that we may have confidence for the day of judgment. . . . There is no fear in love, but perfect love casts out fear . . . whoever fears has not been perfected in love. We love because he first loved us" (1 John 4:17–19).

✵　✵　✵

DAY 98 – SHARING IN THE ANOINTING

(LORD'S DAY 12, Q&A 32, PART 1)

Q. But why are you called a Christian?
A. Because by faith I am a member of Christ and so I share in his
anointing.

In the New Testament, the followers of Jesus are called "Christians" on three occasions: in Acts 11:26, and 26:28, and in 1 Peter 4:16. The common explanation of this term is: Christians are followers of Christ, just like Buddhists follow the doctrine of Buddha. However, the Catechism attaches a much deeper meaning to the term "Christian." A Christian is a member of the body of Christ (1 Cor. 12:12–27), in short: a "member of Christ," says the Catechism. But you can also say: because "Christ" means "anointed," a Christian is someone who shares in the anointing of Christ. This is indeed what the New Testament teaches us: God has "poured out" his Spirit on his people (cf. Acts 2:17; Joel 2:28), which is just another way of saying that God has "anointed" his people with his Spirit, just as he did with Christ (Acts 10:38).

As the apostle Paul puts it: "[I]t is God who establishes us with you in Christ, and has anointed us, and who has also put his seal on us [cf. Eph. 1:13; 4:30] and given us his Spirit in our hearts as a guarantee" (2 Cor. 1:21–22). And the apostle John says, "[Y]ou have been anointed by the Holy One, and you all have knowledge. . . . [T]he anointing that you received from him abides in you, and you have no need that anyone should teach you. But as his anointing teaches you about everything, and is true, and is no lie—just as it has taught you, abide in him" (1 John 2:20, 27). Please note this little detail: you are anointed *by* the Holy One (God), but you are anointed *with* the Holy Spirit.

If we have received the same anointing as Christ, it is understandable that, according to the New Testament, we also have the three *offices* of Christ: prophets, priests, and kings. Paul says of the church service, "[If] *all* prophesy . . . you can *all* prophesy . . ." (1 Cor. 14:24, 31). Peter says that believers "are being built up to be a holy priesthood . . . [and] a royal priesthood" (1 Pet. 2: 5, 9). And John says that the Lord has "made us a kingdom, priests to his God and Father" (Rev. 1:6; cf. 5:10; 20:6). This will be worked out in the rest of this Q&A.

✳   ✳   ✳

DAY 99 – OUR PROPHETIC OFFICE
(LORD'S DAY 12, Q&A 32, PART 2)

A. . . . I am anointed to confess his name.

Interestingly, the Catechism does not explicitly refer to the three offices of believers—prophet, priest, and king—although it is quite obvious that these are the three that are listed in this Q&A. The sentence, "I am anointed to confess his [i.e., Christ's] name," is a reference to the believer's prophetic office.

In Ephesians 4:11, the prophets are just one out of five different ministries that Christ has given to his church, in Romans 12:6–8 one out of seven, and in 1 Corinthians 12:28 even one out of eight. In all these cases, the New Testament refers to prophets in a narrower sense, such as we find them in the book of Acts (11:27; 13:1; 15:32; 21:10). However, in a wider sense, all Christians could be said to have a prophetic office, for instance, in the sense of Peter's statement: "As each has received a gift, use it to serve one another, as good stewards of God's varied grace: whoever speaks, as one who speaks oracles of God" (1 Pet. 4:10–11). And Paul says, "[T]he one who prophesies speaks to people for their upbuilding and encouragement and consolation" (1 Cor. 14:3). He even supposes that this could happen to all believers: "[If] *all* prophesy . . . you can *all* prophesy . . ." (vv. 24, 31).

The prophet proclaims God as well as his Word as it has been commissioned by God. Therefore, in the broadest sense all believers are prophets because they are all witnesses of Christ, that is, they all render their testimony about Christ (cf. Matt. 24:14; Acts 4:33; Rev. 12:11, 17; 20:4); "[f]or the testimony of Jesus is the spirit of prophecy" (Rev. 19:10). It is virtually unthinkable to be a believer in Christ, and not a confessor of Christ: "[I]f you confess with your mouth that Jesus is Lord and believe in your heart that God raised him from the dead, you will be saved. For with the heart one believes and is justified, and with the mouth one confesses and is saved" (Rom. 10:9–10). If there is nothing prophetic about me, that is, if I—in my own way, according to my own talents—am not a confessor of Christ, people may rightly wonder whether I am a Christian (cf. Matt. 10:32).

✢   ✢   ✢

DAY 100 – OUR PRIESTLY OFFICE
(LORD'S DAY 12, Q&A 32, PART 3)

A. . . . I am anointed . . . to present myself to him as a living sacrifice of thanks.

One essential task of the priests in the Old Testament was to bring sacrifices, or to help the ordinary Israelites bringing their sacrifices. The priesthood of Christ is closely connected with his self-sacrifice (Heb. 1:17; 9:26; 10:12), and the priesthood of the believer involves bringing sacrifices as well: "Through him [i.e., Christ] let us continually offer up a sacrifice of praise to God, that is, the fruit of lips that acknowledge his name. Do not neglect to do good and to share what you have, for such sacrifices are pleasing to God" (vv. 13:15–16). This is a reference to Hosea 14:2 (NIV: ". . . that we may offer the fruit of our lips"), while the expression "sacrifice of praise" reminds us of the "sacrifice of thanksgiving" (Lev. 7:12–15; 22:29; Ps. 50:14, 23). Notice, by the way, how in this passage, in one breath, our lofty sacrifices of praise are linked with down-to-earth sacrifices of material goods!

Peter has his own way of describing our priesthood, as being both holy and royal: "[Y]ou yourselves like living stones are being built up as a spiritual house, to be a *holy* priesthood, to offer spiritual sacrifices acceptable to God through Jesus Christ. . . . [Y]ou are a chosen race, a *royal* priesthood, a holy nation, a people for his own possession, that you may proclaim the excellencies of him who called you out of darkness into his marvelous light" (1 Pet. 2:5, 9). The royal and priestly elements are also brought together by John, who explains that the Lord "made us a kingdom, priests to his God and Father" (Rev. 1:6; cf. 5:10; 20:6).

The Catechism mentions the aspect of our priesthood that is emphasized by Paul: "I appeal to you therefore, brothers, by the mercies of God, to present your bodies as a living sacrifice, holy and acceptable to God, which is your spiritual worship" (Rom. 12:1). Here, the sacrifice is not something we bring (praise, thanksgiving, material goods), but we ourselves are the sacrifice: with all that I have and all that I am I consecrate myself to God, as a "living sacrifice." We may certainly call this the loftiest part of our priesthood!

✦ ✦ ✦

DAY 101 – OUR ROYAL OFFICE (I)
(LORD'S DAY 12, Q&A 32, PART 4)

A. . . . I am anointed . . . to strive with a free conscience against sin and the devil in this life, and afterward to reign with Christ over all creation for eternity.

Here we come to the third office of Christians: it is kingship. The first aspect that the Catechism mentions is what we could call the warrior king. We have been anointed, that is, granted the Holy Spirit, in order to function as kings. One day, we will "reign with Christ over all creation for eternity" (Rev. 22:5). But today we have to reign, as far as it is given us, over the powers in our lives: sin and the devil. "I write to you, young men," says John, "because you are strong, and the word of God abides in you, and you have overcome the evil one" (1 John 2:14). "Put on the whole armor of God," says Paul, "that you may be able to stand against the schemes of the devil. For we do not wrestle against flesh and blood, but against the rulers, against the authorities, against the cosmic powers over this present darkness, against the spiritual forces of evil in the heavenly places" (Eph. 6:11–12). It is one kingdom over against the other: the kingdom of Satan versus the Kingdom of God (Matt. 12:25–28).

The notion of the warrior-king comes out also in Paul's word to Timothy: "Fight the good fight of the faith. Take hold of the eternal life to which you were called and about which you made the good confession. . . . I charge you in the presence of God, who gives life to all things, and of Christ Jesus, who in his testimony before Pontius Pilate made the good confession, to keep the commandment unstained and free from reproach until the appearing of our Lord Jesus Christ, which he will display at the proper time—he who is the blessed and only Sovereign, the King of kings and Lord of lords" (1 Tim. 6:12–15). What was the "good confession" of Christ to Pilate? About his Kingdom! Jesus said, "My kingdom is not of this world. If my kingdom were of this world, my servants would have been fighting, that I might not be delivered over to the Jews. But my kingdom is not from the world" (John 18:36). The Roman kingdom was earthly and material; Jesus' Kingdom is heavenly and spiritual. Romans fought with worldly weapons; Jesus' followers are warrior-kings fighting with spiritual weapons.

✦ ✦ ✦

DAY 102 – OUR ROYAL OFFICE (II)
(Lord's Day 12, Q&A 32, part 5)

A. . . . I am anointed . . . to strive with a free conscience against sin and the devil in this life, and afterward to reign with Christ over all creation for eternity.

The road of every disciple of Christ goes through the valley to the mountain top. Paul says, "[I]f we endure, we will also reign with him" (2 Tim. 2:12), and as he says elsewhere, ". . . provided we suffer with him in order that we may also be glorified with him" (Rom. 8:17). And Peter says, "[R]ejoice insofar as you share Christ's sufferings, that you may also rejoice and be glad when his glory is revealed" (1 Pet. 4:13). "For the joy that was set before him" Jesus "endured the cross, despising the shame, and is seated at the right hand of the throne of God" (Heb. 12:2). This is also the "race" for us (v. 1): through sufferings to glory, from the warrior-king to the ruler-king. For many years, David was the anointed warrior-king before he became the anointed ruler-king.

In the fights of our present-day lives it is good to be reminded of what we will be one day. For instance, because the Corinthian believers had quarrels among themselves, Paul linked these strifes with their future: "When one of you has a grievance against another, does he dare go to law before the unrighteous instead of the saints? Or do you not know that *the saints will judge the world*? And if the world is to be judged by you, are you incompetent to try trivial cases? Do you not know that *we are to judge angels*? How much more, then, matters pertaining to this life!" (1 Cor. 6:1–3).

The book of Revelation tells us that believers are kings who will "reign on [or, over] the earth" (5:10). The resurrected saints will "reign with Christ for a thousand years" (20:4, 6), but also: "they will reign forever and ever" (22:5). So what is it: a thousand years, or forever and ever? That does not have to bother us right now. The great thing is: we *will* reign together with Christ over the "world to come" (Heb. 2:5–8)! But reigning as kings *then* should already affect us *now*. If you are a king, behave as one! In the greatest misery, Jesus always spoke and acted royally, so that even on the cross it was written, "This is the King of the Jews" (Luke 23: 38). So we too, let's be kings, even in misery!

✦   ✦   ✦

DAY 103 – THE ONLY SON

(Lord's Day 13, Q&A 33, part 1)

Q. Why is he called God's "only begotten Son" when we also are God's children?
A. Because Christ alone is the eternal, natural Son of God.

In the New Testament, there are two words that are relevant here. The one is *monogenes*, which in older translations is rendered "only begotten," and in newer translations just "only" (John 1:18; 3:16, 18; 1 John 4:9). The other word is *prototokos*, which is usually translated "firstborn," sometimes just "first," indicating not so much a time sequence as ranking (Rom. 8:29; Col. 1:15, 18; Heb. 1:6). The term *monogenes* underscores the absolute uniqueness of Jesus as the Son of God, while the term *firstborn* emphasizes Jesus' association with others: with creation, or with the church, or with resurrected humans, among whom he is always the first (highest).

In this latter sense—Christ as the firstborn—we can truly say that the Son of God became a human, in order that humans could become sons of God, Jesus being the "first(born) among many brothers" (Rom. 8:29), that is, humans who are sons of God like him: "For all who are led by the Spirit of God are sons of God. For you did not receive the spirit of slavery to fall back into fear, but you have received the Spirit of adoption as sons, by whom we cry, 'Abba! Father!'" (vv. 14–15).

As the "only begotten Son," Jesus is unique. He was and is the eternal Son of the eternal Father, from eternity "the only God [or, the only Son], who is at the Father's side [literally, in the Father's bosom]" (John 1:1–3, 18). Viewed as a human, he *became* "Son of God" by being fathered by the Holy Spirit (Luke 1:35). As to his present position, he "was declared to be the Son of God in power according to the Spirit of holiness by his resurrection from the dead" (Rom. 1:4). However, as to his divinity, he has been "the Father's Son" (2 John 1:3) from eternity. As such, we cannot compare ourselves with him. *We* were conceived in time; we have no eternity behind us. *He* had been eternally "the Son," but in "the fullness of time" (Gal. 4:4), the Word "*became* flesh" (John 1:14). With us it was the opposite: we were "flesh" from the earliest moment of our existence, but in due time we became what we had been eternally predestined for: *sons* (Eph. 1:5).

✳ ✳ ✳

DAY 104 – BIRTH AND ADOPTION

(Lord's Day 13, Q&A 33, part 2)

A. . . . *Christ alone is the eternal, natural Son of God. We, however, are adopted children of God.*

For the way believers are related to God, the New Testament uses at least two different metaphors. Although the Catechism does not seem to see much difference between "children" (Greek, *teknoi* or *paidia*) and "sons" (*huioi*), I think that the first metaphor, that of "birth," is linked with "children," and the second metaphor, that of "adoption," with "sons." On the one hand, we are *"children* of God, who were *born*, not of blood nor of the will of the flesh nor of the will of man, but of God" (John 1:12–13). Compare this wonderful word: "See what kind of love the Father has given to us, that we should be called children of God" (1 John 3:1). "Of his own will he *brought us forth* by the word of truth, that we should be a kind of firstfruits of his creatures" (James 1:18).

On the other hand, "you did not receive the spirit of slavery to fall back into fear, but you have received the Spirit of *adoption as sons*, by whom we cry, 'Abba! Father!'" (Rom. 8:15; cf. v. 23). "Adoption as sons" is one word, *huiothesia*, which we also find elsewhere: ". . . to redeem those who were under the law, so that we might receive *adoption as sons*. And because you are sons, God has sent the Spirit of his Son into our hearts, crying, 'Abba! Father!' So you are no longer a slave, but a son, and if a son, then an heir through God" (Gal. 4:5–7). God "predestined us for *adoption as sons* through Jesus Christ" (Eph. 1:5).

When I think of children, I think especially of birth, of kinship, of consanguinity, and therefore of similarity, of resemblance. If God is light (1 John 1:5), his children are light: "[N]ow you are light in the Lord. Walk as children of light" (Eph. 5:8). Be "blameless and innocent, children of God without blemish in the midst of a crooked and twisted generation, among whom you shine as lights in the world" (Phil. 2:15). However, when I think of adoption, I think of position, of heritage, of maturity, and therefore of worship: "Abba, Father!" Jesus himself, *the* Son of God, said, "Abba! Father" (Mark. 14:36). God made us sons that we, by the Spirit of adoption, could say the same (Rom. 8:15).

✦   ✦   ✦

DAY 105 – ADOPTED BY GRACE
(Lord's Day 13, Q&A 33, part 3)

A. . . . *adopted by grace through Christ.*

I miss in the ESV the words "(un)to himself," which we do find in other translations: ". . . having predestined us to adoption as sons by Jesus Christ *to Himself,* . . . to the praise of the glory of His grace, by which He made us accepted in the Beloved" (Eph. 1:5–6 NKJV). Some Christians seem to think that everything God did was entirely *for us,* as if there was nothing in it for himself. Most people desire to have sons (and daughters). As they have been created in the image of God, we assume that God is like that. The Father has one eternal Son, and the love between them was sufficient for both of them. And yet, in God's heart there was room for *millions* of sons (including daughters), "predestined to be conformed to the image of his Son" (Rom. 8:29), for *his own* pleasure, sons whom he could love, but who also would return this love, as reverberates in the words: "Abba, Father!" (v. 15; Gal. 4:6).

Similarly, Jesus desired a bridal church "that he might present her . . . *to himself* in splendor, without spot or wrinkle or any such thing, that she might be holy and without blemish" (Eph. 5:27). Jesus did not just give himself away for his church; he desired her *for himself* as his bride.

Notice the words "through Christ" which the Catechism mentions, and which we also found in Ephesians 1:5. Whether it is a small or a great privilege, it can never be given to us apart from Christ and his work on the cross. This also means that we can never merit even the smallest blessing. Each is a gift of God's grace: "sons by Jesus Christ to Himself, . . . to the praise of his glorious *grace,* with which he has blessed us in the Beloved. In him we have redemption through his blood, the forgiveness of our trespasses, according to the riches of his *grace*" (vv. 6–7). It is all grace in Ephesians: "God, being rich in mercy, . . . made us alive together with Christ—by *grace* you have been saved— . . . so that . . . he might show the immeasurable riches of his *grace* in kindness toward us in Christ Jesus. For by *grace* you have been saved through faith. And this is not your own doing; it is the gift of God" (2:5–8).

❖　❖　❖

DAY 106 – NOT WITH GOLD OR SILVER
(Lord's Day 13, Q&A 34, part 1)

Q. *Why do you call him "our Lord"?*
A. *Because—not with gold or silver, but with his precious blood—he has set us free . . .*

The thought of the Catechism is this: we call Jesus "our Lord" because he has bought us, and thus made us his very own. He is our Master, our Possessor, our Owner. It is even more precious if we are able to say *"my* Lord," as did Elizabeth, Mary Magdalene, Thomas, and Paul (Luke 1:43; John 20:13, 28; Phil. 3:8). This points to a very personal, very precious relationship: "I count everything as loss because of the surpassing worth of knowing Christ Jesus my Lord. For his sake I have suffered the loss of all things and count them as rubbish, in order that I may gain Christ" (Phil. 3:8).

In order to buy us the Lord Jesus paid a price. It is obvious that the Catechism is alluding here to 1 Peter 1:18–19: you know "that you were ransomed from the futile ways inherited from your forefathers, not with perishable things such as silver or gold, but with the precious blood of Christ, like that of a lamb without blemish or spot." Two means of redemption are excluded here. First, we have not been set free "with gold or silver." In itself, this is not such a condemnable thought at all. In Numbers 31 we read that the army leaders who had gained the victory over Midian "brought the LORD's offering, what each man found, articles of gold, armlets and bracelets, signet rings, earrings, and beads, to make *atonement* for ourselves before the LORD. And Moses and Eleazar the priest received from them the gold, all crafted articles" (vv. 50–51). However, it is obvious that gold and silver are at best *allusions* to the only price that has eternal value before God: the precious blood of Christ.

Second, it is equally obvious that animal blood will not suffice either: "For it is impossible for the blood of bulls and goats to take away sins" (Heb. 10:4). Even more clearly than in the case of gold and silver, this animal blood is at best an *allusion* to the only price that is valid before God: the blood of Christ. In Revelation 5 the heavenly saints say to him, "[Y]ou were slain, and by your blood you ransomed people for God from every tribe and language and people and nation" (v. 9; cf. 1:5–6).

✦ ✦ ✦

DAY 107 – SET FREE
(Lord's Day 13, Q&A 34, part 2)

A. . . . he has set us free from sin and from the tyranny of the devil.

In a certain sense, Jesus could be compared to a benevolent slave trader who goes to the market to set free slaves who are under the tyranny of dark enemies (in our case these were sin, the devil, and death). He pays the price that is demanded for these slaves, and thus purchases them for himself. Because he is such a good person, who strives for the best interests of these slaves, being a slave of this man is experienced as freedom, even as the utmost happiness. Strikingly enough, believers indeed remain slaves: slaves of righteousness (Rom. 6:18), slaves of God (v. 22), slaves of Christ (1 Cor. 4:1; Phil. 1:1). Some translations have "servants," but the literal meaning is "slaves." But what happy slaves, who love their Master, and are loved by their Master! Slaves, and yet perfectly free! What a lovely paradox: formerly we were *unfree* slaves, in bondage and under tyranny. Now we are *free* slaves: "For freedom Christ has set us free; stand firm therefore, and do not submit again to a yoke of slavery" (Gal. 5:1).

Everything depends on the master you have. If you have a master who oppresses you, who makes you feel miserable and unhappy, who constantly demands things that you hate, then you are in pitiful bondage. You need deliverance. But if you have a Master who loves you, who serves your best interests, who first made *himself* a slave *for you* (Phil. 2:7), who gives you orders that fit in perfectly with the desires of your new nature—then you are the happiest person in the world.

Jesus made us indeed "turn from darkness to light and from the power of Satan to God" (Acts 26:18). Jesus came in order "that through death he might destroy the one who has the power of death, that is, the devil, and deliver all those who through fear of death were subject to lifelong slavery" (Heb. 2:14–15). The Father "has delivered us from the domain of darkness and transferred us to the kingdom of his beloved Son" (Col. 1:13–14). "[Y]ou are . . . a people for his own possession, that you may proclaim the excellencies of him who called you out of darkness into his marvelous light" (1 Pet. 2:9).

✧   ✧   ✧

DAY 108 – BOUGHT TO BE HIS OWN

(Lord's Day 13, Q&A 34, part 3)

A. . . . he has . . . bought us, body and soul, to be his very own.

In Q&A 1 we heard it already: "I am not my own, but belong—body and soul, in life and in death— to my faithful Savior, Jesus Christ." Your bodies belong to him, therefore you are called to "present your bodies as a living sacrifice, holy and acceptable to God" (Rom. 12:1). And Paul hoped "that with full courage now as always Christ will be honored in my body, whether by life or by death" (Phil. 1:20). "[Y]ou were bought with a price. So glorify God in your body" (1 Cor. 6:20; cf. 7:23). And of course, your soul is involved: "You shall love the Lord your God with all your heart and with all your soul and with all your strength and with all your mind" (Luke 10:27). Mary said, "My soul magnifies the Lord, and my spirit rejoices in God my Savior" (Luke 1:46–47).

Jesus paid the ransom for our deliverance and freedom. Don't ask to *whom* he paid the ransom—to God? to the devil?—because either way you run into theological trouble. You are stretching the metaphor. We cannot say that Jesus paid the price to God because we did not have to be freed from *God's* captivity but Satan's. Nor can we say that Jesus paid the price to the devil because he did not owe the devil anything; he simply *triumphed* over him. Yet, the Bible uses the image of a ransom to express what it cost Jesus to set us free. He gave himself as a ransom for "all" (1 Tim. 2:6) because all people may come to receive his salvation. It is offered to the whole world. And Jesus gave his life as a ransom for "many" (Matt. 20:28), that is, for the many who actually believe in him.

The result is great: Jesus "gave himself for us to redeem us from all lawlessness and to purify for himself a people for his own possession who are zealous for good works" (Titus 2:14). Jesus wanted to have a people "for himself, for his own possession," people who would belong to him, who would love him, serve him, please him. He gave *everything* he had for them, and now he expects that they will give *everything* they have for him. Is it not perfectly fair and righteous that he expects this from them? Does he not *deserve* it?

✤ ✤ ✤

DAY 109 – HE REMAINS GOD

(Lord's Day 14, Q&A 35, part 1)

Q. What does it mean that he "was conceived by the Holy Spirit and born of the virgin Mary"?
A. That the eternal Son of God, who is and remains true and eternal God, took to himself . . . a truly human nature.

It has always been difficult for many people to properly maintain the truth of the two natures of Christ. From eternity the Son was God (John 1:1–3), in the fullness of time (Gal. 4:4) he became flesh (John 1:14a), in order to remain forever both God and Man. There are at least three errors one could make here. The Catechism addresses especially the first error (Jesus *is* God) and the second one (Jesus *remains* God), but for completeness' sake I will add a third one.

First, some deny the eternal pre-existence of Christ, and thus also his true deity. However, the New Testament clearly testifies to both his pre-existence (see, e.g., John 1:1–3, 18; 16:28; 17:5, 24; Col. 1:17) and to the fact that Jesus is God (see, e.g., John 10:30–36; 20:28; Rom. 9:5; Titus 2:13; 2 Pet. 1:1; 1 John 5:20).

Second, some think that when the Son became Man, he laid aside his deity for a while. They argue that Jesus *was* in the form of God, and at incarnation *took* the form of a servant (Phil. 2:6–7), and *thus* laid aside the form of God. But this is a mistake. Here on earth he was in the form of *both* God and a servant. To be sure, Jesus did *conceal* his divine glory to a large extent behind the "veil" of his humanity, although his followers could look through it (John 1:14b). But he remained God, also on earth. Only in this way can we understand, for instance, that Jesus could forgive sins (Mark 2:7) and could accept people falling down before him and worshiping him (Matt. 14:33; 28:9, 17; Luke 5:8, 12; 8:28; 17:16; John 9:38; for a contrast, cf. Acts 10:25–26; Rev. 19:10).

The third error is that some think that when Jesus returned to heaven, he laid aside his humanity. Such people forget that, today, Jesus is still the Son of Man, and that one day he will return as the Son of Man (Matt. 10:23; 16:27; 24:27; 25:31). Paul writes in the present tense, "[I]n him [i.e., Christ] the whole fullness of deity dwells *bodily*" (Col. 2:9). With his glorified body he is seated at the right hand of God. Just as he remained God on earth, and will remain God forever, he will remain Man forever.

✳   ✳   ✳

DAY 110 – THE VIRGIN BIRTH
(Lord's Day 14, Q&A 35, part 2)

A. . . . the eternal Son of God . . . took to himself, through the working of the Holy Spirit, . . . a truly human nature.

The Catechism does not explicitly say so, but of course it is implied here that Jesus had no earthly father; he was "fathered," so to speak, by the Holy Spirit: "When [Jesus'] mother Mary had been betrothed to Joseph, before they came together she was found to be with child from the Holy Spirit . . . an angel of the Lord appeared to [Joseph] in a dream, saying, '. . . that which is conceived in [Mary] is from the Holy Spirit" (Matt. 1:18, 20). The angel Gabriel told Mary, "The Holy Spirit will come upon you, and the power of the Most High will overshadow you; therefore the child to be born will be called holy—the Son of God" (Luke 1:35).

This truth of the so-called Virgin Birth involved the truth that Mary was still a virgin when she gave birth to Jesus. This is of the greatest importance. It is not some myth that at a later stage was introduced into the New Testament, as some have asserted. On the contrary, this truth is already implied by Paul in an early letter: "[W]hen the fullness of time had come, God sent forth his Son, *born of a woman*"—not of a father (Gal. 4:4). Because God was his Father, he did not need an earthly father—but because he was to be a true Man he needed an earthly mother.

Notice the interesting word "overshadow" in Luke 1:35. It is a term that we find, for instance, in the Greek translation of Exodus 40:35, where it is said that the "cloud" (the *Shekinah*, God's holy presence, which in the New Testament is comparable to the Holy Spirit) "overshadowed" the newly built tabernacle. Jesus called his body a "temple," and compared it to the temple in Jerusalem (John 2:19–22) because in him dwelt the *Shekinah*; or, as Paul puts it, "in him all the fullness of God was pleased to dwell" (Col. 1:19). Jesus received his body through Mary but because of his divine origin ("conceived by the Holy Spirit") the fullness of the Godhead dwelt in this Man. In such a way, the fullness of God could never dwell in us because we are ordinary humans. But though he had a human body, he *was* God himself; in this human body even the entire fullness of God could dwell.

✳   ✳   ✳

DAY 111 – FROM THE FLESH OF MARY
(Lord's Day 14, Q&A 35, part 3)

*A. . . . the eternal Son of God . . . took to himself . . . from the flesh
and blood of the virgin Mary, a truly human nature.*

The Catechism emphasizes that the "truly human nature" that the Son
of God "took to himself" was "from the flesh and blood of Mary."
What exactly does this mean? What do Mary's *own* flesh and blood have
to do with *Jesus'* flesh and blood? The Belgic Confession (Art. 18) refers to
"the heresy of the Anabaptists who deny that Christ assumed human flesh
from his mother." I remember a believing French medical doctor (a paedobaptist) who adjured me that "the womb of Mary did not contribute anything to the body of Jesus." On a different occasion, a believing Scottish-
Australian medical doctor (also a paedobaptist) told me exactly the same
thing! You see, baptism cannot be the problem here. This subject seems to
be a specialty of medical doctors . . . although this is first and foremost a
theological question. (Let me emphasize this, being both a biologist and a
theologian myself.)

Let me, with the greatest reverence, put it in explicit terms: Did the
body of Jesus in the womb of Mary develop from an ovum of Mary, or not?
To be sure, the Son "became flesh" (John 1:14), and: "Since . . . the children
share in flesh and blood, [the Son] himself likewise partook of the same
things" (Heb. 2:14). God sent "his own Son in the likeness of sinful flesh"
(Rom. 8:3), that is, in human flesh that *in us* is stained by sin. Thus, we
know for sure that Jesus had a genuine human body, a body of real flesh
and blood. But I do not know of any Bible verse telling us what contribution *Mary's* "flesh and blood" made to Jesus' flesh and blood. I have heard
the most solemn theological arguments pleading for the ovum theory, and
similar serious arguments pleading for the non-ovum theory. My answer
to this is that it is sometimes wiser to leave holy matters alone.

Think of the foolish men of Beth-shemesh who curiously "looked
upon [or, into] the ark of the LORD," and were "struck" for it (1 Sam. 6:19).
The ark is a striking image of Christ, the gold referring to his divine nature, and the wood to his human nature. Don't irreverently look into the
ark! There are mysteries that are simply beyond us.

✳ ✳ ✳

DAY 112 – DAVID'S DESCENDANT
(Lord's Day 14, Q&A 35, part 4)

*A. . . . the eternal Son of God . . . took to himself . . . from the flesh
and blood of the virgin Mary, a truly human nature so that he might
also become David's true descendant.*

Jesus was "David's true descendant." He is often identified this way (e.g.,
Matt. 1:1; 9:27; 12:23; 15:22; 20:30–31; 21:9, 15). This descent is of great
importance, because it gives Christ title to the throne of David. As the angel told Mary, "[T]he Lord God will give to him the throne of his father
David, and he will reign over the house of Jacob forever, and of his kingdom there will be no end" (Luke 1:32–33), and it is prophesied of him, "Of
the increase of his government and of peace there will be no end, on the
throne of David and over his kingdom, to establish it and to uphold it with
justice and with righteousness from this time forth and forevermore" (Isa.
9:7). Paul speaks of "the gospel of God . . . concerning his Son, who was
descended from David according to the flesh" (Rom. 1:3).

Now the question arises: *how* did he descend from David? One might
conclude from our Q&A that this was "through Mary." This may very well
be. However, it is interesting that Joseph is repeatedly said to be of the house
of David, but never Mary. She is said to be a relative of Elizabeth, who was
a Levite (Luke 1:5, 36). It has been argued that the genealogy of Luke 3 is in
fact that of Mary (so that she would be a descendant of David), but many
have objected to this far-fetched idea. However, the most important objec-
tion is this: how could Jesus ever be entitled to David's throne if he descended from David only through a *woman*?

It is far more likely that Jesus was entitled to David's throne because
Joseph, who was of Davidic descent (Matt. 1:1, 16, 20; Luke 1:27; 2:4), was
his *legal* father. Jesus was born within the marriage of Joseph and Mary,
and thus was fully entitled to Joseph's inheritance (cf. Luke 2:48, "your father and I"). In Jerusalem, a rabbi once told me that I could not have it both
ways: Mary's Son Jesus was either the Son of God, but then he could not be
Son of David; or he was Son of David, but then he could not be Son of God.
My answer was: Jesus' Virgin Birth underscores his being the Son of God;
but the *legal* fatherhood of Joseph made Jesus truly Son of David.

✣   ✣   ✣

DAY 113 – LIKE US EXCEPT FOR SIN
(Lord's Day 14, Q&A 35, part 5)

*A. . . . the eternal Son of God . . . took to himself . . . a truly human
nature so that he might also become David's true descendant, like his
brothers and sisters in every way except for sin.*

Jesus was "like his brothers and sisters in every way," as it is said: "Since
. . . the children share in flesh and blood, he himself likewise partook of
the same things. . . . For surely it is not angels that he helps, but he helps
the offspring of Abraham. Therefore he had to be made like his brothers in
every respect" (Heb. 2:14, 16–17; his "brothers and sisters" are here specifically Israel). Paul says that Jesus was "born in the likeness of men" (Phil.
2:7), and: "By sending his own Son in the likeness of sinful flesh and for sin
[or, as a sin offering], [God] condemned sin in the flesh" (Rom. 8:3).

Jesus was exactly like us. He was a Man of flesh and blood. He could
be "wearied" (John 4:6; others translate: "tired"), he could be hungry
(Matt. 4:2) and thirsty (John 4:7; 19:28). "[H]e himself has suffered when
tempted" (Heb. 2:18). "For we do not have a high priest who is unable to
sympathize with our weaknesses, but one who in every respect has been
tempted as we are, *yet without sin*" (4:15). Here is the great exception: he
knew weaknesses and temptation, just like we do. But there is this difference: because we have a sinful nature we can *fall* into the temptations. He
could not because he had no sinful nature. The New Testament insists on
this: Jesus "committed no sin" (1 Pet. 2:22; this refers to his deeds), more
strongly: he "knew no sin" (2 Cor. 5:21), even more strongly: "in him there
is no sin" (1 John 3:5; this refers to his nature). He was and is "holy, innocent, unstained, separated from sinners" (Heb. 7:26).

Look now at Romans 8:3 again: Jesus came "in the likeness of sinful
flesh." This can only mean that Jesus came in perfectly human flesh, exactly like our flesh, with this difference: *in us* this flesh is stained by sin, in
him it was not. And it *had* to be this way, otherwise Jesus could never have
become our Redeemer, or the true "sin offering." Only a perfect human
Mediator can redeem imperfect human beings. Both were essential conditions for our redemption: he had to be fully human *like* us, and he had to be
sinless *unlike* us (cf. Q&As 15 and 16).

✤   ✤   ✤

DAY 114 – OUR MEDIATOR
(Lord's Day 14, Q&A 36, part 1)

Q. How does the holy conception and birth of Christ benefit you?
A. He is our mediator and, in God's sight, he covers with his inno-
cence and perfect holiness my sinfulness in which I was conceived.

It is a nice feature of the Catechism that, once in a while, it asks what practical use the specific elements of the Apostles' Creed have for us. It does
not give us primarily *theological* teaching, but *existential* instruction. For
instance, the Creed says, "I believe in . . . the forgiveness of sins"—but if
it is asked, "How does this benefit us?", our answer is: "I believe that God,
because of Christ's satisfaction, will no longer remember any of *my* sins"
(Q&A 56). That is very personal! Likewise, you may consider it an interesting fact that Christ came into this world through the Virgin Birth without
this fact really touching your heart and life. But this cannot be the intention
of the Creed; it is supposed to be the confession of *your personal* faith. The
believer is existentially involved in every element of it.

Thus, the holy conception and birth of Christ are important for us too,
because they guaranteed that Jesus would be both perfectly human and perfectly sinless. It was vital that he was fully human *like* us, and it was equally
vital that he was sinless *unlike* us. He had to fulfill at least these two conditions in order to become our Mediator (cf. 1 Tim. 2:5–6; Heb. 9:13–15).
(A third condition was that he was God.) Jesus was and is "holy, innocent,
unstained, separated from sinners" (Heb. 7:26). If he had not been innocent,
that is, without sin, he would have needed redemption himself.

His innocent life was the necessary preparation for his sacrificial death.
The Mosaic law did not prescribe any burnt offering without a grain offering. The non-bloody grain offering speaks of the perfect *life* of Jesus, which
preceded his perfect, atoning *death*, depicted in the bloody burnt offering
(cf. Lev. 1 and 2). By nature, we were *sin*, and he was *righteousness*. But on
the cross, he was made *sin*, so that we could become the *righteousness* of God
(2 Cor. 5:21). And now we have been clothed with the "innocence" (righteousness and holiness) of Christ (cf. 1 Cor. 1:30, "Christ Jesus . . . became to
us wisdom from God, righteousness and sanctification and redemption").

✦   ✦   ✦

DAY 115 – HIS HOLINESS

(Lord's Day 14, Q&A 36, part 2)

A. . . . in God's sight, he covers with his innocence and perfect holiness my sinfulness in which I was conceived.

The original English version of the Catechism (1611) said "sins" here, but the original German version said "sin" (singular), in the sense of "original sin," and this is what this Q&A is actually all about. The present revised edition of the Catechism has solved this problem by the rendering "sinfulness." The reason why the reference here must be to what theologians have called "original sin" is because the text implicitly quotes Psalm 51:5, "Behold, I was brought forth in iniquity, and in sin did my mother conceive me." David confesses here not only that he had done sinful things—think of his gross sins against Bathsheba and Uriah (2 Sam. 11)—but that he was sinful all the way to his very core. He was a sinner since his conception and birth, just like us all. We are not sinners because we sin, but we sin because we are sinners. It's our nature. It can be changed only by a radical *transformation* of our being, which is called "rebirth," "regeneration," even becoming a "new creation."

You see how the Catechism moves here from the *holy* conception and birth of Jesus to our own *unholy* conception and birth. The latter fact is witnessed many times in the Bible, for instance: "[T]he intention of man's heart is evil *from his youth*" (Gen. 8:21). "Who can bring a clean thing out of an unclean? There is not one" (Job 14:4). "What is man, that he can be pure? Or he who is *born* of a woman, that he can be righteous?" (15:14). "The wicked are estranged *from the womb*; they go astray *from birth*, speaking lies" (Ps. 58:3). Humans are conceived and born as sinful beings, whereas Jesus was conceived and born in a perfect, divine way. *His* human nature was pure from the start, *our* human nature is rotten from the start. For a Mediator, we not only needed one who led a perfect life, but one who had a perfect *beginning* as Man on earth.

Thank God, our old condition is now covered with Christ's righteousness and holiness: "Blessed is the one whose transgression is forgiven, whose sin is covered" (Ps. 32:1; cf. Rom. 4:7). "In God's sight" the believer now is as righteous and holy as Christ is!

❖　　❖　　❖

DAY 116 – CHRIST'S SUFFERING
(Lord's Day 15, Q&A 37, part 1)

Q. What do you understand by the word "suffered"?
A. That during his whole life on earth, but especially at the end,
Christ sustained in body and soul the wrath of God.

There is no doubt that Jesus had to suffer during his entire life. For his perfectly pure soul it must have been terrible to live among wicked sinners: "Consider him [i.e., Jesus] who endured from sinners such hostility against himself" (Heb. 12:3). Peter says, "[E]ven if you should suffer for righteousness' sake, you will be blessed" (1 Peter 3:14), and Jesus said, "Blessed are those who are persecuted for righteousness' sake" (Matt. 5:10). Well, if there ever was one who suffered "for righteousness' sake" it was the righteous Jesus in the midst of so many unrighteous. One might put it this way: during his whole life on earth, Christ sustained the wrath of wicked, hostile *sinners*—but "at the end," that is, on the cross, "Christ sustained the wrath of *God*."

During his life on earth, Jesus always enjoyed the fellowship with his Father. Twice, the Father said, "This is my beloved Son, with whom I am well pleased" (Matt. 3:17; 17:5). No wrath, but pleasure. No wonder; Jesus could say, "I always do the things that are pleasing to him [i.e., his Father]" (John 8:29), and: "My food is to do the will of him who sent me and to accomplish his work" (4:34). Even on the brink of going to the cross he could still say to his disciples, "[Y]ou will leave me alone. Yet I am not alone, for the Father is with me" (16:32). Thus, Father and Son went together, like once Abraham and Isaac, discussing the lamb for the burnt offering (Gen. 22:6–8).

However, during the three hours of darkness on the cross, "he was pierced for our transgressions; he was crushed for our iniquities; upon him was the chastisement that brought us peace, and with his wounds we are healed" (Isa. 53:5). When Peter quotes these words, he explicitly says that Jesus "bore our sins in his body *on the tree*," that is, on the cross (1 Pet. 2:24). During these horrible hours, we do not hear about the fellowship between the Father and the Son, but we hear this holy Man complaining, "My God, my God, why have you forsaken me?" (Matt. 27:46; Mark 15:34; cf. Ps. 22:1). What a dreadful moment it was!

✦　　✦　　✦

DAY 117 – THE WRATH OF GOD
(Lord's Day 15, Q&A 37, part 2)

A. . . . during his whole life on earth, but especially at the end, Christ sustained in body and soul the wrath of God against the sin of the whole human race.

What a dark, sobering expression is this: "the wrath of God." Literally, we never read that Jesus sustained the wrath of God against sin, but implicitly the thought is clearly there. The Bible says that the wrath of God dwells on the sinner who refuses to repent (John 3:36), and that this wrath "is revealed from heaven against all ungodliness and unrighteousness of men, who by their unrighteousness suppress the truth" (Rom. 1:18). The day of judgment will be a "day of wrath" (2:5; cf. 3:5; 5:9; 12:19; 13:4–5; Eph. 5:6; Col. 3:6; 1 Thess. 5:9; Rev. 14:10, 19; 19:15). Unrepentant sinners are called "vessels of wrath" (9:22). If God's judgment on the wicked is described as the "wrath of God," it is obvious that, when Jesus vicariously underwent God's judgment for us, this judgment may be called the "wrath of God" as well.

"Wrath" is equivalent to anger, fury, ire. We could hardly say that, on the cross, God was angry with Jesus. But we certainly can say that he was angry with "the sin of the whole human race." There can never be any person who is as angry with sin as God is. In his sight, even the smallest sin is a thousand times worse than it is in our sight. At the same time, there can never be any person who loves sinners as much as God does. He loves even our own beloved ones more than we do.

This is a great mystery because we ourselves hardly manage to keep the two apart. That is, if we detest a malice that a certain person has committed we can hardly avoid detesting that malicious person as well. But God so loved the world that he gave his only Son for her (John 3:16), not *because of* her wickedness, but *in spite of* it. His hatred toward sin was counterbalanced by his love for sinners. God rather preferred to let his wrath come down upon his beloved Son than that millions of sinners would have to suffer eternal destruction. God's hatred toward sin was proven by the full vicarious punishment Jesus had to undergo. God's love toward sinners was proven by the fact that not we, but his beloved Son had to undergo this punishment. What a great God we have!

❖   ❖   ❖

DAY 118 – DELIVERED FROM ETERNAL CONDEMNATION

(LORD'S DAY 15, Q&A 37, PART 3)

A. . . . This he did in order that, by his suffering as the only atoning sacrifice, he might deliver us, body and soul, from eternal condemnation.

What it really *meant* that Jesus endured the "wrath of God" on the cross we cannot even begin to surmise. No wonder the scene on Calvary was hidden in darkness before the eyes of the spectators. His enemies were dead silent. It now was entirely a matter between a holy and righteous God and this perfect Man who had been made sin for us (2 Cor. 5:21). Perhaps one could say that the eternity in hell that unrepentant sinners will have to undergo was condensed into three hours for Jesus. He suffered in three hours what the wicked will have to suffer in the ages of ages. But at least the wicked will know *why* they will suffer. But Jesus could rightly ask, "*Why* have you forsaken me?" There was for him no personal reason why God should forsake him. However, two verses later in Psalm 22, Jesus himself gives the answer: "Yet you are holy" (v. 3). At the moment when he was made sin for us, a holy and righteous God had to turn away his face from him because God is "of purer eyes than to see evil and cannot look at wrong" (Hab. 1:13).

Jesus was the atoning sacrifice who died in our stead (Rom. 3:25; 1 John 2:2; 4:10), so that we do not have to suffer in hell forever. He commanded his disciples to "fear him who can destroy both soul and body in hell" (Matt. 10:28). For Jesus were the tortures of hell, for us there is atonement, redemption, eternal salvation: "There is therefore now no condemnation for those who are in Christ Jesus" (Rom. 8:1).

Everything that *humans* did to Jesus during the last days of his life did not at all contribute to our salvation; it only increased human guilt. No, it was what *God* did to him on the cross that saved us: "[I]t was the will of the LORD to crush him; he has put him to grief" (Isa. 53:10). "'Awake, O sword, against my shepherd, against the man who stands next to me,' declares the LORD of hosts" (Zech. 13:7). "*You* lay me in the dust of death" (Ps. 22:15). Jesus' "wounds" with which we are healed (Isa. 53:5; 1 Pet. 2:24) are not the wounds that Roman soldiers inflicted upon him, but the wounds with which God smote him on the cross!

✳   ✳   ✳

DAY 119 – GAINING GOD'S GRACE
(Lord's Day 15, Q&A 37, part 4)

A. . . . This he did in order that . . . he might deliver us . . . from eternal condemnation, and gain for us God's grace, righteousness, and eternal life.

Sometimes we are focused too much on the negative side of redemption. It involves the things from which we have been delivered. We have been set free from the power of sin and death, and therefore there is "now no condemnation for those who are in Christ Jesus" (Rom. 8:1). We have been delivered from the power of Satan (e.g., Acts 26:18). If someone has been deeply subjugated to these powers, and to the fear of death (Heb. 2:15), we can imagine how happy such a person is when he or she is set free. When in ordinary life a person is released from prison, this is his first thought: "I am free! I am no longer in captivity!" But now he has to discover what his life of freedom is going to be. Will he have a family, a job, a house, an income?

From the moment we had been set free from sin, the devil, and death, we also had to learn to consider the positive side of this redemption. What did we *gain*? One of the biblical answers is that "God blessed us in Christ with every spiritual blessing in the heavenly places" (Eph. 1:3). Some of them are enumerated here. First, there is God's grace. This is not only the grace of redemption as such; *all* our new blessings are tokens of grace as well: God "predestined us for adoption as sons through Jesus Christ, . . . to the praise of his glorious *grace*, with which he has blessed us in the Beloved. In him we have redemption through his blood, the forgiveness of our trespasses, according to the riches of his *grace*, which he lavished upon us, . . . making known to us the mystery of his will, according to his purpose, which he set forth in Christ as a plan for the fullness of time, to unite all things in him, things in heaven and things on earth" (vv. 5–10). It's all grace!

It is the same with righteousness: we have "become the righteousness of God" (2 Cor. 5:21), or, "Christ Jesus became to us righteousness" (1 Cor. 1:30). Every blessing we received we have in Christ. We have eternal life in him (John 5:24), and he himself is to us "the true God and eternal life" (1 John 5:20). All these things will be worked out in later Q&As.

✢   ✢   ✢

DAY 120 – PONTIUS PILATE
(Lord's Day 15, Q&A 38, part 1)

Q. Why did he suffer "under Pontius Pilate" as judge?
A. So that he, though innocent, might be condemned by an earthly judge.

Apart from Jesus Christ himself, only two human beings are mentioned in the Apostles' Creed: Mary the mother of Jesus, and Pontius Pilate. That Mary is referred to is understandable—but why Pilate? Is this not too much honor for this cowardly and dishonest man? He was only a little governor in a little corner of the mighty Roman Empire. And now his name is known to billions of people, and for many centuries already. Of course he did not deserve this attention. That's not the point of his being mentioned. The point is that the reference to Pilate helps us to realize that Jesus' life and death belong to genuine world history. They are not part of some mythology, some pious religious fabrication. Pontius Pilate was a real figure in Roman history, a man who served under the emperor Tiberius and was the prefect of the Roman province of Judaea from AD 26 to 36. We know his name and a few facts of his life from several authors: Roman (Tacitus) and Jewish (Philo of Alexandria, Flavius Josephus) writers, several apocryphal works, and the famous Pilate Stone, found at Caesarea in 1961. Even Pilate's wife, mentioned in Matthew 27:19, is known to us by the name of Claudia Procula. In the Eastern Orthodox Church, she is commemorated as a saint because of her alleged conversion.

Jesus' condemnation is not a story from some dark prehistoric past. It is part and parcel of Roman and Judaean history. The Jews were famous for their *law*, which God had given to them. But they abused this law to claim that, according to it, Jesus deserved the death penalty (John 19:7). The Greeks were famous for their *wisdom*; the Greek word "philosophy" means "love of wisdom." But this wisdom did not stop them from calling the cross mere foolishness (1 Cor. 1:20–25). The Romans were famous for their *justice*; Roman law is still widely studied. But this justice did not prevent some of them from committing the greatest injustice of world history: sentencing Jesus to death (Luke 23:13–24; John 19:4, 12–16). Against this black background of human wickedness the gold of God's grace is shining.

✤　✤　✤

DAY 121 – CONDEMNED TO SET US FREE
(LORD'S DAY 15, Q&A 38, PART 2)

A. . . . *[Jesus], though innocent, [was] condemned by an earthly judge, and so [freed] us from the severe judgment of God that was to fall on us.*

The Catechism draws an interesting parallel between Jesus' condemnation by the unfair earthly judge Pontius Pilate and the severe judgment that fell on Jesus from a holy and righteous heavenly Judge. It is indeed striking to see how these two histories are interwoven. On the one hand, there is the story of the wickedness of some Romans and Jews, sentencing Jesus to death. On the other hand, there is the story of God's judgment that we had deserved but that fell on Jesus. In his wisdom God had provided that the moment at which humanity's stupidity and wickedness came to light at their worst coincided with the moment at which God's grace and mercy were revealed at their best.

Never did humanity's evil become more evident than on Good Friday— and *never* did God's goodness become more evident than on Good Friday. *Pilate* condemned Jesus in his own court, and thus helped bring humanity's misery to its deepest point. On the very same day, *God* laid his "severe judgment" on Jesus during the hours of darkness on the cross, and thus led humanity to the summit of God's saving grace. Pilate's condemnation involved the greatest possible increase of human guilt—God's judgment took away that guilt fully for all those who would believe. *Pilate* laid on Jesus the chastisement that would eventually lead to the decline of the pagan Roman Empire. *God* laid on Jesus the chastisement that brings us peace (cf. Isa. 53:5).

A superficial reading might lead one to conclude that the Catechism suggests that Pilate's condemnation of Jesus *as such* was a contribution to our salvation. But that cannot possibly be its intention. Pilate's judgment did not take away our guilt; it only *increased* humanity's guilt. Pilate was at best an indirect instrument in God's hand to bring Jesus to the cross, where God would deal with Jesus in his own way (a fact that did not diminish Pilate's own responsibility, of course). Consider the two sides in Acts 2:23, "[T]his Jesus, delivered up according to the definite plan and foreknowledge of God [in view of redemption], *you* crucified and killed by the hands of lawless men."

❖   ❖   ❖

DAY 122 – CRUCIFIED
(Lord's Day 15, Q&A 39, part 1)

Q. Is it significant that he was "crucified" instead of dying some other way?
A. Yes.

There are two sides to the death of Jesus. On the one hand, Jesus himself declared, "For this reason the Father loves me, because I lay down my life that I may take it up again. *No one takes it from me*, but I lay it down of my own accord. I have authority to lay it down, and I have authority to take it up again" (John 10:17–18). This is his death as viewed from the divine perspective. However, there is also the other, human side, according to which it is equally true to say that Jesus was killed by wicked humans: "[T]his Jesus, delivered up according to the definite plan and foreknowledge of God, you crucified and killed by the hands of lawless men" (Acts 2:23; cf. 3:15; 5:30). Stephen even spoke of "the Righteous One, whom you have now betrayed and *murdered*" (7:52).

Jesus was murdered by wicked Romans and Jews together. We cannot say that it was actually the Romans who did it, as if the Jews were innocent of it. The words in the four passages in Acts just referred to were all addressed to Jews. Of course not all Jews of all centuries since Calvary are guilty, as has been often claimed. Paul, when speaking to Jews in Pisidian Antioch—far away from Jerusalem—said, "[T]hose who live in Jerusalem and their rulers, because they did not recognize him nor understand the utterances of the prophets, which are read every Sabbath, fulfilled them by condemning him. And though *they* found in him no guilt worthy of death, *they* asked Pilate to have him executed" (13:27–28). At the same time, we can say that Romans and Jews stand, as it were, for humanity in its entirety: it was *humanity*—you and I—that rejected and condemned him.

The book of Acts also refers to the way Jesus was killed: ". . . Jesus, whom you killed by hanging him on a tree" (Acts 5:30). This seems to be a clear reference to the law of Moses: "[I]f a man has committed a crime punishable by death and he is put to death, and you hang him on a tree, his body shall not remain all night on the tree, but you shall bury him the same day, for a hanged man is cursed by God" (Deut. 21:22–23). We come back to this tomorrow.

✤   ✤   ✤

DAY 123 – CURSED
(Lord's Day 15, Q&A 39, part 2)

A. . . . By this [crucifixion] I am convinced that he shouldered the curse which lay on me, since death by crucifixion was cursed by God.

If we ask whether Jesus' way of dying, namely, through crucifixion, was significant, the least we can say is that crucifixion was perhaps the most horrible and cruel death penalty that humanity has ever invented. If Jesus' death should be evidence of the greatest wickedness of humans, we can also imagine that the way they put him to death was the most wicked way possible.

However, there is far more to it. Paul wrote, "Christ redeemed us from the curse of the law by becoming a curse for us—for it is written, 'Cursed is everyone who is hanged on a tree'" (Gal. 3:13, quoting from Deut. 21:23). Of course, this is not a literal application of the Mosaic law. In Deuteronomy, the reference is to a person who was first put to death—generally by stoning—and *then* hanged on a "tree" (or a pole). The rabbis said that only some of the worst criminals underwent this treatment. Such a dead body should not remain on that pole overnight, "but you shall bury him the same day, for a hanged man is cursed by God." This latter phrase is what drew Paul's attention, and which he applied in a rather free way: "Cursed is everyone who is hanged on a tree," not only the *hanged* person under the law of Moses, but also the *crucified* person in New Testament times.

Not only this: the term "curse" here has a specific meaning. Jesus on the cross sustained the curse *for us*, in our stead. The curse is the consequence of not keeping God's commandments (see extensively Deut. 27:13–26). In its deepest meaning, this is not just a providential, but an eternal, curse: "away from the presence of the Lord" (2 Thess. 1:9). There are only two options if we wish to escape from this eternal curse. The one is that we keep God's commandments—but by nature humans are not capable of doing this. The other option is that we find a substitute who becomes a curse for us, in our stead. This is what Jesus did on the cross for all those who believe in him. Vicariously he bore the curse in those hours of darkness on the cross, in order that we would no longer be affected by any curse in eternity.

❖   ❖   ❖

DAY 124 – GOD REQUIRING DEATH
(Lord's Day 16, Q&A 40, part 1)

Q. Why did Christ have to suffer death?
A. Because God's justice and truth require it.

Why did Jesus have to die? In order to save us from the power of death. Was there no easier way to save us? No. Because of our sins, a vicarious sacrifice was demanded. God's "justice and truth" demand the punishment of sin. If we would have to bear the consequences of our sin ourselves, this would imply eternal condemnation. And those who refuse to accept Christ's sacrifice will indeed have to make an eternal payment for their sins. But those who do believe in Christ and his sacrifice may know by faith that Christ underwent God's judgment in their stead. We humans may be able to forgive one another's sin just like that. We say to the other who sinned against us and repents of it: "I forgive you. Forget it."

We can do that. But God cannot do that. No sin can go unpunished, because this would violate his "justice and truth." His justice demands punishment, either the punishment of the trespasser, or the punishment of an innocent, vicarious sacrifice. There is no other way. "[W]ithout the shedding of blood there is no forgiveness of sins" (Heb. 9:22). There can be no *life* for the sinner without the *death* of the sacrifice. There can be no forgiveness for the sinner without the punishment coming on the head of the sacrifice. Nothing else will do with God: neither our good works, nor our good intentions, nor our begging and beseeching.

God had alluded to this truth already immediately after the Fall: "[T]he Lord God made for Adam and for his wife garments of skins and clothed them" (Gen. 3:21). Apparently, some animals had to die so that the first humans could be covered with the skins. Abel grasped this message, Cain did not. Cain brought to God the fruits of his own labor, and thought he could please God in this way (4:3). But Abel brought a burnt offering from the flock (4:4). Apparently he realized, in whatever weak way that may have been, that he could stand before God only on the basis of an innocent sacrifice dying in his stead. Therefore, "the Lord had regard for Abel and his offering, but for Cain and his offering he had no regard" (vv. 4–5). What a serious lesson!

❖   ❖   ❖

DAY 125 – GOD'S JUSTICE AND TRUTH
(LORD'S DAY 16, Q&A 40, PART 2)

A. . . . God's justice and truth require [death]: nothing else could pay for our sins except the death of the Son of God.

In his letters, the apostle Paul looks at the natural condition of sinners in two different ways, which seem to be contradictory. In the letter to the Romans, he views the sinner as living in sin. There is only one solution for such a sinner: his life in sin must come to an end in the death of Christ: "How can we who died to sin still live in it? Do you not know that all of us who have been baptized into Christ Jesus were baptized into his death? We were buried therefore with him by baptism into death, in order that, just as Christ was raised from the dead by the glory of the Father, we too might walk in newness of life. For if we have been united with him in a death like his, we shall certainly be united with him in a resurrection like his. We know that our old self was crucified with him in order that the body of sin might be brought to nothing, so that we would no longer be enslaved to sin" (Rom. 6:2–6).

In the letter to the Ephesians we have the opposite view: by nature we are *dead* in our sins. There is only one solution for us, which is to be made alive with Christ: "[Y]ou were dead in the trespasses and sins in which you once walked, following the course of this world. . . . But God, being rich in mercy, because of the great love with which he loved us, even when we were dead in our trespasses, made us alive together with Christ—by grace you have been saved—and raised us up with him" (Eph. 2:1–6; cf. Col. 2:13).

You see the point? By faith, the *living* sinner has to come to the point of recognizing that his old life found its end in the death of Christ. By faith, the *dead* sinner must come to the point of recognizing that through the death of Christ he has been made alive and raised to a new life. However you view the matter, the death of Christ was a prerequisite. You were *alive* in sin, but Christ died, and you died with him, in order to find beyond the death of Christ an entirely new life. You were *dead* in sin, but Christ entered into your death, and together with him you returned to life. The death of Christ was the great watershed in your existence.

✢　✢　✢

DAY 126 – JESUS' DEATH
(Lord's Day 16, Q&A 40, part 3)

A. . . . nothing else could pay for our sins except the death of the Son of God.

The first time we hear about death in the Bible is in Genesis 2:17, "[O]f the tree of the knowledge of good and evil you shall not eat, for in the day that you eat of it you shall surely die." This is exactly what happened: at the moment Adam and Eve ate of the forbidden tree they died in the spiritual sense (cf. Eph. 2:1; Col. 2:13). And at the end of a long life—Adam reached the age of 930 (Gen. 5:5)—they underwent physical death: "the wages of sin is death" (Rom. 6:23).

There was still another death waiting for them, beyond physical death: it is called the "second death" (Rev. 20:6, 14). This is the eternal death in the eternal fire (cf. Matt. 18:8; 25:41; Jude 1:7), the "lake of fire" (Rev. 19:20; 20:10, 14–15). From this latter death the first humans were allowed to escape by their faith and by the mercy of God. No one of us can escape spiritual death because we are born with it: we are spiritually dead since our conception and birth. As long as Christ does not return we cannot elude physical death either: "[I]t is appointed for man to die once, and after that comes judgment" (Heb. 9:27). However, thank God, we *can* escape from eternal death, objectively through God's grace and the death of the Son of God, subjectively by faith.

We know that God cannot die; he "alone has immortality" (1 Tim. 6:16). In order to be able to undergo physical death in our stead, as our substitute, he had to assume a mortal body. Imagine: we were born to live; our parents received us that we would live a long life and survive them. But the Son of God became a human being for no other reason than to be able to die: "Since . . . the children share in flesh and blood, he himself likewise partook of the same things, *that through death* he might destroy the one who has the power of death, that is, the devil" (Heb. 2:14). "Being found in human form, he humbled himself by becoming obedient to the point of death, even death on a cross" (Phil. 2:8). The Son was sent by the Father "in the likeness of sinful flesh and for sin" (Rom. 8:3). He became a Man in order to die for sin. Wonderful Lord!

✤　　✤　　✤

DAY 127 – WHY BURIED?
(Lord's Day 16, Q&A 41, part 1)

Q. Why was he "buried"?
A. His burial testifies that he really died.

The Catechism connects Jesus' burial with his death, which of course is perfectly correct. However, it is interesting to see that Paul connects Jesus' burial with his resurrection; he points out "that Christ died for our sins in accordance with the Scriptures, that he was buried, that he was raised on the third day in accordance with the Scriptures" (1 Cor. 15:3–4). Twice Paul uses the expression "in accordance with the Scriptures," in such a way that Jesus' burial is connected with his resurrection, not with his death. You can say that we bury people because they have died; the burial is a testimony that the people concerned are really dead. But believers can also say that they bury people in view of the resurrection. We put a seed in the earth expecting that one day a plant will come out of it: "[W]hat you sow is not the body that is to be, but a bare kernel, perhaps of wheat or of some other grain" (v. 37). One day, from this kernel will grow the resurrection body.

Jesus' burial was the end of the horrible process of his suffering and dying: "when they had carried out all that was written of him, they took him down from the tree and laid him in a tomb" (Acts 13:29). "[T]hey made his grave with the wicked and with a rich man in his death" (Isa. 53:9). They had taken his body from the cross and "bound it in linen cloths with the spices, as is the burial custom of the Jews" (John 19:40). He was really dead. And literally no one seems to have had the remotest idea of the possibility of resurrection, although Jesus had mentioned this so often (in Matthew alone five times: 16:21; 17:9, 23; 20:19; 26:32). To the human mind, death and burial are the end of a person. The only thing the women could think of was preparing spices and ointments with a view to caring for the body (Luke 23:56). The only thing the disciples of Emmaus could think of was: "[W]e had hoped that he was the one to redeem Israel"—but no, he died instead (24:21). They were all in for a surprise! "O foolish ones, and slow of heart" (v. 25)—how could his burial ever be the end of him?

✶ ✶ ✶

DAY 128 – THE TESTIMONY OF HIS BURIAL
(Lord's Day 16, Q&A 41, part 2)

A. His burial testifies that he really died.

The Catechism does not contain the question: "How does Christ's burial benefit us?" (cf. Q&As 36, 43, 45, 49, and 51). So let *us* squeeze this question in. Paul speaks twice of *our* burial with Jesus, and connects this with baptism: "Do you not know that all of us who have been baptized into Christ Jesus were baptized into his death? We were buried therefore with him by baptism into death, in order that, just as Christ was raised from the dead by the glory of the Father, we too might walk in newness of life" (Rom. 6:3–4). And: "In him [i.e., Christ] also you were circumcised with . . . the circumcision of Christ, having been buried with him in baptism, in which you were also raised with him through faith in the powerful working of God, who raised him from the dead" (Col. 2:11–12).

The aspect of burial is not mentioned in Q&As 69–74 (dealing with baptism), so I mention it here. Paul says that we have been baptized into the death of Christ, and even that we were "buried" with him by baptism into death. Most Christians are familiar with the idea that we have "died" with Christ (Rom. 8:4; Col. 2:20; 2 Tim. 2:11), and that we have been "raised" with Christ (Eph. 2:6; Col. 2:12; 3:1). But Paul argues that we have also been "buried" with him, as is depicted in baptism: buried in water.

We find a beautiful example of this in the mother of Moses (Exod. 2). When she received her child, she realized that the judgment of death was upon him. All children had to be thrown into the Nile, the river of death. So she indeed entrusted her boy to the river, but in a safe way: within the secure confines of a basket of bulrushes. This is what happens when we bring a person into the water of baptism. We recognize that the person has deserved death, and we actually entrust him or her to death as depicted by the water. But we do it in the only safe way: we bury the person into death—but not his or her own death, but the death of Christ! The grave of Christ is the only safe place on earth, because God's judgment has raged there already, and has no more power over the baptized. A wonderful escape!

✤   ✤   ✤

DAY 129 – WHY STILL DIE?
(Lord's Day 16, Q&A 42, part 1)

Q. Since Christ has died for us, why do we still have to die?
A. Our death does not pay the debt of our sins. Rather, it puts an
end to our sinning.

It is indeed very important to realize that the physical death of Christians *to them* is not the wages of sin (Rom. 6:23). Death is the *consequence* of sin, but it can never be a *payment* for the debt of our sins. It cannot be this for the unbeliever, for "[t]ruly no man can ransom another, or give to God the price of his life" (Ps. 49:7), either someone else's life or one's own life. And it cannot be this for the believer, because Christ paid this debt for him. The death of a believer is nothing but the transition to a higher form of life.

Therefore, in a certain sense our physical death cannot be called "death" anymore. Jesus said, "[W]hoever hears my word and believes him who sent me has eternal life. He does not come into judgment, but has passed from death to life" (John 5:24)—not just at resurrection but at the moment one comes to faith. And: "I am the resurrection and the life. Whoever believes in me, though he die, yet shall he live, and everyone who lives and believes in me shall never die" (11:25–26). First, Jesus said, "though he die, yet shall he live," but then he puts it even more strongly: actually the believer's death is not death anymore—he "shall never die." This is why, when it comes to believers, the New Testament likes to use the term "sleep" or "fall asleep" where physical death is meant: "[W]e do not want you to be uninformed, brothers, about those who are asleep, that you may not grieve as others do who have no hope. For since we believe that Jesus died and rose again, even so, through Jesus, God will bring with him those who have fallen asleep" (1 Thess. 4:13–14; cf. Matt. 9:24; 27:52; John 11:11–13; Acts 7:60; 13:36; 1 Cor. 15:6, 18, 20, 51).

"Christ Jesus . . . abolished death and brought life and immortality to light through the gospel" (2 Tim. 1:10). "'Death is swallowed up in victory. O death, where is your victory? O death, where is your sting?' The sting of death is sin, and the power of sin is the law. But thanks be to God, who gives us the victory through our Lord Jesus Christ" (1 Cor. 15:54–56; cf. Isa. 25:8; Hos. 13:14).

❖   ❖   ❖

DAY 130 – ENTRANCE INTO LIFE
(Lord's Day 16, Q&A 42, part 2)

A. *Our death . . . puts an end to our sinning and is our entrance into eternal life.*

Our physical death is not an end point; it is a transition. Interestingly, Jesus himself said that the believer "does not come into judgment, but has passed from death to life" (John 5:24)—not just at physical death or resurrection, but at the moment one comes to faith. Actually, there are three great transitions in the New Testament. The first is the one just quoted: the transition at the moment of faith. Here, eternal life is not a future thing but a present possession: whoever believes in Christ *has* eternal life (3:15–16, 36; 6:40, 47, 54; 1 John 3:15; 5:13).

The second transition is the one that the Catechism refers to. As Paul puts it: "My desire is to depart and be with Christ, for that is far better" (Phil. 1:23). At death, we lose our physical life, but at the same time we move to a higher manner of existence, whose precise nature we cannot yet fathom. Yet, what can be better than to "be *with Christ* in Paradise" (Luke 23:43)? One day, Paul "was caught up into Paradise . . . and he heard things that cannot be told, which man may not utter" (2 Cor. 12:3–4). Theologians call this the "intermediate state," that is, the state between physical death and physical resurrection. It is not the end goal of the believer; it is "just" the intermediate state. Yet, it is a state in which we will no longer sin, as the Catechism says, and in which we will no longer deal with the weaknesses of the body and the mind.

The third transition is the one at the moment of resurrection (or the moment Christ returns; 1 Cor. 15:51; 1 Thess. 4:15). The words of the criminal on the cross clearly seem to imply that, to him, resurrection was the moment that Christ would "come into his kingdom," and he himself hopefully together with Christ (Luke 43:42). For believing Jews, the term "eternal life" was apparently linked with the Messianic Kingdom: inheriting eternal life implied entering into the Kingdom (Matt. 19:16, 29; 25:46; Luke 18:18; cf. Ps. 133; Dan. 12:2). Physical death is in view of the resurrection, and resurrection is in view of the Kingdom. This is what we are heading for!

❋   ❋   ❋

DAY 131 – FURTHER BENEFIT
(Lord's Day 16, Q&A 43, part 1)

Q. What further benefit do we receive from Christ's sacrifice and death on the cross?
A. By Christ's power our old selves are crucified, put to death, and buried with him.

When it comes to salvation, we like to distinguish between the objective and the subjective side of it. The objective aspect involves what happened almost two thousand years ago, on the cross of Calvary: Jesus died for our sins, and in him we died as well. I heard about a Reformed brother (from the Netherlands) meeting an Evangelical brother (in the United States), who asked him: "When were you saved?" His answer was: "In AD 30. . . ." Of course, this is true, but it is only a half-truth. There is a time during our lives where this objective truth must become our practical subjective possession. Through faith, I *realize* in my heart that I have died with Christ. This was already true in AD 30 (some would say: 33), but it *became* practically true for me when I began to believe.

When was our old self crucified with Christ (Rom. 6:6; Gal. 2:20; 6:14)? In AD 30. It is very important that we realize this. God did not begin to act for us at the moment of our soul's earliest spiritual exercises. He began acting for us already hundreds of years before we were even born, namely, on the cross. And actually, he began even much earlier: when God planned our salvation—and this planning is from eternity—not only the Lamb was "foreknown before the foundation of the world" (1 Pet. 1:19–20), but we as well. *Our names were in his mind*: "[H]e chose us in him before the foundation of the world, that we should be holy and blameless before him. In love he predestined us for adoption as sons through Jesus Christ, according to the purpose of his will" (Eph. 1:4–5).

God thought of us in eternity past. What a wonderful grace! God thought of us at the cross of Christ. Again, what a grace! And God thought of us after we were born and he began working in our souls. And when, by God's grace and through his Spirit, we received the assurance of salvation, our death on the cross became a spiritual reality for us in faith. I repeat: what an extraordinary grace that God has been thinking of us from eternity past until this very day, and that we will be in his heart forever!

❊   ❊   ❊

DAY 132 – THE OLD SELF
(Lord's Day 16, Q&A 43, part 2)

A. By Christ's power our old selves are crucified, put to death, and buried with him.

Yesterday we saw that God thought of us in eternity, he thought of us at the cross, and he thought of us during our lives when leading us to faith. What has happened objectively on the cross becomes a subjective reality for our hearts by faith. Now we go one step further. In this subjective part, there are again two phases, so to speak. When we came to faith, we realized: Christ died for me, and I died with him. This refers to our *position* in Christ: we are in him, and nothing is ever going to change this. But what is positionally true must become practically true in our everyday life. I *was* crucified with Christ; that's passive. But there is also an *active* crucifixion on our behalf: "[T]hose who belong to Christ Jesus have crucified the flesh with its passions and desires" (Gal. 5:24).

This is quite remarkable. First I realize that I *was* crucified; then I realize I must work this out during my Christian life in the power of the Holy Spirit. In faith I acknowledge God's judgment over my flesh by actively "crucifying the flesh with its passions and desires." Or, as Paul says elsewhere: "[B]y the Spirit you put to death the deeds of the body" (Rom. 8:13). "Put to death therefore what is earthly in you: sexual immorality, impurity, passion, evil desire, and covetousness, which is idolatry" (Col. 3:5). Or in more positive words: "[P]ut on the Lord Jesus Christ, and make no provision for the flesh, to gratify its desires" (Rom. 13:14).

Notice the distinction in the tenses here. It is true that the believer *has* crucified the flesh (past tense). But it is equally true that he (repeatedly) *puts* to death the things of the flesh, and that he *puts* on the Lord Jesus (present tense). When you come to faith, you begin hating sin. You say as it were, I will have nothing to do with the workings of the flesh anymore. Once and for all you do away with the flesh. But sooner or later—usually sooner—you find out it is still there, and it still yields its evil products if you are not vigilant enough. This is the moment you *again* put to death the deeds of the flesh!

✦ ✦ ✦

DAY 133 – THE EVIL DESIRES
(Lord's Day 16, Q&A 43, part 3)

A. By Christ's power our old selves are crucified, put to death, and buried with him, so that the evil desires of the flesh may no longer rule us.

What a great declaration of the Catechism: ". . . so that the evil desires of the flesh may no longer rule us." You may say that this will be reality only when we will be with Christ in eternity. But the Catechism states it as a *present* fact, and this may be a difficulty to some of us. You may say, I still experience the presence of those evil desires of the flesh as a tangible reality every day of my life. You are right—I experience that too. But notice the important word "rule" in the Catechism's wording!

This is an important point that we must understand well. Paul says that "God shows his love for us in that *while we were still sinners*, Christ died for us" (Rom. 5:8). Such a formulation can mean nothing less than that, for Paul, believers are not "sinners" anymore. Does this mean that the sinful flesh is no more in us? We know better ("we all stumble in many ways," James 3:2). But Paul makes a clear distinction between still having the flesh in us and being "ruled" by the flesh. How else could we understand him saying that we have been "set free from sin" (Rom. 6:7, 18, 22; 8:2)? This means we are no longer under the *power* of sin. We still have the sinful flesh in us, and we experience how at certain times it produces its evil effects. However, if we "walk by the Spirit," we will no longer "gratify the desires of the flesh" (Gal. 5:16).

Paul is very clear on this: "Let not sin therefore reign in your mortal body, to make you obey its passions. Do not present your members to sin as instruments for unrighteousness, but present yourselves to God as those who have been brought from death to life, and your members to God as instruments for righteousness. For *sin will have no dominion over you*, since you are not under law but under grace" (Rom. 6:12–14). John says, "If we say we have no sin, we deceive ourselves" (1 John 1:8). But he also says, "No one born of God makes a practice of sinning, for God's seed abides in him, and he cannot keep on sinning because he has been born of God" (3:9). Unfortunately, we still may sin. But that's not our Christian lifestyle: we serve God!

✦ ✦ ✦

DAY 134 – A SACRIFICE OF GRATITUDE
(Lord's Day 16, Q&A 43, part 4)

A. By Christ's power our old selves are crucified, put to death, and buried with him, so that . . . we may offer ourselves as a sacrifice of gratitude to him.

First we had the negative side: "By Christ's power our old selves are crucified, put to death, and buried with him, so that the evil desires of the flesh may no longer rule us." Now we get the positive side: ". . . so that we may offer ourselves as a sacrifice of gratitude to him." We are not preoccupied with avoiding sin all the time. Not only is this a negative mentality, but it will not help us either. It is far better to be focused on what is positive: on Christ himself, and on loving and serving him. If I may put it in a rather extreme form: if we would be full of Christ all the time, we would have no time and no opportunity to sin. If we are filled with the Spirit (Eph. 5:18), we cannot be filled with sin. If we concentrate on God, we cannot be concentrated on Satan.

The Catechism has its own interesting way of putting this. It speaks of a "sacrifice of gratitude [or, thankfulness]," which reminds us of the "sacrifices of thanksgiving" in the Old Testament (Lev. 7:12–15; 22:29). "The one who offers thanksgiving as his sacrifice glorifies me; to one who orders his way rightly I will show the salvation of God!" (Ps. 50:23; cf. v. 14). Hebrews 13 refers to such sacrifices: "Through him [i.e., Christ] then let us continually offer up a sacrifice of praise to God, that is, the fruit of lips that acknowledge his name" (v. 15).

Paul goes a step further: we do not bring only our praises and thanksgiving to God—our "spiritual sacrifices" (1 Pet. 2:5)—but we present *ourselves* as such a sacrifice: "I appeal to you therefore, brothers, by the mercies of God, to present your bodies as a living sacrifice, holy and acceptable to God, which is your spiritual worship" (Rom. 12:1). In this respect, Christ is our example: "[W]alk in love, as Christ loved us and gave himself up for us, a fragrant offering and sacrifice to God" (Eph. 5:2). You do the same thing: love him, give yourself up for him, a fragrant offering and sacrifice to God! This is the true Christian life of gratitude: in love following him, treading in his footsteps, serving him, praising him.

✢　✢　✢

DAY 135 – DESCENDED TO HELL
(Lord's Day 16, Q&A 44, part 1)

Q. Why does the creed add, "He descended to hell"?

What numerous controversies have surrounded these few words in the Apostles' Creed! To begin with, some have argued that the words do not belong to the Creed at all; they were allegedly added at a much later stage in church history. Others have claimed that the words have been adopted from Ephesians 4:9 ("descended into the lower parts of the earth"), and that they thus refer to Christ's burial in the earth, and have nothing to do with hell. Still others have also objected to the term "hell" as being a wrong translation of the original Greek and Latin versions. They prefer a translation such as: "he descended into the realm of death," or, "of the dead." That is, Jesus died, and then spent three days among the dead before he rose again. Others, such as Roman Catholics and Anglicans, have maintained the rendering "hell."

About one thing there can be no doubt, and that is the order of the Apostles' Creed: Jesus' descent to hell is clearly presented as having occurred *after* his death and burial, and *before* his resurrection. Of course, this presents a problem. Where was Jesus between his death and his resurrection? There are three answers: first, he was in Paradise (Luke 23:43). Second, he was in the tomb (John 19:42). Third, Acts 2:27 seems to suggest he was in Hades (the "underworld"), which is *not* the same as hell (cf. Rev. 20:14, which says that Hades was thrown into the lake of fire). It nowhere says in the Bible that, between his death and resurrection, Jesus was in *hell*.

Of course, people have often referred to Peter's words: in the spirit (or, Spirit), Jesus "went and proclaimed to the spirits in prison, because they formerly did not obey, when God's patience waited in the days of Noah" (1 Pet. 3:18–20). The problem is that there are dozens of interpretations of this verse. At any rate, this passage does not prove that Jesus "descended into hell" between his death and resurrection. So instead of "hell" we should read either the tomb, or the realm of the dead—or we think, with the Catechism, in a very different direction. This we will discuss tomorrow.

❖   ❖   ❖

DAY 136 – OUR HELLISH EXPERIENCES
(Lord's Day 16, Q&A 44, part 2)

A. [I am assured] . . . that Christ my Lord, by suffering unspeakable anguish, pain, and terror of soul, on the cross but also earlier, has delivered me from hellish anguish and torment.

Yesterday we saw what problems we encounter if we think of some descent into hell by Jesus between his death and resurrection. Therefore, a very different solution was sought. The order of death—descent—resurrection was ignored, and the "descent to hell" was viewed as having occurred during Christ's sufferings on the cross. It has been argued that, if unrepentant sinners will go to hell, it was necessary for our redemption that Christ, our substitute, would undergo in our stead on the cross "unspeakable anguish, pain, and terror of soul," and "hellish anguish and torment." In other words, Jesus "descended to hell," *not* during the time between his death and resurrection, but during his sufferings on the cross, during the three hours of darkness. He was for us in the anguish and torment of hell in order that we would never have to experience this anguish and torment.

One of the main characteristics of hell is that it is the place of being totally forsaken by God. In the new heavens and the new earth God will be "all in all" (1 Cor. 15:28), with one exception: "*Outside* are the dogs and sorcerers and the sexually immoral and murderers and idolaters, and everyone who loves and practices falsehood" (Rev. 22:15). God will be "all in all" except for one place: the place of total forsakenness. *This* is what Jesus experienced on the cross: "My God, my God, why have you forsaken me?" (Matt. 27:46; Mark 15:34; cf. Ps. 22:1). This being forsaken by God was pure hell for Jesus.

Hell is also called "outer darkness" (Matt. 8:12; 22:13; 25:30), and this darkness was represented by the literal darkness on the cross. Jesus could say, "You have put me in the depths of the pit, in the regions dark and deep" (Ps. 88:6). At the same time, hell is described as "fire" (the lake of fire, Rev. 20:10–15; the eternal fire, Matt. 18:8; 25:41), and this too was what Jesus experienced on the cross: "How long, O Lord? Will you hide yourself forever? How long will your wrath burn like fire?" (89:46). On the cross, Jesus was in hell for us, so that we never will have to be in hell!

✣　✣　✣

DAY 137 – JESUS EXPERIENCING HELL
(Lord's Day 16, Q&A 44, part 3)

A. [I am assured] during attacks of deepest dread and temptation that Christ my Lord . . . has delivered me from hellish anguish and torment.

In the literal sense, no believers will ever experience hell, either during their life or after their physical death or after their resurrection. They are never forsaken by God: "I have been young, and now am old, yet I have not seen the righteous forsaken" (Ps. 37:25). Yet, we have to realize that the Psalms that I quoted yesterday are records of real experiences. In Psalm 22:1, David was not literally forsaken by God, but he certainly *felt* that way. The sons of Korah *felt* as if they had been put "in the depths of the pit, in the regions dark and deep: (88:6). Ethan the Ezrahite *felt* as if God's wrath burned upon him like fire (89:46). As they wrote this, they were driven by the Holy Spirit, who "predicted the sufferings of Christ and the subsequent glories" (1 Pet. 1:11). Inspired by the Spirit they described experiences that went beyond them because in fact they were depicting those of Christ on the cross.

Yet, we take such utterances by the psalmists very seriously. At least they had experiences that came close to what Jesus experienced. Precisely this is our consolation: when we are in "attacks of deepest dread and temptation," we realize that Jesus has been there before—to an extent that we cannot even begin to fathom. "[W]e do not have a high priest who is unable to sympathize with our weaknesses, but one who in every respect has been tempted as we are, yet without sin. Let us then with confidence draw near to the throne of grace, that we may receive mercy and find grace to help in time of need" (Heb. 4:15–16).

The psalmist once said, "The snares of death encompassed me; the pangs of Sheol laid hold on me; I suffered distress and anguish. Then I called on the name of the LORD: 'O LORD, I pray, deliver my soul!'" (Ps. 116:3–4). "In the days of his flesh, Jesus offered up prayers and supplications, with loud cries and tears, to him who was able to save him from death, and he was heard because of his reverence" (Heb. 5:7). God's answer was to raise Jesus from the dead. God's ultimate answer to us will be the same: resurrection. Only then will all misery be over.

✤ ✤ ✤

DAY 138 – CHRIST'S RESURRECTION
(Lord's Day 17, Q&A 45, part 1)

Q. How does Christ's resurrection benefit us?
A. First, by his resurrection he has overcome death.

What would Good Friday be without Easter? Just before his death Jesus said, "It is finished" (John 19:30), but of course this was only in anticipation (just as in 17:4, where he already said, I have "accomplished the work that you gave me to do"). If, after these words, Jesus had not died, his work would certainly *not* have been finished. And if he had not risen on the third day, it would not have been finished either. If Jesus would still be in the tomb today, we could not possibly know whether he had really conquered sin, the devil, and death: "[I]f Christ has not been raised, your faith is futile and you are still in your sins. . . . If in Christ we have hope in this life only, we are of all people most to be pitied. But in fact Christ has been raised from the dead, the firstfruits of those who have fallen asleep" (1 Cor. 15:17, 19–20).

Please note this term "risen" (cf. Matt. 27:64; 28:6–7; Luke 24:6, 34). This is Christ's divine side: Jesus "rose" from the dead in his own divine power. He "took up again" the life that he had "laid down" at the moment of death (John 10:17–18). There is also the human side: the Man Jesus was "raised" from the dead by the glory of the Father (Rom. 6:4; cf. Matt. 16:21; 17:9, 23; 20:19; 26:32; 27:52 etc.). This was the core of the great message of salvation preached by the early disciples in Acts 2–5: God "raised Jesus up" (2:24, 32; 3:7, 15, 26; 4:10; 5:30). "[O]ur Savior Christ Jesus . . . abolished death and brought life and immortality to light through the gospel" (2 Tim. 1:10). "Remember Jesus Christ, risen from the dead" (2:8). Jesus "was declared to be the Son of God in power according to the Spirit of holiness by his resurrection from the dead" (Rom. 1:4). God "has caused us to be born again to a living hope through the resurrection of Jesus Christ from the dead" (1 Pet. 1:3).

"'Death is swallowed up in victory.' 'O death, where is your victory? O death, where is your sting?' The sting of death is sin, and the power of sin is the law. But thanks be to God, who gives us the victory through our Lord Jesus Christ" (1 Cor. 15:54–56).

✦ ✦ ✦

DAY 139 – DEATH AND JUSTIFICATION
(LORD'S DAY 17, Q&A 45, PART 2)

A. . . . by his resurrection he has overcome death, so that he might make us share in the righteousness he obtained for us by his death.

Apparently, the Catechism is alluding here to Romans 4:24–25: faith "will be counted to us who believe in him who raised from the dead Jesus our Lord, who was delivered up for our trespasses and raised for our justification." Many Christians will understand the first of these two truths: Jesus was "delivered up for our trespasses": Jesus had to bear our sins on the cross, and as a consequence had to die for us. All the Old Testament bloody sacrifices testify to this (cf. Heb. 2:17; 9:22, 28; 10:12). Jesus died so that we could live.

However, the second truth is far less known and understood: Jesus was "raised for our justification." Think here of another verse: "[O]ne who has died has been set free [literally, has been justified] from sin" (Rom. 6:7). Such a person is beyond death, and thus beyond the entire problem of sin. It has forever been dealt with. One day Jesus will appear, "not to deal with sin" (Heb. 9:28); that is, the problem of sin has been dealt with once and forever through his death and resurrection. Not only that: *we* have nothing to do with the problem of sin anymore, because *in Christ* we have died and have been raised as well. We are forever associated with a dead and risen Christ, beyond the realm of sin. He has "obtained righteousness for us by his death," says the Catechism. God looks at me as being incorporated *in* the dead and risen Christ, who has put aside the problem of sin. God does not see any sin in me anymore; he views me as precisely as righteous as Christ is himself.

Of course, *in practice* we know that the flesh is still in us, and that it can still produce evil deeds—and it often does. But this is another matter. Here, Paul is referring to our *position*, to what we formally *are* in Christ, as being one with the dead and risen Christ. He has become our righteousness (1 Cor. 1:30). We went with him through death, and arrived at the realm of resurrection, where sin is a defeated enemy. Christ was raised, and we have been raised with him (Eph. 2:6; Col. 2:12), so that we too have arrived at the realm where sin is forever a thing of the past.

✳   ✳   ✳

DAY 140 – RAISED TO NEW LIFE
(Lord's Day 17, Q&A 45, part 3)

A. . . . Second, by his power we too are already raised to a new life.

On Day 126, we saw that the Bible knows three very different meanings of the word "death." Similarly, we are now reminded of the fact that there are two kinds of "resurrection" (not three, because no one can "rise" from eternal death). The second resurrection is the physical resurrection from the dead that we will discuss tomorrow. The first one is the spiritual resurrection from our natural condition of spiritual death. Paul speaks of it several times: "God, being rich in mercy, . . . when we were dead in our trespasses, made us alive together with Christ—by grace you have been saved—and *raised us up* with him and seated us with him in the heavenly places in Christ Jesus" (Eph. 2:4–6). "In him [i.e., Christ] also you were circumcised . . . by the circumcision of Christ, having been buried with him in baptism, in which you were also *raised with him* through faith in the powerful working of God, who raised him from the dead. And you, who were dead in your trespasses and the uncircumcision of your flesh, God made alive together with him, having forgiven us all our trespasses" (Col. 2:11–13). "If then you have been *raised with Christ*, seek the things that are above, where Christ is, seated at the right hand of God. . . . For you have died, and your life is hidden with Christ in God" (3:1–3). Also compare Romans 6: "We were buried therefore with him by baptism into death, in order that, just as Christ was raised from the dead by the glory of the Father, we too might walk in newness of life" (v. 4).

From John 3 it seems that rebirth is rather connected with our "old nature" and receiving a "new nature" ("That which is born of the flesh is flesh, and that which is born of the Spirit is spirit," v. 6). Being "made alive" (as the older translations said, "quickened") is linked with our natural condition of spiritual death. And being "raised with Christ" seems to emphasize the thought that we are snatched away from the company of the dead. We died *with Christ*, we were *made alive* with Christ, we were raised *with Christ*, and *in him* we have even been seated in the heavenly places!

✵ ✵ ✵

DAY 141 – OUR OWN RESURRECTION
(Lord's Day 17, Q&A 45, part 4)

A. . . . Third, Christ's resurrection is a sure pledge to us of our blessed resurrection.

Because Christ has been raised from the dead, I first know that death is a defeated enemy. Second, I know that a holy and righteous God has received full satisfaction from Christ, and thus that I fully share in the righteousness of the risen Christ. Third, I know that I have been raised with him, as this is illustrated in baptism: with him I now am spiritually on the other side of death and tomb. I am in the realm where the risen and glorified Christ has all authority, and where sin, the devil, and death cannot enter. He defeated them all.

We now come to a fourth point: because God raised Christ from the dead, I can be sure that, if I were to pass away before the return of Christ, one day my dead body will be raised just like Christ's dead body was raised. Paul makes this link in a direct way: "If the Spirit of him who raised Jesus from the dead dwells in you, he who raised Christ Jesus from the dead will also give life to your mortal bodies through his Spirit who dwells in you" (Rom. 8:11). Some have explained this as referring to our spiritual resurrection, but most agree that Paul speaks here of our bodily resurrection.

In his well-known chapter on the resurrection Paul says, "Christ has been raised from the dead, the firstfruits of those who have fallen asleep. For as by a man came death, by a man has come also the resurrection of the dead. For as in Adam all die, so also in Christ shall all be made alive" (1 Cor. 15:20–22). Even the resurrection of the wicked is guaranteed by the resurrection of Christ! As Jesus said to the Father: "[Y]ou have given him authority over all flesh" (John 17:2). And at an earlier occasion: "[A]s the Father raises the dead and gives them life, so also the Son gives life to whom he will. . . . An hour is coming when all who are in the tombs will hear his [i.e., the Son of Man's] voice and come out, those who have done good to the resurrection of life, and those who have done evil to the resurrection of judgment" (John 5:21, 28–29). Through his own death and resurrection Christ secured the resurrection of all humans!

✤   ✤   ✤

DAY 142 – ASCENDED TO HEAVEN
(Lord's Day 18, Q&A 46, part 1)

Q. What do you mean by saying, "He ascended to heaven"?
A. That Christ, while his disciples watched, was taken up from the earth into heaven.

Most Christians know about the meaning of Christ's death, fewer realize what is the redemptive meaning of his resurrection, and still fewer are aware of the redemptive meaning of his ascension. This important event is described in Luke 24:50–51 ("he parted from them and was carried up into heaven") and in Acts 1:9–11 ("he was lifted up, and a cloud took him out of their sight"). Amazingly, Matthew and John, who were there, did not mention it (except in a general sense: "[N]ow I am leaving the world and going to the Father," John 16:28). The ascension is described only by Luke, though he was *not* present when it happened. The Holy Spirit decided what each New Testament author had to write, and what not. Paul, who hadn't been present either, quoted Psalm 68:18 saying, "'When he ascended on high he led a host of captives, and he gave gifts to men.' (In saying, 'He ascended,' what does it mean but that he had also descended into the lower regions, the earth? [i.e., Jesus' burial] He who descended is the one who also ascended far above all the heavens, that he might fill all things.)" (Eph. 4:8–10).

Jesus' ascension was the summit of his tremendous victory: God "raised him from the dead and seated him at his right hand in the heavenly places, far above all rule and authority and power and dominion, and above every name that is named, not only in this age but also in the one to come. And he put all things under his feet" (Eph. 1:20–22). Peter speaks of "the resurrection of Jesus Christ, who has gone into heaven and is at the right hand of God, with angels, authorities, and powers having been subjected to him" (1 Pet. 3:21–22). The suffering Christ was on the cross, the dead Christ was in the tomb, the risen Christ was for forty days among his disciples (Acts 1:1–8), the ascended Christ is at the right of God in heaven above all powers, human and angelic, good and evil.

The Old Testament verse quoted most frequently in the New is this one: "The Lord says to my Lord: 'Sit at my right hand, until I make your enemies your footstool'" (Ps. 110:1). It says it all!

❊   ❊   ❊

DAY 143 – AT GOD'S RIGHT HAND
(Lord's Day 18, Q&A 46, part 2)

A. . . . Christ . . . was taken up from the earth into heaven and remains there on our behalf . . .

"O n our behalf"! What a great statement this is. Jesus at the right hand of God is not just resting and enjoying himself there. He is *working*. Like the slave in Exodus 21:1–6 he has become a "slave forever." He came to serve (Matt. 20:28; Luke 22:27), and he is still serving his people today in everything he does for them. One important aspect is the intercession that he makes for us, a subject that will be dealt with in Q&A 49. Let us look today and tomorrow at seven other important aspects.

First, because Jesus is at the right hand of God, we know that the work of atonement is complete: "God exalted him at his right hand as Leader and Savior, to give repentance to Israel and forgiveness of sins" (Acts 5:31). "After making purification for sins, he sat down at the right hand of the Majesty on high" (Heb. 1:3); "when Christ had offered for all time a single sacrifice for sins, he sat down at the right hand of God" (10:12).

Second, because Jesus is at the right hand of God, we know that we do not have to fear the powers of darkness anymore because Jesus has prevailed over them. He is seated at God's right hand, "far above all rule and authority and power and dominion" (Eph. 1:20). Jesus "has gone into heaven and is at the right hand of God, with angels, authorities, and powers having been subjected to him" (1 Pet. 3:21–22). This was the great message Jesus gave the apostles to preach: "All authority in heaven and on earth has been given to me" (Matt. 28:18).

Third, only because Jesus is at the right hand of God, the Holy Spirit could be given to us: "Being therefore exalted at the right hand of God, and having received from the Father the promise of the Holy Spirit, he has poured out this that you yourselves are seeing and hearing" (Acts 2:33). The Spirit was sent by the Father in the name of the glorified Jesus (John 14:26; cf. 15:26): "He will glorify me, for he will take what is mine and declare it to you. All that the Father has is mine; therefore I said that he will take what is mine and declare it to you" (16:14–15). The Spirit is *the* witness to the glorified Christ!

❖   ❖   ❖

DAY 144 – ON OUR BEHALF

(Lord's Day 18, Q&A 46, part 3)

A. . . . Christ . . . was taken up from the earth into heaven and remains there on our behalf.

Let us continue looking at several respects in which Jesus is sitting at the right hand of God "on our behalf" (for our benefit):

Fourth, because Jesus is at the right hand of God, our actual spiritual life belongs to that sphere: "If you have been raised with Christ, seek the things that are above, where Christ is, seated at the right hand of God. Set your minds on things that are above, not on things that are on earth. For you have died, and your life is hidden with Christ in God. When Christ who is your life appears, then you also will appear with him in glory" (Col. 3:1–4). Where Christ is, is your real life—not down here but above! (See also Q&A 49.)

Fifth, the spiritual gifts and ministries in the church come from the glorified Christ: "[G]race was given to each one of us according to the measure of Christ's gift . . . He who descended [into the earth] is the one who also ascended far above all the heavens, that he might fill all things. And he gave the apostles, the prophets, the evangelists, the shepherds and teachers" (Eph. 4:7–11). Every officer in the church is a gift from the throne of God, where Christ is!

Sixth, "we have such a high priest, one who is seated at the right hand of the throne of the Majesty in heaven, a minister in the holy places" (Heb. 8:1–2). Here the word for "minister" is *leitourgos*; Jesus is the "leader of the liturgy." Jesus at the right hand of God represents his worshiping church on earth. It is "through him" that we "draw near to God" (7:25), and "through him" that we "continually offer up a sacrifice of praise to God" (13:15).

Seventh, because Jesus is at the right hand of God, we know that our weary race will also end at that glorious place: "[L]et us run with endurance the race that is set before us, looking to Jesus, the founder and perfecter of our faith, who for the joy that was set before him endured the cross, despising the shame, and is seated at the right hand of the throne of God" (Heb. 12:1–2). Jesus went through the dark valleys to the bright summit; if we are still in the gloomy valleys, we know we will reach the glorious summit too.

✢ ✢ ✢

DAY 145 – HIS COMING AGAIN
(Lord's Day 18, Q&A 46, part 4)

A. . . . Christ . . . was taken up from the earth into heaven . . . until he comes again to judge the living and the dead.

Jesus' ascension occurred because of what happened *before*—his atoning death and resurrection—and occurred in view of what is *going* to happen: his return from heaven (often called his "second coming"). Jesus told his judges: "[F]rom now on you will see the Son of Man seated at the right hand of Power and coming on the clouds of heaven" (Matt. 26:64). The first phrase was an allusion to Psalm 110:1, and the second phrase an allusion to Daniel 7:13, "[B]ehold, with the clouds of heaven there came one like a son of man." To the bewilderment of his judges, Jesus implied that he was the fulfillment of both passages.

After Jesus had ascended to heaven, two angels told the staring disciples: "Men of Galilee, why do you stand looking into heaven? This Jesus, who was taken up from you into heaven, will come in the same way as you saw him go into heaven" (Acts 1:11). He will perhaps come even at the same *place*, if we may interpret Zechariah 14:1–5 this way.

We read of Stephen that "he, full of the Holy Spirit, gazed into heaven and saw the glory of God, and Jesus standing at the right hand of God. And he said, 'Behold, I see the heavens opened, and the Son of Man standing at the right hand of God'" (7:55–56)—standing, not sitting! As if Jesus were on the brink of coming again, if his people had only believed in him at the testimony of Stephen.

Paul wrote, "[T]o this end Christ died and lived again, that he might be Lord both of the dead and of the living" (Rom. 14:9); and to Timothy: "I charge you in the presence of God and of Christ Jesus, who is to judge the living and the dead, and by his appearing and his kingdom . . ." (2 Tim. 4:1). Peter said of the wicked, "[T]hey will give account to him who is ready to judge the living and the dead" (1 Pet. 4:5). None of those who will be alive at the moment of Christ's return, and none of those who will be dead at that time, will escape from Christ the Supreme Judge: "For we must all appear before the judgment seat of Christ, so that each one may receive what is due for what he has done in the body, whether good or evil" (2 Cor. 5:10).

✶ ✶ ✶

DAY 146 – CHRIST WITH US
(Lord's Day 18, Q&A 47, part 1)

Q. But isn't Christ with us until the end of the world as he promised us?
A. Christ is true human and true God.

At a few places, the Catechism enters into a polemic with other Christians without always saying so. To those who know the history of the Reformation, in Q&As 47 and 48 obviously a controversy with the Lutherans is implied. Already at an early stage, Lutherans and Calvinists broke up because of their different views of the Lord's Supper. Tying in more closely with Roman Catholic thinking, the Lutherans argued that Christ was *bodily* present under the emblems of bread and wine. The Calvinists answered that this was impossible because the glorified body of Christ is in heaven. Also, after his resurrection and ascension, Jesus' body is not omnipresent; it can only be at one specific place. In other words, according to his divine nature Jesus is omnipresent, but according to his human nature he is not.

Now we have to realize that the precise relationship between the divine and the human natures of Christ has always been controversial. No wonder—basically it is a mystery, which theologians cannot fully map out. There have always been Christians who accused other Christians of "separating" the two natures. And those other Christians accused the former ones of "confusing" the two natures. The Lutherans accused the Calvinists of "dividing" the two natures by claiming that the one involved omnipresence, and the other did not. The Calvinists accused the Lutherans of "merging" the two natures by claiming that a certain *divine* feature—omnipresence—must be attributed to Christ's human nature as well.

One sometimes feels that both parties wanted to know more than they could really account for. Is this not another example of wishing to "look into the ark"? (See Day 111 above.) Yet, if I would have to choose, I would choose the Calvinist side: there is not the slightest biblical evidence that Christ's glorified body is omnipresent. This view is called the *extra calvinisticum* (literally, the Calvinistic beyond or outside; see Q&A 48): the *infinite* divine nature remains "distinct" from (or, "beyond, outside") the human nature, even though the two are inseparably and intimately united forever.

✢　　✢　　✢

DAY 147 – AS MAN OMNIPRESENT?
(Lord's Day 18, Q&A 47, part 2)

A. Christ is true human and true God. In his human nature Christ is not now on earth.

This is the continuation of yesterday. The divine and the human natures are inseparably and intricately united, they may not be separated, yet they have to be clearly distinguished. That which is divine in Christ does not acquire human features, and that which is human in him does not obtain divine features. Omnipresence is a divine attribute, not a human one, and the human nature can never take it on, even in the case of Christ. In other words, Christ is omnipresent according to his divine nature, not according to his human nature—just as, for instance, he is corporeal as Man, not as God; or omniscient as God, not as Man (cf. Mark 13:32).

Therefore, the Calvinists argued against the Lutherans that the *body* of Christ cannot be literally present under the emblems of bread and wine. His body ascended to heaven (Acts 1:9–11); it does not descend, so to speak, every time we celebrate the Lord's Supper. Jesus will descend only at his second coming; in the meantime, his glorified body is at the right hand of God: ". . . Jesus, whom heaven must receive until the time for restoring all the things" (Acts 3:20–21).

Of course, there is a certain tension here, because Jesus promised on the one hand: "[B]ehold, I am with you always, to the end of the age" (Matt. 28:20). On the other hand, he said, "[I]t is to your advantage that I go away, for if I do not go away, the Helper will not come to you. But if I go, I will send him to you" (John 16:7). Jesus had to go, otherwise the Helper, that is, the Holy Spirit, could not come. Jesus left, and the Spirit came. And this Spirit would be with Christ's followers forever, promised the Lord (14:16).

But if this is so, how could Jesus say, "*I* am with you always" (Matt. 28:20)? Why did he not say "the Spirit"? The answer is that, although the second and the third persons in the Godhead are distinct, the Holy Spirit is the Spirit of Jesus (Acts 16:7), the Spirit of Christ (Rom. 8:9; 1 Pet. 1:11), the Spirit of Jesus Christ (Phil. 1:19), the Spirit of God's Son (Gal. 4:6). Where the Holy Spirit is, there Jesus is as well.

✢ ✢ ✢

DAY 148 – IN THE SPIRIT OMNIPRESENT
(Lord's Day 18, Q&A 47, part 3)

A. . . . In his human nature Christ is not now on earth; but in his divinity, majesty, grace, and Spirit he is never absent from us.

Yesterday we saw that the Holy Spirit is often connected with Christ through various names, such as the Spirit of Jesus, of (Jesus) Christ, or of God's Son. Of course, the Spirit is equally connected with the Father: "[I]t is not you who speak, but the Spirit of your Father speaking through you" (Matt. 10:20); "the Father . . . may grant you to be strengthened with power through *his* Spirit" (Eph. 3:14–16). Within the triune God, the Father is the Father of the Son, the Son is the Son of the Father, the Spirit is the Spirit of the Father and of the Son.

The union between Christ and the Spirit is so strong that Jesus could say, "I will not leave you as orphans; I will come to you" (John 14:18), where we would have expected him to say: "the Holy Spirit will come to you." Just as in John 14:3 the reference is clearly to the second coming of Christ, in verse 18 the reference is, I believe, to the coming of the Spirit on the Day of Pentecost (Acts 2). First, Jesus came into this world when he was born in Bethlehem. Second, he came into this world in the form of the Holy Spirit. Third, he will come to this world again as the glorified Man when he will return on the clouds of heaven. At each of the three comings, Jesus appears with all "his divinity, majesty, grace, and Spirit," as the Catechism puts it (though they were "veiled," concealed, at his first coming).

In the meantime, Christ is with us in the person of the Holy Spirit. If you say, But the person of the Son must be discerned from the person of the Spirit, you are perfectly right. However, you cannot separate the two persons either. Scripture is very clear on this point: when the Holy Spirit came, it is the same as saying that Christ came, because the Spirit is the Spirit of Christ. Don't confuse the persons—but don't separate them either. Jesus said, "[W]here two or three are gathered in my name, there am I among them" (Matt. 18:20). That was true then, and it is true now. Christ is not *bodily* present among the "two or three"—his glorified body is in heaven—but *spiritually*, that is, in the Spirit, he *is* present.

❉ ❉ ❉

DAY 149 – THE TWO NATURES
(Lord's Day 18, Q&A 48, part 1)

Q. If his humanity is not present wherever his divinity is, then aren't the two natures of Christ separated from each other?
A. Certainly not. Since divinity is not limited and is present everywhere, it is evident that Christ's divinity is surely beyond the bounds of the humanity that has been taken on.

The question that the Catechism asks here is in fact a Lutheran question. The Lutherans blamed the Calvinists for separating the two natures of Christ by attributing omnipresence to Christ's divine nature, but not to his glorified human nature. They argued, if we want to keep the two natures together, we cannot say that the glorified Christ at the right hand of God is spiritually but not bodily omnipresent. The Calvinists would answer—and I suppose many Evangelicals with them—first, that there is no biblical ground for the allegation that Christ is also omnipresent according to his human nature, that is, that Christ's glorified *body* is, or can be, everywhere in the universe at the same time. Second, in itself there is nothing wrong with the view that Jesus' divine nature remains fully divine forever, and Jesus' human nature remains fully human forever. We have no need, nor reason, to deify his (glorified) human nature, or to humanize his divine nature.

About God's omnipresence as such there is hardly any discussion: "Where shall I go from your Spirit? Or where shall I flee from your presence? If I ascend to heaven, you are there! If I make my bed in Sheol, you are there! If I take the wings of the morning and dwell in the uttermost parts of the sea, even there your hand shall lead me" (Ps. 139:7–10). God asks, "Am I a God at hand, . . . and not a God far away? Can a man hide himself in secret places so that I cannot see him? . . . Do I not fill heaven and earth?" (Jer. 23:23–24).

If God is omnipresent, then God the Father is omnipresent, God the Son is omnipresent (cf. Eph. 1:23, Christ "who fills all in all"), and God the Spirit is omnipresent. But the *Man* Christ Jesus as such is *not* omnipresent. When Jesus said, "[I]t is to your advantage that I go away, for if I do not go away, the Helper will not come to you" (John 16:7), one of these advantages is that Christ on earth could only be at one place, whereas the Spirit is everywhere. The Bible gives us no reason to assume that this was any different with the *glorified* body of Christ.

✣   ✣   ✣

DAY 150 – THE DIVINE NATURE
(LORD'S DAY 18, Q&A 48, PART 2)

A. . . . at the same time [Christ's] divinity is in and remains personally united to his humanity.

Could God truly become Man? Yes: "the Word *became* flesh" (John 1:14)—which is a mighty testimony against any heresy that denies the true humanity of Christ. He did not just adopt a human form for a while, like the three angelic figures who visited Abraham (Gen. 18). No, he *became* human forever and ever, and *remained* divine at the same time. Forever his divinity and his humanity will remain united: one person, two natures. It is the *Man* Christ Jesus who is at the right hand of God in his glorified body: "in him the whole fullness of deity dwells [present tense!] *bodily*" (Col. 2:9). It is the *Son of Man* who will come with the clouds of heaven (Dan. 7:13; Matt. 26:64), who at the same time will be God (cf. Zech. 14:5).

The Holy Spirit carefully guards against any form of separation. He does so, for instance, by using *divine* names when clearly the *human* nature of Christ is meant, and the reverse: "[C]oncerning that day or that hour, no one knows, not even the angels in heaven, *nor the Son*, but only the Father" (Mark 13:32): the *Man* Jesus, who does not know all that the Father knows, is described here by the name "the Son"—obviously one of his divine names. If Paul says that the Son of *God* gave himself for him (Gal. 2:20), it is obvious that it was the *Man* Jesus who died for Paul; God cannot die. Yet, the person who died for us *is* the Son of God.

Conversely, Jesus says explicitly that it was the *Son of Man* who "descended from heaven" (John 3:13; cf. 1 Cor. 15:47, "the second man is from heaven"), whereas, of course, it was the Son of God who *became* Man, and had not yet been Man when he was still in heaven. Older translations even add the words ". . . who is in heaven." That is, as Jesus was speaking with Nicodemus, he was the Son of Man who at the same time was "in the bosom of the Father" (John 1:18). However, it is clear that, when the Son was in the bosom of the Father, he was there as the Son of *God*, not as the Son of *Man*. But in order that we would not separate the two natures it is said "Son of Man." Keep the two natures together in the *one* person of the Christ!

✦ ✦ ✦

DAY 151 – THE BENEFIT OF HIS ASCENSION

(LORD'S DAY 18, Q&A 49, PART 1)

Q. How does Christ's ascension to heaven benefit us?
A. First, he is our advocate in heaven in the presence of his Father.

Christ is our "advocate" in heaven in the presence of his Father. The term "advocate" is the literal rendering of the Greek *paraklētos*. This word is often used in John 14–16 for the Holy Spirit, and is then rendered "Helper" in the ESV. But in 1 John 2:1 it is used for Christ: "My little children, I am writing these things to you so that you may not sin. But if anyone does sin, we have an *advocate* with the Father, Jesus Christ the righteous." The advocate (literally, one who is "called along") is a helper, a representative, a counselor. He jumps in when you are in trouble. John insists that believers should not sin (cf. 3:4–9; 5:18). But thank God, if it does happen, we have a representative in heaven who always pleads for us on the basis of his blood (cf. 1:7).

Paul connects this even more clearly with Christ's ascension: "Christ Jesus is the one who died—more than that, who was raised—who is at the right hand of God, who indeed is interceding for us" (Rom. 8:34). And Hebrews 7 says that Jesus "is able to save to the uttermost those who draw near to God through him, since he always lives to make intercession for them. For it was indeed fitting that we should have such a high priest, holy, innocent, unstained, separated from sinners, and *exalted above the heavens*" (vv. 25–26). "Christ has entered, not into holy places made with hands, which are copies of the true things, but into heaven itself, now to appear in the presence of God *on our behalf*" (9:24).

In 1 John 2 the emphasis is on sins that believers might still commit. In Hebrews the emphasis is more on weaknesses and temptations. We do *not* necessarily *fall* into them, but we do certainly need help so that such falling may be prevented: "For because he himself has suffered when tempted, he is able to help those who are being tempted" (Heb. 2:18). "[W]e do not have a high priest who is unable to sympathize with our weaknesses, but one who in every respect has been tempted as we are, yet without sin. Let us then with confidence draw near to the throne of grace, that we may receive mercy and find grace to help in time of need" (4:15–16).

✢   ✢   ✢

DAY 152 – A SURE PLEDGE
(Lord's Day 18, Q&A 49, part 2)

A. . . . Second, we have our own flesh in heaven as a sure pledge that Christ our head will also take us, his members, up to himself.

It is beautiful that the Catechism speaks here of Christ as "our head," and of believers as "his members." We know this imagery from the apostle Paul in Ephesians (1:22; 4:15; 5:23) and Colossians (1:18; 2:10, 19). It very fittingly functions here as an argument that we, too, will one day be taken up to be where he is. For how could the head and the members be separated? Husband and wife can, at times, be separated for 6,000 miles (my wife and I have experienced this), but a body's head and members cannot be separated one inch for one second. For Paul, the link between head and body is so close that it is self-evident that, if Christ was raised and seated at God's right hand in the heavenly places, we have been raised and seated there together with him. "In Christ Jesus" Paul sees us already in heaven (Eph. 2:5–6).

Other passages do not go that far, but they underscore the same basic idea: where the risen and glorified Christ is, *that* is the place where we belong as well: "In my Father's house are many rooms . . . for I go to prepare a place for you. And if I go and prepare a place for you, I will come again and will take you to myself, that *where I am you may be also*" (John 14:2–3). "Father, I desire that they also, whom you have given me, may be with me *where I am*, to see my glory that you have given me because you loved me before the foundation of the world" (17:24).

Jesus not only accomplished vital things *for* us, he also united himself forever *with* us. We are inseparable from him. Where he will be, we will eternally be. As the *Son of God*, he has associated many sons and daughters with himself (cf. Rom. 8:29). As the *Man* Christ Jesus he is the head of the body, forever united with his members. We died with him, we were raised with him, we were seated with him, we will dwell with him, we will enjoy with him, we will reign with him.

Even in the "intermediate state"—between death and resurrection—this will be the essential thing: we will be *with Jesus* (Luke 23:42–43), we will be *with Christ* (Phil. 1:23), we will be *with the Lord* (2 Cor. 5:6–7).

✦　✦　✦

DAY 153 – THE SPIRIT AS PLEDGE
(Lord's Day 18, Q&A 49, part 3)

A. . . . Third, he sends his Spirit to us on earth as a corresponding pledge.

The word "pledge" is used in several translations of Ephesians 1:13–14, "In Him, you also, after listening to the message of truth, the gospel of your salvation . . . you were sealed in Him with the Holy Spirit of promise, who is given as a pledge of our inheritance, with a view to the redemption of [God's own] possession, to the praise of His glory" (NASB). "Now He who establishes us with you in Christ and anointed us is God, who also sealed us and gave [us] the Spirit in our hearts as a pledge" (2 Cor. 1:21–22 NASB). "Now He who prepared us for this very purpose is God, who gave to us the Spirit as a pledge" (5:5 NASB). The word "pledge" is also rendered as "earnest," "down payment," or "guarantee."

In modern Greek, the original word seems to be used for an engagement ring. The man tells his fiancée as it were, "Now I give you this ring as a down payment; one day I will give *myself* to you." Likewise, the Lord tells us, "Now I give you the Holy Spirit as a down payment; one day I will give you the complete inheritance."

The point of the Catechism is the connection between Christ's ascension and the "descent" of the Spirit. While Jesus departs, the Spirit comes: "[I]t is to your advantage that I go away; for if I do not go away, the Helper will not come to you; but if I go, I will send him to you" (John 16:7).

There are at least three reasons why it is better that Jesus left and the Spirit came. First, Jesus was bodily bound to one place, somewhere in Israel, whereas the Spirit is everywhere in and with believers: "He abides with you and will be in you" (14:17)—wherever they are. Second, without the Spirit we would not understand what the Lord was teaching us: "What I do you do not realize now, but you will understand hereafter" (13:7), that is, after the coming of the Spirit. Third, without the Spirit we would have no spiritual power: "[Y]ou are to stay in the city until you are clothed with power from on high" (Luke 24:49). "[Y]ou will receive power when the Holy Spirit has come upon you; and you shall be my witnesses" (Acts 1:8).

✦　✦　✦

DAY 154 – SEEKING THE THINGS ABOVE
(Lord's Day 18, Q&A 49, part 4)

A. . . . By the Spirit's power we seek not earthly things but the things above, where Christ is, sitting at God's right hand.

For every Christian, it is important to understand the difference between worldly things and earthly things. In general, the *worldly* things are wrong because they are linked with sin, the devil, and death (cf. Rom. 12:2; 1 John 2:15–17; Titus 2:12; Jude 1:19). The *earthly* things are the good things of God's creation: "[E]verything created by God is good, and nothing is to be rejected if it is received with thanksgiving, for it is made holy by the word of God and prayer" (1 Tim. 4:4–5). However, *setting your mind on the earthly things is worldly as well!* "[M]any . . . walk as enemies of the cross of Christ. Their end is destruction, their god is their belly, and they glory in their shame, with minds set on earthly things" (Phil. 3:18–19).

Elsewhere, Paul uses the words that the Catechism obviously alludes to: "If then you have been raised with Christ, seek the things that are above, where Christ is, seated at the right hand of God. Set your minds on things that are above, not on things that are on earth. For you have died, and your life is hidden with Christ in God. When Christ who is your life appears, then you also will appear with him in glory" (Col. 3:1–4). The "things that are on earth" are in themselves alright, but do not set your mind on them. They can never be your actual life because your true life is connected with Christ, and with the place where he is: "above, at the right hand of God."

Paul wrote to Timothy, "[G]odliness with contentment is great gain, for we brought nothing into the world, and we cannot take anything out of the world. But if we have food and clothing, with these we will be content. . . . *Take hold of the eternal life* to which you were called. . . . As for the rich in this present age, charge them not . . . to set their hopes on the uncertainty of riches, but on God. . . . They are to do good, to be rich in good works, to be generous and ready to share, thus storing up treasure for themselves as a good foundation for the future, so that they may *take hold of that which is truly life*" (1 Tim. 6:6–19). This is the life that really matters!

✦ ✦ ✦

DAY 155 – HEAD OF THE CHURCH
(Lord's Day 19, Q&A 50, part 1)

Q. Why the next words: "and is seated at the right hand of God"?
A. Because Christ ascended to heaven to show there that he is head of his church.

The matter of Christ's headship plays a great role in the letters to the Ephesians and the Colossians. The term functions in these letters in two ways. First, "Christ is the head of the church, his body" (Eph. 5:23; cf. 4:15); "he is the head of the body, the church" (Col. 1:18); ". . . not holding fast to the Head, from whom the whole body . . . grows" (2:19). Second, Christ "is the head of all rule and authority" (Col. 2:10). The Catechism refers here to both meanings at once.

The two meanings come together nicely in Ephesians 1:22–23. God raised Christ "from the dead and seated him at his right hand in the heavenly places, far above all rule and authority and power and dominion, and above every name that is named, not only in this age but also in the one to come. And he put all things under his feet and gave him as head over all things to the church, which is his body, the fullness of him who fills all in all." Christ is here "head over all things," and at the same time, he is head of his body. God esteems the church so highly that he gave to her the best present that could be imagined: he gave to her him who is the "head over all things" to be *her* head. (She was not given to *him*, as a bride is given by her father to a bridegroom, but *he* was given to *her*!)

Notice that the church does *not* belong to "all the things" that have been put "under his feet" (cf. Heb. 2:5–8; Ps. 8:6)! One exception to this "all things" is obviously God himself (1 Cor. 15:27), and the other exception is the church. She is the "last Eve," so to speak, alongside the "last Adam" (v. 45); they will reign together. When God said to Adam and Eve, "[F]ill the earth and subdue it, and have dominion" (Gen. 1:28), these verbal forms are plural, that is, they include Eve. Not just a "head" will rule over everything, but a "head" *with* his "body," or, the last Adam *and* the last Eve. Believers will reign with Christ (2 Tim. 2:12; Rev. 20:4, 6; cf. 1 Cor. 6:2–3). "The one who conquers, I will grant him to sit with me on my throne, as I also conquered and sat down with my Father on his throne" (Rev. 3:21).

✦   ✦   ✦

DAY 156 – CREATION AND THE BODY
(Lord's Day 19, Q&A 50, part 2)

A. . . . Christ ascended to heaven to show there that he is head of his church, the one through whom the Father rules all things.

In Colossians 1, we find the double headship of Christ as well, as we saw yesterday in Ephesians 1. We are told three things about Christ in relation to God's creation, on the one hand, and in relation to God's New Testament people, on the other hand.

First, on the one hand, Christ is the head of the *universe*. That is, in him, through him, and for him all things have been created, and "he is before all things, and in him all things hold together" (vv. 15–17). On the other hand, "he is the head of the *body*, the *church*. He is the beginning, the firstborn from the dead, that in everything he might be preeminent" (v. 18). Christ is preeminent not only in creation but also in the church. The head of all things is the same person as the head of the body (cf. Eph. 1:22–23).

Second, on the one hand, Christ is the Reconciler of the *universe*: "For in him all the fullness of God was pleased to dwell, and through him to reconcile to himself all things, whether on earth or in heaven, making peace by the blood of his cross" (vv. 19–20). On the other hand, he is the Reconciler of all *believers*: "And you, who once were alienated and hostile in mind, doing evil deeds, he has now reconciled in his body of flesh by his death, in order to present you holy and blameless and above reproach before him" (vv. 21–22).

Third, on the one hand, Paul had become the "minister" of the *universe*, so to speak. He refers to "the hope of the gospel that you heard, which has been proclaimed in all creation under heaven, and of which I, Paul, became a minister" (v. 23). On the other hand, Paul had become the "minister" of the *church*: "Now I rejoice in my sufferings for your sake, and in my flesh I am filling up what is lacking in Christ's afflictions for the sake of his body, that is, the church, of which I became a minister according to the stewardship from God that was given to me for you, to make the word of God fully known" (vv. 24–25).

In this Lord's Day, we have a wonderful picture of the two aspects that the Catechism underscores: Christ's headship of the universe, and his headship of the church.

✢   ✢   ✢

DAY 157 – THE FATHER RULES
(Lord's Day 19, Q&A 50, part 3)

*A. Christ ascended to heaven to show there that he is . . . the one
through whom the Father rules all things.*

In John 5, Jesus gives a wonderful exposé of the power and authority
that the Father has entrusted to him: "The Father judges no one, but
has given all judgment to the Son, that all may honor the Son, just as they
honor the Father. . . . And he has given him authority to execute judgment,
because he is the Son of Man" (vv. 22–23, 27; cf. 17:2, "you have given him
authority over all flesh").

Notice carefully how Jesus deals with his own names and titles here.
Do not forget that the God who ruled, and rules, the universe is the triune
God: Father, Son, and Holy Spirit. Nevertheless, Jesus speaks here of a *given*
authority, given "because he [i.e., Jesus] is the Son of *Man*"! The eternal Son
of the eternal Father became flesh (1:14); he became the Son of Man. Because
of the work that he, *as a Man*, has accomplished on the cross, he has received
as a *Man* what he had possessed from eternity as the *eternal Son*. It is now a
Man who rules the universe: "All authority in heaven and on earth has been
given to me" (Matt. 28:18).

Only in this light can we understand John 17: "Father, the hour has come;
glorify your Son that the Son may glorify you, since you have *given* him authority over all flesh, to give eternal life to all whom you have given him. . . . I
glorified you on earth, having accomplished the work that you gave me to do.
And now, Father, glorify me in your own presence with the glory that I had
with you before the world existed" (vv. 1–5). "And now" is here "And *therefore*": *because* I accomplished—*as a Man!*—the great work of restoring the
universe to you, Father, I ask you to glorify me *as a Man* with the glory that I,
as the Son, possessed from eternity.

The tremendous importance of this is that only in this way he could
share his glory with *us*: "The glory that you have given me I have given to
them" (v. 22). "When Christ who is your life appears, then you also will appear with him in glory" (Col. 3:4); if "we suffer with him in order that we
may also be glorified with him" (Rom. 8:17; cf. v. 30). One day, the Father
will rule all things through Christ *and his church*!

✦   ✦   ✦

DAY 158 – THE SON RULES

(Lord's Day 19, Q&A 50, part 4)

A. *Christ ascended to heaven to show there that he is . . . the one through whom the Father rules all things.*

Basically, there are two ways in which we can speak of the Kingdom of God. First, this Kingdom is simply the general rule of God over the universe: "The LORD will reign forever and ever" (Exod. 15:18). "God is the King of all the earth" (Ps. 47:7). "[T]he LORD is a great God, and a great King above all gods" (95:3). "Great and amazing are your deeds, O Lord God the Almighty! Just and true are your ways, O King of the nations!" (Rev. 15:3).

The second meaning is much more specific. From the outset, it was God's plan to put his divine Kingdom under the feet of a Man (cf. Ps. 8:6, and its prophetic explanation in Heb. 2:5–8). The first Adam and the first Eve, who had been installed as first royal rulers (or viceroys, if you like; Gen. 1:26–28), failed miserably in this respect (Gen. 3). However, from the start God looked beyond them, and saw from afar the "last Adam" (1 Cor. 15:45), and the "last Eve" at his side.

During the Old Testament, believers looked forward to this King, the Messiah, that is, the anointed King of Israel, and in fact of the entire world (cf. Ps. 2:6 and 8). When Jesus was born, it was heathen men who asked: "Where is he who has been born king of the Jews?" (Matt. 2:2). When the Pharisees were discussing the Kingdom of God, Jesus said, "The kingdom of God is not coming in ways that can be observed, nor will they say, 'Look, here it is!' or 'There!' for behold, the kingdom of God is in the midst of you" (Luke 17:20–21), namely, *in his person*. As he performed miracles, Jesus could say, "[I]f it is by the Spirit of God that I cast out demons, then the kingdom of God has come upon you" (Matt. 12:28). To Pilate, Jesus spoke of "my kingdom" (John 18:36). And when he was about to leave this world, he told his disciples, "All authority in heaven and on earth has been given to me" (Matt. 28:18).

As the Son of Man, Jesus could speak of "*his* kingdom" (13:41)—and two verses later he called it the "kingdom of their Father." It is the same thing. This is what the Catechism says: Christ is "the one through whom the Father rules all things"—now and for evermore.

✳   ✳   ✳

DAY 159 – GIVER OF GIFTS

(Lord's Day 19, Q&A 51, part 1)

Q. How does this glory of Christ our head benefit us?
A. First, through his Holy Spirit he pours out gifts from heaven upon us his members.

The Catechism touches here upon one of the most remarkable aspects of Christ's glorification at the right hand of God, as described by Paul: "[G]race was given to each one of us according to the measure of Christ's gift. Therefore it says [Ps. 68:18], 'When he ascended on high . . . he gave gifts to men' . . . He is the one who ascended far above all the heavens, that he might fill all things. And he gave the apostles, the prophets, the evangelists, the shepherds and teachers, to equip the saints for the work of ministry, for building up the body of Christ" (Eph. 4:7–12).

Christians, especially in Pentecostal and Charismatic circles, often speak of the "gifts of the Spirit," because Paul says, "[T]here are varieties of gifts [*charismata*], but [it is] the same Spirit. . . . To each is given the manifestation of the Spirit for the common good. For to one is given through the Spirit the utterance of wisdom . . . [etc.]. All these are empowered by one and the same Spirit, who apportions to each one individually as he wills" (1 Cor. 12:4, 7–11). This emphasis on the Holy Spirit as the One through whom the gifts and ministries function is quite important. However, in Ephesians 4 the emphasis is rather on the glorified Christ at God's right hand who has granted them to the church, his body.

Notice three things here. There are five ministries mentioned here, and only a minority of Christians have one of these five ministries. However, verse 7 says that "to *each* one of us" was given "grace," namely, for a certain task in the Kingdom of God; as Peter says, "As each has received a gift, use it to serve one another, as good stewards of God's varied grace" (1 Pet. 4:10). Second, each gift, task, or ministry comes directly from him who is above all the heavens and fills all things. If you consider this, you will never despise even the smallest task in the church. Third, it is not the church that is given to the pastor or teacher, but the pastor or teacher is given to the *church* as a present from the glorified Christ. It is not the minister who expends his time and energy, but the church expends *him*.

✣   ✣   ✣

DAY 160 – HEAD AND MEMBERS
(Lord's Day 19, Q&A 51, part 2)

A. . . . through his Holy Spirit [Christ] pours out gifts from heaven upon us his members.

In Paul's letters we find four lists of gifts, tasks, and ministries within the church. The first one is this: "Having gifts that differ according to the grace given to us, let us use them: if prophecy, in proportion to our faith; if service, in our serving; the one who teaches, in his teaching; the one who exhorts, in his exhortation; the one who contributes, in generosity; the one who leads [or, gives aid], with zeal; the one who does acts of mercy, with cheerfulness" (Rom. 12:6–8). The emphasis here is this: although we are "one body in Christ" (v. 5), we are all very different, which comes to light in the many different tasks in the church.

In 1 Corinthians 12 the emphasis is the opposite: although we have many different gifts and tasks, we have one Spirit and we are one body: "Now there are varieties of gifts, but the same Spirit; and there are varieties of service, but the same Lord; and there are varieties of activities, but it is the same God who empowers them all in everyone. To each is given the manifestation of the Spirit for the common good. For to one is given through the Spirit the utterance of wisdom, and to another the utterance of knowledge according to the same Spirit, to another faith by the same Spirit, to another gifts of healing by the one Spirit, to another the working of miracles, to another prophecy, to another the ability to distinguish between spirits, to another various kinds of tongues, to another the interpretation of tongues. All these are empowered by one and the same Spirit, who apportions to each one individually as he wills" (vv. 4–11).

The third list is found in the same chapter: "God has appointed in the church first apostles, second prophets, third teachers, then miracles, then gifts of healing, helping, administrating, and various kinds of tongues" (v. 28).

The fourth and final list we considered yesterday: Christ "gave the apostles, the prophets, the evangelists, the shepherds [or, pastors], and teachers, to equip the saints for the work of ministry, for building up the body of Christ" (Eph. 4:11–12).

✣ ✣ ✣

DAY 161 – HE KEEPS US
(Lord's Day 19, Q&A 51, part 3)

A. . . . Second, by his power he defends us and keeps us safe from all enemies.

Sometimes we may be amazed about ourselves. We wholeheartedly believe that Christ is at God's "right hand in the heavenly places, far above all rule and authority and power and dominion" (Eph. 1:20–21), and that he "has gone into heaven and is at the right hand of God, with angels, authorities, and powers having been subjected to him" (1 Pet. 3:22). All powers of darkness are under his feet! Yet, at the same time, we may have difficulty believing that the dark powers *in our own lives* are also under his feet. We may be intimidated by those who take a hostile attitude to us because we are followers of Christ, and we may tend to forget that *our* enemies are *his* enemies, and that God said to Christ, "Sit at my right hand until I make your enemies your footstool" (Ps. 110:1; cf. Luke 20:43; Acts 2:35; Heb. 1:13; 10:13). We have nothing to worry about. If Satan comes, and, for instance, whisperingly reminds us of our past, we need only remind him of his future: "The God of peace will soon crush Satan under your feet" (Rom. 16:20).

What is greater than Jesus' own promise: "My sheep hear my voice, and I know them, and they follow me. I give them eternal life, and they will never perish, and no one will snatch them out of my hand. My Father, who has given them to me, is greater than all, and no one is able to snatch them out of the Father's hand" (John 10:27–29)?

Christ is above, at God's right hand in the heavenly places, and we are here below. Interestingly, however, Paul places our spiritual battle in the same realm: "Put on the whole armor of God, that you may be able to stand against the schemes of the devil. For we do not wrestle against flesh and blood, but against the rulers, against the authorities, against the cosmic powers over this present darkness, against the spiritual forces of evil in the heavenly places" (Eph. 6:11–12). That is, Christ's "defending and keeping us" does not make us passive; we ourselves are warriors, involved in the battle against our spiritual enemies. But no one less than the glorified Christ empowers us to engage in this battle.

❖ ❖ ❖

DAY 162 – AWAITING THE JUDGE
(Lord's Day 19, Q&A 52, part 1)

Q. How does Christ's return "to judge the living and the dead" comfort you?
A. In all distress and persecution, with uplifted head, I confidently await the very judge who has already offered himself to the judgment of God in my place and removed the whole curse from me.

Jesus will be the judge of the living and the dead (Acts 10:42; Rom. 14:9; 2 Tim. 4:1; 1 Pet. 4:5). Paul says, "[W]e must *all* appear before the judgment seat of Christ, so that each one may receive what is due for what he has done in the body, whether good or evil" (2 Cor. 5:10). This includes believers. But what a difference! The wicked have every reason to *fear* the coming of the judge. But believers know that he who is the judge has undergone the judgment of God on the cross for them! He saved us from the wrath of God (Rom. 5:9); he delivers us from the wrath to come (1 Thess. 1:10; cf. 5:9). He redeemed us from the curse of the law by becoming a curse for us (Gal. 3:13). So indeed, "with uplifted head" we can "confidently await" the judge. When we are in "all distress and persecution," we look forward to his coming even more eagerly.

We may wonder why believers must appear at all before the judgment seat of Christ. Is it only to hear that they are saved? They know that already! (The "sheep" in Matthew 25:31–40 do *not* yet know that, but we can't enter now into this difficult passage.) I see at least two important reasons for our appearance before Christ's judgment seat. One is that only then, when all my deeds will come to light, will I realize who I really was (then "I shall know fully, even as I have been fully known," 1 Cor. 13:12), and how many sins were forgiven me, and I will never love the Lord more than at that moment (as Jesus said, "[H]er sins, which are many, are forgiven—for she loved much. But he who is forgiven little, loves little," Luke 7:47).

The other reason is that there will be rewards according to the measure of our faithfulness. In the imagery of Luke 19:11–27, some receive authority over ten, others over five cities. Scripture also speaks of a "crown of life" for the martyrs (James 1:12; Rev. 2:10), an "imperishable wreath" for those who have run the race (1 Cor. 9:25), a "crown of righteousness" for those who have "loved his appearing" (2 Tim. 4:8), and a "crown of glory" for faithful shepherds (1 Pet. 5:4).

✤　✤　✤

DAY 163 – ETERNAL CONDEMNATION
(Lord's Day 19, Q&A 52, part 2)

A. . . . Christ will cast all his enemies and mine into everlasting condemnation.

When the Catechism asks how Christ's return comforts us, it may sound rather harsh to answer that he will cast all enemies into everlasting condemnation. God so loved the world (John 3:16), and we should love our fellow humans as well. How, then, could we look forward to the destruction of our enemies? Some will argue that such an attitude is in conflict with the Christian gospel.

Yet, there is another side; David said, "Do I not hate those who hate you, O Lord? And do I not loathe those who rise up against you? I hate them with complete hatred; I count them my enemies" (Ps. 139:21–22). We cannot easily get rid of such words by saying this is "just" Old Testament language! The book of Revelation is full of God's wrath, anger, and fury against his (and our) enemies as well (e.g., 14:10; 16:19; 19:15). And Paul says, "God considers it just to repay with affliction those who afflict you, . . . when the Lord Jesus is revealed from heaven with his mighty angels in flaming fire, inflicting vengeance on those who do not know God and on those who do not obey the gospel of our Lord Jesus. They will suffer the punishment of eternal destruction, away from the presence of the Lord and from the glory of his might, when he comes on that day to be glorified in his saints, and to be marveled at among all who have believed" (2 Thess. 1:6–10).

It is the *Old* Testament that says, "If your enemy is hungry, give him bread to eat, and if he is thirsty, give him water to drink" (Prov. 25:21; cf. Rom. 12:20), and Jesus said, "Love your enemies" (Matt. 5:44). But there is an end to this love and patience. If enemies stubbornly choose to remain God's—and thus our—enemies, then in the end this means condemnation. God's patience is never infinite. It may last 120 years (Gen. 6:3), or 400 years (15:13), or 2,000 years (since the cross), but in the end, "the way of the wicked will perish" (Ps. 1:6; cf. 37:20; 68:2). We will not rejoice in their condemnation as such, but we *will* rejoice in the honor and justice of God that in the end will be vindicated through the righteous judgment of Christ.

✳   ✳   ✳

DAY 164 – INTO JOY AND GLORY
(LORD'S DAY 19, Q&A 52, PART 3)

A. . . . Christ . . . will take me and all his chosen ones to himself into the joy and glory of heaven.

The emphasis in this answer is on the words "to himself." In the Bible, places have no glory of themselves; heaven is glorious only because it is filled with the glory of God and of his Christ. Islam tells us much about the alleged beauties of Paradise, and very little about Allah in connection with this. In the Bible it is the opposite: there is little about the beauties of the place, much about the glory of God and Christ. The thrill of going to heaven at his second coming is that we will be there *with him*, and will be *seeing* him: "[W]e know that when he appears we shall be like him, because we shall see him as he is" (1 John 3:2).

Jesus promised his disciples: "In my Father's house are many rooms. . . . [I]f I go and prepare a place for you, I will come again and will take you to myself, that *where I am* you may be also" (John 14:2–3). This is not referring to the believer's death; the angels may come and fetch you when you have passed away (Luke 16:22), but it is not the Lord himself who is "coming again" at that moment. But when he *will* come, it will be to take his entire church to himself at once: "[W]e who are alive, who are left until the coming of the Lord, will not precede those who have fallen asleep. For the Lord himself will descend from heaven with a cry of command, with the voice of an archangel, and with the sound of the trumpet of God. And the dead in Christ will rise first. Then we who are alive, who are left, will be caught up together with them in the clouds to meet the Lord in the air, and so we will always be *with the Lord*" (1 Thess. 4:15–17).

This will be entirely according to Jesus' own wishes: "Father, I desire that they also, whom you have given me, may be with me *where I am*, to see my glory that you have given me because you loved me before the foundation of the world" (John 17:24). Even of the "intermediate state" it is said that "to depart and be *with Christ* is far better" than staying on this earth (Phil. 1:23). How much better will it be to be with Christ after his second coming, in our resurrected and glorified bodies!

✦ ✦ ✦

DAY 165 – GOD THE SPIRIT
(Lord's Day 20, Q&A 53, part 1)

Q. What do you believe concerning "the Holy Spirit"?
A. First, that the Spirit, with the Father and the Son, is eternal God.

The Holy Spirit is mentioned twice in the Apostles' Creed: Jesus "was conceived by the Holy Spirit," and: "I believe in the Holy Spirit." The latter statement is remarkably brief in comparison to all that has been said about the Son of God. People have tried to make up for this by subsuming the following phrases under it—"the holy catholic church, the communion of saints, the forgiveness of sins, the resurrection of the body, and the life everlasting"—but I see no convincing reasons for this.

Perhaps the Creed is brief on the Spirit simply because at the time it originated, the church had little to say about him. The one thing it knew very well—a truth firmly established at the Council of Constantinople in AD 381—is that the Holy Spirit is a divine person, just like the Father and the Son. There is only one God. We do not have the slightest hesitation to confess with Israel that the LORD our God, the LORD is one (or, the LORD our God is one LORD) (Deut. 6:4). And yet, we distinguish between God the Father, God the Son, and God the Holy Spirit.

Already Jesus himself commanded that his apostles should baptize their converts in the name of the Father and of the Son and of the Holy Spirit (Matt. 28:19; cf. John 16:14–15; 1 Cor. 12:4–6; 2 Cor. 13:14). The Spirit is not just the Spirit of God in the same sense as we can speak of a human's spirit. No, the Spirit *as such* is a person, who helps, encourages, comforts, wills, teaches, testifies, sends, dwells, searches, thinks, feels—and this activity clearly occurs distinct from the Father and the Son (see extensively John 14–16). The Greek word for "spirit," *pneuma*, is neuter, yet, the Spirit is referred to as a "he" (15:26; 16:13–14). In comparison to the Son he is the "other Helper" (14:16). He can say "I" and "me" (Acts 13:2). In Acts 5:3–4 lying against the Holy Spirit is the same as lying against God. The Spirit is the LORD God of the Old Testament (Acts 28:25–27 [cf. Isa. 6:10]; 2 Cor. 3:16–17). These are just a few reasons to fully maintain that the Holy Spirit is eternal God, along with the Father and the Son.

✣   ✣   ✣

DAY 166 – THE SPIRIT GIVEN
(Lord's Day 20, Q&A 53, part 2)

A. Second, [I believe] that the Spirit is given also to me.

It is a tremendous fact that the Holy Spirit has been "given" to believers to "dwell" in them: God has "given us his Spirit in our hearts" (2 Cor. 1:22). "God has sent the Spirit of his Son into our hearts, crying, 'Abba! Father!'" (Gal. 4:6). The Spirit "dwells" in believers in two respects: both individually ("your body is a temple of the Holy Spirit within you, whom you have from God," 1 Cor. 6:19) and collectively: "[Y]ou [plural!] are God's temple and God's Spirit dwells in you. . . . God's temple is holy, and you are that temple" (3:16–17). In Christ, the whole church, "being joined together, grows into a holy temple in the Lord. In him you also are being built together into a dwelling place for God by the Spirit" (Eph. 2:21–22). The (New Testament) church is the present home of the Holy Spirit; it is *there* that he dwells.

Besides Christ himself, the Holy Spirit is the greatest gift God could ever give to his people. Of course, the "gift" (the being-given, Greek *dorea*) of the Spirit (Acts 2:38; 10:45) must be distinguished from the "gifts" (*charismata*) of (i.e., worked by) the Spirit (1 Cor. 12: 4–11; Heb. 2:4). It is primarily the Holy Spirit *himself* who is a divine gift to believers.

In the Old Testament, it was rare to hear about the Spirit having been given to certain believers—usually judges or prophets. It is all the more special that Joel prophesied that one day the Spirit would be "poured out on all flesh," that is, on the entire people of God (2:28; cf. Acts 2:17). Formerly, only priests, kings, and prophets received the anointing with *oil*. Today, *all* believers receive the anointing with the *Holy Spirit* (2 Cor. 1:21–22; 1 John 2:20, 27; cf. Acts 10:38; Isa. 61:1). One could also say: *all* believers have now become priests, kings, and prophets (cf. Q&A 32). It is the faith of these believers that has been sealed with the Holy Spirit (Eph. 1:13; cf. 4:30).

At Christmas and Easter we commemorate what Christ did *for* us; at Pentecost something happened *with* us! In this sense, Pentecost is the summit of all Christian feasts.

✳   ✳   ✳

DAY 167 – SHARING IN CHRIST
(Lord's Day 20, Q&A 53, part 3)

A. . . . *through true faith, [the Spirit] makes me share in Christ and all his benefits.*

Try to think of one single benefit that we have received from God in Christ apart from the Holy Spirit! You will have a difficult time finding one. . . . Think of your rebirth: it was worked in you by the Spirit (John 3:5); Paul speaks of "the washing of regeneration and renewal of the Holy Spirit" (Titus 3:5). Think of any spiritual wisdom you may have: it is because of the "Spirit of wisdom" (Eph. 1:17). Think of your access to the Father (cf. Rom. 5:2): it is through the "one Spirit" (Eph. 2:18). Think of the unity of believers: it is that of the Spirit (4:3). Think of your worship: it is through the Spirit (5:18–20).

Think of your spiritual power: it is that of the Spirit (Luke 24:49; Acts 1:8; Eph. 3:16). Think of your power in fighting: it is through the Spirit (Eph. 6:17; cf. 2 Cor. 10:4; 1 Pet. 4:14; 1 John 4:2–4). Think of your power in praying: it is through the Spirit (Eph. 6:18; Jude 1:20; cf. Rom. 8:26; Zech. 12:10). Think of your power in walking in faith: it is through the Spirit (Gal. 5:16–18; cf. Rom. 8:14). Think of your power in witnessing: it is through the Spirit (Mark 13:11; Acts 1:8; 1 Cor. 12:3). Think of your spiritual fruit for God: it is through the Spirit (Gal. 5:22).

If you wish to "put to death the deeds of the body" (that is, the activities of your sinful nature), it is through the Spirit (Rom. 8:13). If, by the grace of God, you are sure you are a child of God, it is through the Spirit (v. 16). If you need help in your weakness, it will come from the Spirit (v. 26). If you lead a life of obedience and dedication, it is through the Spirit (Acts 8:29; 10:19; 13:2, 4; 15:28; 16:6–7; Rom. 8:4). If you wish to become like Christ, this can only happen through the Spirit (2 Cor. 3:17–18). If you need power for preaching, it can only come from the Spirit (1 Cor. 2:3–5; 1 Thess. 1:5; 1 Pet. 1:12).

So, if you are not filled with the Spirit, remember the words of Jesus: "If you then, who are evil, know how to give good gifts to your children, how much more will the heavenly Father give the Holy Spirit to those who ask him" (Luke 11:13).

✤   ✤   ✤

DAY 168 – THE COMFORTER

(Lord's Day 20, Q&A 53, part 4)

A. . . . [the Spirit] comforts me.

Luke tells us about the early church: "[W]alking in the fear of the Lord and in the comfort [or, encouragement, exhortation] of the Holy Spirit, it multiplied" (Acts 9:31). This is one of those wonderful things that the Spirit does: he comforts.

When Martin Luther translated the New Testament in 1522, he decided to render the Greek word *paraklētos* as *Tröster*, that is, "Comforter." This rendering was taken over by the ancient Protestant translations in other languages. The word *paraklētos* is derived from a verb that indeed can mean "to comfort," but also "to encourage," "to admonish." It can even mean something like "to assist." The verb literally means "to call along," as you do with an "advocate"; this word comes from Latin and means exactly the same as *paraklētos*. Therefore, in more modern translations this word is usually no longer rendered as "Comforter," but as "Advocate, Helper (in court), Counselor, Intercessor, Standby," even "Companion, Friend."

The Holy Spirit guards our interests, he seeks the best for us, he assists us, he encourages us, he admonishes us if necessary, and, yes, he comforts us too, as the circumstances require. He is our Permanent Assistant. Look at what Jesus told his disciples about the Paraclete: "I will ask the Father, and he will give you another Helper, to be with you forever" (John 14:16–17). "[T]he Helper, the Holy Spirit, whom the Father will send in my name, he will teach you all things and bring to your remembrance all that I have said to you" (v. 26). "[H]e will bear witness about me" (15:26). "I will send [the Helper] to you. And when he comes, he will convict the world concerning sin and righteousness and judgment" (16:7–8).

Interestingly, the work of the Paraclete has sometimes been linked in particular with the inspiration of the New Testament: he brought to the apostles' remembrance the words of Jesus (the Gospels; 14:26), he bore witness about Jesus (the Acts; 15:26), "he will guide you into all the truth" (the Epistles; 16:13a), and "he will declare to you the things that are to come" (Revelation; 16:13b).

✦ ✦ ✦

DAY 169 – THE REMAINING SPIRIT
(Lord's Day 20, Q&A 53, part 5)

A. . . . [the Spirit] will remain with me forever.

Many Christians little realize the enormous impact of Jesus' words in John 14:16–17, "I will ask the Father, and he will give you another Helper, *to be with you forever*, even the Spirit of truth. . . . [H]e dwells with you and *will be in you*." Before Pentecost, the Holy Spirit could rest upon special men and women of God in view of a special ministry (e.g., Exod. 31:3; Isa. 61:1–3; Micah 3:8). But none of them could claim the Spirit dwelling in them forever. The Spirit *worked* here on earth right from the beginning (Gen. 1:2), but he never had a *permanent address* here below. Since the Day of Pentecost he has such an address: it is the church of God (1 Cor. 3:16; Eph. 2:20–22), and every believer individually (1 Cor. 6:19).

This was unknown before. Therefore, David, on whom the Spirit of prophecy rested (2 Sam. 23:1–2), could pray: "[T]ake not your Holy Spirit from me" (Ps. 51:11). We could not literally pray such a thing, except in one respect. We have to understand that the Spirit is not only a person but also a power, of which you can have much or little. This is why the Spirit is compared to water (of which you can have a droplet or an ocean), to wind (a breeze or a hurricane), and to fire (a spark or an inferno). As a person, the Spirit dwells in us one hundred percent; as a power, he may be just a droplet, a breeze, a spark in us. This is why we need the exhortation to be "filled" with the Spirit (Eph. 5:18; cf. Acts 2:4; 4:8, 31; 13:52). *Have* yourself filled with the Spirit by closing yourself to the things of the world and opening up to this tremendous power.

If we apply David's prayer to ourselves, we could pray: "Take not the *fullness* of your Spirit from me," so that only a droplet would remain. And if this happens nonetheless, we remember Jesus' words: "[T]he heavenly Father [will] give the Holy Spirit to those who ask him" (Luke 11:13), if you confess your sins and open up to him. However, the *person* of the Spirit has made your body a temple in which he will dwell forever. You may *grieve* the Spirit (Eph. 4:30), and you will have to confess this—but he will never leave you.

✷ ✷ ✷

DAY 170 – THE GATHERING SON
(Lord's Day 21, Q&A 54, part 1)

Q. What do you believe concerning "the holy catholic church"?
A. I believe that the Son of God through his Spirit and Word . . . gathers [the church].

The English word "church" comes from Greek *kyriakē*, an adjective ("lordly") that we find in expressions such as "the Lord's supper" (1 Cor. 11:20) and "the Lord's day" (Rev. 1:10). The "church" is "the Lord's people." The Greek word for "church" is *ekklēsia*, which is preserved in the French église, the Spanish *iglesia*, etc. It literally means "called out" in the sense of "called together," like the "congregation" of Israel in the wilderness (Acts 7:38) and the city assembly of Ephesus (19:39). Jesus was the first to refer to it in its present meaning: "[O]n this rock I will build my church, and the gates of hell [or rather, Hades] shall not prevail against it" (Matt. 16:18). Jesus loved to have his own *ekklēsia*, not that of Israel or the nations, one that would be imperishable and invincible. Somewhat later, he used the word in a practical, local sense: "If [some evildoer] refuses to listen to [some believing witnesses], tell it to the *ekklēsia*. And if he refuses to listen even to the *ekklēsia*, let him be to you as a Gentile and a tax collector," that is, an outsider (18:17).

Jesus also referred to "his" *ekklēsia* (without using this term) in John 10: "I have other [viz., Gentile] sheep that are not of this fold [i.e., Israel]. I must bring them also, and they will listen to my voice. So there will be one flock, one shepherd" (v. 16). Jesus would die for all his own, and "gather *into one* the children of God who are scattered abroad," that is, among Israel and the nations (11:52). This is the company he "obtained with his own blood" (Acts 20:28; cf. Titus 2:14). The church, then, is not just the sum of all Jesus-believers but much more than that. This marvelous unity is described as the body of Christ of which he is the head (Eph. 5:23; Col. 1:18; 2:19), as the temple of God in which the Holy Spirit dwells (1 Cor. 3:16; Eph. 2:20–22), as the bride or wife of Christ (2 Cor. 11:2; Eph. 5:23–32; Rev. 19:7; 21:9; 22:17), as the city of God (Rev. 21:9–27), etc. All these names illustrate certain aspects of this most wonderful company the world has ever seen.

✧ ✧ ✧

DAY 171 – OUT OF ALL HUMANITY
(Lord's Day 21, Q&A 54, part 2)

A. I believe that the Son of God . . . out of the entire human race, from the beginning of the world to its end, gathers [the church].

At the end of time, there will be only two kinds of people: those who have been saved by the blood of Christ, "from the beginning of the world to its end," and the wicked, who will be lost forever. All the saved ones, in Old and New Testaments, share in the prophecy of Genesis 3:15, that is, they are the (spiritual) "offspring of the woman." And since Abraham, they *all* belong to the "families" that are blessed in this chosen vessel (12:3), and in his "offspring" (22:18; 26:4), which is basically a reference to Christ (Gal. 3:16). *All* believers, of all ages, have the same life from God, and share the same salvation. *All* of them are "ransomed people for God" (Rev. 5:9). *All* will eventually share in the blessings of the New Covenant (Jer. 31:31–34; Heb. 8).

At the same time, looking at the characteristics of the church as described by the Catechism, we see particularly New Testament features: "catholic" (i.e., universal or worldwide); a "community chosen for eternal life" (which implies knowing God *and* Jesus Christ, John 17:3; cf. 1 John 5:20), "united in true faith," which is the Christian faith; a community with "members"—an image reminding us of the body of Christ (Rom. 12:4–5; 1 Cor. 12:12–27; Eph. 3:6; 5:30). We find the same tension in the Belgic Confession (Art. 27): the church is "a holy congregation and gathering of true Christian believers, awaiting their entire salvation in Jesus Christ . . . sealed by the Holy Spirit." This is thoroughly New Testament language; yet, it is added: "This church has existed from the beginning of the world and will last until the end."

The New Testament church has its own special characteristics: in Matthew 16:18 it was still a future thing, to be born on the Day of Pentecost. It is the company of saints that is viewed as unified with its glorified head in heaven (Eph. 1:20–2:6). As the dwelling-place of the Holy Spirit (1 Cor. 3:16; Eph. 2:20–22) it is a post-Pentecost phenomenon. It is important to always emphasize the *continuity* of Old and New Testaments, but also keep an eye on the special features of the New Testament church.

✣ ✣ ✣

DAY 172 – A CHOSEN COMMUNITY
(Lord's Day 21, Q&A 54, part 3)

A. I believe that the Son of God . . . gathers, protects, and preserves for himself a community chosen for eternal life.

The term "eternal life" is rather ambiguous. It is often simply used for the blessed life in the hereafter. But in the Old Testament, the expression refers to the future restoration of Israel: "[A]t that time [of trouble] your people shall be delivered, everyone whose name shall be found written in the book. And many of those who sleep in the dust of the earth shall awake, some to everlasting life, and some to shame and everlasting contempt" (Dan. 12:1–2; cf. Ps. 133:3, ". . . there [in Zion] the LORD has commanded the blessing, life forevermore"). Similarly, the faithful in Israel looked forward to "eternal life" as the blessed life of the "world to come," the Messianic Kingdom: "Teacher, what good deed must I do to have eternal life? . . ." "[E]veryone who has left houses or brothers or sisters or father or mother or children or lands, for my name's sake, will receive a hundredfold and will inherit eternal life" (Matt. 19:16, 29; cf. Luke 10:25).

However, with John the emphasis is quite different: "[T]his is eternal life, that they know you the only true God, and Jesus Christ whom you have sent" (John 17:3). "That which was from the beginning . . .—the life was made manifest, and we have seen it, and testify to it and proclaim to you the eternal life, which was with the Father and was made manifest to us—that . . . we proclaim also to you, so that you too may have fellowship with us; and indeed our fellowship is with the Father and with his Son Jesus Christ" (1 John 1:1–3). "[W]e are in him who is true, in his Son Jesus Christ. He is the true God and eternal life" (5:20). In whatever meaning we take the term "eternal life," Jesus is both the source and the glorious content of it.

Notice that we were *chosen* for this life: "[A]s many as were appointed to eternal life believed," says Luke (Acts 13:48). And Paul wrote, "Paul, . . . for the sake of the faith of God's elect, . . . in hope of eternal life, which God, who never lies, promised before the ages began . . ." (Titus 1:1–2; cf. Rom. 8:29; 9:23; Eph. 1:4–5). This is the greatest election for the greatest life ever, for evermore!

✤ ✤ ✤

DAY 173 – UNITED IN FAITH
(Lord's Day 21, Q&A 54, part 4)

A. I believe that the Son of God . . . gathers, protects, and preserves for himself a community . . . united in true faith.

The term "faith" has two different meanings in the New Testament. It may refer to the attitude of the heart, surrender to God and to the gospel of Jesus Christ: we are "saved through faith" (Eph. 2:8). "Faith" can also refer to what Christians believe, the Christian truth: ". . . the faith that was once for all delivered to the saints" (Jude 1:3). Sometimes we find the two meanings together: ". . . holding faith and a good conscience. By rejecting this, some have made shipwreck of their faith" (1 Tim. 1:19). Here we have "faith" initially in the first, then in the second meaning.

Now, which of the two meanings is intended in what the Catechism says: "united in true faith"? We cannot deny that the second meaning must be included. How could we be "church" in a very practical way if we did not at least agree on the fundamentals of Christianity? We may regret it if we differ about the Millennium, or about predestination, but we would not easily claim that those who think differently about such matters could not be true Christians. For other subjects it is the same, but there we have to make practical decisions: within one congregation we must generally think alike on, say, baptism, or the functioning of women. But again, we would not easily doubt the salvation of those who think differently about such matters. However, if a person would deny the deity of Christ, or the atoning value of his sacrifice, we would doubt whether such a person could at all be called a Christian. So, indeed, we have to agree on the basics: the things that are a matter of life and death, salvation and condemnation.

However, a common confessional basis is not enough. Paul exhorts us "to maintain the *unity of the Spirit* in the bond of peace" (Eph. 4:3). This goes much further than a common confessional basis: *this* unity is a matter of the heart, of "sincere faith" in a "pure heart" (1 Tim. 1:5), in the power of the Holy Spirit; not an organizational, but an organismic unity, so to speak. Faith as "truth" without inner faith leads to confessionalism; inner faith without confessional interests leads to sectarianism.

✤   ✤   ✤

DAY 174 – A LIVING MEMBER
(Lord's Day 21, Q&A 54, part 5)

A. . . . And of this community I am and always will be a living member.

The image of a "member" of God's church ties in most clearly with the image of the church as the "body" of Christ: "[W]e, though many, are one body in Christ, and individually members one of another" (Rom. 12:5). "[J]ust as the body is one and has many members, and all the members of the body, though many, are one body, so it is with Christ" (1 Cor. 12:12; cf. vv. 18, 25). "[Y]ou are the body of Christ and individually members of it" (v. 27). Believers from "the Gentiles are fellow heirs, members of the same body" together with believers from Israel (Eph. 3:6); "we are members of his body" (5:30).

In Romans 12, the emphasis is on the horizontal relationships between these members, and on the variability that exists within the same body. We belong together, and we are one in Christ, yet all very different. In 1 Corinthians 12, the emphasis is again on the horizontal relationships between the members (here, the "head' is just one of the "members," 1 Cor. 12:21), and this time on the unity that the various members display, in spite of their differences. We belong together, and though very different, yet are one in Christ ("members of Christ," 6:15).

In Ephesians 1–5, the emphasis is on the vertical relationship between the "head" (i.e., Christ) and the "body," with a special accent on the glories of the body. Only a glorious head is fitting for such a glorious body. (But it also says, "we are members one of another," 4:25). In Colossians 1–3, the emphasis is again on the vertical relationship between the "head" and the "body," this time with a special accent on the glories of the head (i.e., Christ). Only a glorious body is fitting for such a glorious head.

I always *will be* a member of the body of Christ. This means that the body of Christ *will exist* forever. In Revelation 21, John is shown "the Bride, the wife of the Lamb"—and what he sees is the New Jerusalem (vv. 9–10). Even in the new heaven and the new earth, this New Jerusalem will be the center of all (v. 1–2). To stick with the imagery: the church will be the eternal capital of God's new world!

✤   ✤   ✤

DAY 175 – SHARING IN CHRIST
(Lord's Day 21, Q&A 55, part 1)

Q. What do you understand by "the communion of saints"?
A. First, that believers one and all, as members of this community, share in Christ and in all his treasures and gifts.

It is interesting that the Apostles' Creed speaks first of the "holy catholic church," and then, as a separate matter, of the "communion of saints." Indeed, it is one thing to speak of this one church of God, another to speak of the mutual relationships within that church. The church is "catholic," that is, universal, worldwide. This is a great thought to contemplate: almost everywhere in the world we can find Christians. On paper Christians make up one third of the world population (but that's on paper). However, most of us do not travel that much. It is nice to know there are Christians on the other side of the globe, but we will probably never meet them.

However, when we think of the "communion of saints," we think of what the church means *to us*: our own local church, where we worship, where we hear the Word, and where we know a good number of fellow members. These are the people with whom we laugh and cry, whose sorrows and joys we know, and with whom we can enjoy everything we have in common in Christ. Here are the pastors and elders who look after us when we are in need, and we ourselves fill our little niche in this community to be of service to others.

Don't think you can manage on your own. Perhaps you are dissatisfied with your church, but please, don't decide to stay home. God made you in such way that you can spiritually survive only in communion with fellow believers. You need them. But what is at least as important: they need you. God gave you your unique qualities and talents to be of benefit to others. This is the way a local church functions. It is not a theater where you only watch what is happening up front. It is not a restaurant, where you come to eat without bothering about the other guests. It is a *family* of children of God, enjoying Christ's treasures and gifts—and enjoying each other. John desired "that you too may have fellowship with us; and indeed our fellowship is with the Father and with his Son Jesus Christ" (1 John 1:3). God has "called [you] into the fellowship of his Son, Jesus Christ our Lord" (1 Cor. 1:9). Enjoy Christ's church!

✦ ✦ ✦

DAY 176 – USING THE CHARISMATA
(Lord's Day 21, Q&A 55, part 2)

A. . . . Second, . . . each member should consider it a duty to use these gifts readily and joyfully.

Believers, as members of the community of saints, share in Christ and in all his treasures and gifts, and should use these gifts for the service of others. What are these "treasures and gifts"? The original Latin version only speaks of "good things," then says that we have to serve others with these "gifts." The good things of God, which we possess in Christ, are the "true riches" that Jesus spoke about (Luke 16:11). Paul spoke about the Lord as the One "bestowing his riches on all who call on him" (Rom. 10:12); he spoke about "the unsearchable riches of Christ" (Eph. 3:8), and about "all the riches of full assurance of understanding and the knowledge of God's mystery, which is Christ" (Col. 2:2). The expressions in the last part of the Apostles' Creed—"the Holy Spirit, the holy catholic church, the communion of saints, the forgiveness of sins, the resurrection of the body, and the life everlasting"—cover these riches adequately. Think further about the new life of Christ and the fellowship with him, think about believers being sons and heirs of God, being righteous and holy in the eyes of God, and having received the power of the Holy Spirit in order to lead a righteous and holy life.

Now the Catechism asks the question: What are you going to do with these blessings? Are you just keeping them for yourself, or are you going to bless other believers with them? We are a community of saints, in which each member serves the other members with what the Lord has entrusted to each of them. It is like the imagery that we find in the parables of the talents (Matt. 25:14–30) and the minas (Luke 19:11–27): the Lord has entrusted a treasure to us, and we have to "trade" with it. Every time another person, Christian or non-Christian, accepts the treasure that I try to share with him or her, the treasure is not halved but doubled: my mina has made one mina more! If I share the treasure with ten, or a thousand others, my mina has made ten, or a thousand. The parables show us, each in their own way, how the Lord appreciates it if we thus share the riches that he has granted us!

✣　✣　✣

176

DAY 177 – SERVING OTHERS
(Lord's Day 21, Q&A 55, part 3)

A. . . . Second, . . . each member should consider it a duty to use these gifts readily and joyfully for the service and enrichment of the other members.

It seems as if the language of the Catechism shifts here, from the "gifts" (spiritual blessings) that the Lord has given to all of us alike, to the "gifts" (qualities, callings, ministries) that each of us has received in a distinct way. The glorified Christ "gave the apostles, the prophets, the evangelists, the shepherds and teachers, to equip the saints for the work of ministry, for building up the body of Christ, until we all attain to the unity of the faith and of the knowledge of the Son of God, to mature manhood, to the measure of the stature of the fullness of Christ" (Eph. 4:11–13).

On the one hand, we must say that only a few of us are apostles (if any—it depends how you define them) or prophets, evangelists, pastors, or teachers. On the other hand, Ephesians 4:7 as well as Romans 12 and 1 Corinthians 12 show that each believer has his or her own ministry or task in the church of God. And perhaps we could even say that, in the widest sense, all who have a task of leadership, belong to the apostolic category. All who are allowed to speak a word of "upbuilding and encouragement and consolation" to others on behalf of the Lord (cf. 1 Cor. 14:3) belong to the prophetic category. All who take part in evangelistic and missionary work belong to the category of evangelists. All who are involved in pastoral work and counseling belong to the shepherds' category. And all who are occupied with some form of teaching in the church are found in the teachers' category.

Generally speaking, only very few believers could honestly say that there is no place for them in any of these five areas of Christian activity, both inwardly (within the church) and outwardly (in missionary work). We are all called upon to take part in using our gifts "readily and joyfully for the service and enrichment of the other members," or "for building up the body of Christ." None of us knows everything, or can do everything. We need each other. Whatever your own calling may be, you need the gifts of others. And if you do not use *your* gift, the church is going to miss something that the Lord had in mind for her!

✳   ✳   ✳

DAY 178 – FORGIVENESS OF SINS
(Lord's Day 21, Q&A 56, part 1)

Q. What do you believe concerning "the forgiveness of sins"?
A. I believe that God, because of Christ's satisfaction, will no longer remember any of my sins or my sinful nature.

It would be a big mistake to think that divine forgiveness is not much more than the work of a bookkeeper coolly crossing out a certain debt, or a judge deciding, in a detached way, that a certain obligation has been met. On the contrary, there is hardly anything in the Bible that shows us more clearly, more touchingly, the love, the grace, and the mercy of God. Nothing lets us look more deeply into God's heart. In comparison with other religions, there is hardly anything that is more characteristic of Christianity than this: forgiveness. God is "merciful and gracious, slow to anger, and abounding in steadfast love and faithfulness, keeping steadfast love for thousands, forgiving iniquity and transgression and sin" (Exod. 34:6–7). If you truly repent, God "forgives all your iniquity. . . . He does not deal with us according to our sins, nor repay us according to our iniquities" (Ps. 103:3, 10). "[T]he blood of Jesus his Son cleanses us from all sin. . . . If we confess our sins, he is faithful and just to forgive us our sins and to cleanse us from all unrighteousness" (1 John 1:7, 9).

The Catechism uses the beautiful word "remember." "[Y]ou have cast all my sins behind your back," said Hezekiah (Isa. 38:17)—but, as someone complained, God only has to turn around, and he will see my sins again. God "will cast all our sins into the depths of the sea," says Micah (7:19). But, said our complainant, God can easily fish them up again. However, God says, "I will forgive their iniquity, and *I will remember their sin no more*" (Jer. 31:34). They will be blotted from his memory so to speak! "[A]s far as the east is from the west, so far does he remove our transgressions from us" (Ps. 103:12).

Because forgiveness has to do with God's own heart, he cannot stand it if his children refuse to forgive one another: "[F]orgive us our debts, as we also have forgiven our debtors" (Matt. 6:12). ". . . So also my heavenly Father will [punish] every one of you, if you do not forgive your brother from your heart" (18:35). You could not offend God's mercy more than by not forgiving your brother!

✻ ✻ ✻

DAY 179 – STRUGGLING ALL MY LIFE
(Lord's Day 21, Q&A 56, part 2)

A. . . . my sinful nature which I need to struggle against all my life.

The wicked are not *willing* to stop sinning, and they are not *able* to. The righteous definitely *are* willing to stop sinning, and by the power of the Holy Spirit they are also *able* to, and to follow Christ. But this addition, "by the power of the Holy Spirit," is vital. Even the reborn Christian as such has the willingness but not the strength to stop sinning and serve God. This strength does not stem from his new life as such, but from another person: the Holy Spirit, dwelling in him. The point, however, is that we do not always *walk* by the Spirit; if it were different, we would not need the exhortation of Galatians 5:16–18. We are not always *filled* with the Spirit; otherwise, we would not need the admonition of Ephesians 5:18. We are not always *led* by the Spirit; if we were, we would not need the encouragement of Romans 8:1–17.

This is where the "struggle" comes in (cf. Rom. 7:21–25). On the one hand, John writes: "If we say we have no sin, we deceive ourselves, and the truth is not in us" (1 John 1:8); no Christian can deny he still has the sinful nature within him. Yet, a few verses later John writes: "My little children, I am writing these things to you so that you may not sin" (2:1a). In Pauline language this is: you may still have the "flesh" in you, but there is no *need* to yield to it. You have been set free from sin, that is, from the *power* of sin (Rom. 6: 7, 18, 22): "Let not sin therefore *reign* in your mortal body, to make you obey its passions" (v. 12). *You* are responsible for not letting this happen (cf. 1 John 3:4–9; 5:18)!

Yet, in practical life things are not that easy. James says, "[W]e all stumble in many ways" (3:2). Solomon says, "Surely there is not a righteous man on earth who does good and never sins" (Eccl. 7:20). Therefore, after his encouragement not to sin, John hastens to add: "But if anyone does sin, we have an advocate with the Father, Jesus Christ the righteous" (1 John 2:1b). He treats us as an exception: "anyone"—but it is available to us all: "*we* have an advocate . . . ." And Paul would say, Make sure you walk by the Spirit!

✤   ✤   ✤

DAY 180 – THE RIGHTEOUSNESS OF CHRIST
(Lord's Day 21, Q&A 56, part 3)

A. . . . Rather, by grace God grants me the righteousness of Christ to free me forever from judgment.

We have seen earlier (Day 139) that God sees us as united with Christ in his death, in his resurrection, in his ascension, and in his glorification at the right hand of God. This risen and glorified Christ is not only perfectly righteous in himself—he was this already *before* his death—but he also brought about the atonement for our sins. Therefore, through his death and resurrection, God sees us in him as perfectly righteous.

Of course, this entails much more than being "free forever from judgment." That is the negative side of it, no matter how important (cf. John 5:24). The positive side is that, by faith, we now are as righteous as the risen and glorified Christ. This was God's plan from the start: "[T]hose whom he foreknew he also predestined to be conformed to the image of his Son, in order that he might be the firstborn among many brothers" (Rom. 8:29). From God, "you are in Christ Jesus, who became to us wisdom from God, righteousness and sanctification and redemption" (1 Cor. 1:30). Notice the connections here: God manifested his wisdom in and through his Son and his work, Christ Jesus brought about redemption through the work on the cross, and through this redemption we have now been justified (made righteous) and sanctified (made holy).

Almost every writer of the New Testament (from Matt. 27:19 to 1 John 2:1) calls Jesus the Righteous One. If he had not accomplished his work on the cross, he would have remained the Righteous One, and we would have remained the unrighteous. However, "Christ suffered once for sins, the righteous for the unrighteous, that he might bring us to God" (1 Pet. 3:18). "We know that our old self was crucified with him in order that the body of sin might be brought to nothing" (Rom. 6:6). The "new self" has been "created after the likeness of God in true righteousness and holiness" (Eph. 4:24). We "have put on the new self, which is being renewed in knowledge after the image of its creator. Here there is not Greek and Jew, circumcised and uncircumcised, barbarian, Scythian, slave, free; but Christ is all, and in all" (Col. 3:10–11).

✺ ✺ ✺

DAY 181 – BODILY RESURRECTION
(Lord's Day 22, Q&A 57, part 1)

Q. How does "the resurrection of the body" comfort you?
A. Not only will my soul be taken immediately after this life to Christ its head.

Already in Roman Catholicism, the end goal of human life was to go, after death, to either heaven or hell. That's it. If you go to heaven, there is nothing to be desired after that. Just read two authors of the most widely read writings of the Middle Ages: Dante Alighieri and Thomas à Kempis. Resurrection hardly played a role in their kind of thinking. If mentioned at all, it was an additional blessing, somewhere at the end of the ages, but of minor importance. As soon as you entered heaven, you would have it all. This viewpoint did not change after the Reformation. The most widely read Protestant author was John Bunyan (*The Pilgrim's Progress*), who gave the same picture: after crossing the River of Death, the New Jerusalem was waiting for the believer. As if the New Jerusalem is not the bride of the Lamb (Rev. 21:9–10) as she will be displayed only *after* Christ's second coming!

In this very common representation of things, the "intermediate state" has become the "end state." Of course, it is a great comfort that we "will be taken immediately after this life to Christ our head," as Jesus promised the criminal on the cross (Luke 23:43, "be with me in Paradise"), and as Paul believed (Phil. 1:23, "be with Christ"). But some people do not realize that we will be in this state in an imperfect, namely, disembodied condition. We will be merely souls (bodiless individuals, cf. Rev. 6:9), just as the unbelievers in the hereafter are called the "spirits in prison" (1 Pet. 3:19). The idea that this would be the "end state" is a product of ancient Greek thinking: the deliverance of the soul from the body is the alleged end goal.

Go through the New Testament, and you will see that believers are never waiting for what awaits them after death, but for the coming of Christ and the Messianic Kingdom (Luke 2:38; 12:36, 40, 46; 1 Thess. 1:10; Titus 2:13; Heb. 9:23; 2 Pet. 3:12–14). We wait for the redemption of our bodies (Rom. 8:23). To the Creator, our body is just as important as our soul. Not physical death but physical resurrection is the believer's end goal!

✦　　✦　　✦

DAY 182 – RISING IN POWER
(Lord's Day 22, Q&A 57, part 2)

A. . . . my very flesh will be raised by the power of Christ.

We will have attained our end goal, not at the moment of our physical death, but only when we will have received our glorified body. Only then will we be complete again. Spiritually we share in the new creation already today (2 Cor. 5:17; Gal. 6:15), but not yet bodily. We have received the "salvation of our souls" (1 Pet. 1:9), but we still wait for the redemption of our bodies (Rom. 8:23). From heaven "we await a Savior, the Lord Jesus Christ, who will transform our lowly body to be like his glorious body, by the power that enables him even to subject all things to himself" (Phil. 3:20–21).

In this passage, and in the Catechism, it is the power of Christ that will transform our body. In Ephesians it is the power of God, who first raised Christ from the dead, and then (spiritually) raised us: Paul speaks of "the immeasurable greatness of [God's] power toward us who believe, according to the working of his great might that he worked in Christ when he raised him from the dead and seated him at his right hand in the heavenly places. . . . And you were dead in the trespasses and sins. . . . But God . . . made us alive together with Christ . . . and raised us up with him" (1:19–20; 2:1, 4–6). By this same power, he will grant us not only our spiritual but also our bodily resurrection. Elsewhere, Paul tells us that the Holy Spirit is involved in this resurrection as well: "If the Spirit of him who raised Jesus from the dead dwells in you, he who raised Christ Jesus from the dead will also give life to your mortal bodies through his Spirit who dwells in you" (Rom. 8:11).

Notice the connection between Christ's resurrection and ours: "Christ has been raised from the dead, the *firstfruits* of those who have fallen asleep" (1 Cor. 15:20), the first of a large harvest: "[U]nless a grain of wheat falls into the earth and dies, it remains alone; but if it dies, it bears much fruit" (John 12:24).

Also notice the splendor of the resurrection body: "What is sown is perishable; what is raised is imperishable." The body is sown in dishonor and weakness; it is raised in glory and power (1 Cor. 15:42–43).

✦   ✦   ✦

DAY 183 – BODY AND SOUL REUNITED

(Lord's Day 22, Q&A 57, part 3)

A. . . . my very flesh . . . reunited with my soul.

I remember asking one of my favorite teachers—many years ago—what he thought of this phrase in the Catechism: body and soul "reunited." I asked him whether this was not a bit of Greek-dualistic thinking that had crept into the Catechism. Scripture never speaks of a body and a soul that are separated at death—the body going into the grave, the soul going to the hereafter—to be "reunited" at resurrection. My Reformed teacher answered that I should not forget that the Catechism is not a theological document, but a confessional one. Do not expect philosophical precision in it, he said; the Catechism speaks the language of the everyday believer, not of the learned thinker (although, thank God, some learned thinkers are also everyday believers).

To be sure, the New Testament is indeed not dualistic. For instance, it says they laid *Jesus* in the tomb (John 19:42), not just the "body of Jesus" (v. 38), or his "remains." At the same time, *Jesus* (not just his soul) was in Paradise (Luke 23:43). Elsewhere, Jesus said that the rich man died and was buried (not just his body), *and* that *he* lifted up his eyes in Hades (not just his soul) (16:22–23). When we die, *we* are buried, and *we* are with Christ; both are true at the same time. However, we have to admit that it is cumbersome to speak this way. So if we want to explain these things, especially to children, it is hardly possible to avoid dualistic language: it is the body that is buried (cf. 23:52–55), and it is the soul or the spirit that is with Christ, or in the "place of torment" (16:28). This is the kind of popular language that the Catechism speaks as well. It may not be ideal, but try to come up with an alternative that is understood just as easily.

My soul is not the kind of "shade" that Isaiah 14:9 speaks of; it is not a ghost. It is my Ego, my personality, my essential being, or whatever you call it. It is thus that we understand Jesus' words: "[D]o not fear those who kill the body but cannot kill the soul. Rather fear him who can destroy both soul and body in hell" (Matt. 10:28).

✦   ✦   ✦

DAY 184 – MADE LIKE CHRIST
(Lord's Day 22, Q&A 57, part 4)

A. . . . my very flesh will be raised by the power of Christ . . . and made like Christ's glorious body.

The New Testament attaches great importance to the fact that we will be "like Christ," also in a bodily respect: he "will transform our lowly body to be like his glorious body" (Phil. 3:21). As John says, "Beloved, we are God's children now, and what we will be has not yet appeared; but we know that when he appears we shall be like him, because we shall see him as he is" (1 John 3:2). Notice three things here: first, what we will be has not yet been manifested to the *world*—but *we* do know it already: we shall be like him! Second, when he will appear, "then you also will appear with him in glory" (Col. 3:4); we will "be glorified with him" (Rom. 8:17). "On that day," he will be "glorified in his saints" (2 Thess. 1:10).

Third, the proof that we will be like him is that we "shall see him as he is." These are two different things: he will always be *more* than we are. He is like us, yet greater. Jesus said to the Father, first, "The glory that you have given me I have given to them" (John 17:22). In *this* sense we are "like him." But then he says, "Father, I desire that they also, whom you have given me, may be with me where I am, to see my glory that you have given me because you loved me before the foundation of the world" (v. 24). This is a glory in him that we will *see* but not share; in this glory he will surpass us. For instance, we are kings like him—but Jesus is the King of kings (Rev. 19:16). We are priests like him—but Jesus is the high priest (thus many times in Hebrews). We are sons of God like him—but he is the "firstborn among many brothers" (Rom. 8:29).

According to his divine nature, he is even the *only* Son (John 1:14; 3:16, 18; 1 John 4:9). He remains unique. The fact that we will be "like him" never means that we enter into the Godhead. 2 Peter 1:4 seems to come very close ("partakers of the divine nature") but it stops short in time. We are "like Christ" only according to his (glorified) human nature. And even in this respect he always surpasses us. We will praise him because we are like him; and we will praise him in all things in which he is greater.

✶   ✶   ✶

DAY 185 – LIFE EVERLASTING

(Lord's Day 22, Q&A 58, part 1)

Q. How does the article concerning "life everlasting" comfort you?
A. Even as I already now experience in my heart the beginning of eternal joy.

L ife everlasting" is a term with various meanings in de Bible. The way it is used in the Apostles' Creed makes it very clear that a *future* eternity of bliss for believers is intended. In Christian tradition, this is usually associated with heaven, but in the Bible it is more clearly connected with the Messianic Kingdom (Dan. 12:2; notice the word "inherit" in Matt. 19:29; Mark 10:17; Luke 10:25).

In John's ministry, the term "eternal life" has the specific meaning of knowing (that is, close intimacy with) God and Jesus Christ (John 17:3). It is the life from Above, which came into this world in the person of Christ: "That which was from the beginning, which we have heard, which we have seen with our eyes, which we looked upon and have touched with our hands, concerning the word of life—the life was made manifest, and we have seen it, and testify to it and proclaim to you the eternal life, which was with the Father and was made manifest to us—that which we have seen and heard we proclaim also to you, so that you too may have fellowship with us; and indeed our fellowship is with the Father and with his Son Jesus Christ. And we are writing these things so that our *joy* may be complete" (1 John 1:1–4).

This is what the Catechism refers to as "the beginning of eternal joy"! Notice what John is telling us. First, "eternal life" descended to us in the person of Jesus Christ (cf. 1 John 5:20, "*He* is the true God and eternal life"). Second, this life was manifested to the apostles (the "we" in this passage). Third, the apostles preach this "eternal life" to the world (whoever believes in Christ receives eternal life, John 3:15–16). Fourth, the purpose of this preaching is that many believers will join the fellowship of the apostles. Fifth, the *character* of this horizontal fellowship is the vertical dimension: fellowship with the Father and with his Son Jesus Christ. Sixth, the purpose of this fellowship is "complete joy" (cf. Rom. 14:17, "the kingdom of God is a matter of . . . righteousness and peace and joy in the Holy Spirit"; also see John 15:11; 16:20–24; 17:13).

✦ ✦ ✦

DAY 186 – PERFECT BLESSEDNESS
(Lord's Day 22, Q&A 58, part 2)

A. . . . after this life I will have perfect blessedness.

The term "after this life" is a bit ambiguous. It seems to refer in particular to the intermediate state, that is, to the state between the believer's physical death and his physical resurrection. Actually, the Bible tells us very little about this state, except that we will be "with Jesus" (Luke 23:42–43; cf. 16:19–31), "with Christ" (Phil. 1:23), or "with the Lord" (2 Cor. 1:10, if this indeed refers to the "intermediate state").

In the New Testament, we instead see believers waiting for the return of Christ, and for the glory that awaits them after this. At the moment of Christ's coming again, we will receive our glorified resurrection body (1 Cor. 15:35–56; Phil. 3:20–21), with which we will dwell "with the Lord" (1 Thess. 4:17), in the Father's house with its many rooms (John 14:1–3). We will receive our "inheritance" (Rom. 8:17; Eph. 1:9, 14; Col. 1:12; 1 Pet. 1:4; Rev. 21:7). We will rest from our labors, and be "blessed," which means here: "happy" (Rev. 14:13). We will be in the place of comfort (Luke 16:25), of the joy of the Lord (Matt. 25:21, 23), of perfect understanding (1 Cor. 13:10, 12).

Everything in this blessed eternal state will center around the glory of God and of his Christ. We will behold (John 17:24; 1 John 3:2), and forever reflect, the glory of the Lord (2 Cor. 3:18; 4:6; cf. Matt. 13:43; Rev. 21:9–11), as well as the glory of God (Matt. 5:8; Heb. 12:14; Rev. 22:4). We will recline at God's table (in the figurative sense), eat, and enjoy him (Luke 12:37; cf. Rev. 2:7; 7:17; 19:9). We will enjoy the fellowship with the Father, and with his Son Jesus Christ (1 John 1:1–3; cf. John 17:3). We will serve God, and reign with Christ forever (Rev. 22:3–5). We will worship God and the Lamb forever (Rev. 4:10; 5:14; 11:16; 14:7; 15:4; 19:4). We will forever enjoy what we will praise; we will forever praise what we will enjoy. God will be "all in all" (1 Cor. 15:28), and Christ will forever be the One who "fills all in all" (Eph. 1:23), as he also will forever be "all, and in all" in us, that is, everything in all believers (Col. 3:11).

✦ ✦ ✦

DAY 187 – NEVER DREAMED OF
(Lord's Day 22, Q&A 58, part 3)

A. . . . perfect blessedness such as no eye has seen, no ear has heard, no human heart has ever imagined.

Of course, the Catechism's answer here is an allusion to 1 Corinthians 2:7–10, "[W]e impart a secret and hidden wisdom of God, which God decreed before the ages for our glory. None of the rulers of this age understood this, for if they had, they would not have crucified the Lord of glory. But, as it is written, 'What no eye has seen, nor ear heard, nor the heart of man imagined, what God has prepared for those who love him'—these things God has revealed to us through the Spirit."

There are things—the "secret and hidden wisdom of God"—that the world cannot understand; as John says, "The reason why the world does not know us is that it did not know him" (1 John 3:1b; cf. John 14:17). "The natural person does not accept the things of the Spirit of God, for they are folly to him, and he is not able to understand them because they are spiritually discerned" (1 Cor. 2:14). To explain this further, Paul says, "it is written." This has always amazed expositors, for there is no Old Testament passage where we literally find what is "quoted" here. The thought that Paul expresses most nearly resembles Isaiah 64:4, "From of old no one has heard or perceived by the ear, no eye has seen a God besides you, who acts for those who wait for him."

The point that Paul apparently wishes to make is that "what God has prepared for those who love him," that is, their eternal blessedness, does not go back to human observation ("the eye"), or to human history ("the ear"), or to human understanding (what "the heart of man imagined"). You could even say that neither science, nor religious tradition, nor philosophy could have ever imagined the wonderful things that God had in mind from eternity for his children to enjoy forever. The fact that we do know about these things is due to *divine revelation* through the Spirit: God *told* us about them (the objective part). Moreover, he enlightened our minds by the same Spirit (the subjective part): "'[W]ho has understood the mind of the Lord?' [cf. Isa. 40:13; Rom. 11:34]. But we have the mind [the thinking, the insight, the understanding] of Christ" (1 Cor. 2:16).

✢   ✢   ✢

DAY 188 – PRAISE GOD FOREVER
(Lord's Day 22, Q&A 58, part 4)

A. . . . a blessedness in which to praise God forever.

The Westminster Larger Catechism begins with the question: "What is the chief and highest end of man?" The answer is: "Man's chief and highest end is *to glorify God*, and fully to enjoy him forever." Man is called upon to glorify (praise, honor, worship) God, and at the same time this is a privilege. It will be part of saved humanity's eternal blessedness that it will praise God forever.

Leah is the first one mentioned in the Bible who praised God: "[S]he conceived again and bore a son, and said, 'This time I will praise the Lord.' Therefore she called his name Judah" (Gen. 29:35). Judah is from the verb *yada*, "to praise" or "to give thanks." The name "Judah" gave rise to the name "Judean," which later became "Jew." So you could describe a Jew as "one praising God." It is an essential part of Israel's identity that the righteous praise God: "Seven times a day I praise you for your righteous rules" (Ps. 119:164). "It is good to give thanks to the Lord, to sing praises to your name, O Most High" (92:1; cf. 147:1). Of Daniel it is said, "He got down on his knees three times a day and prayed and gave thanks before his God" (Dan. 6:10).

Jesus said, "[T]he hour is coming, and is now here, when the true worshipers will worship the Father in spirit and truth, for the Father is *seeking* such people to worship him" (John 4:23). The Father seeks (longs for, strives after) worshipers! The book of Revelation is full of such worship: "[T]he twenty-four elders fall down before him who is seated on the throne and worship him who lives forever and ever" (4:10; cf. 5:14; 19:4). "And the twenty-four elders who sit on their thrones before God fell on their faces and worshiped God, saying, 'We give thanks to you, Lord God Almighty, who is and who was'" (11:16–17). "Fear God and give him glory, because the hour of his judgment has come, and worship him who made heaven and earth, the sea and the springs of water" (14:7). "All nations will come and worship you, for your righteous acts have been revealed" (15:4). Heaven and earth will resound with God's praises forever!

✤　✤　✤

DAY 189 – WHY BELIEVE?

(Lord's Day 23, Q&A 59, part 1)

Q. What good does it do you, however, to believe all this?
A. In Christ I am righteous before God.

We have come to the end of the Apostles' Creed; now it's time to look back. What did we learn? And how do the Christian truths that we have learned about benefit us? Repeatedly the Catechism asked this question, and now it asks it in a general way: "What good does it do you to believe all this?" You may wonder why the Catechism does this here. Apparently, the answer is that it wants to introduce to us the subject of justification, to be covered in Q&As 59–64. At first, the answer is given here in a very brief way: "In Christ I am righteous before God and heir to life everlasting."

Please realize what a tremendous statement this is! *I am righteous before God.* Already the Old Testament testifies: "Can mortal man be in the *right* before God? Can a man be pure before his Maker?" (Job 4:17). "What is man, that he can be pure? Or he who is born of a woman, that he can be *righteous*?" (15:14). "How then can man be in the *right* before God? How can he who is born of woman be pure?" (25:4). "None is *righteous,* no, not one" (Rom. 3:10–12; cf. Ps. 14:1–3; 53:1–3). "If you, O LORD, should mark iniquities, O Lord, who could stand?" (Ps. 130:3). "Enter not into judgment with your servant, for no one living is *righteous* before you" (143:2). "Surely there is not a *righteous* man on earth who does good and never sins" (Eccl. 7:20).

Yet, we do explicitly hear about righteous persons in the Gospels (apart from Jesus): Joseph (Matt. 1:19), Zechariah and Elizabeth (Luke 1:6), Simeon (2:25), Joseph of Arimathea (23:50). Others were identified as righteous implicitly: Mary, Anna, Nicodemus. What was their secret? First, regeneration (cf. John 3:3–5); second, love for God, for his Torah, and for their neighbors; third, an upright walk according to God's Torah. By nature, *all* are unrighteous. By the grace of God, *some become* righteous: "Noah found *favor* [or, grace] in the eyes of the LORD. . . . Noah was a righteous man, blameless in his generation. Noah walked with God" (Gen. 6:8–9). This is the message today as well: you can be "justified [i.e., made righteous] by the grace of God" (Rom. 3:24; Titus 3:7)!

※　　※　　※

DAY 190 – RIGHTEOUS AND HEIR
(Lord's Day 23, Q&A 59, part 2)

A. In Christ I am righteous before God and heir to life everlasting.

By the grace of God, we have been made not only righteous, but also "heirs to life everlasting." Paul often speaks about this: "The Spirit himself bears witness with our spirit that we are children of God, and if children, then heirs—heirs of God and fellow heirs with Christ, provided we suffer with him in order that we may also be glorified with him" (Rom. 8:16–17). "[B]ecause you are sons, God has sent the Spirit of his Son into our hearts, crying, 'Abba! Father!' So you are no longer a slave, but a son, and if a son, then an heir through God" (Gal. 4:6–7); ". . . giving thanks to the Father, who has qualified you to share in the inheritance of the saints in light. He has delivered us from the domain of darkness and transferred us to the kingdom of his beloved Son" (Col. 1:12–13).

In Ephesians 1:11 we read, "In [Christ] we have obtained an inheritance"; this is more correct than, for instance, the ASV: ". . . in whom also we were made a heritage." *We* are not the inheritance, we *receive* one, in association with Christ, in the "world to come." I like the rendering in *The Voice*: "With immense pleasure, [God] laid out His intentions *through Jesus,* a plan that will climax when the time is right *as He returns to create order and unity*—both in heaven and on earth—when all things are brought together under the Anointed's *royal rule.* In Him we stand to inherit even more. As His heirs, we are predestined *to play a key role* in His *unfolding* purpose that is energizing everything to conform to His will" (vv. 9–11).

Such a rendering underscores that our being heirs of God is connected with the Kingdom of Christ (cf. Col. 1:12–13), the "world to come" (Heb. 2:5) in the "age to come" (6:5), which will be precisely what the Catechism calls the unfolding of "life everlasting." I see this prophetically in Psalm 133: "Behold, how good and pleasant it is when brothers dwell in unity! It is like . . . the dew of Hermon, which falls on the mountains of Zion! For there the Lord has commanded the blessing, *life forevermore.*" This is the bliss to be inherited with Christ!

✢ ✢ ✢

DAY 191 – BY TRUE FAITH
(Lord's Day 23, Q&A 60, part 1)

Q. How are you righteous before God?
A. Only by true faith in Jesus Christ.

In the "justification of the ungodly" (Rom. 4:5), three parties are involved. First, justification (the making righteous) is by the grace of God (Rom. 3:24; Titus 3:7; cf. Gal. 5:4; Gen. 6:8–9). That is, there is not the slightest element of human merit involved in it. The only thing *we* "contributed" to it were our sins. Justification goes forth from God, is by the power of his Spirit, and is for his glory.

Second, justification is "through the redemption that is in Christ Jesus, whom God put forward as a propitiation by his blood" (Rom. 3:24–25). That is, a holy and righteous God demanded a just, adequate, and satisfactory *ground* for justification. To this end, he himself "put forward" Christ, who made propitiation by his work on the cross, and thus redeemed us.

Third, there is the sinner himself who is involved. He cannot contribute anything to his own salvation and justification; yet, if he would not believe he would not receive it. Faith is the means by which he receives his justification. Paul speaks of "the righteousness of God through faith in Jesus Christ for all who believe. . . . [T]he redemption that is in Christ Jesus [is] . . . to be received by faith. . . . [God is] just and the justifier of the one who has faith in Jesus" (Rom. 3:22–26). "[W]e know that a person is not justified by works of the law but through faith in Jesus Christ, so we also have believed in Christ Jesus, in order to be justified by faith in Christ" (Gal. 2:16).

We must be careful not to turn this faith into a kind of merit or a good work after all: "[B]y grace you have been saved through faith. And this is not your own doing; it is the gift of God" (Eph. 2:8). It is all God's work. In no way is my righteousness "a righteousness of my own that comes from the law"; rather, it is "that which comes through faith in Christ, the righteousness from God that depends on faith" (Phil. 3:9). Faith is nothing but opening a window in a dark room to let the sunlight flood in. Such opening is not a merit, it does not add anything to the sunlight as such, yet it is an absolute condition for seeing the light!

✦　　✦　　✦

DAY 192 – OUR CONSCIENCE
(Lord's Day 23, Q&A 60, part 2)

A. . . . *Even though my conscience accuses me of having grievously sinned against all God's commandments, of never having kept any of them, and of still being inclined toward all evil.*

The believer, that is, the person who has been justified in Christ, by faith, has a good conscience as far as his *position* in Christ is concerned. This conscience has been purified "from dead works to serve the living God" (Heb. 9:14); "our hearts [have been] sprinkled clean from an evil conscience and our bodies washed with pure water" (10:22). However, in the *practical* sense we always have to "take pains to have a clear conscience toward both God and man" (Acts 24:16; cf. Rom. 13:5; 1 Cor. 8:7–12; 10:28). "The aim of our charge is love that issues from a pure heart and a good conscience and a sincere faith" (1 Tim. 1:5; cf. v. 19). If we do not walk in the way of the Lord, our conscience will accuse us again!

Some might be amazed about the Catechism's strong language: have we really sinned against *all* God's commandments? Have we really never kept any of them? Listen to James: "[W]hoever keeps the whole law but fails in one point has become accountable for all of it. For he who said, 'Do not commit adultery,' also said, 'Do not murder.' If you do not commit adultery but do murder, you have become a transgressor of the law" (2:10–11). You might also object that you have never killed anyone, and have never committed adultery. But Jesus made clear that even if you are angry with your brother, and insult him, you are guilty of the sixth commandment (Matt. 5:21–26). And "everyone who looks at a woman with lustful intent has already committed adultery with her in his heart," and is thus guilty of the seventh commandment (v. 28). In this light, who can deny that, by nature, we are guilty of all God's commandments?

You may argue that you, that is, your new self, are *not* "inclined toward all evil" anymore. You are right; Paul says, "[N]ow it is no longer I who do it, but sin that dwells within me" (Rom. 7:17); that is, he clearly distinguishes between his (new) "I" and indwelling sin. Yet, at other places the "I" is the old self: "It is no longer I who live, but Christ who lives in me" (Gal. 2:20). *This* "I," the old self, *always* remains inclined toward all evil!

✵　✵　✵

DAY 193 – CHRIST'S RIGHTEOUSNESS
(Lord's Day 23, Q&A 60, part 3)

A. . . . *nevertheless, without any merit of my own, out of sheer grace, God grants and credits to me the perfect satisfaction, righteousness, and holiness of Christ.*

By his own grace and through the blood of Christ, the *righteous* God has "justified" *me*, that is, has declared *me* to be perfectly righteous. The emphasis on the death and resurrection of Christ is of eminent importance here. My justification cannot for one moment be separated from his person and his work. First, look at the word "satisfaction." We do not find it literally in the Bible with this meaning, but the thought behind it is clearly there. The blood of Christ not only blotted out my sins, but it also gave "satisfaction" to God with respect to his honor and glory that had been violated by my iniquities. As Jesus himself explained, he has not only saved *us*, but he has "glorified" God through his work (John 12:28; 13:31–32; 17:1, 4). God has received so much through Jesus' work that he can now, through his servants, implore people to be reconciled to him (2 Cor. 5:17–20).

Second, God grants and credits me perfect righteousness and holiness, which I can possess only in and through Christ: "[B]ecause of him [or, from him, i.e., God] you are in Christ Jesus, who became to us wisdom from God, righteousness and sanctification and redemption" (1 Cor. 1:30). Jesus *is* my righteousness and holiness, and by faith I myself *am* the "righteousness of God" (2 Cor. 5:21). Jesus was and is the perfectly righteous and holy one (Matt. 27:19, 24; Mark 1:24; Luke 1:35; Acts 3:14; 7:52; 22:14; 1 Pet. 3:18; 1 John 2:1; Rev. 3:7). But now, through my union with him in his death and resurrection, God sees me as just as righteous and holy as Christ himself was and is. My righteousness and holiness derive from the risen Christ.

The prophet Isaiah spoke of the "garments of salvation" and the "robe of righteousness" (61:10). We could say that, in the New Testament, these garments and this robe have received a name: Christ himself is my righteousness. Jeremiah already indicated that the Messiah ("the Branch") would bear the name *Yahweh Tsidkeinu*, "The Lord Is Our Righteousness" (23:5–6; 33:14–16). Jesus Christ is, represents, embodies, all my righteousness and holiness before God.

✦   ✦   ✦

DAY 194 – CHRIST'S OBEDIENCE

(Lord's Day 23, Q&A 60, part 4)

A. . . . God grants and credits to me the perfect satisfaction, righteousness, and holiness of Christ, as if I had never sinned nor been a sinner, and as if I had been as perfectly obedient as Christ was obedient for me.

The obedience of Christ has two distinct, but continuous meanings in the New Testament: he was obedient during his *life*, and he was obedient *unto death*. Both are of great significance for our salvation. First, Jesus was in all things obedient to his Father ("I always do the things that are pleasing to him," John 8:29; cf. 4:34); he "learned obedience through what he suffered" (Heb. 5:8), and his entire life was suffering. At the end of his life, he could have returned to heaven without dying, as the perfect Man, to whom the words, "the wages of sin is death" (Rom. 6:23) did not apply.

Of course, for another reason this was impossible: he had come for the very purpose of honoring God in solving the problem of sin. Not only his deity, but also his perfect life as Man on this earth, made him the single instrument of God that could accomplish this great work of redemption.

So, instead of triumphantly returning to heaven, "he humbled himself by becoming obedient to the point of death, even death on a cross" (Phil. 2:8). He was obedient to the Father's *command* to do so: "For this reason the Father loves me, because I lay down my life that I may take it up again. . . . I have authority to lay it down, and I have authority to take it up again. This *charge* I have received from my Father" (John 10:17–18). "In sacrifice and offering you have not delighted, but you have given me an open ear. Burnt offering and sin offering you have not required. Then I said, 'Behold, I have come; in the scroll of the book it is written of me: I delight *to do your will, O my God*; your law is within my heart' " (Ps. 40:6–8; cf. Heb. 10:5–7).

"Therefore, as one trespass [by Adam] led to condemnation for all men, so one act of righteousness [by Christ] leads to justification and life for all men. For as by the one man's [i.e., Adam's] disobedience the many were made sinners, so by the one man's [i.e., Christ's] obedience the many will be made righteous" (Rom. 5:18–19). Christ was obedient for disobedient sinners, so that disobedient sinners could become obedient servants of God!

✤   ✤   ✤

DAY 195 – ACCEPT IN FAITH

(Lord's Day 23, Q&A 60, part 5)

A. . . . All I need to do is accept this gift with a believing heart.

Can we "do" anything to contribute to our salvation? This is not the way we should understand the word "do" in the Catechism's answer. This doing is not a merit, nor an achievement. If someone who is drowning grabs a rope, is that an achievement? If someone jumps out of a burning house into a safety net, is that a merit? If someone who has a health problem runs to the doctor, is that a good work? This is what faith is. I am in a train that is on its way to an abyss, and by God's grace I am enabled to jump from it. I am in a dark and awful prison, but the Holy Spirit opens my eyes to the one narrow way out. Faith is seizing this one opportunity, this only way out, escaping through the only little window. There is nothing meritorious about it.

Some people object to the word "accept"; they argue that faith is a gift of God, and quote Ephesians 2:8 (rightly or wrongly) in support of their view. They forget that eating and drinking, wealth and possessions are also gifts of God (Eccl. 3:13; 5:19)—and they never seem to hesitate to "accept" these gifts. They are for you! Stretch out your hands, and say "Thank you"! "[T]hose that were sown on the good soil are the ones who hear the word and *accept* it and bear fruit, thirtyfold and sixtyfold and a hundredfold" (Mark 4:20). "[T]o all who believed him and *accepted* him, he gave the right to become children of God" (John 1:12 NLT). "You became imitators of us and of the Lord when you *accepted* the message that came from the Holy Spirit with joy in spite of great suffering" (1 Thess. 1:6 CEB). "[W]e also thank God constantly for this, that when you received the word of God, which you heard from us, you *accepted* it not as the word of men but as what it really is, the word of God, which is at work in you believers" (2:13). "The saying is trustworthy and deserving of full *acceptance*, that Christ Jesus came into the world to save sinners" (1 Tim. 1:15; cf. 4:9).

This is what faith is. You are in an emergency situation, God stretches out a safety net to you, and you gladly and thankfully accept it with a believing heart, and praise him for it!

❖   ❖   ❖

DAY 196 – THROUGH FAITH ALONE
(Lord's Day 23, Q&A 61, part 1)

Q. Why do you say that through faith alone you are righteous?
A. Not because I please God by the worthiness of my faith.

The questions and answers are a bit repetitive here, apparently because of the importance of the subject. Justification is *only* by the grace of God, it is *only* through the redemptive work of Christ, and it is *only* by faith. Yesterday we saw that this faith is no good work, no merit, no achievement. Therefore, it is good to pay some attention to the difference between the word "by" in the expression "by grace," and the word "by" in the expression "by faith." The two are definitely not the same. (The Greek language has a variety of prepositions at its disposal to express the differences.) Justification is *by* the grace of God. This grace is very active: it is God who in his grace brings about this justification. *He* justifies us. Justification is also *by* faith, but this faith is just passive, just receptive. In faith we beggingly stretch out our hands in order to have them filled by God.

God's grace is the active giver, our faith is just the passive receiver. Therefore, it would be a big mistake to speak of the "worthiness" of someone's faith, as if the person had achieved or accomplished something. Look at Abraham in Genesis 15: God is very active in promising to Abraham, and encouraging Abraham. Abraham only passively surrenders to God's promises, or rather, to God himself; this is called "faith" (v. 6). It is God doing everything for Abraham, whereas Abraham can do nothing but throw himself in the arms of God. Or think of Habakkuk, complaining and protesting to God. God explains to him that "the righteous shall live by his faith" (Hab. 2:4; cf. Rom. 1:17; Gal. 3:11; Heb. 10:38). It is as if God says, Just trust me, Habakkuk, I am in control, you don't have to worry. This trust, this confidence, will be the secret of your spiritual life, as it is that of *all* the righteous.

Such a trust is no worthy achievement—we simply have nowhere else to go! We have no other choice than to trust God, for our life down here, and for eternity. Faith is confidence, surrender, commitment. Not a "leap in the dark" but a leap into God's arms. It is the best thing a person could ever do!

✤ ✤ ✤

DAY 197 – CHRIST'S SATISFACTION
(Lord's Day 23, Q&A 61, part 2)

A. . . . It is because only Christ's satisfaction, righteousness, and holiness make me righteous before God.

We might say that there are three ways of being righteous. First, a person could be intrinsically righteous in the eyes of God. This has been true of only three humans: Adam and Eve before the Fall, and Jesus Christ. Second, a person can be *made* righteous (justified) by identification with Christ on the basis of his redemptive work. Such a person is then righteous in the eyes of God, his "new self" is righteous (Eph. 4:24), whereas the "flesh" (the sinful nature) is still in him, which is not righteous, and never will be. Third, a person can have been justified (declared righteous) by God, and set free of the old nature. This is the case with believers after physical death, or perhaps we should say, in the resurrection.

The first and the third categories refer to people who are positionally and practically righteous, whereas the second category refers to one who is positionally righteous, but practically not always. The first category identifies one who is righteous from the start, the second and third categories identify one who has been *made* righteous, by an act of God's redemptive grace, and through the blood of Jesus. This justification is closely associated with the righteousness of Christ himself: first, the righteousness of his life and walk on earth, which made him the right person to accomplish the work of redemption. Second, on the cross he himself was the righteous one. It is Jesus Christ the *righteous* who became the propitiation for our sins (1 John 2:1–2). It is Jesus Christ the *righteous* who died for the unrighteous that he might bring us to God (1 Pet. 3:18).

Third, Jesus Christ was the righteous one in his resurrection, and through his death and resurrection he could share his righteousness with us: he died for our trespasses and was raised in view of our justification (cf. Rom. 4:25–5:1). As the risen one he was "judicially free" from sin, that is, he had nothing to do with the problem of sin anymore (cf. Rom. 6:7). And so it is with us: being identified with Christ in his death *and* in his resurrection, we are "judicially free" from the problem of sin. Because we are "in Christ" God sees us as just as righteous as Jesus himself.

✤　✤　✤

DAY 198 – ACCEPTING THIS RIGHTEOUSNESS
(Lord's Day 23, Q&A 61, part 3)

A. . . . I can accept this righteousness and make it mine in no other way than through faith.

Notice here that people are said to be *able* to accept God's righteousness and make it theirs! Indeed, never belittle the responsibility of humans to do this: they are *commanded* to repent (Acts 17:30); faith is a matter of *obedience* (Rom. 1:5; 16:26). It would be cruel of God to command people to do something if, in fact, they would not be able to do so (albeit in God's strength only). God says, "Accept your righteousness in Christ!", and you respond by accepting it (cf. Mark 4:20; John 1:12; 1 Thess. 1:6; 2:13; 1 Tim. 1:15). And yet, what true believer would not say afterward, It was God's grace that the gospel came to me, and that he opened my eyes to it, and that I took the step to repent and to accept the gospel! "For by grace you have been saved through faith. And this is not your own doing; it is the gift of God" (Eph. 2:8).

There is another important point here. As far as our responsibility is concerned, we are justified by faith, and by nothing else. However, not all faith is true faith. James (2:19) says, "You believe that God is one; you do well. Even the demons believe—and shudder!" In other words, not all faith is *saving* faith (because no demon will ever be saved). First, true faith is connected with *repentance*. For how could you throw yourself in God's arms to be declared righteous by him if you would not first repent of your *un*righteousnesses?

Second, true faith is accepting Christ not only as Savior but also as Lord (Rom. 10:9), with the implication that you accept him as the Master of the rest of your life. For how could you throw yourself in God's arms to be declared righteous by him if you would not be prepared to lead a life, from now on, of dedication and obedience to the Lord, that is, a righteous life in the power of the Holy Spirit? "[N]o one speaking in the Spirit of God . . . can say 'Jesus is Lord' except in the Holy Spirit" (1 Cor. 12:3). "In [Christ] you also, when you heard the word of truth, the gospel of your salvation, and believed in him, were sealed with the promised Holy Spirit" (Eph. 1:13).

✵ ✵ ✵

DAY 199 – OUR "GOOD" WORKS
(Lord's Day 24, Q&A 62, part 1)

Q. *Why can't our good works be our righteousness before God, or at least a part of our righteousness?*
A. *Because the righteousness which can pass God's judgment must be entirely perfect and must in every way measure up to the divine law.*

The Bible speaks of human "works" in three ways. First, there are evil works (John 3:19), works of darkness (Rom. 13:12; Eph. 5:11), etc. Second, there are "dead works" (Heb. 6:1; 9:14). I take these to be works that in themselves may be of benefit to others, and as such may have a certain value in God's providence; but they have no value for eternity. Third, in the Bible the term "good works" is sometimes used only for the works done by believers in the power of the Holy Spirit (see, e.g., Matt. 5:16; Acts 9:36; Heb. 10:24). Believers have been "created in Christ Jesus for good works, which God prepared beforehand, that we should walk in them" (Eph. 2:10). Christ "gave himself for us to redeem us from all lawlessness and to purify for himself a people for his own possession who are zealous for good works" (Titus 2:14).

These good works are a vital and essential part of Christian life! They are the fruits that prove the believer to have a renewed heart, and to live by the power of the Holy Spirit. No believer will ever be saved without such good works. Please note, these works can never be the *ground*, or even *part* of the ground for our salvation (cf. Rom. 3:27–28; 9:32; Gal. 2:16; 3:2, 5). But it is equally true that they must be the necessary *fruits* of our salvation. *This* is what James meant when he said, "What good is it, my brothers, if someone says he has faith but does not have works? Can that faith save him? . . . So also faith by itself, if it does not have works, is dead. . . . You see that a person is justified by works and not by faith alone" (2:14, 17, 24). We are justified (shown to be righteous) by works in the sense that these works testify of God's work in us.

People often ask, But what about the criminal on the cross? He was saved without having the time to bring forth fruit! But notice: first, he recognized that judgment was rightly upon him; second, he gave a good testimony of Jesus; third, he acknowledged Jesus as the Messiah; and fourth, he committed himself to Jesus for his own future. This man clearly exhibited the fruits of the new life that was in him!

❖   ❖   ❖

DAY 200 – IMPERFECT WORKS
(Lord's Day 24, Q&A 62, part 2)

A. . . . the righteousness which can pass God's judgment must be entirely perfect and must in every way measure up to the divine law. But even our best works in this life are imperfect and stained with sin.

The works that we did as unbelievers can never be acceptable to God, not even in the smallest measure. But the works that we did, and do, as believers cannot as such contribute to our salvation either. At best they are the necessary and indispensible *fruit* of our salvation. The reason why our good works cannot "be our righteousness before God, or at least a part of our righteousness" is that they are "imperfect and stained with sin." God is pleased with them just as parents are pleased with the weak and fallible attempts of their little children to do good. But the acts of such children cannot meet the parents' standards; the little ones have to grow up to this end. Similarly, we will be a perfect pleasure to the Father only when we will be with him in glory. Until that time, "even our best works in this life are imperfect and stained with sin." Therefore, we must be thankful that God does not make our eternal salvation dependent on the works that we do even as dedicated believers!

Usually, people refer here to the well-known verse in Isaiah 64:6, "[A]ll our righteous deeds are like a polluted garment." It goes without saying that all our *unrighteous* (wicked) deeds are like a polluted garment—but the prophet says this here of our *righteous* deeds. God has "made perfect those who draw near" (Heb. 10:1), but that only means that the believer has received a cleansed conscience (cf. vv. 2, 22). Paul says, "Not that I . . . am already perfect, but I press on . . ." (Phil. 3:12). The only "perfection" we may have as believers is *maturation*; in the same context, Paul speaks of "those of us who are mature" (v. 15). In Greek, Paul uses the same word for "perfect" and "mature." We *have* a perfect conscience, and we *are* on our way to eternal perfection. In the meantime, we may reach maturity, which, in Paul's thinking, is also a form of "perfection," but *not* in the sense of sinlessness. We will be sinless only when we will have laid down the present body to which the sinful nature is still attached. In the meantime, even our best works could never contribute to our salvation.

❖   ❖   ❖

DAY 201 – PROMISED REWARD

(Lord's Day 24, Q&A 63, part 1)

Q. How can our good works be said to merit nothing when God promises to reward them in this life and the next?
A. This reward is not earned; it is a gift of grace.

This is quite an interesting question. First, the Catechism told us that "even our best works in this life are imperfect and stained with sin" (previous Q&A); now it tells us that God promises to reward our good works. Is there a contradiction here? No. This is explained in the following way. First, the term "reward" is relativized in that we are told that this "reward is not earned; it is a gift of grace" (this Q&A). Yet, we have to take the term "reward" seriously, and this we do by stressing our responsibility as believers: we should not become indifferent and wicked by neglecting this responsibility of ours. On the contrary, we not only must produce fruits of gratitude, but such fruits will be the automatic result of being grafted into Christ (Q&A 64).

So rewards are due to God's grace, and they are only natural for a believer—yet, they are rewards. On the one hand, Jesus said, "So you also, when you have done all that you were commanded, say, 'We are unworthy servants; we have only done what was our duty'" (Luke 17:10). On the other hand, a little later he said in the parable of the ten minas, "The first came before him, saying, 'Lord, your mina has made ten minas more.' And he said to him, 'Well done, good servant! Because you have been faithful in a very little, you shall have authority over ten cities'" (19:16–17).

Elsewhere Jesus said, "Rejoice and be glad, for your reward is great in heaven" (Matt. 5:12). And a little later: "[W]hen you give to the needy, do not let your left hand know what your right hand is doing, so that your giving may be in secret. And your Father who sees in secret will reward you. . . . [W]hen you pray, go into your room and shut the door and pray to your Father who is in secret. And your Father who sees in secret will reward you. . . . [W]hen you fast, anoint your head and wash your face, that your fasting may not be seen by others but by your Father who is in secret. And your Father who sees in secret will reward you" (6:3–6, 16–18). You see? God is good! We just do what is our duty, and yet, God rewards us.

✤   ✤   ✤

DAY 202 – REWARDED BY GRACE
(Lord's Day 24, Q&A 63, part 2)

A. [Our] reward is not earned; it is a gift of grace.

Hebrews 11 says, "[W]hoever would draw near to God must believe that he exists and that he *rewards* those who seek him" (Heb. 11:6). Jesus said, "[W]hoever gives you a cup of water to drink because you belong to Christ will by no means lose his *reward*" (Mark 9:41). "Love your enemies, and do good, and lend, expecting nothing in return, and your *reward* will be great" (Luke 6:35). Paul said, "If the work that anyone has built on the foundation [of Christ] survives, he will receive a *reward*" (1 Cor. 3:14); ". . . knowing that from the Lord you will receive the inheritance as your *reward*. You are serving the Lord Christ" (Col. 3:24). And John said, "Watch yourselves, so that you may not lose what we have worked for, but may win a full *reward*" (2 John 1:8). And: "[T]he time for the dead to be judged, and for *rewarding* your servants, the prophets and saints, and those who fear your name" (Rev. 11:18).

The New Testament speaks a lot about rewards for believers, especially if we also include the references to "wreaths" and "crowns" (1 Cor. 9:25; 2 Tim. 4:8; James 1:12; 1 Pet. 5:4; Rev. 2:10; 3:11; 4:4, 10). The Catechism brings to light a remarkable situation. It is a pure gift of divine grace if we accomplish things that deserve a reward; and it is a pure gift of divine grace if God indeed "promises to reward [such acts] in this life and the next." The underlying problem is the complicated relationship between God's sovereign grace and human responsibility. We have been "created in Christ Jesus for good works, which God prepared beforehand, that we should walk in them" (Eph. 2:10). Christ "gave himself for us to redeem us from all lawlessness and to purify for himself a people for his own possession who are zealous for good works" (Titus 2:14). So it is nothing but our *duty* and *calling* to do good works. Yet, *if* we do them, we find out that it is God's grace that we were enabled to do them. On the one hand, he says, Do them and I will reward you. On the other hand, he says, "[A]part from me you can do nothing" (John 15:5). We will always have to live with this tension!

✳   ✳   ✳

DAY 203 – NO INDIFFERENCE
(Lord's Day 24, Q&A 64, part 1)

Q. But doesn't this teaching make people indifferent and wicked?
A. No.

There is indeed a definite danger of certain Christians arguing as follows: "I have been saved by God's grace, I have been justified by faith, and there is no power in the world that can snatch me out of Jesus' hand and out of the Father's hand (John 10:27–29). So why should I perform good works? What could they add to my salvation? Without good works I will be saved anyway. *Good works are not necessary.*" Indeed, even some Reformed theologians have argued this way. They claim that it is a heresy if we say that one is not simply saved by faith, but saved by faith-producing-good-works. They say that this is nothing but the old Roman Catholic heresy in some new disguise. Good works are being smuggled in again! They assert that this is against the spirit of the Reformation, which always proclaimed that justification is *by faith alone*, and that works have no place in this whatsoever.

How good it is that the Catechism is not disturbed at all by this kind of false reasoning! As strongly as it emphasizes that good works do not contribute anything to our salvation as such, just as strongly does it underscore that good works are a natural *result* of faith, and that otherwise this faith is not true Christian faith at all. To be sure, we are justified by faith alone. But this must be a true Christian faith. And this is a "faith working through love" (Gal. 5:6). "[F]aith by itself, if it does not have works, is dead. . . . I will show you my faith by my works. . . . [F]aith was active along with his [i.e., Abraham's] works, and faith was completed by his works" (James 2:17–18, 22).

Would anyone claim that we are justified "by faith alone," but that it does not matter what faith this is? Can a person be saved by a *dead* faith (James 2:17, 26)? When Jesus "was in Jerusalem at the Passover Feast, many believed in his name when they saw the signs that he was doing. But Jesus on his part did not entrust himself to them, because he knew all people and needed no one to bear witness about man, for he himself knew what was in man" (John 2:23–25). Can any be saved by *this* kind of faith?

✦ ✦ ✦

DAY 204 – IMPOSSIBLE NOT TO BEAR FRUIT
(Lord's Day 24, Q&A 64, part 2)

A. . . . . It is impossible for those grafted into Christ through true faith not to produce fruits of gratitude.

It is impossible that a good tree would not produce good fruits: "For no good tree bears bad fruit, nor again does a bad tree bear good fruit. . . . For figs are not gathered from thornbushes, nor are grapes picked from a bramble bush. The good person out of the good treasure of his heart produces good, and the evil person out of his evil treasure produces evil, for out of the abundance of the heart his mouth speaks" (Luke 6:43–45). It is impossible that a good apple tree would produce plums, or no fruit at all. It is impossible that a typical beaver would not build a dam, or that an average bird would not build a nest in springtime. That would simply be unnatural.

The idea of grafting is taken from Romans 11:16–24. Wild olive shoots are grafted into a cultivated olive tree, "and now share in the nourishing root of the olive tree" (v. 17). A similar image is found in John 15: "I am the true vine, and my Father is the vinedresser. Every branch in me that does not bear fruit he takes away, and every branch that does bear fruit he prunes, that it may bear more fruit. . . . As the branch cannot bear fruit by itself, unless it abides in the vine, neither can you, unless you abide in me. . . . Whoever abides in me and I in him, he it is that bears much fruit, for apart from me you can do nothing. . . . By this my Father is glorified, that you bear much fruit and so prove to be my disciples" (vv. 1–8).

There are three kinds of branches here. First, those without any fruit. Such branches apparently do not receive the juices of life from the vine; they are dead. Second, there are branches with the life of the vine in them, but there is only little fruit. Such a branch needs the vinedresser to prune it, "that it may bear more fruit." Third, there are branches that bear "much fruit." But the pivotal point is this: you are either "grafted into Christ," and then it is impossible to bear no fruit. Or you are not (properly) "grafted into him"; then you are a worthless branch, ready to be burnt. There is a tremendous difference between a little fruit and no fruit. The former points to life, the latter to death!

❖　　❖　　❖

DAY 205 – FRUITS OF GRATITUDE
(Lord's Day 24, Q&A 64, part 3)

A. ... It is impossible for those grafted into Christ through true faith not to produce fruits of gratitude.

It is impossible for a true Christian *not* to produce spiritual fruit: "[N]ow that you have been set free from sin and have become slaves of God, the fruit you get leads to sanctification and its end, eternal life" (Rom. 6:22). Christ "has been raised from the dead, in order that we may bear fruit for God" (7:4). "[T]he fruit of the Spirit is love, joy, peace, patience, kindness, goodness, faithfulness, gentleness, self-control" (Gal. 5:22–23). We must be "filled with the fruit of righteousness that comes through Jesus Christ, to the glory and praise of God" (Phil. 1:11). We must "walk in a manner worthy of the Lord, fully pleasing to him, bearing fruit in every good work" (Col. 1:10).

The fruit of a tree comes naturally. But every image fails in the end. It is natural for apple trees to produce apples, but you could never refer to them as "apples of gratitude." Apples do not know any thankfulness toward the tree—but believers do. Their spiritual fruits are the "natural" products of their faith, but they are not "automatic." There is a strong motivation behind them. They are produced out of gratitude, even as acts of praise and worship. "So, whether you eat or drink, or whatever you do, do all to the glory of God" (1 Cor. 10:31). "[B]e thankful. Let the word of Christ dwell in you richly, teaching and admonishing one another in all wisdom, singing psalms and hymns and spiritual songs, with thankfulness in your hearts to God. And whatever you do, in word or deed, do everything in the name of the Lord Jesus, giving thanks to God the Father through him" (Col. 3:15–17).

This is strong language: *everything* you do or say, let it be an act or word of gratitude, to the glory of God! All too often, our good fruits are mixed with rotten fruits. And if you produce bad fruits only, then you cannot even be a true Christian. Among the bad fruits produced by our sinful nature, there *must* be the "fruits of gratitude." It is impossible that a true Christian would *not* produce them. And if they are there, the Father "prunes" us, that we "may bear more fruit" (John 15:2).

✤   ✤   ✤

DAY 206 – THROUGH FAITH ALONE
(Lord's Day 25, Q&A 65, part 1)

Q. It is through faith alone that we share in Christ and all his benefits: where then does that faith come from?
A The Holy Spirit produces it in our hearts by the preaching of the holy gospel.

Of course, the Catechism does not wish to detract at all from our own human responsibility. God *appeals* to our responsibility: "Believe in the Lord Jesus, and you will be saved" (Acts 16:31). God *warns* us if we do not believe: "Whoever believes in the Son has eternal life; whoever does not obey the Son shall not see life, but the wrath of God remains on him" (John 3:36). Believing, then, is a matter of *obedience* to God's appealing; Paul speaks of "the command of the eternal God, to bring about the obedience of faith" (Rom. 16:26; cf. 1:5). God "commands all people everywhere to repent" (Acts 17:30); as Jesus said, "[R]epent and believe in the gospel" (Mark 1:15). If you do this, you will "share in Christ and all his benefits." If you do not do this, you will be lost, and you will only blame yourself for it.

And yet, what true believer would ever boast that his faith was all his own accomplishment? *You* believe; yes, that is true. But would you ever have been able to believe apart from the Holy Spirit? Were you born again by your own power, or by the Holy Spirit (cf. John 3:5; Titus 3:5)? Luke says, "One who heard us was a woman named Lydia. . . . *The Lord opened her heart* to pay attention to what was said by Paul" (Acts 16:14). The Emmaus disciples walked around in the dark. But the Lord came and opened to them the Scriptures, then he opened their eyes, and finally he opened their minds (Luke 24:31–32, 45). Where would they have been without this opening work of the Lord? "[F]aith comes from hearing, and hearing through the word of Christ" (Rom. 10:17; cf. 1 Pet. 1:23–25)—but what if the Lord, through his Holy Spirit, would not open our ears? The Lord said, "He who has an ear, let him hear what the Spirit says to the churches" (Rev. 2:7, 11, 17, 29; 3:6, 13, 22).

We come, then, to this remarkable conclusion: if someone is lost, it is entirely his own fault, and if someone is saved, it is entirely by God's grace. Of course, this is a paradox. But it is one we have to live with, if we do not want to confuse or detract from God's sovereign grace and human responsibility.

✵ ✵ ✵

DAY 207 – THE SACRAMENTS
(Lord's Day 25, Q&A 65, part 2)

A. The Holy Spirit confirms [our faith] by the use of the holy sacraments.

At this point, an entirely new idea is introduced by the Catechism: the Holy Spirit confirms our faith by the use of holy sacraments. Now what is a sacrament? The word does not occur in the Bible, so we have to find out what Christian tradition understands by it. In the next Q&As, the Catechism enters more deeply into this subject, but let me make some introductory remarks here.

The original meaning of the Latin *sacramentum* was the military oath of the young Roman soldier. He pledged his allegiance to his commander and the emperor, and to the Roman gods. The early Christian church adopted this word because the believer testified, once in baptism, and repeatedly in the Lord's Supper, that from now on he belonged to his Savior and Lord, Jesus Christ. In the Latin Bible, the word *sacramentum* was also used for the Christian "mysteries" (e.g., in Eph. 5:32, which gave rise to the Catholic idea of marriage as a sacrament). In Protestantism, the term "sacrament" was restricted to rituals in which material substances were symbolically applied: water in baptism, bread and wine in the Lord's Supper, oil in anointing the sick (Mark 6:13; James 5:14), and in certain consecrations (implicitly perhaps in Acts 6:6; 13:3). Roman Catholicism distinguished seven sacraments, early Protestantism only two (some would say that they ought to have maintained a third one: anointing the sick) (see Q&A 68).

Apart from movements like the Salvation Army and the Quakers, all Protestants have continued to practice water baptism and the Lord's Supper. Some have reduced them to pure symbols—these were those who discarded the term "sacrament" as well—others have maintained that sacraments "do" something to us. God works through them by his Spirit, thereby giving support to our faith, or to our spiritual life in the wider sense. Those who have been baptized (either as infants or as believers) draw great comfort from it because, through it, they, in a very tangible way, know themselves to be grafted into Christ. And what an encouragement the Lord's Supper can give us, as we will see!

✦   ✦   ✦

DAY 208 – SIGNS AND SEALS
(Lord's Day 25, Q&A 66, part 1)

Q. What are sacraments?
A. Sacraments are visible, holy signs and seals. They were instituted
by God so that by our use of them he might make us understand
more clearly the promise of the gospel, and seal that promise.

Sacraments are visible ceremonies that involve visible materials: water, bread, wine (some would add: oil). Sacraments are holy because they come from the holy God, through them God works, and they are for the glory of God. Sacraments are "signs" because they visibly and symbolically "signify" certain spiritual realities, especially the death of Christ: people are baptized into his death (Rom. 6:3–4), and in the Lord's Supper they "proclaim the Lord's death" (1 Cor. 11:26). Of course, the Lord's resurrection is involved in them: ". . . having been buried with [Christ] in baptism, in which you were also raised with him" (Col. 2:12). And as we celebrate the Lord's Supper, the living Lord himself is present in our midst (cf. Matt. 18:20), and we celebrate it "until he comes" (1 Cor. 11:26).

The sacraments are also "seals" because through them God "seals" (confirms) his promises to us. Usually, a parallel is seen here with Old Testament circumcision: "[I]t shall be a sign of the covenant between me and you" (Gen. 17:11). Abraham "received the sign of circumcision as a seal of the righteousness that he had by faith while he was still uncircumcised" (Rom. 4:11). Similarly, baptism is the entrance into the Kingdom of God (Matt. 28:18–19), and thus "seals" to us all the promises of God for those who are subjects in this Kingdom. The Lord's Supper is an expression of the unity of the Body of Christ (1 Cor. 10:16–17, we all eat of the one loaf), and thus "seals" to us all the promises of God for those who are members of this Body. All these promises are together "the promise of the gospel" in the widest sense of this term: the "good message" of God, containing a tremendous variety of blessings for this time and for eternity.

The sacraments were instituted by God, namely, by his Son: Jesus Christ. Jesus instituted the Lord's Supper during the last night of his earthly life (on the occasion of the Passover celebration), and he instituted baptism between his resurrection and his ascension (on the occasion of the Great Commission). They are from him, through him, and for him.

✤   ✤   ✤

DAY 209 – GOD'S PROMISE
(LORD'S DAY 25, Q&A 66, PART 2)

A. . . . And this is God's gospel promise: to grant us forgiveness of sins and eternal life by grace because of Christ's one sacrifice accomplished on the cross.

Both sacraments—baptism and the Lord's Supper—as instituted by Christ on earth, involved God's forgiveness of sins, which constitutes "God's gospel promise." First, baptism is part of the Great Commission (Matt. 28:18–19), which also involves "repentance and forgiveness of sins" (Luke 24:47). Paul received the order, "[B]e baptized and wash away your sins" (Acts 22:16). He himself explains that baptism means leaving behind a life in sin, and embarking upon a life as connected with the risen Lord: "Are we to continue in sin that grace may abound? By no means! How can we who died to sin still live in it? Do you not know that all of us who have been baptized into Christ Jesus were baptized into his death? We were buried therefore with him by baptism into death, in order that, just as Christ was raised from the dead by the glory of the Father, we too might walk in newness of life" (Rom. 6:2–4).

Second, in the Lord's Supper we find a similar connection between the sacrament and divine forgiveness. The broken bread refers to the body of Jesus, "broken" for us (1 Cor. 11:24 NKJV), and the wine refers to the blood of Jesus poured out for us: "[T]his is my blood of the covenant, which is poured out for many for the forgiveness of sins" (Matt. 26:28). Thus, both sacraments refer to the redemptive work of Christ on the cross, and the effects thereof for us.

If we view baptism as the entrance into the Kingdom of God (cf. Matt. 28:18–19), and we remember how eternal life is sometimes linked in the New Testament with the "inheritance" of the Messianic Kingdom (Luke 10:25; 18:18), we understand how the Catechism can link baptism with eternal life. Similarly, the Lord's Supper is linked with the Kingdom: "And he took a cup, and when he had given thanks he said, 'Take this, and divide it among yourselves. For I tell you that from now on I will not drink of the fruit of the vine until the kingdom of God comes'" (Luke 22:17–18). And Paul says, "For as often as you eat this bread and drink the cup, you proclaim the Lord's death *until he comes*" (1 Cor. 11:26).

✦ ✦ ✦

DAY 210 – FOCUSING FAITH
(Lord's Day 25, Q&A 67, part 1)

Q. Are both the word and the sacraments then intended to focus our faith on the sacrifice of Jesus Christ on the cross as the only ground of our salvation?
A. Yes! In the gospel the Holy Spirit teaches us and by the holy sacraments confirms that our entire salvation rests on Christ's one sacrifice for us on the cross.

There is a Chinese proverb telling us that a picture says more than a thousand words. On the one hand, there is the Word of God that we preach. On the other hand, there are the two (or three) "pictures," which tell their own rich story. The gospel tells us, "Believe in the sacrifice of Jesus Christ on the cross as the only ground of our salvation!" Then comes baptism telling us silently, "Through this sacrament you are now being identified with a dead and risen Christ, and his finished redemptive work!" The gospel tells us, "Jesus gave his body and his blood into death for all those who believe." Then comes the Lord's Supper telling us silently, "Look at this bread! It represents to you the body of Christ that was given for you! Look at this cup! It represents to you the blood of Christ that was poured out for you! Take, eat, drink, and rejoice!"

We *hear* the Word of God as preached by preachers, but we *see* the material substances involved in the sacraments. Moreover, we *feel* the water as we are baptized, we *taste* the bread and the wine as we use the Lord's Supper—and some would add, you *feel*, and perhaps even *smell* the oil on your head when you are being anointed (because of illness, or in view of an office). The Word is for the *ears* ("faith comes from hearing, and hearing through the word of Christ," Rom. 10:17), but the sacraments are, if we may say so, for all the other senses. Together they address the *heart*, that is, the total person, by proclaiming the wonderful truth of the gospel. The preacher says, "Our entire salvation rests on Christ's one sacrifice for us on the cross," and the sacraments "say" the same wonderful truth, but without words. Yet, their language is just as explicit.

It is like the silent message of the celestial bodies: "The heavens declare the glory of God, and the sky above proclaims his handiwork. . . . There is no speech, nor are there words, whose voice is not heard. Their voice goes out through all the earth, and their words to the end of the world" (Ps. 19:1, 3–4). We hear no words, yet, there is a clear message!

✳   ✳   ✳

DAY 211 – CHRIST'S ONE SACRIFICE
(Lord's Day 25, Q&A 67, part 2)

A. In the gospel the Holy Spirit teaches us and by the holy sacraments confirms that our entire salvation rests on Christ's one sacrifice for us on the cross.

From the previous Q&As, we might get the impression that the message of the sacraments is mainly negative: it is about the taking away of sins. 1 Peter 3:21 might strengthen this impression: "Baptism . . . now saves you . . . as an appeal to God for a good conscience, through the resurrection of Jesus Christ." Baptism is a silent prayer: it involves the request that I may walk from now on with a "good conscience," that is, a conscience that will never be burdened with sin anymore. This is walking "in newness of life" from the moment of baptism (Rom. 6:4)—and this is an expression that definitely has very positive connotations as well.

Another such positive element is this: "Repent and be baptized . . . and *you will receive the gift of the Holy Spirit*" (Acts 2:38). Ananias' words to Paul contained two parts: "[T]he Lord Jesus . . . has sent me so that you may regain your sight and be *filled with the Holy Spirit* (Acts 9:17), and: "Rise and be baptized and wash away your sins, calling on his name" (22:16). And here is a third very positive aspect of baptism: "[A]s many of you as were baptized into Christ *have put on Christ*" (Gal. 3:27; cf. Rom. 13:14, "[P]ut on the Lord Jesus Christ, and make no provision for the flesh, to gratify its desires"). Not only is the garment of sin taken away—symbolically in baptism—but you are clothed with the garment of Christ.

Similarly, the Lord's Supper contains very positive elements (all resting "on Christ's one sacrifice for us on the cross"): "The bread that we break, is it not a participation in the body of Christ? Because there is one bread, we who are many are one body, for we all partake of the one bread" (1 Cor. 10:16–17). The one bread points not only to the physical body of Christ, which was delivered for us unto death, but also to the mystical Body of Christ, his church. As all believers take little pieces of the bread, they testify thereby that they themselves are little pieces of the Body of Christ. Being conscious of the death of Jesus' physical body, we realize what a privilege it is to belong to his Body, the church!

✤ ✤ ✤

DAY 212 – HOW MANY SACRAMENTS?
(Lord's Day 25, Q&A 68, part 1)

Q. *How many sacraments did Christ institute in the New Testament?*
A. *Two: holy baptism and the holy supper.*

The Bible tells us nowhere that there are precisely two sacraments, just as it does not tell the Catholics that there are seven. The Bible does not even mention the word "sacrament," or a synonymous term. So if we want to determine how many sacraments there are, everything depends on our definition of a sacrament.

The characteristics of a sacrament are as follows. First, it is an institution given by Jesus Christ, in order to be kept by all Christians in all ages. Second, it is an institution that involves certain material substances, such as water, bread, wine, anointing oil. Third, such an institution is not just symbolic. God is present in it with his Holy Spirit; the sacrament *does* something to those who make use of it. It is not the substances themselves that have a certain effect; in other words, they do not work in a magical way. *God* works through them, speaks through them, shows through them his presence and his love. However, they can never *replace* God's Word and God's Spirit; in other words, they borrow their significance from what God's Word and Spirit are doing in and through them, and never work independently of them.

There have been many discussions about whether there were sacraments in the Old Testament, or whether everything in the universe at a certain moment might not have a sacramental character, or whether there are also sacraments in some secondary sense such as preaching, pastoral care, evangelization, worship. Are there not many things that God can use as signs and seals? Or can we say that Christ himself is *the* sacrament as the point of intersection between God and humanity? We will not enter into these controversies here.

Let us keep it simple. What the Catechism refers to is what Protestants generally have accepted as sacraments: baptism and the Lord's Supper. When Jesus said, "This is my body, which is given for you. Do this in remembrance of me" (Luke 22:19; cf. 1 Cor. 11:24–25), he instituted the Lord's Supper. And when he said, "Go . . . and make disciples of all nations, baptizing them . . ." (Matt. 28:19), he instituted baptism.

✦   ✦   ✦

DAY 213 – ANOINTING THE SICK
(Lord's Day 25, Q&A 68, part 2)

Q. How many sacraments did Christ institute in the New Testament?
A. Two: holy baptism and the holy supper.

Before closing this introduction to the sacraments, let us ask one more question. Several theologians have argued that anointing the sick should be called a sacrament just like baptism and the Lord's Supper. Do they have good arguments? Let us look at the characteristics mentioned by the Catechism.

Anointing the sick is visible and holy: it is given by the Lord, for we read that the disciples "cast out many demons and anointed with oil many who were sick and healed them" (Mark 6:13). It is a "sign" that, just like baptism and the Lord's Supper, refers to the death of Christ: "[I]t was our diseases he bore, our pains from which he suffered" (Isa. 53:4 CJB); this refers to literal illnesses: "He took our illnesses and bore our diseases" (Matt. 8:17). Anointing the sick is also a "seal" of the Lord's promises: "[T]hese signs will accompany those who believe: . . . they will lay their hands on the sick, and they will recover" (Mark 16:17–18). "Is anyone among you sick? Let him call for the elders of the church, and let them pray over him, anointing him with oil in the name of the Lord. And the prayer of faith will save the one who is sick, and the Lord will raise him up. And if he has committed sins, he will be forgiven" (James 5:14–15).

These last words show that sickness is sometimes related to forgiveness of sins (in Q&A 66 sacraments are linked with forgiveness). Jesus told the healed invalid: "See, you are well! Sin no more, that nothing worse may happen to you" (John 5:14). Jesus told the paralytic, "Take heart, my son; your sins are forgiven" (Matt. 9:2). James 5 shows that the possibility of sin in the sick person should be investigated. As long as David refused to confess his sins, his "bones wasted away," which points to a physical ailment. But then he did confess, and was healed (Ps. 32).

I do not wish to push this matter any further, but we should be open to the possibility that there are more than two sacraments. We should abandon the notion that the soul is more important than the body. Isaiah 53 shows that even healing is included in the work on the cross!

✦ ✦ ✦

DAY 214 – HOLY BAPTISM
(Lord's Day 26, Q&A 69, part 1)

Q. How does holy baptism remind and assure you that Christ's one sacrifice on the cross benefits you personally?
A. In this way: Christ instituted this outward washing.

In Hebrews 6:2, we find a word that is rendered as "washings" or "baptisms." It indicates the literal meaning of "baptism": a cleansing rite. Ananias told the newly converted Saul, "[B]e baptized and wash away your sins" (Acts 22:16), that is, wash away your sins *through* baptism. It is not baptism as such that intrinsically washes us—as some have asserted—but it refers to the work of Christ through which we are cleansed. Nor is the intention: By faith your sins have been washed away, now you have to testify of this in baptism (as Baptists say). No, it is baptism *itself* that cleanses us, though in a symbolic way. It is baptism that *saves* us (1 Pet. 3:21; cf. Mark 16:16); however, not baptism as such but that to which baptism refers.

This does not mean that every passage about a spiritual "washing" in the New Testament refers to baptism. Roman Catholics believe that a person is re-born when baptized—even as an infant—on the basis of John 3:5 ("born of water and the Spirit") and Titus 3:5 ("the washing of regeneration and renewal of the Holy Spirit"). However, no person, child or adult, is born again by baptism as such, but by the Word of God as applied to the heart and the conscience by the Holy Spirit (see the verses just quoted). As Peter says, "[Y]ou have been born again, not of perishable seed but of imperishable, through the living and abiding *word of God*" (1 Pet. 1:23).

Similarly, Paul says that Christ "sanctifies" his church, "cleansing her by the washing with water *through the word*" (Eph. 5:26 NIV). It reminds us of Jesus' statement: "Already you are clean because of the *word* that I have spoken to you" (John 15:3). This has nothing to do directly with baptism (a sacrament that had not even been instituted yet). It shows us how the *Word* of God, in the power of the Holy Spirit, cleanses us inwardly. However, what we *can* say is that the Word of God, on the one hand, and baptism, on the other, do refer to the same spiritual reality: being brought under all the blessings of Christ's work—through the Word inwardly, and through baptism outwardly.

✦   ✦   ✦

DAY 215 – WASHING AWAY IMPURITY
(Lord's Day 26, Q&A 69, part 2)

A. Christ . . . with [baptism] promised that, as surely as water washes away the dirt from the body, so certainly his blood and his Spirit wash away my soul's impurity, that is, all my sins.

Already the baptism performed by John the Baptist—though differing from Christian baptism—is called "a baptism of repentance for the forgiveness of sins" (Mark. 1:4). Peter told the Jews, "Repent and be baptized every one of you in the name of Jesus Christ for the forgiveness of your sins, and you will receive the gift of the Holy Spirit" (Acts 2:38). We have *inwardly* "died to [the world of] sin," and this was illustrated *outwardly* by being "baptized into Christ Jesus," that is, "baptized into his death" (Rom. 6:2–4). *Inwardly* we have put off "the body of the flesh [i.e., our sinful old self], by the circumcision of Christ [i.e., his redemptive death], having been [*outwardly*] buried with him in baptism" (Col. 2:11–12). "Baptism . . . now saves you, not as a removal of dirt from the body but as an appeal to God for a good conscience," that is, a request to live, from now on, a life without sin (1 Pet. 3:21).

Baptism is not necessary to go to heaven (although some want to read Mark 16:16 and 1 Peter 3:21 this way); what it does is spiritually mark your position before God *on earth*. Christ's blood as applied by the Spirit washes away your "soul's impurity" in rebirth; from a sinner you become a saint. This is an *inward* matter. Water baptism cleanses you *outwardly* in that, before the water grave of baptism (Rom. 6:3–4; Col. 2:11–12), you were one with the world of sinners, but now you are on the side of Christ. Baptism is compared to the Red Sea (1 Cor. 10:1–2): before, you were in "Egypt," the world of sin and devil, now you are in the wilderness, saved from Egypt, following our true "Moses." Baptism is also compared to the flood of Noah (1 Pet. 3:20–21): before, you belonged to the world on which God's judgment rested, now you belong to a new, cleansed world.

Baptism is a real *rite de passage*, as the French call it: a rite through which you pass from the condemned world of sin, the devil, and death to another world: the Kingdom of God, of which Christ is the center (cf. Matt. 28:18–19). The blood of Christ does this inwardly, water baptism does this outwardly.

✤   ✤   ✤

DAY 216 – WASHING AWAY SINS
(Lord's Day 26, Q&A 69, part 3)

A. Christ . . . with [baptism] promised that, as surely as water washes away the dirt from the body, so certainly his blood and his Spirit wash away my soul's impurity, that is, all my sins.

Baptism is not a sign that something *has* happened to you inwardly, which now has to be outwardly expressed, or testified, or affirmed, or confirmed, in baptism. No, in baptism *itself* something happens to you (though outwardly and symbolically). Baptists say, You are saved by faith, so now you have to show this in baptism. No, baptism *itself saves* you (though outwardly and symbolically) (Mark 16:16; 1 Pet. 3:21). Baptists say, Your sins have been washed away, so now you have to affirm this in baptism. No, baptism *itself washes away* your sins (though outwardly and symbolically) (Acts 22:16). Baptists say, You have died with Christ by faith, so now you have to testify of this in baptism. No, baptism *itself* is a burial into the death of Christ (Rom. 6:3–4; Col. 2:11–12). Baptists say, You have put on Christ, so show this now to everybody by being baptized. No, in baptism *itself* a person puts on Christ (though outwardly and symbolically) (Gal. 3:27). For many, this is hard to understand, but it is important enough: every Christian has to answer the question: what *does* baptism do to a person?

Baptists say that, through water baptism, you become a member of the Body of Christ, and quote 1 Corinthians 12:13 in support. However, many expositors believe that this verse does not refer to water baptism but to the baptism of the Spirit (cf. Matt. 3:11; John 1:33; Acts 1:5; 11:16). Literally the text says that people are baptized *in* the Spirit, and thus we read: "[by being baptized] in one Spirit we were all baptized into one body." Just as baptism in the Spirit introduces us into the Body of Christ, baptism in water introduces us into the Kingdom of God. Jesus said, "All authority in heaven and on earth has been given to me. Go *therefore* [that is, in the light of me being the King] and make disciples of all nations, baptizing them in the name of the Father and of the Son and of the Holy Spirit" (Matt. 28:18–19). That is, people become disciples by water baptism. Inwardly they become so by rebirth and faith, outwardly by water baptism. Never confuse these two spiritual realities!

✦ ✦ ✦

DAY 217 – WASHED WITH CHRIST'S BLOOD
(Lord's Day 26, Q&A 70, part 1)

Q. What does it mean to be washed with Christ's blood and Spirit?
A. To be washed with Christ's blood means that God, by grace, has forgiven our sin because of Christ's blood poured out for us in his sacrifice on the cross.

In order to clearly distinguish between the washing with water, as it occurs in baptism, and the washing with the blood of Christ, as it occurs in the moment that our sins are forgiven, the Catechism enters somewhat more deeply into this latter washing. The apostle John tells us about those "coming out of the great tribulation" that they "have washed their robes and made them white in the blood of the Lamb (Rev. 7:14). This is a daring picture! Imagine what happens if you try to wash your clothes in blood! They come out thoroughly red, they are dirtier than they were before, and you will have more trouble making them white than ever. But those who wash their (spiritual) robes in the blood of Christ make them *white*, that is, clean, pure!

In some Greek manuscripts we read about him "who loved us and washed us from our sins in His own blood" (1:5 NKJV). A similar image is that of sprinkling. Peter speaks of "the sanctification of the Spirit, for obedience to Jesus Christ and for sprinkling with his blood" (1 Pet. 1:2), and Hebrews 12 says we have come "to Jesus, the mediator of a new covenant, and to the sprinkled blood that speaks a better word than the blood of Abel" (v. 24; cf. 10:22). Jesus himself spoke of "my blood of the covenant, which is poured out for many for the forgiveness of sins" (Matt. 26:28), and Paul says, "In him we have redemption through his blood, the forgiveness of our trespasses, according to the riches of his grace" (Eph. 1:7); ". . . Christ Jesus, whom God put forward as a propitiation by his blood, to be received by faith" (Rom. 3:24–25); we are "justified by his blood" (5:9). Through Christ, God has made "peace by the blood of his cross" (Col. 1:20).

Some theologians have spoken in a derogatory way of such a "blood theology," which to them is a primitive way of thinking. However, for us it means everything. We believe in the great proclamation of Hebrews 9: "without the shedding of blood there is no forgiveness of sins" (v. 22). You could better dispense with the water of baptism than with the blood of Christ's sacrifice!

✵   ✵   ✵

DAY 218 – WASHED WITH CHRIST'S SPIRIT
(Lord's Day 26, Q&A 70, part 2)

A. . . . To be washed with Christ's Spirit means that the Holy Spirit has renewed and sanctified us to be members of Christ.

The original version of the Catechism does speak in this question about being "washed with the blood and Spirit of Christ," but this apparently means: "washed with the blood of Christ in the power of the Holy Spirit." We cannot speak of being "washed with Christ's Spirit." At best we might speak of being "washed *by* the Spirit"; as Paul says, "[Y]ou were washed . . . in the name of the Lord Jesus Christ and by the Spirit of our God" (1 Cor. 6:11).

We should not confuse the two different biblical images of blood and water: it is said we are washed with the *blood* of Christ when it is a matter of God's holy demands, of satisfaction and propitiation. It is said we are washed with the *water* of the Word when it is a matter of our own conscience and of our testimony to the world, as outwardly expressed in baptism. John summarizes: "This is he who came by water and blood—Jesus Christ; not by the water only but by the water and the blood. And the Spirit is the one who testifies, because the Spirit is the truth. For there are three that testify: the Spirit and the water and the blood; and these three agree" (1 John 5:6–8).

Already the prophet Ezekiel says, "I will sprinkle clean water on you, and you shall be clean from all your uncleannesses, and from all your idols I will cleanse you. And I will give you a new heart, and a new spirit I will put within you. . . . And I will put my Spirit within you, and cause you to walk in my statutes and be careful to obey my rules" (36:25–27).

Jesus told Nicodemus first that he had to be "born again," and then specified: "born of water and the Spirit" (John 3:3, 5). I cannot see how Jesus could possibly speak here of the water of baptism—Christian baptism not being known as yet—and then blame Nicodemus for not understanding these things (v. 10). The "water" may refer here to the Word of God (cf. 15:3; Eph. 5:26), or the meaning simply is: "born of water, namely, the Spirit" (cf. John 7:38–39). Water does not bring about regeneration; it is God's Word in the power of the Holy Spirit that does it.

❖   ❖   ❖

DAY 219 – HOLY AND BLAMELESS LIVES
(Lord's Day 26, Q&A 70, part 3)

A. . . . *renewed and sanctified us to be members of Christ, so that more and more we become dead to sin and live holy and blameless lives.*

Literally speaking, the believer *is* "dead to sin" the moment he is saved. Paul says, "We know that Christ, being raised from the dead, will never die again; death no longer has dominion over him. For the death he died he died to sin, once for all, but the life he lives he lives to God. So you also must consider yourselves dead to sin and alive to God in Christ Jesus" (Rom. 6:9–11). Christ *has* "died to sin," and has nothing to do with the problem of sin anymore. We "have been united with him in a death like his" (v. 5), "our self was crucified with him" (v. 6). So *we* have "died to sin," and thus are not under the power of sin anymore.

However, we do understand the intention of the Catechism. The very fact that Paul has to admonish us that you "must consider yourselves dead to sin," implies that believers had not yet done this, or needed to be reminded of this. And if Paul says that we *have* been "set free from sin" (vv. 7, 18, 22)—we are not under the power of sin anymore—he still has to exhort us: "Let not sin therefore reign in your mortal body, to make you obey its passions . . . present yourselves to God as those who have been brought from death to life, and your members to God as instruments for righteousness. For sin will have no dominion over you, since you are not under law but under grace" (vv. 12–14).

This is the constant tension between what we *are* in Christ (our Christian *position*) and what we practically have to realize (our Christian *practice*). We *are* dead to sin, *and* we have to learn to be "more and more dead to sin" as a practical reality. We *are* holy and blameless the moment we believe (1 Cor. 6:11; Eph. 1:4; Col. 1:22), and we practically have to *learn* to "live holy and blameless lives." Therefore, Peter tells us that we share "in the sanctification of the Spirit" (1 Pet. 1:2), and yet he exhorts us: "[Y]ou also be holy in all your conduct, since it is written, 'You shall be holy, for I am holy'" (vv. 15–16). We "*have* been sanctified" (Heb. 10:10), *and* we have to *strive* for holiness (12:14). This remains true as long as we dwell on this earth.

❖ ❖ ❖

219

DAY 220 – INSTITUTION OF BAPTISM
(Lord's Day 26, Q&A 71, part 1)

Q. Where does Christ promise that we are washed with his blood and Spirit as surely as we are washed with the water of baptism?
A. In the institution of baptism, where he says: "Go therefore and make disciples of all nations, baptizing them in the name of the Father and of the Son and of the Holy Spirit."

This is an exceptional situation in the Catechism: it asks for biblical proof! Of course, everything it says is intended to be in full agreement with the Bible (as far as this is given to fallible humans). Therefore, the Catechism supplies us with Bible references all the time, to underpin what it states. It is all the more remarkable that, here in the question itself, the Catechism asks about "where Christ promises that we are washed with his blood and Spirit as surely as we are washed with the water of baptism." As is so often the case, of course, there is no direct Bible passage at all where this is explicitly stated. We have to deduce the matter indirectly from various passages. To this end, the Catechism refers to four passages.

The first is Matthew 28:19, "Go therefore and make disciples of all nations, baptizing them in the name of the Father and of the Son and of the Holy Spirit." Now in what sense does the Catechism see in this verse a proof "that we are washed with his blood and Spirit as surely as we are washed with the water of baptism"? Remember that the word "baptism" itself means a "(ritual) washing" (Heb. 6:1; cf. 9:10). Jesus is in fact saying this: Make people disciples of me by washing them with water in the name of the Triune God! This is the *outward* aspect of the matter. Outwardly, one becomes a disciple of Christ by water baptism. At the same time, we know that someone becomes *inwardly* a disciple of Jesus by the washing with his blood, as we have seen in previous Q&As.

Please note that in both aspects of the washing, the Holy Spirit is involved. When someone is baptized, it is done in the name of the Holy Spirit (in addition to that of the Father and the Son). The baptized person is placed under the authority of the Spirit. And when someone is justified by faith, we think of Jesus' words: "born of water and the Spirit," which possibly means, "born of water, namely, the Spirit" (John 3:5; cf. 7:38–39). And Peter speaks of "the sanctification of the Spirit, for obedience to Jesus Christ and for sprinkling with his blood" (1 Pet. 1:2).

❋   ❋   ❋

DAY 221 – FAITH AND BAPTISM
(Lord's Day 26, Q&A 71, part 2)

A. . . . *"The one who believes and is baptized will be saved; but the one who does not believe will be condemned."*

The second Bible verse that the Catechism refers to is Mark 16:16. This verse is often quoted by Baptists to prove that a person should first believe before he can be baptized, but that is not the point here. The verse is not at all about the order of faith and baptism. The point is rather that faith and baptism are *two sides of the same coin*. Faith and baptism are both said here to *save* a person, but they do so in different ways. Faith saves a person *inwardly*, and in view of *eternity*. Baptism saves a person *outwardly*, and in view of his position here on earth. (Please note that, when the Lord speaks of condemnation, he speaks only of "not believing," *not* of "not being baptized.")

Similarly, Peter tells us that baptism "saves" a person (1 Pet. 3:21), but this cannot be in view of eternity; no one can be eternally saved by baptism as such. The point is rather that one is "saved" by baptism as Noah and his family were "saved" by the flood (v. 20). The flood brought them from the old world of sin and death to a new world of God's grace, based on the sacrifice (Gen. 8:20–21). Similarly, baptism brings a person, away from the rule of Satan, under the rule of Christ, and this is a "safe place," where God's Word and Spirit reign. Jesus has received all power in heaven and on earth, and when people are baptized they are brought under this authority, and have to learn there all that the Lord has commanded (Matt. 28:18–19).

This is the Kingdom of God in the present age; it is the domain where Christ rules, and where people are taught to follow and serve him. *This* is why we love to bring our children into the "safe place" of this Kingdom of God's blessings when they are young: "Let the children come to me; do not hinder them, for to such belongs the kingdom of God" (Mark 10:14). "Fathers, do not provoke your children to anger, but bring them up in the discipline and instruction of the Lord" (Eph. 6:4). In this sense, the children are "holy" because of the believing parent(s) (1 Cor. 7:14). They are in the safe haven where God's Word is heard and the Spirit is working!

✤   ✤   ✤

DAY 222 – WATER OF REBIRTH

(Lord's Day 26, Q&A 71, part 3)

A. . . . *This promise is repeated when Scripture calls baptism "the water of rebirth" and the washing away of sins.*

Here are the third and the fourth Bible passages to which the Cate-chism refers. Paul says, God "saved us, not because of works done by us in righteousness, but according to his own mercy, by the washing of regeneration [or, the water of rebirth] and renewal of the Holy Spirit" (Titus 3:5). It is questionable whether Paul speaks here literally of baptism because no one of us is regenerated by baptism as such. Moreover, if Paul speaks here of being "saved" in connection with the "renewal of [that is, by] the Holy Spirit," he apparently speaks of *inward* salvation. This is what Peter calls "the salvation of your souls" (1 Pet. 1:9). Thus, the washing is the *inward* washing, to which Paul refers: "[Y]ou were washed, you were sanctified, you were justified in the name of the Lord Jesus Christ and by the Spirit of our God" (1 Cor. 6:11).

At the same time, we can certainly say that baptism is the *outward counterpart* of this inward washing. What sense would the inward wash-ing make if there were no outward passing from the world of Satan to the Kingdom of God? But conversely, what sense would such an outward passing make if, at one time or another, there would not be this inward washing, connected with sanctification and justification?

In this context, we now look at the fourth passage to which the Cat-echism refers. Ananias told Paul, "Rise and be baptized and wash away your sins, calling on his [i.e., Jesus'] name" (Acts 22:16). There is no doubt that Ananias means: Be baptized and *thus* wash away your sins (we find a simi-lar construction in Luke 24:26; John 15:8). Baptism washes away our sins *outwardly*, just as regeneration and faith wash away our sins *inwardly*. Until this point, Paul had stood on the side of the enemies of Christ; now he had to *switch his position*. Through baptism, he would publicly leave this domain (the sins that belonged to that life would no longer cleave to him), and move under the rule of Christ. Not only inwardly, but also outwardly he would become a follower of Christ, not just from the moment of his regeneration, but from the moment of his baptism!

✦   ✦   ✦

DAY 223 – OUTWARD WASHING
(Lord's Day 27, Q&A 72, part 1)

Q. Does this outward washing with water itself wash away sins?
A. No, only Jesus Christ's blood and the Holy Spirit cleanse us from all sins.

The Catechism wants to avoid any thought as if baptism, which is an *outward* washing, is in itself able to wash away sins. Catholics do believe that a person is regenerated by water baptism, Protestants do not. Indeed, baptism does save (1 Pet. 3:21; cf. Mark 16:16), but it does so only outwardly. If there is no inward counterpart, a person is lost forever, in spite of his baptism.

Such an outward salvation is quite important, by the way! Many Christians seem to think that the only thing that matters is inward regeneration, faith, or the salvation of the soul (cf. 1 Pet. 1:9). They say that the only thing that matters is their personal relationship with God; other people allegedly have nothing to do with this. Such Christians are mistaken. Your outward position on earth is very important! Do you still stand on the side of God's enemies, or do you publicly stand on the side of Christ? You are either in the kingdom of Satan, or in the Kingdom of God. And the entrance to this Kingdom is baptism (Matt. 28:18–19). Those who are being baptized are brought under the rule of Christ. The Body of Christ contains individual members, but the Kingdom of God contains entire families. If the parents confess to be followers of Christ, they wish to see their entire family on that same ground. The children are holy (set apart) in the parents (cf. 1 Cor. 7:14). The kids are brought "up in the discipline and instruction of the Lord" (Eph. 6:4). They are (outward) "partakers of the Holy Spirit" (Heb. 6:4 NKJV) because they are in the domain where the Holy Spirit is working. What a privilege!

And yet, no child of believing parents is automatically saved for eternity. The outward washing with water is not enough. "[T]he blood of Jesus his Son cleanses us from all sin. . . . If we confess our sins, he is faithful and just to forgive us our sins and to cleanse us from all unrighteousness" (1 John 1:7, 9). Every child, and every adult, needs to make a personal confession of sins in order to receive the forgiveness of sins. Without inward regeneration, the outward rite is of no avail!

✤   ✤   ✤

DAY 224 – INWARD WASHING

(Lord's Day 27, Q&A 72, part 2)

A. . . . only Jesus Christ's blood and the Holy Spirit cleanse us from all sins.

How can we reconcile this statement by the Catechism with Acts 22:16, where Ananias tells Saul of Tarsus to have himself baptized, and thus have his sins washed away? The answer of the Catechism in various successive Q&As is that baptism is an outward washing—which nevertheless has great spiritual significance—whereas in regeneration and by faith we are washed *inwardly* by the blood of Jesus Christ as applied by the Holy Spirit to the person's heart and conscience. The Catechism says this a little more concisely: "only Jesus Christ's blood and the Holy Spirit," but this is the way we have to read this phrase: "only Jesus Christ's blood as applied by the Holy Spirit" (cf. Day 218).

Please notice carefully the combination of these two phrases. The blood of Jesus, poured out almost two thousand years ago, is the *objective* part of our salvation. The application by the Holy Spirit is the *subjective* element; it happens somewhere during our lifetime. The blood is not enough; it needs the working of the Holy Spirit to awaken a person's conscience, make him repent of his sins, bring him to the confession of these sins, and to the acceptance of the redemptive work of Christ in faith. But the Holy Spirit is not enough either; whatever its operations in a person's heart and conscience, it must have a solid and acceptable *foundation* to grant a person God's forgiveness of sins. This foundation is supplied by the blood of Christ, that is, the redemptive work of Christ on the cross.

"[T]he blood of Jesus his Son cleanses us from all sin" (1 John 1:7). Yes, but it does not cleanse *all* people from their sins, only those who truly and honestly confess their sins (v. 9). And it needs the work of the Holy Spirit to bring a person to such a confession. Conversely, we are sanctified by the Spirit (cf. 1 Pet. 1:2), and we were washed, sanctified, and justified by the Spirit of our God (1 Cor. 6:11). Yes, but only if we are spiritually sprinkled with the blood of Christ (see the rest of 1 Pet. 1:2). It is "the Spirit and the water and the blood; and these three agree" (1 John 5:8).

✦ ✦ ✦

DAY 225 – BAPTISM IS WASHING

(LORD'S DAY 27, Q&A 73, PART 1)

Q. Why then does the Holy Spirit call baptism the water of rebirth and the washing away of sins?
A. God has good reason for these words. To begin with, God wants to teach us that the blood and Spirit of Christ take away our sins just as water removes dirt from the body.

This is the sequel to the previous Q&A: "Q. Does this outward washing with water itself wash away sins? A. No, only Jesus Christ's blood and the Holy Spirit cleanse us from all sins. Q. Why then does the Holy Spirit call baptism the water of rebirth and the washing away of sins?" Here again, the Catechism emphasizes the close relationship between the outward sign and the inward spiritual reality. This is quite common with respect to the sacraments. Think of the controversy between Luther and other Protestants about the little word "is" in Jesus' words, "This *is* my body" (Luke 22:19; 1 Cor. 11:24). Catholic transubstantiation, and even Lutheran consubstantiation, go too far into the direction of identifying bread and body, whereas symbolism ("the bread is just a symbol") goes too far to the other extreme. The truth is in between, as we will see.

Similarly, one may wonder how far oil and the Holy Spirit are identified in the anointing of the sick (James 5:14–15). Prophets in the Old Testament were sometimes anointed with oil (1 Kings 19:16); one of them could even say, "The Spirit of the Lord GOD is upon me, *because* the LORD has anointed me" (Isa. 61:1; cf. Acts 10:38). When David was anointed with oil, "the Spirit of the LORD rushed upon David from that day onward" (1 Sam. 16:13). This illustrates how close oil (the matter representing) and the Spirit (the matter represented) are related, already in the Old Testament.

Similarly, the outward sign (baptism) and the inward spiritual reality are very close because baptism is not just a "symbol" of something. God himself meets us in baptism, and accepts us as no longer belonging to "the evil world"; he welcomes us in the company of Christ's followers. The Catechism emphasizes the *distinction* between baptism ("representing" rebirth and the washing away of sins) and rebirth, the washing away of sins, as such, which is accomplished by the blood of Christ (Rom. 3:24; 5:9; Rev. 1:5; 7:14). But it also emphasizes the spiritual reality of baptism itself. It is God stretching out his hand to the person baptized.

❄   ❄   ❄

DAY 226 – WASHED OF OUR SINS
(Lord's Day 27, Q&A 73, part 2)

A. . . . *But more important, God wants to assure us, by this divine pledge and sign, that we are as truly washed of our sins spiritually as our bodies are washed with water physically.*

A "pledge" is a beautiful term for baptism. It corresponds with terms such as "earnest," "guarantee," "down payment," "deposit," which we find in various translations (2 Cor. 1:22; 5:5; Eph. 1:14). God promises or guarantees us certain things in baptism. He speaks, as it were, through the sign of baptism, saying, "As surely as this water physically washes your body and takes away the dirt, just as surely the blood of Christ spiritually washes your soul and takes away your sins, *if only* you honestly confess them before me, and entrust yourself to the accomplished work of Christ."

As surely as the ark of Noah transferred Noah and his family from the old world of sin, the devil, and death to a new world, based on the sacrifice (1 Pet. 3:20–21), just as surely does baptism transfer a person from the rule of Satan to the rule of Christ in the Kingdom of God. As surely as Israel went through the Red Sea—being "baptized into Moses in the cloud and in the sea" (1 Cor. 10:1–2)—and thus left Egypt, a picture of the world of sin, the devil, and death, just as surely does baptism transfer a person from this old world to the "wilderness," and in the end to the promised Canaan (the Messianic Kingdom).

However, notice that, as we have to assume, not all members of Noah's family were saved, although they had all been in the ark. Similarly, not all those who went through the Red Sea were necessarily saved: "God was not pleased with most of them; their bodies were scattered in the wilderness" (1 Cor. 10:5). No person who was baptized will be saved for eternity if there is not the concomitant work in the soul by the blood of Christ and the Spirit of God. You may put on Christ outwardly in baptism (Gal. 3:27), but it is worth nothing if you do not put him on spiritually (Rom. 13:14). You may have been baptized into the death of Jesus (Rom. 6:3–4), but if there is not the inward surrender of faith to the dead and risen Jesus, it will not benefit you eternally. You may have risen outwardly in baptism (Col. 2:12), but if you are not risen with Christ by faith, what is the lasting value of it?

✦ ✦ ✦

DAY 227 – INFANT BAPTISM
(Lord's Day 27, Q&A 74, part 1)

Q. Should infants also be baptized?
A. Yes. Infants as well as adults are included in God's covenant and people, and they, no less than adults, are promised deliverance from sin through Christ's blood and the Holy Spirit who produces faith.

It is highly interesting that the question whether infants should also be baptized comes only at the end of this part of the Catechism—almost as an afterthought. Rightly so. First we had to establish the actual meaning of baptism. Many Christians think that the main issue around baptism is whether we should baptize believers as well as the children of believers, or only believers. But no, the real issue is what baptism *in itself* stands for.

Take the age-old difference of opinion between Reformed paedobaptists and Reformed credobaptists (such as John Bunyan, Charles H. Spurgeon, Joseph C. Philpot, and other Strict Baptists in England). Whatever their differences were, they were all Reformed, they all accepted covenant theology, and assumed a link between the (new) covenant and baptism. Paedobaptists will emphasize the close link, as they see it, between the Abrahamic covenant and the new covenant, and thus refer to, for instance, Genesis 17:7, where God says, "I will establish my covenant between me and you and your offspring after you throughout their generations for an everlasting covenant." Credobaptists, however, will emphasize that the new covenant contains only true believers, and so they baptize only believers: "[T]his is the covenant that I will make with the house of Israel after those days . . . : I will put my law within them, and I will write it on their hearts. And I will be their God, and they shall be my people. And no longer shall each one teach his neighbor and each his brother, saying, 'Know the Lord,' for they shall all know me, from the least of them to the greatest. . . . For I will forgive their iniquity, and I will remember their sin no more" (Jer. 31:33–34; cf. Heb. 8:10–12).

Interestingly, within the Catechism, the covenant, which plays such a great role in Reformed thinking (paedo- and credobaptist), appears only here, and briefly in Q&A 82. Actually, this is quite fitting insofar as in the New Testament, baptism is never explicitly linked with the Abrahamic covenant or the new covenant (I will discuss Acts 2:38–39 and Col. 2:11–12 next).

✤   ✤   ✤

DAY 228 – INCORPORATED INTO THE CHURCH

(Lord's Day 27, Q&A 74, part 2)

A. . . . *Therefore, by baptism, the sign of the covenant, they too should be incorporated into the Christian church and distinguished from the children of unbelievers.*

There can be no doubt that children of believers are part of the Christian community. Jesus said explicitly that the Kingdom of heaven belonged to the little children (Matt. 19:14), that is, the children of believers, for it was they who brought their children to Jesus. Paul says, "[T]he unbelieving husband is made holy because of his wife, and the unbelieving wife is made holy because of her husband. Otherwise your children would be unclean, but as it is, they are holy," that is, set apart (1 Cor. 7:14). Believers do not view their children as pagans until they are saved, but they "bring them up in the discipline and instruction of the Lord" (Eph. 6:4). They deal with them as Christians, until the sad moment when they would turn their backs to the gospel.

For Reformed paedobaptists, such passages supply enough ground for baptizing the children of believers, and understandably so. Reformed credobaptists argue that children are indeed part of the Christian community, but have to make a personal commitment to Christ before they can be baptized. Paedobaptists point to the complete "houses" (households) that were baptized (Acts 16:15, 31–33; 18:8; 1 Cor. 1:16), and that is certainly a strong argument. Credobaptists argue that there is no proof that there were infants in these families. On the contrary, they point out that Crispus "believed in the Lord, together with his entire household" (Acts 18:8). Acts 16:34 is ambiguous: the jailer "rejoiced along with his entire household that he had believed in God" (ESV), or ". . . having believed in God with all his household" (NKJV).

Paedobaptists refer to Acts 2:38–39, where Peter says, "[T]he promise is for you and for your children and for all who are far off, everyone whom the Lord our God calls to himself." They like to think here of the Abrahamic promise; credobaptists instead think of verse 33, which speaks of "the promise of the Holy Spirit." Moreover, "children" does not always mean "infants," they say; often, it simply means "descendants." Paedobaptists see no reason to exclude the infants from "the promise."

✦   ✦   ✦

DAY 229 – CIRCUMCISION AND BAPTISM
(Lord's Day 27, Q&A 74, part 3)

A. . . . This [distinguishing] was done in the Old Testament by circumcision, which was replaced in the New Testament by baptism.

There is undoubtedly a certain parallel between circumcision in the Old Testament, and baptism in the New Testament. The circumcised males of Israel were part of God's people, uncircumcised males were not. Similarly, baptized persons in the New Testament are part of the New Testament people of God, and non-baptized persons are not. Circumcision implied joining God's people then; baptism implies joining God's people now.

I notice, though, that nowadays Reformed theologians have become a little careful in saying that circumcision "was replaced in the New Testament by baptism." It sounds too much like "Israel was replaced by the church"—as if there would be no future for ethnic Israel as such in the counsel of God. This doctrine is called supersessionism or replacement theology. Since the seventeenth century many Reformed theologians did accept a literal interpretation of the biblical prophecies, and believed in a future for ethnic Israel in its own land.

We cannot pursue this interesting subject here any further. Let us instead look at the passage that is always quoted when a link between baptism and the covenant is sought: Colossians 2:11–12. Paul says, In Christ "you were circumcised with a circumcision made without hands, by putting off the body of the flesh, by the circumcision of Christ, having been buried with him in baptism, in which you were also raised with him." Paedobaptists argue that this passage says that we have been "circumcised" in the sense that we were baptized. Baptism is the new word for "circumcision," so to say. Credobaptists will object that Paul speaks here of circumcision *not* as an outward ritual but as an *inward* spiritual work: the "circumcision of Christ" (his work on the cross, in which he underwent God's judgment on the "flesh") is applied to us on account of faith. Baptism is the *outward counterpart* of this. If the inward "circumcision" is on account of faith, then baptism as well, they argue.

Both parties seem to have strong arguments at their disposal. Will the ongoing, often heated controversy on this matter ever die here on earth?

✢   ✢   ✢

DAY 230 – THE HOLY SUPPER
(Lord's Day 28, Q&A 75, part 1)

*Q. How does the holy supper remind and assure you that you share
in Christ's one sacrifice on the cross and in all his benefits?
A. In this way: Christ has commanded me and all believers to eat
this broken bread and to drink this cup in remembrance of him.*

This sacrament involves a spiritual place (the Lord's table; 1 Cor. 10:21), where we have the meal, and the meal itself, called the Lord's Supper (1 Cor. 11:20), or the Last Supper (because it was the last meal Jesus had with his disciples before he died), or the Holy Supper. The Catechism reminds us of the very first meaning of the Holy Supper: we eat the bread and drink the wine "in remembrance of *him*" (Luke 22:19; 1 Cor. 11:24–25). We do not primarily commemorate our salvation when celebrating the Lord's Supper, it is not primarily "Christ's one sacrifice on the cross and all his benefits" that stand before us, but *Christ himself.* When a person is baptized, it is in view of *Christ*, under whose authority the person is brought. When a person takes part in the Holy Supper, it is *Christ* who stands primarily before him. (We may add: when a sick person is anointed with oil, it is *Christ* under whose healing power the person is brought.)

We see this especially in Christ's own words of institution concerning baptism (Matt. 28:18–19). He says as it were, "I am the King; go therefore, and baptize people into this King (cf. Rom. 6:3; Gal. 3:27), or, in the name of this King (cf. Acts 2:38; 8:16; 10:48; 19:5)." In baptism, you are *added to Christ.* Similarly he says as it were (1 Cor. 11:24–25), "This bread represents my body, which is given for you; every time you eat it, think of *me*; this cup represents my blood; every time you drink it, think of *me*."

However, it is clear that it is not *just* the person of Christ who is in view; it is Christ as the One who delivered up his body unto death *for us*, the One who poured out his blood *for us*. We commemorate Christ as the One who sacrificed himself on the cross in view of *our* eternal salvation. Jesus indicates this by saying about his blood that it "is poured out for many for the forgiveness of sins" (Matt. 26:28). Jesus asks us to eat the bread and drink the cup time and again, so that we would never forget what he accomplished for us on the cross. At the Holy Supper, we "proclaim the Lord's *death*" (1 Cor. 11:26), that is, his death *for us*.

✣　✣　✣

DAY 231 – IN REMEMBRANCE OF HIM
(Lord's Day 28, Q&A 75, part 2)

A. . . . With this command come these promises: First, as surely as I see with my eyes the bread of the Lord broken for me and the cup shared with me, so surely his body was offered and broken for me and his blood poured out for me on the cross. . . .

The term "command" is strong; we might prefer to say that Jesus' request is a gentle desire, not an order. At the beginning of the Passover meal Jesus said to his disciples, "I have earnestly *desired* to eat this Passover with you before I suffer" (Luke 22:15), and he expects, as our response, that *we* will earnestly desire to eat the Holy Supper, time and again. It is, as it were, the last wish of a dear, dying friend or relative.

Yet, "command" is a correct term. He is the *Lord* (it is no coincidence that this word occurs seven times in 1 Cor. 11:20–27), and as such he is in the position to command. "Be baptized" (Acts 2:38; 10:48; 22:16) is not just a kind request, it is a command. "Take, eat, drink" is a command as well—a lovely command by a lovely Master; but still a command. If you wish to be a disciple of Jesus, the proper way to do so is to be baptized. If you wish to proclaim the Lord's death until he comes, the proper way to do so is to celebrate the Holy Supper. He is the Master; he determines the rules. You cannot simply become the Lord's disciple or proclaim the Lord's death in a way you choose yourself.

The Catechism adds that it is a command that involves promises, or perhaps we should say: guarantees. Just as we saw for baptism, the Lord speaks through the emblems of bread and the cup; he is present in them through the Holy Spirit. He says as it were, Look at this bread that you break—it is "the bread that *we* break," not just the pastor (1 Cor. 10:16)—and that I first broke for you (11:24); take it, eat it, realize that this bread speaks of my body, and remember that I delivered my body up into death *for you*. Look at this cup for which you give thanks ("say a blessing," 1 Cor. 10:16) and from which you drink, realize that the wine speaks of my blood, and remember that I poured out my blood on the cross *for you*. As surely as you eat of this bread and drink from this cup, just as surely do you share in the work of redemption that I accomplished for you on the cross. What a wonderful "language" of forgiveness and redemption the Lord's Supper speaks!

❧   ❧   ❧

DAY 232 – SURE SIGNS
(Lord's Day 28, Q&A 75, part 3)

A. . . . Second, as surely as I receive from the hand of the one who serves, and taste with my mouth the bread and cup of the Lord, given me as sure signs of Christ's body and blood, so surely he nourishes and refreshes my soul for eternal life with his crucified body and poured-out blood.

We have seen that "Christ has commanded me and all believers to eat this broken bread and to drink this cup in remembrance of him. With this command come these promises: First, . . . his body was offered and broken for me and his blood poured out for me on the cross." Now comes the second promise: through the Lord's Supper, Jesus Christ "nourishes and refreshes my soul for eternal life with his crucified body and poured-out blood."

It is obvious that the Catechism's words here are an allusion to John 6, where Jesus calls himself the "bread of life" (vv. 35, 48), the "bread from heaven" (vv. 32–33, 41, 50–51, 58), and says, "Whoever feeds on my flesh and drinks my blood has eternal life, and I will raise him up on the last day. For my flesh is true food, and my blood is true drink. Whoever feeds on my flesh and drinks my blood abides in me, and I in him. As the living Father sent me, and I live because of the Father, so whoever feeds on me, he also will live because of me. This is the bread that came down from heaven, not like the bread the fathers ate, and died. Whoever feeds on this bread will live forever" (vv. 54–58).

For two reasons, many expositors have wondered whether these words could indeed be a direct reference to the Lord's Supper. First, at the time the Holy Supper had not yet been instituted, so how could Jesus have spoken of it? Second, for the greater part Jesus refers here to the way a person can *receive* eternal life by "feeding" on him, whereas the Holy Supper is certainly not the means to *receive* life. It is for those who *have* received eternal life. Yet, the Greek form of verses 54 and 56–58 (present tense) refers to events that are still going on: here it is *believers* spiritually "feeding" on Christ. Even if the chapter does not refer to the Holy Supper directly, what we find here is certainly represented by the Holy Supper: eating of the bread and drinking from the cup represents a spiritual "eating" of Christ's flesh and "drinking" of his blood as a nourishment of the soul (see Q&A 76). We "feed" on him as Israel daily ate the manna (vv. 31, 49).

✢ ✢ ✢

DAY 233 – EATING HIS BODY
(Lord's Day 28, Q&A 76, part 1)

Q. What does it mean to eat the crucified body of Christ and to drink his poured-out blood?
A. It means to accept with a believing heart the entire suffering and death of Christ and thereby to receive forgiveness of sins and eternal life.

This is the sequel of Q&A 75, and the reference is again to Jesus' words in John 6. Of course, the Catechism cannot be saying here that by using the Lord's Supper as such a person will *receive* forgiveness of sins and eternal life. The Holy Supper is not a means to get saved—it is for those who, by the grace of God, may know that they *have* received salvation in Christ. However, in the Lord's Supper we "relive" this, so to speak: I eat the bread, I think of Christ's finished work on the cross, as if I realize for the first time that he died *for me*, accomplished redemption *for me*. No matter how often we celebrate the Lord's Supper, we eat and drink as if it were the first time.

Just as Israel in celebrating the Passover "relives" that last night in Egypt (Exod. 12), we "relive" what happened on the cross of Calvary for us, and proclaim the Lord's death (1 Cor. 11:26). We are like mourners, as if Jesus had just died (cf. Jer. 16:7, ". . . break bread for the mourner, to comfort him for the dead, nor shall anyone give him the cup of consolation to drink for his father or his mother"). At the same time, we rejoice because the risen and glorified Lord is in our midst through his Spirit. We celebrate our salvation, we celebrate the forgiveness of our sins and the reception of eternal life, as if these blessings had just been given to us. I have celebrated the Lord's Supper perhaps two thousand times in my life—yet, I try to celebrate it each time as if it were the first. I eat the bread as if I had received eternal life *just now*, I drink from the cup as if I had received the forgiveness of my sins *just now*.

In John 6:53 ("unless you eat the flesh of the Son of Man and drink his blood, you have no life in you"), the verbal form refers to an event that takes place only once: there was *one* time in his life that a person, through appropriating (personally accepting) Christ as his Savior, received eternal life. But in verses 54 and 56–58 believers eat and drink time and again, and enjoy every time afresh the life that they now may have in and through Jesus Christ, their Lord!

✦   ✦   ✦

DAY 234 – UNITED TO HIS BODY
(Lord's Day 28, Q&A 76, part 2)

A. . . . But it means more. Through the Holy Spirit, who lives both in Christ and in us, we are united more and more to Christ's blessed body. . . .

It is highly interesting how the Catechism moves here from the one meaning of the bread of the Holy Supper—the physical body of Christ—to the other meaning of it: the "mystical" Body of Christ, that is, his worldwide church. This is fully in line with Paul's teaching: "The cup of blessing that we bless, is it not a participation in the blood of Christ? The bread that we break, is it not a participation in the body of Christ? Because there is one bread, we who are many are one body, for we all partake of the one bread" (1 Cor. 10:16–17). Whereas in verse 16 we might still think that the apostle is referring to the physical body of Christ, which he delivered up unto death, in verse 17 he unmistakably refers to the Body of Christ, that is, the church. We participate in the body of Christ in two ways: we participate in the physical body of Christ because he delivered this body unto death for our eternal redemption. And we participate in the mystical Body of Christ because, by eating and drinking together, we express our unity as members of the same worldwide church of Christ.

Celebrating the Lord's Supper is not just an individual matter, for our personal benefit only. For instance, we do not break the bread for ourselves at home. It is a collective matter: by eating a piece of the one loaf I bring to expression in a very practical way that I am a piece of Christ's universal church. In the Holy Supper, we look *back* to the cross, where Christ died. We look *forward* because we eat and drink "until he comes" (1 Cor. 11:26). We look *upward* to the living Lord to thank and to praise him. We look *inward* to check whether we have the right attitude (see Q&A 81). But we also look *outward* to those with whom we celebrate the Holy Supper. We eat the same loaf, and thus we demonstrate that we are one church. This is not just our own local congregation, or our own denomination; the one loaf speaks of the unity and fellowship of the "one single catholic or universal church," the "holy congregation and gathering of true Christian believers" (Belgic Confession, Art. 27).

✦ ✦ ✦

DAY 235 – FLESH OF HIS FLESH
(Lord's Day 28, Q&A 76, part 3)

A. . . . *And so, although he is in heaven and we are on earth, we are flesh of his flesh and bone of his bone. . . .*

The Catechism pursues here the notion of the loaf as representing not only the physical body of Christ, but also the Body of Christ in the sense of the church of God. Paul says, "Christ loved the church and gave himself up for her. . . . [N]o one ever hated his own flesh, but nourishes and cherishes it, just as Christ does the church, because we are members of his body. 'Therefore a man shall leave his father and mother and hold fast to his wife, and the two shall become one flesh.' This mystery is profound, and I am saying that it refers to Christ and the church" (Eph. 5:25, 29–32). Here Paul is quoting Genesis 2:24, while the Catechism is referring to verse 23, in which Adam says of the newly created Eve, "This at last is bone of my bones and flesh of my flesh."

In Paul's words, two images are intertwined: the image of a marriage (Christ and his church are like husband and wife), and the image of head and body. The image of a marriage underscores the love between Christ and his church: he sanctifies her, cleanses her (v. 26), nourishes her, and cherishes her (v. 29). The image of head and body emphasizes the unity of Christ and his church: Head and Body are inseparable. By the way, the expression "bone of my bones and flesh of my flesh" relates to both images.

The Catechism points out that Christ, the Head, is in heaven (glorified at the right hand of God), whereas we (his Body, the church) are still on earth. Yet, the two are inseparable, as Paul brings out quite remarkably: God "raised us up with [Christ] and seated us with him in the heavenly places in Christ Jesus" (Eph. 2:6). Christ is there, and in him we are already there as well!

What does this have to do with the Lord's Supper? The Catechism argues: when celebrating the Lord's Supper, we focus on the loaf, and we see not only the physical body of Christ, delivered up for me, but also that other Body of Christ, his church. It reminds us of the fact that we, the members of that Body, are one with our glorified Head. And at the same time, I can never forget that this person was also the Christ who died for me on the cross!

✤　　✤　　✤

DAY 236 – ONE SPIRIT
(Lord's Day 28, Q&A 76, part 4)

A. . . . And we forever live on and are governed by one Spirit, as the members of our body are by one soul.

Here, the Catechism uses an image that it apparently has developed itself. The Body of Christ has a "Head," which is the glorified Christ. It also has a "soul," which is the Holy Spirit. As Paul puts it succinctly, "I therefore, a prisoner for the Lord, urge you to walk in a manner worthy of the calling to which you have been called, . . . eager to maintain the *unity of the Spirit* in the bond of peace. There is one body and one Spirit" (Eph. 4:1–4).

Please notice that there is a difference between the *formal* unity of the Body and the *practical* unity of the Spirit, although both expressions refer to the same fellowship of believers. Some Christians speak of the enormous dissension within the Christian world, and describe it as a "ruptured body," a body "torn apart." I regret the denominational division of Christianity, but I reject the imagery used. The glorified Head at the right hand of God is the guarantee that the unity of the Body—that is the "holy congregation and gathering of true Christian believers," no matter how much it is dispersed over many denominations—always remains intact. Beyond all denominational barriers, the members of Christ's body are linked together by Christ himself, by one rebirth and one faith (though perhaps not one creed), by one forgiveness and redemption, by one heavenly goal, and by one Holy Spirit dwelling in them.

However, in the expression "unity of the Spirit" we are dealing with a very practical matter. If all members would be filled with the Holy Spirit (cf. Eph. 5:18)—or, as the Catechism puts it, would be "governed by one Spirit"—they would also *display* the most wonderful harmony and unity. If many believers are in fact led by their sinful nature, the *positional* unity of the Body may still be intact—because it lies firmly in Christ's hands—but the *practical* unity of the Spirit is hardly a reality. Precisely at the Lord's Supper, where we express this unity of the Body (1 Cor. 10:16–17), this is a shame. How many sectarian tables there are, simply because we did not manage "to maintain the unity of the Spirit in the bond of peace"!

❈   ❈   ❈

DAY 237 – WHAT BIBLE PASSAGES?
(Lord's Day 28, Q&A 77, part 1)

Q. Where does Christ promise to nourish and refresh believers with his body and blood as surely as they eat this broken bread and drink this cup?
A. In the institution of the Lord's Supper: "The Lord Jesus, on the night when he was betrayed, took a loaf of bread, and when he had given thanks, he broke it and said, 'This is my body that is broken for you. Do this in remembrance of me.' In the same way he took the cup also, after supper, saying, 'This cup is the new covenant in my blood; do this, as often as you drink it, in remembrance of me.' For as often as you eat this bread and drink the cup, you proclaim the Lord's death until he comes."

Just as in the case of baptism (Q&A 71), the Catechism asks here for the biblical basis for what is being said about the Lord's Supper. Interestingly, what the Catechism asks for— "Where does Christ promise to nourish and refresh believers with his body and blood as surely as they eat this broken bread and drink this cup?"—is not stated at all in the passages quoted. We could say, however, that the *developed thoughts* of the Catechism ("nourishing and refreshing believers with his body and blood") find their *basis* and *root* in the two passages (1 Cor. 11:23–26; 10:16–17).

The Lord's Supper is described in all three synoptic Gospels (Matt. 26:26–28; Mark 14:22–24; Luke 22:19–20), although only in Luke do we read about a real *institution* of the Lord's Supper because of the words, "[D]o this in remembrance of me," that is, as an event repeated also *after* Jesus would have left them (cf. 1 Cor. 11:24). This is indeed what we find later in the book of Acts: after the pouring out of the Holy Spirit, we read that the disciples "devoted themselves to the apostles' teaching and the fellowship, to the *breaking of bread* and the prayers" (Acts 2:42), and that they were "breaking bread in their homes" (v. 46). About Troas we read, "On the first day of the week, when we were gathered together *to break bread*, Paul talked with them. . . . And when Paul had gone up and had *broken bread* and eaten, he conversed with them a long while . . ." (20:7, 11). There is no doubt that the expression "breaking of bread" refers to the Lord's Supper; what use would it be to stress that the early disciples devoted themselves to their daily meals!?

✤   ✤   ✤

DAY 238 – PAUL'S RENDERING
(Lord's Day 28, Q&A 77, part 2)

A. . . . This promise is repeated by Paul in these words: "The cup of blessing that we bless, is it not a sharing in the blood of Christ? The bread that we break, is it not a sharing in the body of Christ? Because there is one bread, we who are many are one body, for we all partake of the one bread."

The Catechism sees Christ's "promise to nourish and refresh believers with his body and blood as surely as they eat this broken bread and drink this cup" reflected in 1 Corinthians 10:16–17 as well. Again, the connection between this passage and what is here called Christ's promise is not easy to see. Let us therefore look first at the context of these words of Paul.

The apostle compares Christians with Israel, whom he describes as a people characterized by what we would now call "sacraments": Israel was "baptized" into Moses by going through the Red Sea, and "all ate the same spiritual food, and all drank the same spiritual drink"—an allusion to the Lord's Supper (vv. 2–5). However, these "sacraments" did not keep them from terrible sins: idolatry, sexual immorality, putting God to the test, and grumbling, which is rebellion (vv. 7–10). Paul says as it were, You, Corinthian believers, are in the same danger. You have been baptized (1 Cor. 1:13–17) and you participate in the blood and the body of Christ at Holy Supper (10:16–17). But at the same time, you participate in idolatrous ceremonies: "[W]hat pagans sacrifice they offer to demons and not to God. I do not want you to be participants with demons. You cannot drink the cup of the Lord and the cup of demons. You cannot partake of the table of the Lord and the table of demons" (10:20–21).

The "table of the Lord" was an ancient name for the golden or bronze altar in Jerusalem (Ezek. 41:22; 44:16; Mal. 1:7, 12). In New Testament language the Lord's table is the spiritual place where you celebrate the Lord's Supper. In terms of the Catechism: at the Lord's table you are "nourished and refreshed" with Christ, at the "table of the demons" (an idolatrous altar) you feed yourself with the world of sin, the devil, and death. It is unthinkable that you try to live in two opposing worlds! The idolatrous "altars" of our own time may look very different, but they are still linked with the same demonic world. We have to choose! We cannot partake of Christ, and at the same time sneakily partake of the world that is hostile to him!

✣ ✣ ✣

DAY 239 – TRANSUBSTANTIATION
(Lord's Day 29, Q&A 78, part 1)

Q. Do the bread and wine become the real body and blood of Christ?
A. No.

This Q&A is an allusion to the Roman Catholic doctrine of transubstantiation. This word means that allegedly the "substance" of the bread and wine of the Eucharist (the Catholic term for the Lord's Supper) is transformed into the "substance" of the body and blood of Christ, while the outward appearance of the bread and wine remain the same. This is not biblical language at all; the terminology goes back to the Greek philosopher Aristotle. The entire idea of transubstantiation was developed in the high Middle Ages. It is still the official doctrine of the Roman Catholic Church, although many Catholic theologians and philosophers reject the Aristotelian roots of it.

When the Protestant Reformation arose in the sixteenth century, transubstantiation was rejected by all Protestants. However, the Roman Catholic Church reaffirmed the doctrine at the Council of Trent (1551). The Protestants in turn were not very sure how *they* should reformulate the doctrine. They were quite aware of the fact that the Apostolic Father, Ignatius of Antioch, wrote as early as AD 106: "I desire the bread of God, which is the flesh of Jesus Christ." What do we make of this little word "is"? Hadn't Jesus himself clearly said, "This *is* my body" (Matt. 26:26; Mark 14:22; Luke 22:19; 1 Cor. 11:24)?

Yes, but think. Jesus poured out his blood into death. He carried his blood into the heavenly sanctuary, as the high priest of old did with animal blood (Heb. 9:12). In Jesus' resurrection body, the blood is not even mentioned anymore ("flesh and bones," Luke 24:39). How, then, can we say that the wine at the Eucharist changes into the blood that Jesus had *before his death*? When Jesus said, "This is my body," to what body did he refer? To the body he had at that moment, of course. However, that "lowly body" has been replaced by his "glorious body" (Phil. 3:21). So, if the bread is transformed into the body of Christ, what body is meant? It is changed into a body that no longer exists? Or is it changed into the glorious body that Christ possesses now, at the right hand of God? Either way we land in absurdities.

✦   ✦   ✦

DAY 240 – SIGN AND ASSURANCE
(LORD'S DAY 29, Q&A 78, PART 2)

A. . . . *Just as the water of baptism is not changed into Christ's blood and does not itself wash away sins but is simply a divine sign and assurance of these things, so too the holy bread of the Lord's Supper does not become the actual body of Christ.*

Yesterday, we looked at the Roman Catholic doctrine of transubstantiation, and rejected it. The Protestants, however, were not so sure how *they* should formulate the relationship between the bread of the Lord's Supper and the body of Christ. In 1529, an infamous debate took place at the German city of Marburg, where Martin Luther wrote the little word "is" ("This IS my body") with huge letters on the lectern. He insisted that, although transubstantiation should be rejected, in some way the identity of the bread and the body of Christ should be maintained.

Of course, Luther forgot two things. First, in the Hebrew or Aramaic language that Jesus spoke with his disciples the word "is" as a copula does not even exist. So what value can we attach to this word as we have it in the Greek New Testament? Second, Paul writes that the Israelites "drank from the spiritual Rock that followed them, and the Rock was Christ" (1 Cor. 10:4). Would Luther insist that the rock from which Israel drank (Exod. 17:6; Num. 20:11) was Christ in person, because of the little word "was"? All expositors agree that such an expression means: "the rock was a representation (image, picture) of Christ," or "prefigured Christ."

In the words of the Catechism: the water of baptism is not transformed either, and I would add, the oil in the anointing of the sick is not either. Water and oil, and similarly bread and wine, are symbols, "divine signs and assurances" of certain spiritual realities. Similarly, Christ's "wife," the church, is washed with "water" (Eph. 5:26)–not literal water, but the Word of God. Regeneration is a "washing," but not a literal washing (Titus 3:5). Hebrews 10 says, "[L]et us draw near with a true heart in full assurance of faith, with our hearts sprinkled clean from an evil conscience and our bodies washed with pure water" (v. 22). Who would take such words literally? Have our hearts been sprinkled with blood? Of course they haven't. It's a picture, referring to a deep spiritual reality. It is the same with bread and wine in the Lord's Supper.

✷   ✷   ✷

DAY 241 – NATURE OF THE SACRAMENTS
(Lord's Day 29, Q&A 78, part 3)

A. . . . *the holy bread of the Lord's Supper does not become the actual body of Christ, even though it is called the body of Christ in keeping with the nature and language of sacraments.*

What the Catechism wishes to say here is that the little word "is" in the expression "This is my body" should be plain to every common Bible reader. No need for secular philosophy here. The Catechism explains that this kind of language is "in keeping with the nature and language of sacraments," and, I would add, in keeping with our everyday language.

Consider this example. I point to a photograph and say, "This is my mother." Now what person in his right mind would be so silly as to reply, "No, that is not your mother, that is only a picture of your mother"? Or the reverse: "If this is your mother, I take you at your word, and conclude from it that you were born from a piece of paper." So, if the Lord said, "This is my body," who of the disciples at that moment would have taken these words literally, given the fact that Jesus himself was still present in his human body? Were there *two* bodies of Christ at that moment: one reclining *at* the table, and one lying *on* the table?

So why did Luther emphasize so strongly that little word "is"? Because although he did reject transubstantiation, he did not wish to fall into the other extreme either: that of "memorialism." This is the view that the Lord's Supper is only a memorial meal, and that bread and wine are only symbols. In some way or another—and *this* is the problem: in *what* way precisely?—faith realities become visible in the form of bread and wine. Or, to put it a bit more strongly, *God's* world becomes tangibly present within our material world, as represented by the bread and wine. This is like walking on the razor's edge: every formulation slides either more in the direction of transubstantiation, or more in the direction of a mere memoralism. Over against the former, Protestants do not accept any material-physical transformation of the emblems. Over against the latter, many Protestants maintain the real presence of Christ in connection with bread and wine (and leave aside the involved question how this word "connection" has to be understood). When we celebrate the Lord's Supper, *Christ himself is there.*

✥   ✥   ✥

DAY 242 – CHRIST'S BODY AND BLOOD
(Lord's Day 29, Q&A 79, part 1)

Q. Why then does Christ call the bread his body and the cup his blood, or the new covenant in his blood, and Paul use the words, a sharing in Christ's body and blood
A. Christ has good reason for these words. He wants to teach us that just as bread and wine nourish the temporal life, so too his crucified body and poured-out blood are the true food and drink of our souls for eternal life.

It has often been pointed out that there is a parallel here with Q&A 73: "Q. *Why then does* the Holy Spirit *call* baptism the water of rebirth and the washing away of sins? A. God *has good reason for these words.* To begin with, God *wants to teach us that* the blood and Spirit of Christ take away our sins *just as* water removes dirt from the body. *But more important,* God *wants to assure us, by this divine pledge and sign, that we* are as truly washed of our sins spiritually as our bodies are washed with water physically." The words that correspond in Q&As 73 and 79 are in italics. Thus, the Catechism wishes to emphasize the deep bonds between the two sacraments dealt with: baptism and the Lord's Supper.

The Catechism asks, Why does the Bible speak about the Lord's Supper the way it does? The answer is that bread and wine, as representing "his crucified body and poured-out blood," are our spiritual food. That is, Christ himself is the spiritual food of the believer. Of course, this is true in our everyday lives, not just at the Lord's Supper (although there in a special way). When the Catechism alludes here to John 6, we notice that Jesus compares himself there with the manna, the "bread from heaven" (Ps. 105:40), which Israel ate in the wilderness (vv. 31–33, 49–51). They ate it *every day.* Jesus says as it were, I am the *true* bread of life that has descended from heaven, and you need me every day as well: "Whoever feeds [time and again! present tense] on my flesh and drinks [time and again!] my blood has eternal life. . . . Whoever feeds [time and again!] on my flesh and drinks [time and again!] my blood abides in me, and I in him" (vv. 54–56).

What you feed on, you will smell like afterward. In the Song of Solomon, the girl compares her friend to an apple tree (2:3) and wishes to be fed with apples (2:5). He says, "[T]he scent of your breath [is] like apples" (7:8). She had been feeding on him! Dwight Moody wrote in the margin of his Bible something like this: Imagine how she would have smelled if she had been feeding on the leeks, the onions, and the garlic of Egypt . . . (Num. 11:5)!

✤ ✤ ✤

DAY 243 – SIGN AND PLEDGE

(Lord's Day 29, Q&A 79, part 2)

A. . . . *But more important, he wants to assure us, by this visible sign and pledge, that we, through the Holy Spirit's work, share in his true body and blood as surely as our mouth receive these holy signs in his remembrance, and that all of his suffering and obedience are as definitely ours as if we personally had suffered and made satisfaction for our sins.*

Celebrating the Lord's Supper is a form of being "assured" by God concerning our eternal salvation, says the Catechism. Do those who celebrate it by definition *need* this assurance? Are they such doubters? Is it not enough for them to believe the promises of God's Word? John says, "If we confess our sins, he is faithful and just to forgive us our sins and to cleanse us from all unrighteousness" (1 John 1:9). If I confess my sins, and believe this statement of God's Word, do I not have sufficient ground to be assured of God's forgiveness? Paul says, "[I]f you confess with your mouth that Jesus is Lord and believe in your heart that God raised him from the dead, you will be saved. For with the heart one believes and is justified, and with the mouth one confesses and is saved. For the Scripture says, 'Everyone who believes in him will not be put to shame'" (Rom. 10:9–11; cf. Isa. 28:16). If I believe in my heart and confess with my mouth the things mentioned here, then *I am saved.* What else do I need? What does celebrating the Lord's Supper *add* to this? How can our assurance of salvation be based on eating bread and drinking wine anyway? Could not the hypocrites who take part in this celebration even derive a *false* assurance from it?

This is all perfectly true. And yet. Mr. and Mrs. Johnson assure me that I am their child. My name is on their marriage certificate. The county records also identify me as a child of Mr. and Mrs. Johnson. All fine. I am assured of my ancestry. And yet. Mrs. Johnson kisses and caresses me, and says, "My sweet boy!" That's great! It is better than any formal record! The Lord's Supper is such a kiss by my heavenly Father, and by my dear Lord. I sit at the Lord's table, and I feel enveloped by his love and warmth. I eat the bread, and I realize afresh in my heart, "He died *for me!*" I am touched by it. I drink the cup, and it makes me aware once again: "He poured out his blood *for me!*" It makes me feel warm inside. I know, it is not a judicial proof. But it is better than all formal arguments for the assurance of my salvation!

✣ ✣ ✣

DAY 244 – THE CATHOLIC MASS
(Lord's Day 30, Q&A 80, part 1)

Q. How does the Lord's Supper differ from the Roman Catholic Mass?

A. The Lord's Supper declares to us that all our sins are completely forgiven through the one sacrifice of Jesus Christ, which he himself accomplished on the cross once for all.

This is perhaps the most controversial of all Q&As in the Heidelberg Catechism! It was totally absent from the first edition of the Catechism, was present in a shorter form in the second edition, and in its present version in the third edition. Synod 2006 of the Christian Reformed Church of North America "directed that this Q&A remain in the CRC's text of the Catechism but that the last three paragraphs be placed in brackets to indicate that they do not accurately reflect the official teaching and practice of today's Roman Catholic Church and are no longer confessionally binding on members of the CRC. The Reformed Church in America retains the original full text, choosing to recognize that the Catechism was written within a historical context that may not accurately describe the Roman Catholic Church's current stance."

Take the first sentence: "The Lord's Supper declares to us that all our sins are completely forgiven through the one sacrifice of Jesus Christ, which he himself accomplished on the cross once for all." This is indeed what we read in Hebrews 7: Jesus "has no need, like those high priests [of old], to offer sacrifices daily, first for his own sins and then for those of the people, since he did this *once for all* when he offered up himself" (v. 27). A bit later we read, "[H]e entered *once for all* into the holy places . . . by means of his own blood, thus securing an eternal redemption. . . . [H]e has appeared *once for all* at the end of the ages to put away sin by the sacrifice of himself" (9:12, 26). "[W]e have been sanctified through the offering of the body of Jesus Christ *once for all*" (10:10). And Paul says, "[T]he death he died he died to sin, *once for all*" (Rom. 6:10).

As a Roman Catholic bishop told me once, "Hebrews 7–10 is also in *our* Bibles, Willem!" Of course it is. During the Eucharist, Christ's sacrifice is not "repeated," but only "presented" to believers afresh. There are enough matters in which Protestants do differ from Rome. But let us begin with presenting each other's views in a fair way! I will come back to this point.

�֍   ✤   ✤

DAY 245 – GRAFTED INTO CHRIST
(Lord's Day 30, Q&A 80, part 2)

A. . . . It also declares to us that the Holy Spirit grafts us into Christ, who with his true body is now in heaven at the right hand of the Father where he wants us to worship him.

There is something remarkable about the Lord's Supper. It has something in it of both a mourning character and of an exultation. We *remember* the Lord in his sufferings and his death (1 Cor. 11:25), we *proclaim* his death (v. 26). It is like breaking bread for the mourner, to comfort him for the dead, or drinking the cup of consolation for a beloved one (cf. Jer. 16:7). At the same time we know that the Lord has risen and "is now in heaven at the right hand of the Father where he wants us to worship him," as the Catechism puts it. The Roman Catholic name for the Lord's Supper is "Eucharist." This comes from a Greek verb that we find in Matthew 26:27, Jesus "took a cup, and when he had *given thanks* he gave it to them" (cf. Mark 14:23). "[H]e took a cup, and when he had *given thanks* he said, 'Take this, and divide it among yourselves.' And he took bread, and when he had *given thanks*, he broke it and gave it to them, saying, 'This is my body, which is given for you. Do this in remembrance of me'" (Luke 22:17, 19; cf. 1 Cor. 11:23–24).

In Catholic eyes, this is what the Lord's Supper essentially is: *thanksgiving, praise, worship* to the triune God, in particular to Christ himself. Also notice 1 Corinthians 10:16, "The cup of blessing that we bless. . . ." I wonder whether the idea is really that we bless *the cup*. Nor is the meaning that we ask God's blessing on the cup (AMP, CEV). It is rather the "cup of thanksgiving for which we give thanks" (NIV; cf. many other translations). The CJB says, the "cup of blessing" over which we make the *b'rakhah*, that is, the Jewish blessing of God. We do not bless the cup; we bless (praise, worship) God! This is what Jesus did when he "gave thanks" for bread and wine; he said, *Barukh atah, Adonai Eloheinu, Melekh ha'Olam*, "Blessed are you, Lord, our God, sovereign of the universe. . . ."

This is an often neglected but very important aspect of the Lord's Supper: it is *worship!* It is exclaiming and pronouncing his greatness as our Savior, as the Lord of the universe at the right hand of the Father. We *remember* the dead Lord, and we *praise* the living Lord!

✣   ✣   ✣

DAY 246 – A DAILY OFFERING?
(Lord's Day 30, Q&A 80, part 3)

A. But the Mass teaches that the living and the dead do not have their sins forgiven through the suffering of Christ unless Christ is still offered for them daily by the priests.

It is amazing how, in the heat of a controversy, people accuse each other of things that are highly unfair. This is human, so it may be understandable; but it cannot be excused. Thus, the Council of Trent (sixteenth century) stated that those who teach that a person is justified by faith alone are cursed. This judgment was based on the idea that Protestants taught that it does not matter how you live—you only have to believe. Protestants never taught this (although Luther may sometimes have given this impression). Because of this misunderstanding, Catholics falsely accused the Lutherans, who in turn misunderstood the background of the Council's judgment. Centuries later, they found out that their views were not that different after all; both parties believe that a person is justified by faith, but then, a "faith working through love" (Gal. 5:6).

It is very similar with respect to the Eucharist, or the Lord's Supper. Protestants quote the Council of Trent on this matter, often without taking into consideration the background of certain statements. At any rate, *today* no Catholic theologian would ever assert that Christ still has to be "offered daily by the priests" to guarantee the forgiveness for the participants. Their own Bibles state very clearly that Jesus was offered on the cross *once for all* (Rom. 6:10; Heb. 7:27; 9:12, 26; 10:10). This sacrifice of Christ is not "repeated" daily, but is "presented" as a living spiritual reality during the Eucharist time and again.

Actually, the real problem does not lie here at all. It lies far more in the fact that in Roman Catholicism the priest is of essential importance in mediating salvation by means of administering the sacraments, whereas Protestantism in general believes in a far more direct, personal relationship between God and the believer. However, this is a relative distinction: many Catholic believers today know this personal relationship just as well, whereas many Protestants—Lutheran, Calvinist, Charismatic, and others— are in practice far too dependent on their pastors as (unofficial) mediators of salvation!

✤   ✤   ✤

DAY 247 – A CONDEMNABLE IDOLATRY?
(Lord's Day 30, Q&A 80, part 4)

A. . . . It also teaches that Christ is bodily present under the form of bread and wine where Christ is therefore to be worshiped. Thus the Mass is basically nothing but a denial of the one sacrifice and suffering of Jesus Christ and a condemnable idolatry.

This is the most unfair statement in the entire Catechism, and fortunately, is therefore rejected by many Protestants today. "Idolatry" means worshiping a creature instead of the Creator (cf. Rom. 1:23). The accusation of "condemnable idolatry" (older version: "accursed idolatry") would be correct only if Roman Catholics would worship bread and wine, but that is not what they do at all. What they do believe is that the bread and the wine before which they kneel down strictly speaking are not bread and wine anymore, but the body and blood of Christ. According to their deepest conviction, they therefore worship Christ, and Christ only. It is their firm conviction—as it is ours—that only the triune God may be worshiped.

Protestants do not believe that, during the Eucharist, bread and wine are transformed into the body and the blood of Christ. But that does not give them the right to assert that Roman Catholics worship bread and wine, and therefore are idolators. This is pure slander. People of a different opinion have the right to be evaluated according to their own convictions and according to the intentions behind their actions, not according to the viewpoints of their opponents.

Compare this with an outright unbeliever who blames Protestants for having a "feast meal" together in which every participant with very solemn looks receives just one piece of bread and one sip of wine, and call this a "supper." The infidel judges the situation according to what *he* sees: an ordinary meal in a ridiculous form. Instead, he should judge the situation according to the conviction and intentions of the participants themselves. He does not have to agree with them, but he will not understand them if he does not judge them according to their own intentions and views. It is exactly the same with Protestants when evaluating Roman Catholics. They do not have to agree with them—I do not either—but they have to evaluate them according to their own views and intentions. He who asserts that Catholics worship bread and wine—"a condemnable idolatry"—is either ignorant or condemnable himself.

✳   ✳   ✳

DAY 248 – THE LORD'S TABLE

(Lord's Day 30, Q&A 81, part 1)

Q. Who should come to the Lord's table?
A. Those who are displeased with themselves because of their sins, but who nevertheless trust that their sins are pardoned and that their remaining weakness is covered by the suffering and death of Christ.

In the Old Testament, "the Lord's table" is a name for either the golden or the bronze altar in the temple (Ezek. 41:22; 44:16; Mal. 1:7, 12), and in the New Testament it is a spiritual "altar," in opposition to idolatrous altars (1 Cor. 10:20–21). It is the spiritual place where we celebrate the Lord's Supper (it is not some wooden table in front of the church audience). Paul emphasizes that the bread that we break is also a reference to the mystical Body of Christ, his church, who all participate in the blood of Christ (vv. 16–17). At the Lord's table we express our fellowship as people forgiven by God, and as members of the Body of Christ. This makes very clear "*who* should come to the Lord's table": those who have received the forgiveness of their sins and are true members of the Body of Christ. Who are true members of this Body? "Those who are displeased with themselves because of their sins, but who nevertheless trust that their sins are pardoned and that their remaining weakness is covered by the suffering and death of Christ." In other words, those who have truly and honestly confessed their sins to God, who then cleanses them from all unrighteousness by the blood of Jesus his Son (1 John 1:7, 9).

Believers do not come to the Lord's table because they always feel strong; they often feel very weak, and yet they may come because they are children of God. The Lord's table is not only for his mature children; it is not only for the fathers in Christ, but also for the little children and the young men in Christ (1 John 2:12–14). A table that is reserved only for the strong, the mature, and the spiritual is essentially a sectarian table, because it fixes a boundary narrower than that of the Body of Christ. To be sure, the boundary may not be fixed *wider* either; that would be laxity. We have to supervise the Lord's table so that only true members—as far as we can assess—take part. But we may not fix the boundary *narrower*; sectarianism is just as bad a sin as laxity. ("Sects" are a work of the flesh; Gal. 5:20 YLT; cf. Titus 3:10; 2 Pet. 2:1 YLT).

✤   ✤   ✤

DAY 249 – WHO MAY PARTAKE?
(Lord's Day 30, Q&A 81, part 2)

A. Those who . . . also desire more and more to strengthen their faith and to lead a better life.

All members of the Body of Christ are welcome at the Lord's table, the strong and the weak, spiritual fathers and spiritual babies, the Spirit-filled and the not-so-Spirit-filled. We come to the Lord's table not because we are perfect but because we are forgiven—not boasting in our talents or our good works, but as those who live out of God's grace and boast in the Lord alone.

However, of course this does not mean that the attitude with which you come to the table is an indifferent matter. First, there is a very practical reason. In 1 Corinthians 2:14–3:3, three groups of people are distinguished: the natural, the fleshly, and the spiritual (Spirit-led). The first are not re-born, the second and third groups are regenerated Christians. The problem is, however, that the first and the second groups can often hardly be distinguished! How can we expect to be admitted to the table if we, to a large extent, live, think and speak like the unbelievers?

Second, there is a practical reason for ourselves. How can we expect to truly remember the Lord in his sufferings and death, to enjoy and celebrate our redemption from "Egypt," and to worship God and his Son, if we come with a sinful, negligent attitude? I come to the table to *receive* God's blessing, and to *bring* him my worship. How can I possibly do that? If I come with a fleshly mentality, I am neither open to receiving these blessings, nor to bringing him my worship. Why would I come at all? As a hypocrite, afraid of what others would say if I would *not* come? What an attitude! I come in a humble mood, knowing who and what I am in myself, but also aware of God's infinite grace, and with an earnest desire to be strengthened in my confidence in God, and to leave the table as a better Christian!

Third, what would the implication be for my relationship with the Lord? Can we say he doesn't care about how we come? Obedient and disobedient children are both children of their parents, and welcome at the family table. But this does not mean that the parents do not mind whether the children come either with an obedient or with a disobedient attitude!

✤   ✤   ✤

DAY 250 – THE HYPOCRITES
(Lord's Day 30, Q&A 81, part 3)

A. . . . Hypocrites and those who are unrepentant, however, eat and drink judgment on themselves.

This part of the Catechism's answer is an allusion to 1 Corinthians 11: "Whoever, therefore, eats the bread or drinks the cup of the Lord in an unworthy manner will be guilty concerning the body and blood of the Lord. Let a person examine himself, then, and so eat of the bread and drink of the cup. For anyone who eats and drinks without discerning the body eats and drinks judgment on himself. That is why many of you are weak and ill, and some have died. But if we judged ourselves truly, we would not be judged. But when we are judged by the Lord, we are disciplined that we may not be condemned along with the world" (vv. 27–32).

Let us first notice that the passage does *not* say that the Lord's Supper is not for the unworthy. If it said this, no one of us could take part, for we are all unworthy in ourselves. No, it says we should not take part in an unworthy *manner*. Within the context, this means that such a person does not distinguish between a common meal and the Lord's Supper: eating the bread as if it were regular bread. However, we may certainly extend the principle behind this: everyone who has unconfessed sins on his conscience, both toward the Lord and toward one's neighbor, eats and drinks in an unworthy manner. As Jesus put it: "[I]f you are offering your gift at the altar and there remember that your brother has something against you, leave your gift there before the altar and go. First be reconciled to your brother, and then come and offer your gift" (Matt. 5:23–24).

By the way, there are two kinds of hypocrites. There are the unbelievers who behave as if they are believers, and there are carnal believers who act as though they are spiritual believers. Both groups should repent, and in faith accept God's forgiveness, otherwise they bring judgment on themselves. The Lord will meet with them in his governmental ways; in Corinth this even meant that "many of you are weak and ill, and some have died." If we do not judge *ourselves*, God will apply discipline to us in order to restore us, so that we will not be condemned along with the world. So even his discipline is nothing but grace!

✦ ✦ ✦

DAY 251 – UNGODLY CHURCHGOERS
(Lord's Day 30, Q&A 82, part 1)

Q. Should those be admitted to the Lord's Supper who show by what they profess and how they live that they are unbelieving and ungodly?
A. No, that would dishonor God's covenant and bring down God's wrath upon the entire congregation.

Here we find an important principle that nowadays is greatly neglected in many churches and congregations. It is the principle that we do not participate in the Lord's Supper just on our own responsibility. This is where the responsibility of the elders ("overseers"!) of the congregation comes in, who admit to the table and ban from it (cf. Titus. 1:5–11; 1 Pet. 5:1–3). Paul says, "[W]hat pagans sacrifice they offer to demons and not to God. I do not want you to be participants with demons. You cannot drink the cup of the Lord and the cup of demons. You cannot partake of the table of the Lord and the table of demons. Shall we provoke the Lord to jealousy? Are we stronger than he?" (1 Cor. 10:20–22).

Should these solemn words not be a concern to the entire congregation? If there is unrepentant, gross sin in the congregation, should this not be a concern to all the members? As Paul says, "It is actually reported that there is sexual immorality among you, and of a kind that is not tolerated even among pagans. . . . And you are arrogant! Ought you not rather to mourn? Let him who has done this *be removed from among you*" (1 Cor. 5:1–2; cf. v. 13). The general principle behind this is that, if there is sin that affects the testimony of the entire congregation, the entire congregation should deal with it. "Do you not know that a little leaven leavens the whole lump? Cleanse out the old leaven that you may be a new lump, as you really are unleavened. For Christ, our Passover lamb, has been sacrificed. Let us therefore celebrate the festival, not with the old leaven, the leaven of malice and evil, but with the unleavened bread of sincerity and truth" (vv. 6–8; cf. Gal. 5:9).

Or, to give an Old Testament parallel: "'Offer to God a sacrifice of thanksgiving, and perform your vows to the Most High, and call upon me in the day of trouble; I will deliver you, and you shall glorify me.' But to the wicked God says: 'What right have you to recite my statutes or take my covenant on your lips? For you hate discipline, and you cast my words behind you'" (Ps. 50:14–17; cf. Isa. 1:11–17). Let us take this to heart!

✤   ✤   ✤

DAY 252 – CHURCH DISCIPLINE
(Lord's Day 30, Q&A 82, part 2)

A. . . .*Therefore, according to the instruction of Christ and his apostles, the Christian church is duty-bound to exclude such people, by the official use of the keys of the kingdom, until they reform their lives.*

Jesus had said to Peter, "I will give you the keys of the kingdom of heaven, and whatever you bind on earth shall be bound in heaven, and whatever you loose on earth shall be loosed in heaven" (Matt. 16:19). There has been much discussion on the meaning of the terms "binding" and "loosing" here. Some, including the Catechism, connect it with church discipline. Others have applied it to the ministry of deliverance (delivering people from demons). Nowadays, many expositors believe that the terms have more to do with issuing apostolic commandments of Jesus' followers, or lifting such commandments (cf. the false way in which the scribes and the Pharisees did this, Matt. 23:4).

Church discipline is more the subject of Matthew 18: "If your brother sins against you, go and tell him his fault, between you and him alone. If he listens to you, you have gained your brother. But if he does not listen, take one or two others along with you, that every charge may be established by the evidence of two or three witnesses. If he refuses to listen to them, tell it to the church. And if he refuses to listen even to the church, let him be to you as a Gentile and a tax collector. Truly, I say to you, whatever you bind on earth shall be bound in heaven, and whatever you loose on earth shall be loosed in heaven" (vv. 15–18).

The sinner is not thrown out just like that. He gets a fair chance to confess his sin, and clear up the matter. Only if he does not listen, otherwise people in the congregation get involved. If he refuses to listen to them, only then does it become a matter for the congregation. If he still refuses to repent, he is put out by the entire congregation, and treated as an outsider (cf. 1 Cor. 5:2, 5, 7, 13). No matter how serious the committed sin is, our justice must be fair; it may never be less fair than that of the world! "Brothers, if anyone is caught in any transgression, you who are spiritual should restore him in a spirit of gentleness. Keep watch on yourself, lest you too be tempted" (Gal. 6:1). The goal is not to exclude the impenitent sinner, but ultimately to restore the penitent sinner!

✣　　✣　　✣

DAY 253 – THE KINGDOM'S KEYS
(Lord's Day 31, Q&A 83, part 1)

Q. What are the keys of the kingdom?
A. The preaching of the holy gospel and Christian discipline toward repentance.

The "keys of the kingdom of heaven" are mentioned only in Matthew 16:19, where Jesus says to Peter, "I will give you [singular!] the keys of the kingdom of heaven, and whatever you bind on earth shall be bound in heaven, and whatever you loose on earth shall be loosed in heaven." Please notice that, although the Catechism applies them in a much broader way, these words were first spoken to Peter alone. Indeed, in the book of Acts the apostle Peter played the principal role in opening the Kingdom of God for the various parts of humanity. He was the key figure on the Day of Pentecost, when 3,000 Jews were let in (Acts 2). Together with the apostle John, he played the main role in letting in the (half-Jewish) Samaritans: "[W]hen the apostles at Jerusalem heard that Samaria had received the word of God, they sent to them Peter and John, who came down and prayed for them that they might receive the Holy Spirit" (8:14–15). And in Acts 10, Peter was the "doorkeeper" who used his keys to let the Gentiles in: "Then to the Gentiles also God has granted repentance that leads to life" (11:18).

Although the keys were given to Peter first, most of the words in Matthew 16:19 return in 18:18, where Jesus this time addresses all the apostles: "Truly, I say to you [plural!], whatever you bind on earth shall be bound in heaven, and whatever you loose on earth shall be loosed in heaven." These words have often been related to Jesus' words after his resurrection: "If you forgive the sins of any, they are forgiven them; if you withhold forgiveness from any, it is withheld" (John 20:22–23). Here again, it is the apostles who are addressed. But again, as far as post-apostolic times are concerned, the meaning can be extended to all those who have authority in the church of God. It is they who can admit people to the local congregation, and exclude people from it, who can exercise church discipline, and lift disciplinary measures. This always occurs in cooperation with all the church members (in, e.g., Matt. 18:15–18 and 1 Cor. 5:13, the entire congregation is addressed).

✤   ✤   ✤

DAY 254 – GOSPEL PREACHING
(Lord's Day 31, Q&A 83, part 2)

A. The preaching of the holy gospel and Christian discipline toward repentance. Both of them open the kingdom of heaven to believers and close it to unbelievers.

The traditional Roman Catholic view of Peter as the doorkeeper at the entrance of heaven is based on a misunderstanding. The "Kingdom of heaven" is not heaven; it is a Kingdom *on earth*, in which heaven (i.e., God) rules (cf. Dan. 4:26). The "Kingdom of heaven" is entirely parallel with what Mark and Luke call the "Kingdom of God." In the present age, the Kingdom of God is Christ ruling over the lives of all those who place themselves under his authority. Peter was the apostle who opened the door of this Kingdom of God for the various groups of people, as we saw yesterday.

Matthew 16:19 does not say how many keys Peter received, nor what these keys exactly represented. The Catechism thinks of two keys, which "open the kingdom of heaven to believers and close it to unbelievers." There is no doubt that the "preaching of the holy gospel" is indeed such a key. It was Peter who preached the gospel to Jews in Acts 2 and 3, and to Gentiles in Acts 10. Jesus told his apostles in general: "All authority in heaven and on earth has been given to me. Go therefore and make disciples of all nations, baptizing them in the name of the Father and of the Son and of the Holy Spirit, teaching them to observe all that I have commanded you" (Matt. 28:18–20). "Go into all the world and proclaim the gospel to the whole creation. Whoever believes and is baptized will be saved, but whoever does not believe will be condemned" (Mark 16:15–16). "Thus it is written, that the Christ should suffer and on the third day rise from the dead, and that repentance and forgiveness of sins should be proclaimed in his name to all nations, beginning from Jerusalem" (Luke 24:46–47).

Both Matthew and Mark mention baptism, which is the entrance to the Kingdom of God on earth. Thus, a key to the Kingdom is preaching the gospel as well as baptism. Through baptism, people are brought under the authority of Christ, where they have to learn "to observe all that I have commanded you." "Fathers, do not provoke your children to anger, but bring them up in the discipline and instruction of the Lord" (Eph. 6:4).

✢　　✢　　✢

DAY 255 – OPENING AND CLOSING
(Lord's Day 31, Q&A 83, part 3)

A. The preaching of the holy gospel and Christian discipline toward repentance. Both of them open the kingdom of heaven to believers and close it to unbelievers.

There is a close parallel between Matthew 16:19 and 18:18, so that in fact *all* the apostles opened the Kingdom of God to those who accepted the gospel of Christ. So did the preachers of the gospel after the apostles had departed. In Matthew 18:15–20, the actual subject is church discipline. Therefore, the Catechism mentions what it sees as a second key to the Kingdom of heaven: through church discipline, believers are allowed in, and unbelievers are kept out (as far as it is possible to distinguish between them, for only the Lord "knows the hearts of all," Acts 1:24). But church discipline does also a somewhat different thing: it shuts out "anyone who bears the *name* of brother if he is guilty of sexual immorality or greed, or is an idolater, reviler, drunkard, or swindler. . . . 'Purge the evil person from among you'" (1 Cor. 5:11–13). That is, if someone *calls* himself a Christian—or at least participates in church life—but consistently *behaves* like a non-Christian, he is to be put under discipline. This is all explained in the following Q&As.

In fact, we must distinguish here between the Kingdom of God and the church. We cannot possibly remove every evil person from the Kingdom. In a sense, the Kingdom today contains all of Christianity: about 2.3 billion people! We cannot even begin to dismiss those "Christians" who live like unbelievers. This is why the master of the house says in the *Kingdom* parable of the weeds: Don't try to separate the weeds and the wheat, "lest in gathering the weeds you root up the wheat along with them. Let both grow together until the harvest" (Matt. 13:28–30).

This is the procedure for the Kingdom at large. But this is *not* the procedure for the local church. Here, the apostolic command is: "Purge the evil person from among you"! We cannot purge him from the Kingdom—he can go to a neighboring congregation and be received there, and thus remain within the Kingdom—but at least Christians can fulfill their local duty. It does not matter what a church member *labels* himself, it matters how he *manifests* himself.

✣   ✣   ✣

DAY 256 – OPENING THE KINGDOM
(Lord's Day 31, Q&A 84, part 1)

Q. How does preaching the holy gospel open and close the kingdom of heaven?
A. According to the command of Christ: The kingdom of heaven is opened by proclaiming and publicly declaring to all believers, each and every one, that, as often as they accept the gospel promise in true faith, God, because of Christ's merit, truly forgives all their sins.

The Catechism is still working with the image of "keys." In this context, consider this word of Jesus: "Strive to enter through the narrow door. For many, I tell you, will seek to enter and will not be able. When once the master of the house has risen and shut the door, and you begin to stand outside and to knock at the door, saying, 'Lord, open to us,' then he will answer you, 'I do not know where you come from'" (Luke 13:24–25).

At face value, this seems to differ quite strongly from the common picture of the gospel: the preaching of "repentance and forgiveness of sins" (Luke 24:47), and this all on the basis of the pure grace of God. The idea of God's grace for poor, repentant sinners and the idea of "striving" to enter through the narrow door seem to oppose each other. However, the former picture is that of God's sovereign grace, the latter picture is that of the disciple's responsibility. What Jesus wants to say is that it costs you nothing to *become* a disciple of him, but it will cost you everything to *be* a disciple of him. Discipleship is "striving" and "pursuing." To be sure, this can be done only because of the new life that is in the disciple, and in the power of the Holy Spirit. But this does not change the disciple's own responsibility.

"Striving" and "pursuing" are hard. This is why so many "Christians" (disciples, followers of Christ) fall away (cf. John 6:60, 66). The Gospel of Matthew contains many parables in which we see what a mixed multitude we have in the Kingdom of heaven: wheat and weeds, good and bad fishes (Matt. 13), wise and foolish virgins, good and bad servants (Matt. 25). This is nothing but the distinction between true and false Christians—and it is the responsibility of the church to learn to distinguish between them! It is not so difficult to tell Christians from non-Christians, but it is often quite hard to tell regenerate from unregenerate Christians! The last group is what the Catechism calls "hypocrites." They are a danger to the true believers: "[A] little leaven leavens the whole lump" (1 Cor. 5:6; cf. Gal. 5:9).

✠　✠　✠

DAY 257 – CLOSING THE KINGDOM

(Lord's Day 31, Q&A 84, part 2)

A. . . . The kingdom of heaven is closed, however, by proclaiming and publicly declaring to unbelievers and hypocrites that, as long as they do not repent, the wrath of God and eternal condemnation rest on them.

The church must endeavor to keep two groups of people outside its doors: unbelievers and hypocrites. To be sure, *all* people should be welcomed into our church *gatherings*. All should have the opportunity to hear the Word of God, confess their sins, and believe the gospel. But not all hearers may be church members; the church is the "holy congregation and gathering of true Christian believers" (Belgic Confession, Art. 27).

However, we are not God, who alone "knows the hearts of all" (Acts 1:24). Therefore, *in practice* the church is like a "great house," whose foundation has a two-sided seal. On one side is written: "The Lord knows those who are his," and on the other side, "Let everyone who names the name of the Lord depart from iniquity" (2 Tim. 2:19–20). The former side is that of God's omniscience: he alone knows who are his. The latter side is that of our human responsibility. We cannot see whose *heart* belongs to the Lord, but we definitely can see which confessors of Christ "depart from iniquity," and which do not. This refers to those who *live* in sin, and thus basically do not live differently from non-Christians.

We do not simply throw such people out; no, we do our utmost, with the Lord's help, to bring them to repentance. "Brothers, if anyone is caught in any transgression, you who are spiritual should restore him in a spirit of gentleness" (Gal. 6:1). However, there is a limit to the church's tolerance: "[I]f [the evildoer] refuses to listen even to the church, let him be to you as a Gentile and a tax collector" (Matt. 18:17). "It is actually reported that there is sexual immorality among you. . . . Let him who has done this be removed from among you. For though absent in body, I am present in spirit; and as if present, I have already pronounced judgment on the one who did such a thing. When you are assembled in the name of the Lord Jesus and my spirit is present, with the power of our Lord Jesus, you are to deliver this man to Satan for the destruction of the flesh, so that his spirit may be saved in the day of the Lord" (1 Cor. 5:1–5).

✤   ✤   ✤

DAY 258 – GOSPEL AND JUDGMENT
(Lord's Day 31, Q&A 84, part 3)

A. . . . *the wrath of God and eternal condemnation rest on [the un-believers and hypocrites]. God's judgment, both in this life and in the life to come, is based on this gospel testimony.*

Unbelievers and hypocrites are two different categories of people. Unbelievers are those who live like non-Christians. They are outside the Kingdom of God. They are Jews, or Muslims, or Hindus, etc., or they are agnostics and atheists. Hypocrites, however, are also unbelievers, but they have pretensions about being Christians. They were baptized in church, they marry in church, and in the end they will be buried by their church. Once in a while, or even regularly, they attend church services, they sing psalms and hymns, they say their prayers. They are described as "having the appearance of godliness, but denying its power" (2 Tim. 3:5); the apostle adds, "Avoid such people." Such a person "bears the name of brother" (1 Cor. 5:11), but behind the scenes he lives like the godless.

To both unbelievers and hypocrites it is preached "that, as long as they do not repent, the wrath of God and eternal condemnation rest on them" (cf. John 3:36). However, hypocrites will be judged more severely than the outspoken unbelievers because their responsibility is greater. They are "those who have once been enlightened, who have tasted the heavenly gift, and have shared in the Holy Spirit, and have tasted the goodness of the word of God and the powers of the age to come" (Heb. 6:4–5)—and yet they have never truly embraced the gospel. The fact that they "shared in the Holy Spirit" does not necessarily mean anything more than that they enjoyed some of the blessings of the Spirit's presence without ever being inwardly *renewed* by the Spirit.

"Whoever says 'I know him' but does not keep his commandments is a liar, and the truth is not in him. . . . Whoever says he is in the light and hates his brother is still in darkness" (1 John 2:4, 9). "[I]f we go on sinning deliberately after receiving the knowledge of the truth, there no longer remains a sacrifice for sins, but a fearful expectation of judgment, and a fury of fire that will consume the adversaries" (Heb. 10:26–27). Those who have known the Lord (be it outwardly) but never received him are worse off than those who never knew him!

✦   ✦   ✦

DAY 259 – CHRISTIAN DISCIPLINE
(Lord's Day 31, Q&A 85, part 1)

Q. How is the kingdom of heaven closed and opened by Christian discipline?

A. According to the command of Christ: Those who, though called Christians, profess unchristian teachings or live unchristian lives, and who after repeated personal and loving admonitions, refuse to abandon their errors . . . and who after being reported to the church, that is, to those ordained by the church for that purpose, fail to respond also to the church's admonitions.

This answer is an allusion to Matthew 18:15–20 and 1 Corinthians 5, the two most important passages about church discipline. There are others, however, which show the great importance that is attached to the subject: "[W]atch out for those who cause divisions and create obstacles contrary to the doctrine that you have been taught; avoid them. For such persons do not serve our Lord Christ, but their own appetites, and by smooth talk and flattery they deceive the hearts of the naïve" (Rom. 16:17–18). "[K]eep away from any brother who is walking in idleness and not in accord with the tradition that you received from us. . . . Sometimes, such admonitions also came to individual church leaders (which Timothy and Titus both were). Paul describes those who are "having the appearance of godliness, but denying its power" (2 Tim. 3:5), and adds, "Avoid such people." To Titus Paul writes, "[T]here are many who are insubordinate, empty talkers and deceivers, especially those of the circumcision party. They must be silenced, since they are upsetting whole families by teaching for shameful gain what they ought not to teach. . . . Therefore rebuke them sharply, that they may be sound in the faith" (1:10–13). "[A]void foolish controversies, genealogies, dissensions, and quarrels about the law, for they are unprofitable and worthless. As for a person who stirs up division, after warning him once and then twice, have nothing more to do with him, knowing that such a person is warped and sinful; he is self-condemned" (3:9–11).

John wrote to the "elect lady": "If anyone comes to you and does not bring this teaching, do not receive him into your house or give him any greeting, for whoever greets him takes part in his wicked works" (2 John 1:10–11). So we see that every individual believer has a responsibility in this matter: shun those who pretend to be "Christians" but betray Christianity. They are more dangerous than the outspoken unbelievers!

✤   ✤   ✤

DAY 260 – EXCLUDED FROM THE COMMUNITY
(Lord's Day 31, Q&A 85, part 2)

A. ... Those who, though called Christians, ... fail to respond also to the church's admonitions— such persons the church excludes from the Christian community by withholding the sacraments from them, and God also excludes them from the kingdom of Christ.

In the time of the apostles, excluding a person from the church also implied exclusion from the "Kingdom of Christ." At that time, church and Kingdom were thought to coincide. In the *narrower* sense of the Kingdom, this is the case even today. If rebirth is seen as the entrance to the Kingdom viewed from its true, inner perspective (John 3:3–5), then church and Kingdom do coincide, since both consist of the totality of all born again Christians. But if we look at the Kingdom from its outer perspective, as the totality of all Christian *confessors*, things look very differently. An outward confessor holds to certain Christian principles; he is under the authority of Christ, if only outwardly. In this sense, the Kingdom includes all the 2.3 billion Christians who are counted as such in the present world population. In an even wider sense, given the fact that all authority in heaven and on earth has been given to Christ (Matt. 28:18), of course the entire world population is under his rule. In summary, we can look at the "Kingdom of Christ" in three different ways: it is the true church, it is the Christian world, or it is the entire world.

There is another point we have to consider here. Unfortunately, we all know that a true believer can land in a life of grave sins, both morally and doctrinally. Even though he is a true believer—something only the Lord can assess—his condition may become so bad that we cannot distinguish him from an unbeliever anymore. We deal with him, not according to his inner status—because we cannot know this—but according to his practical outward behavior. We cannot allow him at the Lord's table, we cannot even "greet" him (i.e., proclaim God's blessing on him), "for whoever greets him takes part in his wicked works" (2 John 1:10–11). The only thing we can do is pray for his restoration: "Lord, lead him to repentance, and bring the unbeliever to yourself—and if he was a true believer, bring him *back* to yourself!"

✳   ✳   ✳

DAY 261 – RECEIVED AGAIN

(Lord's Day 31, Q&A 85, part 3)

A. . . . Such persons, when promising and demonstrating genuine reform, are received again as members of Christ and of his church.

It is of the greatest importance to realize that church discipline is not a form of punishment such as an earthly judge may bring upon a criminal. Rather, all discipline is directed at the restoration of the trespasser. That restoration is like the father receiving the prodigal son home again (Luke 15:20–24). As Paul says, "If anyone does not obey what we say in this letter, take note of that person, and have nothing to do with him, that he may be ashamed. [However,] [d]o not regard him as an enemy, but warn him as a brother" (2 Thess. 3:14–15). And James says, "My brothers, if anyone among you wanders from the truth and someone brings him back, let him know that whoever brings back a sinner from his wandering will save his soul from death and will cover a multitude of sins" (5:19–20). "[T]he Lord's servant must . . . [correct] his opponents with gentleness. God may perhaps grant them repentance leading to a knowledge of the truth, and they may come to their senses and escape from the snare of the devil, after being captured by him to do his will" (2 Tim. 2:24–26).

From 2 Corinthians we get the impression that the person who was excommunicated in 1 Corinthians 5 later was restored: "[I]f anyone has caused pain, he has caused it not to me, but . . . to all of you. For such a one, this punishment by the majority is enough, so you should rather turn to forgive and comfort him, or he may be overwhelmed by excessive sorrow. So I beg you to reaffirm your love for him. . . . Anyone whom you forgive, I also forgive. Indeed, what I have forgiven, if I have forgiven anything, has been for your sake in the presence of Christ" (2 Cor. 2:5–10).

With the same determination with which we have to put out the unrepentant sinner, we receive him back "when promising and demonstrating genuine reform," as the Catechism puts it. Such restoration, being received again as a member of the church, was what church discipline was all about from the outset, as we should never forget!

❖   ❖   ❖

DAY 262 – GOOD WORKS
(Lord's Day 32, Q&A 86, part 1)

Q. Since we have been delivered from our misery by grace through Christ without any merit of our own, why then should we do good works?
A. Because Christ, having redeemed us by his blood, is also restoring us by his Spirit into his image, so that with our whole lives we may show that we are thankful to God for his benefits.

We now come to the third major part of the Catechism: after "misery" and "deliverance" it is the part of "gratitude," a term that has to be taken in the widest sense as embracing our entire Christian lives. This third major part contains three minor parts: an introduction (Q&As 86–91), then the Ten Commandments (92–115), and finally the Lord's Prayer (116–129).

The introduction opens with the question why we should do good works. The expression "good works" is a good summary of Christian life: Christians are supposed to think, say, and do what is good, that is, what accords with God's commandments and pleases him: "So, whether you eat or drink, or whatever you do, do all to the glory of God" (1 Cor. 10:31).

The first reason that the Catechism gives for such a life is "that with our whole lives we may show that we are thankful to God for his benefits." This is beautifully illustrated by Paul: "I appeal to you therefore, brothers, by the mercies of God, to present your bodies as a living sacrifice, holy and acceptable to God, which is your spiritual worship. Do not be conformed to this world, but be transformed by the renewal of your mind, that by testing you may discern what is the will of God, what is good and acceptable and perfect" (Rom. 12:1–2). He says as it were, "In the light of all the mercies that God has bestowed upon you, as I have explained in the previous chapters, I now appeal to you to dedicate your lives to God."

You can thank God with words: "[G]ive thanks in all circumstances; for this is the will of God in Christ Jesus for you" (1 Thess. 5:18); "giving thanks always and for everything to God the Father in the name of our Lord Jesus Christ" (Eph. 5:20). But you can also thank God with what you do: *"[B]e thankful.* Let the word of Christ dwell in you richly, teaching and admonishing one another in all wisdom, singing psalms and hymns and spiritual songs, with thankfulness in your hearts to God. And whatever you do, in word or deed, do everything in the name of the Lord Jesus, *giving thanks* to God the Father through him" (Col. 3:15–17).

✦ ✦ ✦

DAY 263 – PRAISED THROUGH US
(Lord's Day 32, Q&A 86, part 2)

A. . . . Christ . . . is restoring us by his Spirit into his image, . . . so that [God] may be praised through us.

In no human being did the image of God come to light as beautifully and perfectly as in his own Son, Jesus Christ. He *is* in his person *the* image of God. Paul describes "the light of the gospel of the glory of Christ, who is the image of God," and "the light of the knowledge of the glory of God in the face of Jesus Christ" (2 Cor. 4:4, 6). Elsewhere he says, Christ "is the image of the invisible God, the firstborn of all creation" (Col. 1:15). Therefore, if the image of God is restored in us through his redemption, this is the same as saying that the image of *Christ* is manifested in us: "[T]hose whom [God] foreknew he also predestined to be conformed to the image of his Son, in order that he might be the firstborn among many brothers" (Rom. 8:29). "[W]e all, with unveiled face, beholding the glory of the Lord, are being transformed into the same image from one degree of glory to another" (2 Cor. 3:18); ". . . my little children, for whom I am again in the anguish of childbirth until Christ is formed in you [or, you truly become like Christ, EXB]" (Gal. 4:19).

One of the great purposes of this image of Christ being reproduced in us is that we will learn to praise God. Jesus is the example: "At that time Jesus, full of joy through the Holy Spirit, said, 'I praise you, Father, Lord of heaven and earth, because you have hidden these things from the wise and learned, and revealed them to little children'" (Luke 10:21 NIV). Hebrews 13 says, "Through [Christ] let us continually offer up a sacrifice of praise to God, that is, the fruit of lips that acknowledge his name" (v. 15; cf. Hos. 14:2). The author is thinking here of the voluntary sacrifices (slaughtered animals) of praise that Israelites could offer up to God (Lev. 7:12–15, usually translated as offerings of thanksgiving; cf. Ps. 50:14, 23; 116:17). He asks his readers to offer up such sacrifices not occasionally, but *continually*, through Christ as the "great priest over the house of God" (Heb. 10:21). We do not just praise God, we become "praisers," worshippers of God! "Glorify God in your body!" (1 Cor. 6:20).

✤   ✤   ✤

DAY 264 – ASSURED OF OUR FAITH

(Lord's Day 32, Q&A 86, part 3)

A. . . . Christ . . . is restoring us by his Spirit into his image, . . . so that we may be assured of our faith by its fruits.

Our assurance of salvation is based on two grounds. The one ground consists of the objective promises of God's Word, such as: "If we confess our sins, [God] is faithful and just to forgive us our sins and to cleanse us from all unrighteousness" (1 John 1:9). "[I]f you confess with your mouth that Jesus is Lord and believe in your heart that God raised him from the dead, you will be saved" (Rom. 10:9). This is the objective ground of God's *Word*.

The other ground for our assurance of salvation is the subjective one: "The *Spirit* himself bears witness with our spirit that we are children of God" (Rom. 8:16). Of course, such a speaking of the Spirit in concurrence with our own human spirit does not take place apart from God's Word. Yet, it is different: it is not the Word coming *to* us, but Word and Spirit speaking *in* us. Now, the Catechism's argument is this: how could we ever expect the Spirit to render such a testimony within us if there would be no spiritual fruit in us (cf. Gal. 5:22–24)? Imagine that people would claim that a certain person is alive. But that person is lying on the ground, ashen-faced, without breathing, with no pulse, etc. What reason do you have to assume that this person is alive? If there are no *signs* of life whatsoever, why assume there is life? It is the same with an alleged believer. If there is life, there are fruits. If there are no fruits, what reason do we have to assume that this person is spiritually alive (cf. John 15:2, 6)?

The fruits are for God in the first place. Of course they are. But they have significance for us also: "[W]e may be assured of our faith by its fruits," says the Catechism. Or put it this way: how do we know we are elect from before the foundation of the world (cf. Eph. 1:4)? Peter gives this answer: "[B]e all the more diligent to *confirm* your calling and election, for if you practice these qualities [cf. vv. 5–9] you will never fall. For in this way there will be richly provided for you an entrance into the eternal Kingdom of our Lord and Savior Jesus Christ" (2 Pet. 1:10–11).

✵   ✵   ✵

DAY 265 – GOOD WITNESSES
(Lord's Day 32, Q&A 86, part 4)

A. . . . Christ . . . is restoring us by his Spirit into his image, . . . so that by our godly living our neighbors may be won over to Christ.

Our "godly living" as believers is for God in the first place, and in the second place for "our neighbors" (and in the third place a blessing for ourselves). Imagine a person producing the ninefold "fruit of the Spirit": "love, joy, peace, patience, kindness, goodness, faithfulness, gentleness, self-control" (Gal. 5:22–23). Imagine what a blessing such a person would be for his environment! He radiates the love of God by *loving* people. He radiates the joy of the Lord by speaking and acting with a happy mood, never grumpy. He radiates the peace of God by exhibiting this inner peace of the soul. He is kind, friendly, gentle, meek. As Jesus said, "Blessed are the meek, for they shall inherit the earth. . . . Blessed are the merciful, for they shall receive mercy. Blessed are the pure in heart, for they shall see God. Blessed are the peacemakers, for they shall be called sons of God" (Matt. 5:5–9).

Imagine what an impression such a person will make on the people around him! He will impress them far more by his behavior than by all the good words of gospel he might speak, however important these are. We live in a world of injustice, war, violence, harshness, rudeness, and sadness. In the midst of this is another domain, which is totally opposite to the former one: "[T]he kingdom of God is a matter of . . . righteousness and peace and joy in the Holy Spirit. Whoever thus serves Christ is acceptable to God and approved by men" (Rom. 14:17–18). Do you see it before you? In the midst of so much injustice there are people who "pursue righteousness" (Isa. 51:1; 1 Tim. 6:11; 2 Tim. 2:22). In the midst of so much violence and war there are people who "[s]trive for peace with everyone" (Heb. 12:14). In the midst of so much sadness, these people have their own sadnesses to cope with, yet they rejoice in the Lord always (Phil. 4:4). What a testimony to those around them! What a way to win people over to Christ! "Keep your conduct among the Gentiles honorable, so that when they speak against you as evildoers, they may see your good deeds and glorify God on the day of visitation" (1 Pet. 2:12).

❖   ❖   ❖

DAY 266 – UNGRATEFUL AND UNREPENTANT
(Lord's Day 32, Q&A 87, part 1)

Q. Can those be saved who do not turn to God from their ungrateful and unrepentant ways?
A. By no means. . . .

This seems quite an astonishing question. How could anyone seriously suppose that those "who do not turn to God from their ungrateful and unrepentant ways" could ever be saved? The reason why the Catechism asks this question is apparently to emphasize the necessity and importance of repentance and gratitude (cf. Q&A 88). These two things are important for both believers and unbelievers: the latter should learn to confess their sins for the first time in their lives, the former should learn to do it repeatedly, whenever necessary.

Why is repentance so important? Well, let's ask a counter-question here: Why would God ever forgive our sins if he sees that we do not wish to change our lives, and that we will just continue sinning? Solomon writes, "Whoever conceals his transgressions will not prosper, but he who *confesses* and *forsakes* them will obtain mercy" (Prov. 28:13). God forgives the sins of those only who truly and honestly regret them, and earnestly wish to lead a different life. Some will say, But only God can work such a repentance and intention in a person's heart. They are perfectly right. However, this does not change a person's responsibility. God's fixed rule is: No contrition, no redemption. No repentance, no deliverance.

David writes, "[W]hen I kept silent [i.e., refused to confess my sins], my bones wasted away through my groaning all day long. For day and night your hand was heavy upon me; my strength was dried up as by the heat of summer." But then, fortunately, there is the change: "I acknowledged my sin to you, and I did not cover my iniquity; I said, 'I will confess my transgressions to the Lord,' and you forgave the iniquity of my sin" (Ps. 32:3–5).

The Catechism speaks not only of "unrepentant" but also of "ungrateful ways." A person refusing to confess his sins is not only stubborn and arrogant toward God; he is also ungrateful. The fact that we are creatures should be sufficient to make us grateful toward our Creator. The fact that God, in Jesus Christ, prepared such a wonderful redemption, should make us even more grateful!

❖   ❖   ❖

DAY 267 – NO WICKED IN THE KINGDOM
(Lord's Day 32, Q&A 87, part 2)

A. . . . *Scripture tells us that no unchaste person, no idolater, adulterer, thief, no covetous person, no drunkard, slanderer, robber, or the like will inherit the kingdom of God.*

It is highly noteworthy that, in general, the Bible does not say, Believers are saved, unbelievers are lost, but: The righteous are saved, the wicked are lost. This is a warning to all those who consider themselves to be righteous, because they allegedly "believe," but who live like the wicked. Paul warns true believers not to "associate with anyone who *bears the name of brother* if he is guilty of sexual immorality or greed, or is an idolater, reviler, drunkard, or swindler" (1 Cor. 5:11). "[D]o you not know that the unrighteous will not inherit the kingdom of God? Do not be deceived: neither the sexually immoral, nor idolaters, nor adulterers, nor men who practice homosexuality, nor thieves, nor the greedy, nor drunkards, nor revilers, nor swindlers will inherit the kingdom of God." It is true, he adds, "[S]uch *were* some of you. But you *were* washed, you *were* sanctified, you *were* justified . . ." (6:9–11). But this does not take away anything from the earnestness of his appeal.

It is the same in Ephesians 5: "[S]exual immorality and all impurity or covetousness must not even be named among you, as is proper among saints. Let there be no filthiness nor foolish talk nor crude joking, which are out of place, but instead let there be thanksgiving. For you may be sure of this, that everyone who is sexually immoral or impure, or who is covetous (that is, an idolater), has no inheritance in the kingdom of Christ and God" (vv. 3–5; cf. Gal. 5:19–21). Again, Paul's message is this: you may claim to be true believers—and for many of you I accept this—but please remember: if you live like the wicked, whatever your confession may be, you may die like the wicked, and go to hell like the wicked, and your confession will prove to be worthless. "Therefore let anyone who thinks that he stands take heed lest he fall" (1 Cor. 10:12). "Do not be deceived: God is not mocked, for whatever one sows, that will he also reap. For the one who sows to his own flesh will from the flesh reap corruption, but the one who sows to the Spirit will from the Spirit reap eternal life" (Gal. 6:7–8).

✢   ✢   ✢

DAY 268 – GENUINE REPENTANCE
(Lord's Day 33, Q&A 88, part 1)

Q. What is involved in genuine repentance or conversion?
A. Two things: the dying-away of the old self.

The New Testament contains basically two words for conversion. The one literally means "turning (back)": ". . . how you turned to God from idols to serve the living and true God" (1 Thess. 1:9). The other word means "repentance"; as John the Baptist and Jesus preached: "Repent, for the kingdom of heaven is at hand" (Matt. 3:2; 4:17). Sometimes the two words occur in one sentence: "Repent therefore, and turn back, that your sins may be blotted out" (Acts 3:19). It was preached to the Jews and "to the Gentiles, that they should repent and turn to God, performing deeds in keeping with their repentance" (26:20). The term for "turning to God" means a drastic change of lifestyle, not serving the idols anymore but God. The term for "repentance" means a drastic change of one's inner being: a radical change of mind.

Words like "drastic" and "radical" are appropriate to describe what is happening. In other Bible passages this is even described in terms of life and death. The *living* sinner must *die*: "We know that our old self was crucified with him in order that the body of sin might be brought to nothing, so that we would no longer be enslaved to sin" (Rom. 6:6). "In [Christ] you were circumcised with a circumcision made without hands, by putting off the body of the flesh, by the circumcision of Christ, having been buried with him in baptism" (Col. 2:11–12). A *life* in sin can only end in *death*, that is, the vicarious death of Jesus—a death that is practically and visibly illustrated in baptism.

God does not trim, revamp, overhaul, or refurbish the old self. *Death* is his only solution for it. Or, to use another term: God has made us a "new creation": "[I]f anyone is in Christ, he is a new creation. The old has passed away; behold, the new has come" (2 Cor. 5:17). "But far be it from me to boast except in the cross of our Lord Jesus Christ, by which the world has been crucified to me, and I to the world. For neither circumcision counts for anything, nor uncircumcision, but a new creation. And as for all who walk by this rule, peace and mercy be upon them" (Gal. 6:14–16).

✦ ✦ ✦

DAY 269 – DYING AND RISING
(LORD'S DAY 33, Q&A 88, PART 2)

A. . . . the dying-away of the old self, and the rising-to-life of the new.

The tremendous change in a person who turns from being a wicked sinner into a beloved child of God could not be described more radically than in terms of death and life. The repentant sinner, who truly confides in Christ and his redemptive work, is brought from death to life. Colossians 2 is one of the few passages where both aspects are mentioned: ". . . having been buried with him in baptism, in which you were also raised with him through faith in the powerful working of God, who raised him from the dead. And you, who were dead in your trespasses and the uncircumcision of your flesh, God made alive together with him" (vv. 12–13). The parallel passage says this: "God, . . . when we were dead in our trespasses, made us alive together with Christ—by grace you have been saved—and raised us up with him and seated us with him in the heavenly places in Christ Jesus" (Eph. 2:4–6).

A bit later Paul speaks of putting "off your old self, which belongs to your former manner of life and is corrupt through deceitful desires, and to be renewed in the spirit of your minds, and to put on the new self, created after the likeness of God in true righteousness and holiness" (4:22–24). And elsewhere: "If then you have been raised with Christ, seek the things that are above, where Christ is, seated at the right hand of God. Set your minds on things that are above, not on things that are on earth. For you have died, and your life is hidden with Christ in God. . . . Put to death therefore what is earthly in you: sexual immorality, impurity, passion, evil desire, and covetousness, which is idolatry" (Col. 3:1–5).

Here we clearly see the two stages in this dying and living. First, at the moment we came to faith, we realized that we *had* died and *had* been raised with Christ, once for all. But second, hereafter, during our Christian life, this has to become practically true in our lives: "you *have* died . . . now put to death!" One day, you put on the new self; but you have to realize this every day anew: keep being renewed, keep putting off and putting on, all the time, as part of your spiritual growth!

✳   ✳   ✳

DAY 270 – DYING-AWAY
(Lord's Day 33, Q&A 89, part 1)

Q. What is the dying-away of the old self?
A. To be genuinely sorry for sin . . .

The "old self" (literally "old human"; see "old man" in the KJV) is the human being in his sinful, unrepentant state. A person will leave this state behind if, through the power of the Holy Spirit, he learns to truly and honestly regret his former sinful life, and turns away from it. He may regret the pain that he, by his sins, caused other people. But the deepest and most significant repentance involves that he realizes that he dishonored *God* by his sins. Whether this concerns a direct sin against God himself (e.g., blasphemy), or a sin against one's neighbor (e.g., stealing, insulting), in both cases it is the holy and righteous *God* who is offended. The reason for this is that he is our Creator, he determines what he may expect of his creatures, and he has laid this down in his commandments. Whether we sin against the Second or against the Seventh Commandment, in both cases it is *God's* commandments that we transgress. David had taken his neighbor's wife and caused this neighbor's death. Yet, he says, "Against *you, you only*, have I sinned and done what is evil in your sight" (Ps. 51:4).

As important as it is to regret and confess our sins, it is just as important to realize that God wholeheartedly forgives: "If you, O Lord, should mark iniquities, O Lord, who could stand? *But with you there is forgiveness, that you may be feared*" (Ps. 130:3–4). "[T]hus says the One who is high and lifted up, who inhabits eternity, whose name is Holy: 'I dwell in the high and holy place, and also with him who is of a contrite and lowly spirit, to revive the spirit of the lowly, and to revive the heart of the contrite'" (Isa. 57:15; cf. 66:2). Therefore, the Lord makes this appeal: "'[R]eturn to me with all your heart, with fasting, with weeping, and with mourning; and rend your hearts and not your garments.' Return to the Lord your God, for he is gracious and merciful, slow to anger, and abounding in steadfast love; and he relents over disaster" (Joel 2:12–13). As Paul says, "[G]odly grief produces a repentance that leads to salvation without regret" (2 Cor. 7:10).

✦ ✦ ✦

DAY 271 – RUN AWAY FROM SIN
(Lord's Day 33, Q&A 89, part 2)

Q. What is the dying-away of the old self?
A. To be genuinely sorry for sin and more and more to hate and run away from it.

Here again we must distinguish between the moment of conversion and coming to faith, on the one hand, and the Christian life that follows upon it, on the other hand. At conversion, we come to "hate" our sins *in principle*, are "genuinely sorry" for them, and are fully prepared to "run away" from them (as Joseph literally did; Gen. 39:12). At the same time we must say: How deeply do we, at that moment, really *fathom* our sinfulness? As somebody once wrote, one sin is in God's eye worse than all the sins of the world are in *our* eyes. However, the more we spiritually grow, the more we learn about the "depths" of sin (cf. Ps. 130:1).

Please note, such learning about the depths of sin should *never* lead us to waver concerning our assurance of salvation. The learning as such does not even *increase* our assurance; what it will increase is our gratitude and our love toward the Lord, who paid such a price for our sins! He once said about the sinful woman, "[H]er sins, which are many, are forgiven—for she loved much. But he who is forgiven little, loves little" (Luke 7:47). We run away from sin not out of any form of legalism or Pharisaism, but because our new self has learned to hate it. God teaches us that he crucified our old self on the cross of Christ (Rom. 6:6), but in response to this, we ourselves "by the Spirit put to death the deeds of the body" (Rom. 8:13). "[T]hose who belong to Christ Jesus have crucified the flesh with its passions and desires" (Gal. 5:24).

"Put to death therefore what is earthly in you: sexual immorality, impurity, passion, evil desire, and covetousness," etc. (Col. 3:5). This is *our* responsibility. In so doing, we acknowledge every day of our lives the righteous judgment of God upon our sins, and even upon our "old self." This does not mean we will never fall into sin again, but we do hate sin. You can scrub a pig clean, but when you let it loose, it will return to the mud. That's its nature. But if a sheep falls in the mud, it hates it, it will stand on its legs as soon as possible, and will try clean itself. That's its nature!

❖   ❖   ❖

DAY 272 – RISING-TO-LIFE

(Lord's Day 33, Q&A 90, part 1)

Q. What is the rising-to-life of the new self?
A. Wholehearted joy in God through Christ . . .

It is striking that the Catechism mentions *joy* as the first aspect of the new self. This is a deep truth. The newly converted Ethiopian eunuch "went on his way rejoicing" (Acts 8:39). The newly converted jailer "rejoiced along with his entire household that he had believed in God" (16:34). The gospel even brought joy to the entire city of Samaria (8:8).

Joy is a typical biblical blessing: "[T]he joy of the LORD is your strength" (Neh. 8:10). The Israelites were commanded once to rejoice at the Feast of Weeks (Deut. 16:11), and three times to rejoice at the Feast of Booths (Lev. 23:40; Deut. 16:14–15). In the New Testament, joy is part of the fruit of the Spirit, mentioned directly after "love" (Gal. 5:22). Joy in the Holy Spirit is even one of three major aspects of the Kingdom of God as described in Romans 14:17. Although Paul was a prisoner at the time, he called upon believers to rejoice in the Lord always (Phil. 2:18, 28; 3:1; 4:4). A believer might not find much joy in his earthly circumstances as such (horizontal joy or sorrow; cf. 2:27); but he will always find joy in the Lord (vertical joy). As Paul says elsewhere, ". . . as sorrowful, yet always rejoicing" (2 Cor. 6:10). "Finally, brothers, rejoice" (13:11).

The believer can say, God is "my exceeding joy" (Ps. 43:4). Israel was supposed to "serve the LORD your God with joyfulness and gladness of heart" (Deut. 28:47; cf. 1 Kings 8:66; Ps. 32:11). We "rejoice in God through our Lord Jesus Christ, through whom we have now received reconciliation" (Rom. 5:11). When Jesus had to leave his disciples behind, he gave them three very personal presents; he called them "*my* peace" (John 14:27), "*my* love" (15:9–10), and "*my* joy": "These things I have spoken to you, that my joy may be in you, and that your joy may be full" (v. 11; cf. 17:13). As the apostle John comments: "[O]ur fellowship is with the Father and with his Son Jesus Christ. And we are writing these things so that our [other manuscripts: your] joy may be complete" (1 John 1:3–4). Eternal joy will be on our heads (Isa. 35:10; 51:11).

✣   ✦   ✣

DAY 273 – JOY, LOVE, DELIGHT

(Lord's Day 33, Q&A 90, part 2)

Q. What is the rising-to-life of the new self?
A. Wholehearted joy in God through Christ, and a love and delight
to live according to the will of God by doing every kind of good work.

Legalism is keeping God's commandments in a pedantic way, as an aim in itself, not in honor of God but for one's own satisfaction, despising others who are less scrupulous, adding all kinds of self-made commandments, etc. This is a work of our sinful flesh. It is characteristic of religious but unregenerate people, but is sometimes also found in regenerate people who are misled, or mislead themselves. Legalism may give some inner satisfaction, but it can never give "joy in God through Christ." Your delight can only be in the law of the Lord if you delight in the Lord himself (Ps. 1:2; Rom. 7:22). This delight is a very clear feature of a person's renewed self: he loves the Lord, and therefore he loves to "live according to the will of God". Loving God and keeping his commandments are always closely connected (Exod. 20;6; Deut. 5:10; 7:9; 11:1, 22; 30:16; Josh. 22:5; Neh. 1:5; Dan. 9:4). The one does not go without the other.

This was the case with Jesus: it was his pleasure to do the things that were a pleasure to his Father (cf. John 8:29) because he loved the Father (14:31). In his prayers, he "overflowed with joy from the Holy Spirit" (Luke 10:21 CEB; cf. ISV: "the Holy Spirit made Jesus extremely joyful"; MSG: "Jesus rejoiced, exuberant in the Holy Spirit"). He could say, "I delight to do your will, O my God; your law is within my heart" (Ps. 40:8; cf. Jer. 31:33; Heb. 8:10; 10:16). He expected the same from his disciples: "Whoever has my commandments and keeps them, he it is who loves me" (John 14:21). "If you keep my commandments, you will abide in my love, just as I have kept my Father's commandments and abide in his love" (15:10).

In fact, there is only one way in which we can prove that we truly love God and his Son, Jesus Christ: "By this we know that we love the children of God, when we love God and obey his commandments. For this is the love of God, that we keep his commandments" (1 John 5:2–3). Therefore, "let us consider how to stir up one another to love and good works" (Heb. 10:24). "Be ready for every good work" (Titus 3:1; cf. 2 Tim. 2:21)!

❖   ❖   ❖

DAY 274 – OUT OF TRUE FAITH

(Lord's Day 33, Q&A 91, part 1)

Q. What are good works?
A. Only those which are done out of true faith.

In this Q&A the Catechism summarizes what we must understand by this important characteristic of Christian life: "good works." Please notice that this term is never used for unbelievers; the highest level the ungodly might ever reach is "dead works" (Heb. 6:1; 9:14). These are works that may be beneficial to others, but that do not come out of the true life *of* God, and do not lead to eternal life *with* God. "Good works" in the biblical sense are "done out of true faith." Good works are those that are pleasing to God, but "without faith it is impossible to please him, for whoever would draw near to God must believe that he exists and that he rewards those who seek him" (Heb. 11:6).

There is more to say about the source of truly good works. Faith as such is a prerequisite, but it is not enough. Jesus said, "Whoever abides in me and I in him, he it is that bears much fruit, for *apart from me you can do nothing*" (John 15:5). So Jesus himself is the origin of good works. You can also say that the Holy Spirit is the source of good works: in opposition to the "works of the flesh" (Gal. 5:19) stands the "fruit of the Spirit," namely, "love, joy, peace, patience, kindness, goodness, faithfulness, gentleness, self-control" (vv. 22–23). You can also say that *God* is the origin of our good works: "[W]e are his workmanship, created in Christ Jesus for good works, which God prepared beforehand, that we should walk in them" (Eph. 2:10). God "who began a good work in you will bring it to completion at the day of Jesus Christ" (Phil. 1:6).

It is obvious that doing good works is the believer's own responsibility; we will even have to account for everything we did, whether good or bad: "[L]et each one test his own work. . . . For each will have to bear his own load" (Gal. 6:4–5; cf. 1 Cor. 4:4–5; 2 Cor. 5:10). But this is only one—though an essential—side of the story. The other side is that in ourselves we have no power, not even as believers, to do any good works: faith is the primary condition, but then we need the power of the Holy Spirit to accomplish good works.

✳   ✳   ✳

DAY 275 – CONFORM TO GOD'S LAW
(Lord's Day 33, Q&A 91, part 2)

Q. What are good works?
A. Only those which . . . conform to God's law . . .

Imagine I hire a carpenter to repair some things in my house. He arrives on Monday morning, sets himself behind my piano, and plays one great work by Chopin after the other. I am thrilled. After an hour or so I say, "Incredible, fantastic—you are fired. This is not what I hired you for." (Of course I should have stopped him long before.) Was what he did not "good"? Yes and no. Making wonderful music is good in itself. But it was not the right thing at the right moment.

Lots of people have clear-cut ideas about what are "good (beautiful, beneficial) works," and in itself this is alright. Paul even says in a very general way, "[W]hatever is true, whatever is honorable, whatever is just, whatever is pure, whatever is lovely, whatever is commendable, if there is any excellence, if there is anything worthy of praise, think about these things," that is, strive for them (Phil. 4:8). Already Solomon said, "Whatever your hand finds to do, do it with your might" (Eccl. 9:10). That is one side of the story. If you hesitate every time you have to act because you wonder whether this or that is really what God wants you to do, you'll not be doing very much at all.

The other side is important too, however. You may spend much time with your poor, young, beautiful widowed neighbor, neglecting your own wife and family. You may think you are a very nice, helpful, social type of person. Yet, every person with any sense can tell you that what you are doing is dangerous and wrong. You are "playing" with the Seventh Commandment. Your intentions may be good (although I would mistrust them in this case), but this is not enough. Your works must always "conform to God's law." And don't look for the "edges" of these commandments, where you might fall overboard! Some things, such as adultery, are *always* wrong. Some things may be sometimes okay, at other times they are not, because God had something else in mind for you. May God "equip you with everything good that you may do his will, working in us that which is pleasing in his sight, through Jesus Christ" (Heb. 13:21)!

✣　✣　✣

DAY 276 – FOR GOD'S GLORY

(Lord's Day 33, Q&A 91, part 3)

Q. What are good works?
A. Only those which are done . . . for God's glory.

Some good works are nice in themselves, in that they benefit people around us, yet they are not for God's glory. This is the case, for instance, if we were doing them primarily for our own glory. For instance, "[t]he one who speaks on his own authority seeks his own glory; but the one who seeks the glory of him who sent him is true" (John 7:18). So, it is not sufficient if our works, such as altruism and generosity, are good in themselves. They must also be done with the proper intentions: not for our own glory, but for God's glory; not out of love for ourselves, but out of love for God. Not even the unselfish love for our neighbors is sufficient; the deepest motive must always be love for God, even if it is our neighbors who are the beneficiaries of our good works.

Paul says, "[W]hether you eat or drink, or whatever you do, do all to the glory of God" (1 Cor. 10:31), and: "[W]hatever you do, in word or deed, do everything in the name of the Lord Jesus, giving thanks to God the Father through him" (Col. 3:17). God is glorified by our obedience! On the one hand, we do good works because this is a characteristic of our new nature. We *love* to do good works. But on the other hand, it always remains true that we *must* do good works (Eph. 2:10; Col. 1:10; 1 Tim. 6:18; 2 Tim. 2:21; Titus 2:7; 3:1, 8; 3:14; Heb. 10:24). These two things go hand in hand in our Christian walk. On the one hand, we never do things simply on our own initiative: we do them in obedience to the Lord's commandments. On the other hand, we never do them *only* because we are told to do them. It also gives us great joy to do them.

This is why the law is called the "law of liberty" (James 1:25; 2:12): we do certain things because we must; that is the law part. But we also do them because we love to honor God through them; that is the liberty part. God's law is the objective motive, that is, *outside* us; our new nature's desire to glorify God through our works is the subjective motive, that is, *inside* us. Having only the former is legalism. Having only the latter is libertinism (if not sentimentalism).

✤　✤　✤

DAY 277 – NOT BASED ON OUR IDEAS
(Lord's Day 33, Q&A 91, part 4)

Q. What are good works?
A. Only those which are . . . not based on our own opinion or human tradition.

There is always the danger that we develop our own rules for what are good works, and what are not. We sometimes hear believers say, "I cannot believe that the Lord would be against what we are going to do." But what value does this personal opinion have? Or they say, "We are used to acting so and so in this or that situation." But what value do their customs and habits have?

Many people wear a bracelet with the letters WWJD, "What Would Jesus Do?" Apparently, those who wear such a wristband wish to express that they love to act always in the same way Jesus would have done. The difficulty, of course, is how, and whether, we can *know* how Jesus would have acted in any given situation. His actions often came as a surprise. He did not condemn the adulterous woman in John 8:1–11, but it is certain that *we* sometimes *have to* condemn adulterous men and women in the church (1 Cor. 5). He said to a paralytic: "Son, your sins are forgiven" (Mark 2:3–5). However, *we* cannot forgive someone's sins that were not committed against *us*, and even in this latter case, there must first be a spoken confession. "What would Jesus do?" is a great question, but first, we usually are not able to answer it; and second, even if we could, we cannot always imitate him. The only certainty we have is that we should always be driven by the same *love* as Jesus was.

Good works must be measured by God's standards, not human standards. Abraham was prepared to kill his son, and Rahab was betraying her own country. According to the laws of our modern nations, both would be guilty of very serious crimes. But in God's eyes, these were good works that proved that Abraham and Rahab were truly righteous (James 2:21–25).

With our own opinions and traditions we are always tempted to add to the Lord's commandments (Deut. 12:32). However, we have no need of the "commandments of men" (Matt. 15:9; cf. Isa. 29:13). All traditionalists should listen to the Lord's warning: "Do not walk in the statutes of your fathers, nor keep *their* rules . . . walk in *my* statutes, and be careful to obey *my* rules" (Ezek. 20:18–19; cf. Col. 2:8).

✶   ✶   ✶

DAY 278 – WHAT IS GOD'S LAW?

(Lord's Day 34, Q&A 92, part 1)

Q. *What is God's law?*
A. *God spoke all these words.*

Here begins the extensive part of the Catechism that deals with the Ten Commandments, or the Decalogue (Q&As 92–115). It begins with a very broad question: "What is God's law?" The Catechism may seem to suggest that God's law contains only the Decalogue, but of course God's law is a much wider concept. The word "law" in Hebrew is *Torah*, which may refer to (a) any commandment of God (cf. Gen. 26:5, "Abraham obeyed . . . my laws"), (b) the entire Mosaic law (e.g., 1 Kings 2:3; Luke 2:22), (c) the five books of Moses (e.g., Luke 24:44; Acts 28:23), or (d) the entire Old Testament (e.g., Rom. 3:19, where the term includes a number of Psalms).

The most common meaning of *Torah* is (b) the Mosaic law, and this is what the Catechism refers to. "God's law" is the totality of all his commandments. There is no doubt that the Decalogue is the summary and kernel of this (Mosaic) law. They are the words that God began with on Mount Sinai (Exod. 20:1–17; cf. Deut. 5:6–21), and that were summarized by Paul as "the law" (Rom. 13:8–10).

It is a sad mistake of some theologians to claim that Jesus would have *abrogated* the Mosaic law. He said himself, "Do not think that I have come to abolish the Law or the Prophets; I have not come to abolish them but to fulfill them" (Matt. 5:17). The term "fulfill" can have a prophetic sense (cf. v. 18; Luke 24:44), and it can mean "observe" the law (cf. Rom. 8:4; 13:8, 10; Gal. 6:2; James 2:8). In the case of Jesus, the word "fulfill" also had the special meaning of him being the "goal" (Rom. 10:4 CEB, CJB), "fulfillment" (GW, NOG), or "culmination" of the law (NIV, ISV). Therefore, Jesus could speak of "*my* commandments" (John 14:15, 21; 15:10) because he brought their most profound meaning to light, as we will see. In this Christian sense, the commandments have great significance: "Bear one another's burdens, and so fulfill the *law of Christ*" (Gal. 6:2). Paul said that he was "under the law of Christ" (1 Cor. 9:21). In such expressions, the "law" is the summary of all the rules for true Christian living. This is why the Catechism pays so much attention to them!

❖   ❖   ❖

DAY 279 – THE "TEN WORDS"
(Lord's Day 34, Q&A 92, part 2)

Q. What is God's law?
A. God spoke all these words.

In the Bible, the Ten Commandments are literally called the "Ten Words" (Exod. 34:28; Deut. 4:13; 10:4 CEB, etc.). It is significant that the Decalogue begins with the words, "I am the Lord your God, who brought you out of the land of Egypt, out of the house of slavery" (Exod. 20:2; Deut. 5:6). Jewish tradition even considers this to be the first of the Ten Words. This first saying, not an imperative at all but an indicative, places the Decalogue in the context of the covenant by referring primarily to the Redeemer God of the covenant. The Ten Words explicitly address a nation redeemed, if not in the full spiritual meaning (cf. 1 Cor. 10:1–5), then at least in the typological sense (vv. 6–12).

Even the famous words, "if a person does [my laws], he shall live by them" (Lev. 18:5), literally do not speak of the problem how to *obtain* eternal life (in spite of the apparent *application* in Rom. 10:5; Gal. 3:12) but of the problem *how to lead a truly blessed life as part of God's redemptive people* (Deut. 4:40; 5:33; 8:1; 11:9; 16:20; 25:15; 30:16; cf. v. 18). The statement in Leviticus 18:5 is again preceded by the declaration "I am the Lord your God" (v. 4) and the implicit reminder of the deliverance from Egypt (vv. 1–3). Israel is addressed as a redeemed and holy nation (Exod. 19:4–6). The statement in Leviticus 18:5 is not about how to *become* holy but about how to *remain* holy.

Thus, the Decalogue is not to be isolated from the rest of the Pentateuch and elevated to some domain of timeless, abstract principles. It stands within the historical framework of Israel's redemption from Egypt, and is closely connected with other imperatives in historical Pentateuchal frameworks, such as: "Go from your country" (Gen. 12:1). "The Lord will fight for you, and you have only to be silent" (Exod. 14:14); "you shall be to me a kingdom of priests and a holy nation" (19:6). God's commands, no matter how abstract they may seem, are always embedded in concrete *events*, in the *course* that God follows with his people through redemptive history. It is the same with Christians and the law of Christ.

✦ ✦ ✦

DAY 280 – GOD'S COMMANDMENTS
(Lord's Day 34, Q&A 92, part 3)

Q. *What is God's law?*
A. *God spoke all these words: "I am the* Lord *your God, who brought you out of the land of Egypt, out of the house of slavery.*

(1) "You shall have no other gods before me.

(2) "You shall not make for yourself a carved image, or any likeness of anything that is in heaven above, or that is in the earth beneath, or that is in the water under the earth. You shall not bow down to them or serve them, for I the Lord your God am a jealous God, visiting the iniquity of the fathers on the children to the third and the fourth generation of those who hate me, but showing steadfast love to thousands of those who love me and keep my commandments.

(3) "You shall not take the name of the Lord your God in vain, for the Lord will not hold him guiltless who takes his name in vain.

(4) "Remember the Sabbath day, to keep it holy. Six days you shall labor, and do all your work, but the seventh day is a Sabbath to the Lord your God. On it you shall not do any work, you, or your son, or your daughter, your male servant, or your female servant, or your livestock, or the sojourner who is within your gates. For in six days the Lord made heaven and earth, the sea, and all that is in them, and rested on the seventh day. Therefore the Lord blessed the Sabbath day and made it holy.

(5) "Honor your father and your mother, that your days may be long in the land that the Lord your God is giving you.

(6) "You shall not murder.

(7) "You shall not commit adultery.

(8) "You shall not steal.

(9) "You shall not bear false witness against your neighbor.

(10)"You shall not covet your neighbor's house, you shall not covet your neighbor's wife, or his male servant, or his female servant, or his ox, or his donkey, or anything that is your neighbor's."

These are the Ten Words in their usual Protestant enumeration (Exod. 20:1–17 ESV; cf. Deut. 5:6–21; Lev. 19:18b; also cf. Rom. 13:19 and Matt. 22:36–40).

✦   ✦   ✦

DAY 281 – THE COMMANDMENTS DIVIDED
(Lord's Day 34, Q&A 93)

Q. How are these commandments divided?
A. Into two tables. The first has four commandments, teaching us how we ought to live in relation to God. The second has six commandments, teaching us what we owe our neighbor.

The Catechism describes here an ancient tradition, which, however, has also been criticized. Some feel that all Ten Commandments were written on each tablet of stone, the one being a copy of the other. Others feel that on each tablet five commandments were written. At face value, the fifth commandment seems rather to fit on the second tablet because parents belong to our horizontal relationships, whereas the relationship with God is a vertical one. But, as some have argued, the fifth commandment is actually a commandment concerning the principle of authority, and therefore refers in the first place to God's authority (cf. Q&A 104). All horizontal authority, that is, between human beings, is only derived authority, deduced from God's authority.

However this may be, we fully appreciate the Catechism's intention: the first group of commandments concerns the relationship between humanity and God, the second group concerns the relationships between people. This is in line with the way Jesus summarizes the entire law. A Pharisee asked him, "Teacher, which is the great commandment in the Law?" Jesus answered, "'You shall love the Lord your God with all your heart and with all your soul and with all your mind.' This is the great and first commandment. And a second is like it: 'You shall love your neighbor as yourself.' On these two commandments depend all the Law and the Prophets" (Matt. 22:35–40).

If the traditional view is correct, then the "great and first commandment," as Jesus calls it, is the subject of the first tablet of stone, and the "second like it" is worked out on the second tablet. The two subjects are closely related: "If anyone says, 'I love God,' and hates his brother, he is a liar; for he who does not love his brother whom he has seen cannot love God whom he has not seen. And this commandment we have from him: whoever loves God must also love his brother. . . . By this we know that we love the children of God, when we love God and obey his commandments" (1 John 4:20–5:2). No love for God, then no love for the neighbors—and vice versa.

❖   ❖   ❖

DAY 282 – NO IDOLATRY

(Lord's Day 34, Q&A 94, part 1)

Q. What does the Lord require in the first commandment?
A. That I, not wanting to endanger my own salvation, avoid and
shun all idolatry, sorcery, superstitious rites, and prayer to saints or
to other creatures . . .

In the law of Moses, no sin is considered to be more serious than idolatry; therefore, the first "You shall" is this: "You shall have no other gods before [or, besides] me." You may say, But how can this be? There is only one God (Deut. 6:4). So how could anyone "have" gods besides the Lord? However, you forget that God is called the "God of gods" (e.g., Deut. 10:17; Ps. 136:2), and that the Bible repeatedly speaks of "gods" as a spiritual reality (e.g., Ps. 86:8; 95:3; 96:4; 135:5)—although we know that these "gods" are nothing but created angels, who have backslidden. They are the thrones, dominions, rulers, and authorities that were originally created by God through Christ (Col. 1:16). In fact, they are demonic powers; idolaters serve demons (cf. Lev. 17:7; Deut. 32:17; 1 Cor. 10:20; Rev. 9:20). The core of all idolatry is replacing the Creator by his creatures (Rom. 1:23), and worshiping them instead of him.

Worshiping such powers alongside God, or even instead of God, is called (spiritual) "adultery." God was "married" to his people on Mount Sinai (cf. Jer. 2:2), and when his people mix with "other gods," this is called "whoring" (e.g., Exod. 34:15–16; Lev. 20:5–6; Deut. 31:16). This is why the false church is called the "great prostitute" (Rev. 17): she has left Christ, and mixes with his adversaries. No offense of God is more gross than idolatry, and its collateral phenomena ("sorcery, superstitious rites," necromancy, divination, etc.; see Deut. 18:9–14). The Catechism even adds "prayer to saints or to other creatures"—an allusion to Roman Catholics (although, of course, not all Roman Catholics pray to saints as if they were gods).

When John writes, "Little children, keep yourselves from idols" (1 John 5:21), he is not necessarily thinking of literal images. *Everything* that threatens to take the place of God or Christ in our minds and lives is in fact a form of idolatry. "What agreement has the temple of God with idols?" (2 Cor. 6:16). Even greed is a form of idolatry because it implies not finding all your sufficiency in God (cf. Eph. 5:5; Col. 3:5).

✢   ✢   ✢

DAY 283 – SERVING THE ONLY GOD

(Lord's Day 34, Q&A 94, part 2)

A. . . . That I rightly know the only true God, trust him alone, and look to God for every good thing humbly and patiently, and love, fear, and honor God with all my heart. . . .

It is striking that eight of the Ten Commandments have a negative form: "You shall *not.*" As we will see, the New Testament shows how, at a deeper level, all these prohibitions go back to a positive ground-form: "The Lord expects of you, his people, that you . . . " Thus, the first commandment could be rendered as follows: "Self-evidently, you will love the Lord, your God, so ardently that you do not even entertain the thought of letting any power, any person, or anything come between you and your God." As the Catechism puts it: you trust no other power or person or thing but God alone; you put all your confidence in him alone. You love, fear (i.e., revere, respect), and honor (praise, worship) no other power or person or thing but God alone.

In John 17:3, Jesus explains that knowing the only true God is eternal life. This knowing does not involve theological knowledge, but relationship, intimacy, fellowship, trust (cf. Jer. 17:5, 7). This again involves "looking to God for every good thing humbly and patiently," instead of expecting any real good from any other source: "Every good gift and every perfect gift is from above, coming down from the Father of lights with whom there is no variation or shadow due to change" (James 1:17). All creatures "look to you, to give them their food in due season. When you give it to them, they gather it up; when you open your hand, they are filled with good things" (Ps. 104:27–28).

It is amazing how in the law of Moses, especially in Deuteronomy, there is so much emphasis on *loving* the Lord (in particular because he loved his people first, 7:7–9, 12; cf. 6:5; 11:1, 11, 22; 13:3; 19:9; 30:6, 16, 20). If we say, "Actually I would like to serve this or that [which in fact is an idol], but unfortunately this is not allowed," we betray the spirit of legalism. If we say, "I love the Lord so much that the thought of serving any idol does not even cross my mind"—and we mean it!—this is the spirit of the law of Christ. "We love because he first loved us" (1 John 4:19). Nothing may affect the intimacy of this relationship!

✦ ✦ ✦

DAY 284 – LIVING BY GOD'S WILL
(Lord's Day 34, Q&A 94, part 3)

A. . . . In short, that I give up anything rather than go against God's will in any way.

It may come as a surprise that, at this point, the Catechism brings in the matter of obedience to God's will. This is perfectly appropriate, however. True love for God excludes all possible idolatry—but what *is* true love for God? It proves itself no more clearly than in obedience. Not obsequious obedience, like that of a slave to his master, but the obedience of love: "Your wish is my command."

At face value, it may sound strange that genuine love for God comes to expression in observing his commandments; yet, it is true. The apostle John expresses it in a sober and persuasive way: "[B]y this we know that we have come to know him, if we keep his commandments. . . . Whoever keeps his commandments abides in God, and God in him. . . . If anyone says, 'I love God,' and hates his brother, he is a liar; for he who does not love his brother whom he has seen cannot love God whom he has not seen. And this commandment we have from him: whoever loves God must also love his brother. . . . By this we know that we love the children of God, when we love God and obey his commandments. For this is the love of God, that we keep his commandments. And his commandments are not burdensome" (2:3; 3:24; 4:20–21; 5:2–3).

Please remember: you can obey God's will because you "have to" (legalism), or because you "love to." Take your pick! Or, to put it more strongly: you can love God because this is a command, but you can also love God out of your own heart—because you *love* to love him! This is why I just quoted from John that God's commandments are not "burdensome"; this is because you love him, and—I may add—because you do so in the power of his Spirit. And likewise you love Jesus, not simply because that is the duty of a disciple, but because he is "altogether lovely" (Song 5:16 NKJV). "Whoever loves father or mother more than me is not worthy of me, and whoever loves son or daughter more than me is not worthy of me" (Matt. 10:37). As a genuine disciple, you love to serve him because you love him, and you even love to love him. He is "distinguished among ten thousand" (Song 5:10)!

✣ ✣ ✣

DAY 285 – WHAT IS IDOLATRY?

(Lord's Day 34, Q&A 95, part 1)

Q. What is idolatry?
A. Idolatry is having or inventing something in which one trusts in place of or alongside of the only true God . . .

It is worthwhile to enter a little more deeply into the subject of the deeper nature of idolatry. There is a beautiful word that Eliphaz spoke to Job. He said it to the wrong person, at the wrong time, but that does not change the fact that this is a wonderful statement: "[I]f you lay gold in the dust, and gold of Ophir among the stones of the torrent-bed, then *the Almighty will be your gold and your precious silver.* For then you will delight yourself in the Almighty and lift up your face to God" (Job 22:24–26). You see the point? If God is your *everything*, if he is more to you than all the treasures of the world, how could there be room in your mind for anyone or anything "in place of or alongside of" him? It is when we begin to be dissatisfied with him, when he is no longer all-sufficient to us, that we start looking for other things (persons, powers) that might fill the gaps. If your spouse is truly the darling of your soul, you will not easily look at other women or men in a wrong way. The believer says, "[A]ll the gods of the people are worthless idols" (1 Chron. 16:26).

It does not matter what kind of idols they are—you reject them out of hand. In Galatians 4, Paul uses the phrase "elementary principles" (or "elemental spirits") both for the pagan idols, and for Jewish legalism, which to him is just another form of idolatry: "[W]e also, when we [i.e., Jews] were children, were enslaved to the elementary principles of the world [i.e., legalism]. . . . Formerly, when you [i.e., Gentiles] did not know God, you were enslaved to those that by nature are not gods. But now that you have come to know God, or rather to be known by God, how can you turn back *again* to the weak and worthless elementary principles of the world, whose slaves you want to be *once more*?" (4:3, 8–9).

Notice the words "again" and "once more"! You *came* from (pagan) idolatry, argues Paul, and now you are *returning* to idolatry (Jewish, this time). The one is just as bad as the other. Pagan images or Jewish legalism—both draw you away from the true God of the Bible. Let God alone be your true treasure!

✧   ✧   ✧

DAY 286 – THE ONLY TRUE GOD
(Lord's Day 34, Q&A 95, part 2)

A. . . . the only true God, who has revealed himself in the Word.

What do we know about the false gods, other than the myths that the pagans tell us about them? The Bible reveals the true nature not only of the only true God, but also of the false gods. For instance, the Bible tells us about Chemosh, the god of the Moabites (Num. 21:29) and Ammonites (Judg. 11:24), and what he did for his peoples. These things are not pagan myths but spiritual realities, as God sees them! These are the gods of the nations who in Psalm 82 are called on to account for what they have done for their people, and are condemned for it.

In Daniel 10, they are not called "gods" but "princes" (or "rulers"): the prince of the kingdom of Persia and the prince of Greece (vv. 13, 20), and even Michael, the prince of Israel (v. 21; 12:1). The former two are not earthy kings, but what Ephesians 6:12 calls "the rulers, the authorities, the cosmic powers over this present darkness, the spiritual forces of evil in the heavenly places," and what the pagans themselves call their gods. It follows that the gods are high angelic powers, and we know that in the beginning all angels were created by God (Col. 1:16). However, they fell into the sin of rebellion; they are now called "demons," angels of Satan (Matt. 25:41; Rev. 12:7, 9; cf. 2 Cor. 11:14).

It is only God's Word that reveals the true character of the gods of the nations, just as it reveals to us the true character of the "God of gods": "[T]he LORD your God is God of gods and Lord of lords, the great, the mighty, and the awesome God" (Deut. 10:17). "There is none like you among the gods, O Lord, nor are there any works like yours" (Ps. 86:8). "[T]he LORD is a great God, and a great King above all gods" (95:3). "[G]reat is the LORD, and greatly to be praised; he is to be feared above all gods. For all the gods of the peoples are worthless idols, but the LORD made the heavens" (96:4–5). "[Y]ou, O LORD, are most high over all the earth; you are exalted far above all gods" (97:9). "Give thanks to the God of gods" (Ps. 136:2). Such a God, who is far above all the gods, is the only One to be served and praised!

✷   ✷   ✷

DAY 287 – THE SECOND COMMANDMENT
(Lord's Day 35, Q&A 96, part 1)

Q. *What is God's will for us in the second commandment?*
A. *That we in no way make any image of God . . .*

In the First Commandment, God commands his people to serve the one true God only. In the Second Commandment, he commands his people to serve him in the proper way. By making images of God, we run at least two risks. First, it is a very small step from images of God to images of the gods. When Aaron made the golden calf for Israel, he suggested that he was preparing a "feast for the Lord" (Exod. 32:5); but the Israelites took the golden calf for what they wanted it to be: a representation of the bull god of Egypt. When king Jeroboam put up the two golden calves in Bethel and Dan, he too suggested that these were the gods who had led Israel out of Egypt (1 Kings 12:28). The festival that he introduced around these calves was an imitation of the Feast of Booths (cf. v. 32 and Lev. 23:33). But in fact the whole thing was pure idolatry (cf. 1 Kings 13:1–6). In short: serving any image, no matter how piously intended, easily leads to idolatry.

Moreover, what *kind* of images could you possibly make? We do not know what God looks like! So, inadvertently, the image we come up with can hardly be anything else than "a carved image, or any likeness of anything that is in heaven above, or that is in the earth beneath, or that is in the water under the earth" (Exod. 20:4). When the Lord spoke to Israel out of the midst of the fire, they "heard the sound of words, but *saw no form*; there was only a voice" (Deut. 4:12): "Since you *saw no form* . . . beware lest you act corruptly by making a carved image for yourselves, in the form of any figure, the likeness of male or female. . . . Take care, lest you . . . make a carved image, the *form* of anything that the Lord your God has forbidden you" (vv. 15–16, 23).

The second reason why we should not make images of God is that such images tend to *replace* God. We begin to worship these images, instead of the God who is thought to be portrayed by these images. The images themselves will grow ever more important, instead of being *only* representations. The portrayals become the real thing. That's why God says so rigorously, "No images at all!"

✤   ✤   ✤

DAY 288 – FALSE IMAGES OF GOD

(Lord's Day 35, Q&A 96, part 2)

A. . . . nor worship him in any other way than has been commanded in God's Word.

The phrase "images of God" can be a very broad concept. We should not think only of material images: images of wood or stone, of gold or silver. There is also such a thing as mental images. Each religion, but also each movement within Christianity, and even each Christian, tends to develop its/his/her own specific image of God. All the theories that theologians develop about God can become images of God that they, and their followers, begin to venerate. C. S. Lewis says somewhere that the deepest places in hell are reserved for those theologians who find their images of God more important than God himself! In the opera *Moses and Aaron* by the Jewish composer Arnold Schoenberg, Moses scolds Aaron for having made an image of God. But Aaron retorts that the pillar of cloud, or the two tablets of stone, are images of God as well. . . . Why are certain images allowed, and others forbidden? Did Moses himself not have golden cherubim and a bronze serpent made?

This is a fair question: *anything* can become an image of God, and as such can take the place of God himself. For instance, the Israelites had begun making offerings to the bronze serpent (called Nehushtan), and therefore king Hezekiah destroyed this serpent (2 Kings 18:4). Even presumption (1 Sam. 15:23) and covetousness (Eph. 5:5; Col. 3:5) can push God from his place, and as such can become forms of idolatry. God wants us to "worship him" in no other way "than has been commanded in God's Word," says the Catechism. Jesus said, "[T]he hour is coming, and is now here, when the true worshipers will worship the Father in spirit and truth, for the Father is seeking such people to worship him. God is spirit, and those who worship him must worship in spirit and truth" (John 4:23–24), that is, in a spiritual and truthful way. Image veneration is neither spiritual, nor truthful. God killed the two sons of Aaron, who "offered unauthorized fire before the LORD, which he had not commanded them" (Lev. 10:1)—that was enough to arouse his wrath! Don't worship him in a way that he has not commanded you. In worship, *he* is the One determining the rules, not you!

✦   ✦   ✦

DAY 289 – NO IMAGES AT ALL?

(Lord's Day 35, Q&A 97)

Q. May we then not make any image at all?
A. God cannot and may not be visibly portrayed in any way. Although creatures may be portrayed, yet God forbids making or having such images if one's intention is to worship them or to serve God through them.

Where is the limit to this prohibition against visibly portraying God in any way? In Western culture, God has often been displayed: in the visual arts, in music, and in literature. Is it wrong to depict God in a painting, as Michelangelo did in the famous ceiling fresco of the Sistine chapel in Rome, or as William Blake did in his *God Judging Adam*? In classical oratorios we rarely hear God's voice. The famous *Messiah* of Handel does begin with God's words "Comfort ye my people" (Isa. 40:1), sung by the tenor, but actually it is only a quotation (". . . saith your God"). Mendelssohn, when quoting God, used the voice of the soprano in his oratorio *Elijah*, to avoid the idea of imaging God. Likewise, when he impersonated the voice of Jesus in his oratorio *St. Paul*, he used the women's choir! Apparently, he felt a certain reluctance to represent God in a direct way. (With the voice of Christ, composers usually had less trouble; this voice is heard several times in Bach's cantatas.) In some theatre plays, though, such as the German tragedy *Faust* by Goethe, we do hear the voice of God in a very direct way (although we do not see him on the stage). In Stravinsky's musical play *The Flood*, the role of God is sung by a duet of two basses.

Like Mendelssohn, some Christians have a problem with such representations, and understandably so. They do not like seeing God visibly represented by an actor, such as in the movie *Bruce Almighty*. Yet, the Catechism adds an important condition: don't make such images (pictures, representations) "if one's intention is to worship them or to serve God through them." In general this is certainly not the intention of art. But art can do another despicable thing: in the visual arts, including theatre plays and cinematography, God can be represented only in some human form, and many Christians experience this as something derogatory with respect to God. God created humans after his image—but we do not like to see a "God" created after our own human image. Perhaps we could call the latter "creations" a very sophisticated form of idolatry.

✣　✣　✣

DAY 290 – NO IMAGES IN CHURCHES?
(Lord's Day 35, Q&A 98)

Q. But may not images be permitted in churches in place of books for the unlearned?
A. No, we should not try to be wiser than God. God wants the Christian community instructed by the living preaching of his Word—not by idols that cannot even talk.

This is obviously another allusion to Roman Catholic practice in the days when the Catechism was written. In the fire of the sixteenth-century battle, one cannot expect a very balanced and fair judgment on Catholic customs, such as putting up in churches images of biblical figures and of so-called "saints" from later church history. In general, Protestants do not tolerate such images in their church buildings, and for good reason. But they do have children's Bibles with many pictures of biblical figures, and they do appreciate the many biblical representations by the (Protestant!) painter Rembrandt and many others. What is the difference between these, on the one hand, and images and icons in Roman Catholic and Eastern Orthodox churches, on the other? The answer is this: people kiss the icons in Orthodox churches, and they bow before the images in Catholic churches, which is utterly rejected by Protestants.

However, we must be fair here. Roman Catholic theology makes a clear distinction between adoration and veneration. Only God (the Father, the Son, and the Holy Spirit) may be adored (worshiped), and not "saints," who are just human beings—not even Mary the mother of Jesus. They may only be venerated (honored; cf. Luke 1:48 NLV, "honor me"). Worship belongs to God alone, and is therefore refused by godly humans (Acts 10:25–26) and by angels (Rev. 19:10). Therefore, in the light of Catholic and Orthodox theology it is unfair to say that Catholic and Orthodox Christians treat the images in their churches as idols, because they do not worship them.

And yet . . . in both Roman Catholic and Eastern Orthodox countries I have often been sitting in churches, quietly observing believers coming in. I have seen numerous people, especially women, going past the statue of Christ to bow down before the statue of Mary. And I have often wondered how many of them knew the fine distinction between adoration and veneration, or between praying to statues or to the saints represented by these statues. So I do understand the Catechism: better to have no statues at all in church, and "instruct the people by the living preaching of God's Word."

✢ ✢ ✢

DAY 291 – THE THIRD COMMANDMENT
(Lord's Day 36, Q&A 99, part 1)

Q. What is the aim of the third commandment?
A. That we neither blaspheme nor misuse the name of God by curs-
ing, perjury, or unnecessary oaths, nor share in such horrible sins by
being silent bystanders . . .

The Third Commandment seems to refer to some quite different sins. First, there is cursing, using the Lord's name in a thoughtless, sloppy, trivial way, simply as an expletive, as an utterance of rage, or to enforce one's language, without any respect for God ("unnecessary oaths"; cf. James 5:12, "[D]o not swear, either by heaven or by earth or by any other oath, but let your 'yes' be yes and your 'no' be no, so that you may not fall under condemnation"). Second, people sometimes take oaths in a light and rash way, without thinking of the consequences; they connect the name of the Lord with enterprises that they cannot accomplish. Third, people take false oaths; they commit perjury: they know that what they assert under oath is false. They too misuse the name of God, attaching his name to their lies. Fourth, there is outright blasphemy, in which the evildoer offends the name of God, and *intends* to offend it (cf. Lev. 24:10–16). The latter is the grossest transgressing of the Third Commandment.

Interestingly, the Catechism refers to another form of transgression: "If anyone sins in that he hears a public adjuration to testify, and though he is a witness, whether he has seen or come to know the matter, yet does not speak, he shall bear his iniquity" (Lev. 5:1). That is, you hear someone take an oath in support of what *you* know to be perjury. If you do not raise your voice, you yourself become guilty of that perjury (cf. Prov. 29:24).

Jesus said, "Do not take an oath at all, either by heaven, for it is the throne of God, or by the earth, for it is his footstool, or by Jerusalem, for it is the city of the great King. . . . Let what you say be simply 'Yes' or 'No'; anything more than this comes from evil" (Matt. 5:34–37). He did not necessarily mean that we should not take official oaths, for instance, in court, or when you are sworn into a certain office. What he apparently did mean is: You should not need to enforce your promises and allegations by lightly attaching God's name to it. You should not need to do that. You should simply be known as a thoroughly honest and reliable person.

❖   ❖   ❖

DAY 292 – USING THE NAME OF GOD
(Lord's Day 36, Q&A 99, part 2)

A. . . . In summary, we should use the holy name of God only with reverence and awe, so that we may properly confess God, pray to God, and glorify God in all our words and works.

Because of the Third Commandment, godly Jews went so far as to avoid the holy name of God ("Yahweh") altogether; they rather refer to him as Adonai ("Lord"), or Elohim ("God"), or HaShem ("The name"), or the Eternal One. Even in the New Testament we sometimes seem to encounter a certain reluctance to use the word "God." Thus, the prodigal son says, "I have sinned against heaven" (Luke 15:18), where he simply means "God." Even the expression "kingdom of heaven" in Matthew could be viewed as a euphemism for "kingdom of God" (cf. Dan. 4:26, "Heaven rules," which means, "God rules").

Yet, we should not be ashamed to use terms such as "God," "Father," "Lord," etc., as long as we do it "with reverence and awe," says the Catechism. There is even room for "swearing" here: "If you remove your detestable things from my presence, and do not waver, and if you swear, 'As the Lord lives,' in truth, in justice, and in righteousness, then nations shall bless themselves in him, and in him shall they glory" (Jer. 4:1–2). We are even *encouraged* to use the name of God in confession and praise, as a public testimony to the world around us: "[E]veryone who acknowledges me before men, I also will acknowledge before my Father who is in heaven" (Matt. 10:32). Confess with your mouth that Jesus is Lord (Rom. 10:9–10). "I will praise you, O Lord, among the nations, and sing to your *name*" (Ps. 18:49). "[M]agnify the Lord with me, and let us exalt his name together!" (Ps. 34:3).

In Ezekiel 20 and 36, God often speaks of the Israelites who "profaned" his name among the nations—quite an efficient way to summarize the essence of the Third Commandment. But in connection with the Messianic Kingdom, God says, "[M]y holy name I will make known in the midst of my people Israel, and I will not let my holy name be profaned anymore. And the nations shall know that I am the Lord, the Holy One in Israel" (39:7). "For at that time I will change the speech of the peoples to a pure speech, that all of them may call upon the name of the Lord and serve him with one accord" (Zeph. 3:9).

✦   ✦   ✦

DAY 293 – BLASPHEMY
(Lord's Day 36, Q&A 100)

Q. Is blasphemy of God's name by swearing and cursing really such serious sin that God is angry also with those who do not do all they can to help prevent and forbid it?
A. Yes, indeed. No sin is greater or provokes God's wrath more than blaspheming his name. That is why God commanded it to be punished with death.

Here we have the Third Commandment in its most serious form: "blasphemy." The word comes from the Greek words *blapto* ("to damage") and *phemi* ("to say"). Blasphemy is (deliberately) saying slanderous things about God, insulting him, offending him. If it is done inadvertently, and it is subsequently regretted and confessed, it is still bad enough, but it will be forgiven. But if it is done deliberately, and not regretted and confessed, it will inevitably "provoke God's wrath." Jesus said that blasphemy in general, or even against his person, would in principle be pardonable (cf. 1 Tim. 1:13). But blasphemy against the Holy Spirit—for instance, by equating him with Satan—would be counted as an outright act of rebellion: "[T]he blasphemy against the Spirit will not be forgiven. And whoever speaks a word against the Son of Man will be forgiven, but whoever speaks against the Holy Spirit will not be forgiven, either in this age or in the age to come" (Matt. 12:31–32).

In Leviticus 4 we find such a case: a certain man "blasphemed the Name, and cursed. Then they brought him to Moses. . . . And they put him in custody, till the will of the LORD should be clear to them. Then the LORD spoke to Moses, saying, 'Bring out of the camp the one who cursed, and let all who heard him lay their hands on his head, and let all the congregation stone him. And speak to the people of Israel, saying, "Whoever curses his God shall bear his sin. Whoever blasphemes the name of the LORD shall surely be put to death." All the congregation shall stone him. The sojourner as well as the native, when he blasphemes the Name, shall be put to death'" (Lev. 24:11–16).

In the New Testament, we do not apply the death penalty anymore; it is replaced by expulsion from the Christian community, or even worse: Paul speaks of two heretics, "whom I have handed over to Satan [thus causing sickness?] that they may learn not to blaspheme" (1 Tim. 1:20). Even fundamental heresies concerning the Father, the Son, or the Holy Spirit are considered to be forms of blasphemy (cf. 2 Pet. 2:2, 10–12; Jude 1:8–10). Let us beware!

✣   ✣   ✣

DAY 294 – SWEARING IN GOD'S NAME
(Lord's Day 37, Q&A 101)

Q. But may we swear an oath in God's name if we do it reverently?
A. Yes, when the government demands it, or when necessity requires it, in order to maintain and promote truth and trustworthiness for God's glory and our neighbor's good. Such oaths are grounded in God's Word and were rightly used by the people of God in the Old and New Testaments.

Interestingly, several groups such as the Mennonites take the Third Commandment so seriously that they even refrain from official oaths as demanded by the government or in courtrooms. The Catechism does not go that far, and rightly so. Moses makes clear that, under certain circumstances, the Israelite may certainly "swear" by the name of the Lord (Deut. 6:13; 10:20). Hebrews 6 does assume that "people swear by something greater than themselves, and in all their disputes an oath is final for confirmation" (v. 16). Abraham took an oath when he made a covenant with king Abimelech (Gen. 21:22–24). Joshua did the same in his covenant with the Gibeonites (Josh. 9:15). David swore to his wife Bathsheba concerning their son Solomon (1 Kings 1:29–30).

When the high priest Caiaphas said to Jesus, "I adjure you by the living God, tell us if you are the Christ, the Son of God" (Matt. 26:63), this in effect was the same as putting Jesus under oath. Jesus took this very seriously, so that he felt obliged to answer the question (v. 64), whereas just before he had remained silent (v. 63a; cf. Luke 23:9, Jesus before Herod; John 19:9, Jesus before Pilate).

Even God occasionally took oaths: "[W]hen God made a promise to Abraham, since he had no one greater by whom to swear, he swore by himself, saying, 'Surely I will bless you and multiply you'" (Heb. 6:13–14); as it is said in Genesis, "By myself I have sworn, . . . because you have done this and have not withheld your son, your only son, I will surely bless you" (22:16–17). This was the second time God swore, after his first oath taken already in Ur of the Chaldeans (24:7; 26:3; 50:24; etc.). God also swore to David "a sure oath from which he will not turn back: 'One of the sons of your body I will set on your throne'," referring to Solomon (Ps. 132:11). Finally, God swore even to Jesus: "The LORD has sworn and will not change his mind, 'You are a priest forever after the order of Melchizedek'" (Ps. 110:4; cf. Heb. 5:6). There is nothing wrong with swearing as such, as long as it is done in the right attitude, and for the glory of God!

✤   ✤   ✤

DAY 295 – SWEARING BY SAINTS
(Lord's Day 37, Q&A 102)

Q. May we also swear by saints or other creatures?
A. No. A legitimate oath means calling upon God as the only one who knows my heart to witness to my truthfulness and to punish me if I swear falsely. No creature is worthy of such honor.

Jesus said, "Do not take an oath at all, either by heaven, for it is the throne of God, or by the earth, for it is his footstool, or by Jerusalem, for it is the city of the great King. And do not take an oath by your head, for you cannot make one hair white or black" (Matt. 5:34–36; cf. 23:16–22; James 5:12). In the first three of these four examples, the person was still swearing by God, though indirectly (heaven is the throne of God, the earth is his footstool, Jerusalem is his city). But in the fourth case, the person is swearing by his own head (i.e., his life), and this is even worse. Would you put your own head at risk, just to enforce your statements? If one takes an oath at all, it can be only by the highest authority: "the only one who knows my heart to witness to my truthfulness and to punish me if I swear falsely." If you call upon the name of God when you are swearing, this means: God is my witness that what I say is true, and God may punish me if I am not telling the truth.

In earlier centuries, swearing by the (Roman Catholic) saints—deceased believers who had been canonized—was very common: in Shakespeare's *Hamlet* someone swears by St. Patrick, and in his *Romeo and Juliet*, someone swears "by St. Peter's church and Peter too." Many other examples from Western literature could be mentioned. Some say that the English term "bloody" in its vulgar meaning comes from "by our Lady," that is, Mary. The Holy Virgin was, and is, called upon more than any other saint.

However, be honest about it: what can the saints really do for you? The Catechism rightly says, "No creature is worthy of such honor," that is, the honor of being invoked. The saints are not your witnesses that what you say is true, nor are they able to chastise you if you are not telling the truth right now. At best you may believe—although I think you would be wrong—that the saints can intercede for you with God. You use them as intermediaries. But even then, it is God who is your only true helper. "The Father himself loves you," says Jesus—you don't need any intermediaries (John 16:26–27)!

✢ ✢ ✢

DAY 296 – SATURDAY OR SUNDAY?
(Lord's Day 38, Q&A 103, part 1)

Q. What is God's will for you in the fourth commandment?

This is how the Fourth Commandment begins: "Remember the Sabbath day, to keep it holy." The question arises: What is the Sabbath day? Interestingly, the Catechism does not at all enter into the question which day of the week this is: Saturday or Sunday. The reason is that apparently this was self-evident to its readers: the "Sabbath" under the New Covenant is Sunday. This is not a specifically Reformational view, because Roman Catholic and Eastern Orthodox Christians have always maintained the same standpoint. The new Sabbath is Sunday.

However, not only Seventh Day Adventists, but also a growing number of Evangelicals and so-called Messianic Jews are convinced that the Sabbath was never moved from Saturday to Sunday. So they argue that, if you wish to keep the Fourth Commandment, you ought to celebrate Saturday as the day of rest and worship, not Sunday. Others argue that we are indeed under the law of Christ (Gal. 6:2), but that this law is not identical with the Ten Commandments, which were given to Israel only. They argue that, in the present Christian age, no special day of rest and worship has been set aside by God at all.

Whatever the case may be, there can be no doubt that Sunday, the "first day of the week," is a special day, and that Christians from the beginning viewed it as such. Most importantly, it was the day on which Jesus rose from the dead. With a little calculation we can figure out that it was also the day on which the Holy Spirit was poured out (Lev. 23:15). It was the day on which the Gentile believers in Troas were accustomed to assembling and breaking bread (Acts 20:7). "On the first day of every week, each of you is to put something aside and store it up" (1 Cor. 16:2), and this money for the poor was probably collected on the same day. No wonder that the Christians from the Gentiles began to view this day as the most appropriate day to come together. Even if not all Christians are convinced that the New Testament gives us any reason to view this day as the new "Sabbath," at least Sunday is a special day!

✢   ✢   ✢

DAY 297 – THE GOSPEL MINISTRY
(Lord's Day 38, Q&A 103, part 2)

Q. What is God's will for you in the fourth commandment?
A. First, that the gospel ministry and education for it be maintained.

If we do agree that the Sunday is a special day for Christians—even if we do not agree on calling it the "Sabbath"—the first thing that we can say is that it is a day for the churches to *come together*. Of the first period after the pouring out of the Spirit, we are told that the early Christians "devoted themselves to the apostles' teaching and the fellowship, to the breaking of bread and the prayers. . . . And day by day, attending the temple together and breaking bread in their homes, they received their food with glad and generous hearts" (Acts 2:42, 46). Notice the difference between "breaking bread" and "receiving food": the latter refers to the common meals, but the former to the celebration of the Lord's Supper (cf. Matt. 26:26).

The enthusiasm of the early period—breaking bread together every day—was not maintained; in Acts 20 we read about the church of Troas: "On the first day of the week, when we [i.e., the local believers, plus at least Paul and Luke] were gathered together to break bread, Paul talked with them, . . . and he prolonged his speech until midnight. . . . And when Paul . . . had broken bread and eaten, he conversed with them a long while, until daybreak, and so departed" (vv. 7, 11). At least in Troas, it apparently had become customary to meet and celebrate the Lord's Supper every first day of the week. Of course, this is presented as a historical fact, not as a rule for all churches. Roman Catholic priests still celebrate the Eucharist every day, whereas many Protestant churches celebrate it every month or every three months.

Apart from the Lord's Supper, it is a good custom for Christians to meet on Sundays, to hear God's Word. Those who proclaim the Word should be adequately *trained* for this: "[W]hat you [i.e., Timothy] have heard from me [i.e., Paul] in the presence of many witnesses entrust to faithful men who will be able to teach others also" (2 Tim. 2:2; cf. 1 Tim. 3:13–17). "Let the elders who rule well be considered worthy of double honor, especially those who labor in preaching and teaching" (1 Tim. 5:17). Honor and respect preachers!

✤ ✤ ✤

DAY 298 – ATTENDING CHURCH SERVICES
(Lord's Day 38, Q&A 103, part 3)

A. First, . . . that, especially on the festive day of rest, I diligently attend the assembly of God's people to learn what God's Word teaches, to participate in the sacraments, to pray to God publicly, and to bring Christian offerings for the poor.

In this answer, the Catechism mentions four things that believers are supposed to do on the first day of the week, at a minimum. First, listen to the teaching and preaching of God's Word. Second, participate in the sacraments (the Lord's Supper in particular, of course). Third, pray to God publicly, that is, during church services (this also includes worship, praise, thanksgiving). And fourth, bring Christian offerings for the poor. Three of these four elements are mentioned in Acts 2:42, "the apostles' teaching, the breaking of bread, and the prayers." In writing to the Corinthian Christians, Paul gives a wider array: "When you come together, each one has a hymn [viz., as part of praise and worship], a lesson [i.e., a piece of teaching], a revelation [i.e., a new insight from God], a tongue [i.e., a message in an unknown language], or an interpretation [viz., of the latter message]. Let all things be done for building up. . . . [Y]ou can all prophesy [i.e., bring a word from the Lord for 'upbuilding and encouragement and consolation,' v. 3] one by one, so that all may learn and all be encouraged" (1 Cor. 14:26, 31; cf. 1 Tim. 4:13; Col. 3:16). It would bring us too far afield to discuss how this all works out in our day. Suffice to say that church meetings do exhibit many different aspects, which are divided into two main categories: (a) what God has to say to us, and (b) what we have to bring to God.

As far as the "Christian offerings for the poor" are concerned, in 1 Corinthians 16:2 Paul commands that on the first day of the week alms for the poor must be collected. Also notice Hebrews 13, where we first read of our spiritual offerings of praise and worship: "Through [Christ] let us continually offer up a sacrifice of praise to God, that is, the fruit of lips that acknowledge his name" (v. 15)—immediately followed by material offerings: "Do not neglect to do good and to share what you have, for such sacrifices are pleasing to God" (v. 16). The two belong together, and must not be separated. Never forget the poor!

✦ ✦ ✦

DAY 299 – THE ETERNAL SABBATH
(Lord's Day 38, Q&A 103, part 4)

A. . . . Second, that every day of my life I rest from my evil ways, let the Lord work in me through his Spirit, and so begin in this life the eternal Sabbath.

Here, the Catechism touches upon quite a different aspect of the weekly day of rest: every Sabbath is a joyful foreshadowing of the "eternal Sabbath." Hebrews 4 speaks very clearly of this: "[T]here remains a Sabbath rest for the people of God, for whoever has entered God's rest has also rested from his works as God did from his. Let us therefore strive to enter that rest, so that no one may fall by the same sort of disobedience" (vv. 9–11).

Jesus once said, "Come to me, all who labor and are heavy laden, and I will give you rest" (Matt. 11:28). I take it that this is (or at least includes) rest for the *conscience*, which a soul receives who comes with the burdens of his sins to Jesus. Immediately after this he says, "Take my yoke upon you, and learn from me, for I am gentle and lowly in heart, and you will find rest for your souls" (v. 29). This is the rest for the *soul* that a believer finds who faithfully follows Jesus, submitting to his yoke, and daily learning from him. The former rest corresponds with this: "[S]ince we have been justified by faith, we have *peace with God* through our Lord Jesus Christ" (Rom. 5:1). The latter rest corresponds with this: "[I]n everything by prayer and supplication with thanksgiving let your requests be made known to God. And the *peace of God*, which surpasses all understanding, will guard your hearts and your minds in Christ Jesus" (Phil. 4:6–7).

The "Sabbath rest" of Hebrews 4 is the third type of rest: the eternal rest we are looking forward to, which begins at Jesus' second coming. This rest, too, corresponds to peace, namely, the peace of the Messianic Kingdom: "Of the increase of his government and of peace there will be no end, on the throne of David and over his kingdom, to establish it and to uphold it with justice and with righteousness from this time forth and forevermore" (Isa. 9:7). Every weekly day of rest and peace reminds us of, and helps us to look forward to, the eternal "day" of rest and peace, through him, the "Prince of Peace" (v. 6). "To him be the glory both now and to the day of eternity" (2 Pet. 3:18).

✦　✦　✦

DAY 300 – THE FIFTH COMMANDMENT

(Lord's Day 39, Q&A 104, part 1)

Q. What is God's will for you in the fifth commandment?
A. That I honor, love, and be loyal to my father and mother . . .; that I
submit myself with proper obedience to all their good teaching and disci-
pline; and also that I be patient with their failings . . .

The Fourth and the Fifth Commandments are the only ones among the Ten with a positive form; these do not say "You shall not," but: "Remember the Sabbath day," and: "Honor your father and your mother" (for the negative form of the Fifth Commandment see, e.g., Exod. 21:17; Prov. 20:20). The apostle Paul comments: "Children, obey your parents in the Lord, for this is right. 'Honor your father and mother' (this is the first commandment with a promise), 'that it may go well with you and that you may live long in the land.' Fathers, do not provoke your children to anger, but bring them up in the discipline and instruction of the Lord" (Eph. 6:1–4; cf. Col. 3:20–21). The latter phrase shows there is also the other side of the coin: it is not just children honoring their parents, but also parents fulfilling toward their children their responsibility of disciplining and teaching.

The commandment says, "Honor," whereas Paul says, "Obey," and also the Catechism uses the term "proper obedience." This is because these latter two address "children," whereas the Fifth Commandment addresses the entire nation. When people are grown up, they should be able to find their own way, and take responsibility for their own lives. But the honor and respect for their parents should always remain, and they should keep paying attention to the latter's advice: "Listen to your father who gave you life, and do not despise your mother when she is old" (Prov. 23:22).

We should honor our parents if they are good educators, but also if they are less good ("be patient with their failings," says the Catechism), simply because they are the people from whom we were born. We find this principle in 1 Peter 2:18, "Servants, be subject to your masters with all respect, not only to the good and gentle but also to the unjust." When you are under some form of authority (governments, bosses, parents, elders), you may have your private opinion about the good or less good way they are fulfilling their duties toward you—but they remain that authority above you, to which you are subject. This principle is of eminent importance!

✦ ✦ ✦

DAY 301 – ALL AUTHORITIES
(Lord's Day 39, Q&A 104, part 2)

A. That I honor, love, and be loyal to . . . all those in authority over me.

The Fifth Commandment speaks only about the relationship of children toward their parents, but the Catechism rightly sees behind this commandment a wider principle, namely, subjection to *every* form of authority that is placed above us. In the end, all authority comes from God. All human authorities above us have only some form of derived or bestowed authority. First, there is governmental authority above us, and the Bible is very clear about how we should behave toward it: "Let every person be subject to the governing authorities. For *there is no authority except from God*, and those that exist have been instituted by God. Therefore whoever resists the authorities resists what *God has appointed*, and those who resist will incur judgment. . . . [The person] who is in authority . . . is *God's servant* for your good. . . . For he is the *servant of God*, an avenger who carries out God's wrath on the wrongdoer. Therefore one must be in subjection, not only to avoid God's wrath but also for the sake of conscience. . . . [T]he authorities are *ministers of God*. . . . Pay to all what is owed to them: taxes to whom taxes are owed, revenue to whom revenue is owed, respect to whom respect is owed, *honor to whom honor is owed*" (Rom. 13:1–8; cf. Titus 3:1).

Paul places the entire subject of obedience to the government against the background of authority in general, and our duties in general. Compare Jesus' word, "[R]ender to Caesar the things that are Caesar's, and to God the things that are God's" (Matt. 22:21). And Peter says, "Be subject for the Lord's sake to every human institution, whether it be to the emperor [or, king] as supreme, or to governors as sent by him to punish those who do evil and to praise those who do good" (1 Pet. 2:13–14). We could easily widen this principle: employees, respect your employers; church members, respect your elders; wives, respect your husbands; and similarly, children, respect your parents (cf. Eph. 5:21–6:9; Col. 3:18–4:1). The principle is this: if you are a person under some form of authority, respect that authority, because it is God-given.

✳ ✳ ✳

DAY 302 – INSTITUTED BY GOD
(Lord's Day 39, Q&A 104, part 3)

A. That I honor, love, and be loyal to my father and mother and all those in authority over me . . . for through them God chooses to rule us.

None of us can choose his or her own parents; we have to accept what God chose for us. I may choose a company I would like to work for, but I have no influence on who is going to be my direct boss. In a democracy, I have some influence on who will be the authorities in my country or in my town, but it is very limited. And even if the party I voted for indeed becomes the ruling party—or not—I have to accept those who are in power as placed there by God himself: "there is no authority except from God, and those that exist have been instituted by God . . . [they are] what God has appointed. [The person] in authority . . . is God's servant. [T]he authorities are ministers of God" (Rom. 13:1–6). It does not matter in what way they came to power: in a democratic or in an autocratic way. I have to accept the final result from the hand of God. Even if I don't like the authorities, I have to accept them as God-given, and thus subject myself to them as if I subject myself directly to God himself. This is what Paul told the Roman believers in a time that the cruel emperor Nero was in power there.

Some people do not like their parents because father and mother are nasty people, who do not show much love to their children. However, even if the power they have over me would be taken from them by the authorities because of their bad behavior, I will remain obliged to honor, even to love them, and to be loyal to them, says the Catechism. I have to obey the government, I have to obey my boss, but I am never called upon to love them (apart from the general rule to love our neighbors). With parents it is different: you have to *love* them. Actually, I am not aware of any Bible verse telling me so (at best in some negative sense: "Whoever loves father or mother more than me is not worthy of me," Matt. 10:37); yet, I believe the Catechism is perfectly right. Your parents may never have done much to win you over to their side; but your love may be the means in God's hands to win them over to *your* side! "Let your father and mother be glad; let her who bore you rejoice" (Prov. 23:25).

✤ ✤ ✤

DAY 303 – THE SIXTH COMMANDMENT
(Lord's Day 40, Q&A 105, part 1)

Q. What is God's will for you in the sixth commandment?
A. I am not to belittle, hate, insult, or kill my neighbor—not by my
thoughts, my words, my look or gesture, and certainly not by actual
deeds—and I am not to be party to this in others; rather, I am to put
away all desire for revenge.

Already the rabbis said that the Ten Words do not refer to individual commandments but to ten *categories* of commandments. Thus, the Sixth Commandment refers to all kinds of both physical and mental violence against a fellow human. In the positive form of such commandments, they imply *respect* for God and the neighbor: respect for God in the First through Third Commandments, respect for God's Sabbath in the Fourth, respect for one's parents in the Fifth, respect for the neighbor's life in the Sixth, respect for marriage in the Seventh, respect for the neighbor's sacrosanctity in the Eighth, respect for truth in the Ninth, and respect for the neighbor's possessions in the Tenth Commandment.

God's commandments in their positive form even imply *love* for the neighbor: you shall love your neighbor so much that you protect his life; you shall love your wife so much that you are prepared to give your life for her; you shall love your neighbor so much that you share your possessions with him; you serve him with the truth, and you desire the best for him. In all these respects, Jesus is the great example, as we will see.

The Sixth Commandment is the non-violence commandment in the widest sense: as the Catechism says, no belittling, no hatred, no insults, no "killing" by thoughts, words, look, or gesture, "and certainly not by actual deeds." In the Sermon on the Mount Jesus explained the depth of this commandment: "You have heard that it was said to those of old, 'You shall not murder; and whoever murders will be liable to judgment.' But I say to you that everyone who is angry with his brother will be liable to judgment; whoever insults his brother will be liable to the council; and whoever says, 'You fool!' will be liable to the hell of fire" (Matt. 5:21–22). What Jesus does is, first, *sharpen* the commandment: even thoughts of revenge make you guilty of it (cf. Rom. 12:19; Deut. 32:35; Prov. 25:21–22). But he does more: he turns the commandment into a *positive* one, and presents himself as the great example of fulfilling it. This we will see extensively in the coming days.

✢ ✢ ✢

303

DAY 304 – SUICIDE; THE GOVERNMENT

(Lord's Day 40, Q&A 105, part 2)

A. I am not to harm or recklessly endanger myself either. Prevention
of murder is also why government is armed with the sword.

In one sentence the Catechism also implies the prohibition of self-mutilation and suicide ("I am not to harm myself"). But we cannot mention this difficult matter without adding that, today, we have much more knowledge of the mental disorders that may cause such terrible problems. Of course, this does not mean approval—it means understanding, comprehension. Instead of simply forbidding these things, we try to help those who suffer from the underlying disorders. You shall not kill yourself—but we will help you, as far as we can, so that you will never actually do it.

Another point is that homicide is condemned not only by God's law but also by all civilized governments: "Would you have no fear of the one who is in authority? Then do what is good, and you will receive his approval, for he is God's servant for your good. But if you do wrong, be afraid, for he does not bear the sword in vain. For he is the servant of God, an avenger who carries out God's wrath on the wrongdoer" (Rom. 13:3–4; cf. Gen. 9:6). "Be subject for the Lord's sake to every human institution, whether it be to the emperor as supreme, or to governors as sent by him to punish those who do evil and to praise those who do good" (1 Pet. 2:13–14; cf. Titus 3:1). Similarly, the laws of civilized countries forbid perjury, rape, theft, and even some forms of slander (cf. the Third and the Seventh through Tenth Commandments).

To that extent, one might think that the Ten Commandments do no more than all civilized countries do, whether or not they are Christian. However, in the New Testament we find the true depth of the Ten Commandments: governments do not, and cannot, forbid murderous thoughts (except those coming to light in conspiracies) and hatred (except when coming to the surface in, e.g., anti-Semitism). Judicial systems do not deal with our thoughts, but God judges the deepest thoughts of the heart (cf. Mark 7:21; 1 Cor. 4:5). Moreover, he encourages us to *further* and *protect* our neighbor's life: Jesus "laid down his life for us, and we ought to lay down our lives for the brothers" (1 John 3:16).

❖   ❖   ❖

DAY 305 – ENVY, HATRED, ANGER . . .
(Lord's Day 40, Q&A 106, part 1)

Q. Does this commandment refer only to murder?
A. By forbidding murder God teaches us that he hates the root of murder: envy, hatred, anger, vindictiveness.

God goes to the root of things. He does not condemn just homicide, he condemns the motives behind it: "evil, . . . malice . . . envy, murder, strife, . . . maliciousness" (Rom. 1:29); ". . . enmity, strife, jealousy, fits of anger, rivalries, dissensions, divisions, envy . . . and things like these. I warn you . . . that those who do such things will not inherit the kingdom of God" (Gal. 5:20–21). John says in a very direct way, "Whoever says he is in the light and hates his brother is still in darkness" (1 John 2:9; cf. v. 11). Such a person "is a murderer, and you know that no murderer has eternal life abiding in him" (3:15). "If anyone says, 'I love God,' and hates his brother, he is a liar; for he who does not love his brother whom he has seen cannot love God whom he has not seen" (4:20).

Earthly judges can issue verdicts regarding actual deeds of people; God can judge our deepest thoughts, which sometimes are even concealed to ourselves: "The heart is deceitful above all things, and desperately sick; who can understand it? 'I the Lord search the heart and test the mind, to give every man according to his ways, according to the fruit of his deeds'" (Jer. 17:9–10). "Oh, let the evil of the wicked come to an end, and may you establish the righteous—you who test the minds and hearts, O righteous God!" (Ps. 7:9).

Children in Christian families develop a certain sense of what *sins* are. More mature Christians develop a sense of what *sin* is, in the sense of "sinfulness." And the most mature are those who learn to discern their deeper motives, as far as this ability is given to creatures. They even learn to pray: "Who can discern his errors? Declare me innocent from hidden faults" (Ps. 19:12). Psychoanalysis claims to have laid bare much of our unconscious emotions and motives; but Christians, if they are led by God's Word and God's Spirit, have had knowledge of these things all along. If you are not a stranger to your own heart, you know that "the intention of man's heart is evil from his youth" (Gen. 8:21). It is only the Holy Spirit who can, and does, change the direction of your heart!

❖   ❖   ❖

DAY 306 – DISGUISED MURDER

(Lord's Day 40, Q&A 106, part 2)

A. . . . envy, hatred, anger, vindictiveness. In God's sight all such are disguised forms of murder.

In the judicial systems of civilized countries, it makes a tremendous difference whether you hate a person or kill a person. We all experience it as fair that vindictiveness is punished in a different way—if at all—than actually taking revenge is punished. Don't think that in the Bible it is otherwise. It clearly distinguishes between "great" sinners, "worse" sinners, and smaller sinners (Gen. 13:13; Luke 13:2, 4; cf. Rev. 20:12). Jesus said, "[T]hat servant who knew his master's will but did not get ready or act according to his will, will receive a severe beating. But the one who did not know, and did what deserved a beating, will receive a light beating. Everyone to whom much was given, of him much will be required, and from him to whom they entrusted much, they will demand the more" (Luke 12:47–48).

So there is clear difference in judgment: "[W]e must all appear before the judgment seat of Christ, so that each one may receive what is due for what he has done in the body, whether good or evil" (2 Cor. 5:10; cf. Ps. 62:12; Jer. 17:10; 32:19). "[T]he Son of Man is going to come with his angels in the glory of his Father, and then he will repay each person according to what he has done" (Matt. 16:27; cf. Rom. 2:6). "[A]ll the churches will know that I am he who searches mind and heart, and I will give to each of you according to your works" (Rev. 2:23; cf. 22:12).

But then, if there is such difference in judgment, how can the Catechism say that "envy, hatred, anger, vindictiveness" in God's sight "are disguised forms of murder"? If we take this literally, it seems to suggest that all these evils are punished in the same measure, which is clearly not the case. The answer is suggested by James 2:10, "[W]hoever keeps the whole law but fails in one point has become accountable for all of it." To become an evildoer—leaving aside your sinful nature—it is enough to commit the smallest sin. This one sin suffices to make you a condemnable sinner. Seen from *this* viewpoint, envy and hatred are enough to make you a murderer *in principle*. How serious are God's commandments!

✤   ✤   ✤

DAY 307 – MORE THAN MURDER
(Lord's Day 40, Q&A 107)

Q. Is it enough then that we do not murder our neighbor in any such way? A. No. By condemning envy, hatred, and anger God wants us to love our neighbors as ourselves, to be patient, peace-loving, gentle, merciful, and friendly toward them, to protect them from harm as much as we can, and to do good even to our enemies.

Here, the Catechism touches upon the core of the matter. When God gave the Ten Commandments to his people, they hardly knew themselves; they readily claimed: "All that the LORD has spoken we will do" (Exod. 19:8; cf. 24:3, 7). So, God gave them his commandments in a *minimal* form in order to prove that they would not be able to keep them even in terms of this mildest wording. However, this form never fully represented God's mind. As his thoughts were revealed by and by, the negative "You shall not murder" was viewed in the light of this fundamental rule: "[Y]ou shall love your neighbor as yourself" (Lev. 19:18; quoted nine times in the New Testament). It is ludicrous to claim you show this love (patience, gentleness, friendliness) by not killing the neighbor. No, in a positive sense you "protect the neighbor from harm as much as you can," and you do good to him, even if he behaves like an enemy toward you.

In its deepest sense, the Sixth Commandment turns out to mean: "You shall love your neighbor so much that you even put your own life at risk for him." As John says, "By this we know love, that he laid down his life for us, and we ought to lay down our lives for the brothers" (1 John 3:16). Jesus was the perfect example. Moses gave God's commandments to the people, but he could neither keep them himself, nor give the people the strength to keep them. Jesus, the "new Moses," did and does both. "Christ loved us and gave himself up for us, a fragrant offering and sacrifice to God. . . . Christ loved the church and gave himself up for her" (Eph. 5:2, 25); ". . . the Son of God, who loved me and gave himself for me" (Gal. 2:20). As Jesus said, "This is my commandment, that you love one another as I have loved you. Greater love has no one than this, that someone lay down his life for his friends" (John 15:12–13). Jesus gave to believers the power of the Holy Spirit, so that they, against their old nature, are now both prepared and able to make themselves available for their brothers and sisters (cf. 2 Cor. 8:5, "they gave themselves first to the Lord and then . . . to us").

✠   ✠   ✠

DAY 308 – THE SEVENTH COMMANDMENT
(Lord's Day 41, Q&A 108, part 1)

Q. What does the seventh commandment teach us?
A. That God condemns all unchastity, and that therefore we should thoroughly detest it and live decent and chaste lives.

What God condemns should always be something that we learn to detest. One form of legalism is that you do keep God's law but in fact desire to do what the law forbids. In such a case, the law is a "yoke" (Acts 15:10). But if we *love* God's law (Ps. 119:97; cf. 1:2), and have it in our *hearts* (Ps. 40:8; Jer. 31:33), we condemn what God condemns, and detest what God detests. And so we do condemn and "thoroughly detest" "all unchastity." Unchastity refers not only to all sexual intercourse outside the confines of (husband–wife) marriage, but also to all sexual *desires* outside these boundaries (cf. Q&A 109).

The sexual drive is very strong in most people. It is like hunger and thirst. These are very normal human drives, but they have to be "channeled": God condemns gluttons and drunkards (cf. Deut. 21:20; Prov. 23:20–21; Matt. 11:19). Similarly, God has "channeled" the sexual drive: it belongs to the sphere of marriage. Among the several institutions God gave to humanity, marriage has a special place because it originated before the Fall: "[M]ale and female he created them. And God blessed them. And God said to them, 'Be fruitful and multiply'" (Gen. 1:27–28). "Therefore a man shall leave his father and his mother and hold fast to his wife, and they shall become one flesh" (2:24).

Paul says, "[B]ecause of the temptation to sexual immorality, each man should have his own wife and each woman her own husband. The husband should give to his wife her conjugal rights, and likewise the wife to her husband. . . . Do not deprive one another, except perhaps by agreement for a limited time, that you may devote yourselves to prayer; but then come together again, so that Satan may not tempt you because of your lack of self-control" (1 Cor. 7:1–5). "[T]his is the will of God, your sanctification: that you abstain from sexual immorality; that each one of you know how to control his own body in holiness and honor, not in the passion of lust like the Gentiles who do not know God. . . . For God has not called us for impurity, but in holiness" (1 Thess. 4:3–7; cf. Heb. 13:4).

✦　✦　✦

DAY 309 – DECENT LIVES
(Lord's Day 41, Q&A 108, part 2)

A. . . . live decent and chaste lives, within or outside of the holy state of marriage.

Just like most other commandments, the Seventh Commandment has a negative form: "You shall *not* . . . " but its deepest intention is a positive one. In order to understand this, we have to realize that, in its original form, the Seventh Commandment primarily served the interests of the deceived husband (cf. Lev. 18:20; 20:10). The two wives (the one deceived, the other seduced) came second. Compare the Tenth Commandment: "[Y]ou shall not covet your neighbor's wife"; the emphasis is on "neighbor"! The feelings of the deceived wife are never mentioned in the Pentateuch.

However, in Malachi 2, at the end of Old Testament redemptive history, we are in a different sphere: "[T]he LORD was witness between you and the wife of your youth, to whom you have been faithless, though she is your companion and your wife by covenant. . . . So guard yourselves in your spirit, and let none of you be faithless to the wife of your youth" (vv. 14–15). The deceived wife has entered the picture! "How could you do this to her!?"

In the New Testament, we go another step forward. The (young) wives are told once to love their husbands (Titus 2:4), and the husbands are told even more than once: "Husbands, love your wives, as Christ loved the church and gave himself up for her" (Eph. 5:25; cf. vv. 28, 33). "Husbands, love your wives, and do not be harsh with them" (Col. 3:19).

Notice the three steps: first, do not humiliate your neighbor by sleeping with his wife. Second, do not be unfaithful to your *own* wife. Third, love your wife as much as Christ has loved the church and has given himself for her. Only after Christ (and his church) had been brought in, the full depth of the Seventh Commandment could be revealed. "You shall not commit adultery" then becomes: "You shall love your own wife so much that you are prepared to surrender your life for her." Again, Christ is the great example *and* the One giving us the strength to do this. No culture has ever demanded any man to put his life at risk for his wife. However, such a commandment is perfectly fitting within the holy framework of the law of Christ!

✦   ✦   ✦

DAY 310 – TEMPLES OF THE SPIRIT
(Lord's Day 41, Q&A 109, part 1)

Q. Does God, in this commandment, forbid only such scandalous sins as adultery?
A. We are temples of the Holy Spirit, body and soul, and God wants both to be kept clean and holy.

In 1 Corinthians 6, Paul links sexual (im)morality with the vital truth that our bodies are temples of the Holy Spirit: "Flee from sexual immorality. Every other sin a person commits is outside the body, but the sexually immoral person sins against his own body. Or do you not know that your body is a temple of the Holy Spirit within you, whom you have from God? You are not your own, for you were bought with a price. So glorify God in your body" (vv. 18–20). It has often been pointed out that, of course, *every* sin involves the body. However, no sin affects the sacrosanct character of the body as much as sexual immorality does. This is the very body that, in the case of the believer, is a "temple" (a sacred dwelling-place) of the Holy Spirit. The Lord has bought us with a price; we are his, so our bodies are his. "Do you not know that your bodies are members of Christ? Shall I then take the members of Christ and make them members of a prostitute? Never!" (v. 15).

Elsewhere, Paul says, "[S]exual immorality and all impurity or covetousness must not even be named among you, as is proper among saints. . . . For you may be sure of this, that everyone who is sexually immoral or impure, . . . has no inheritance in the kingdom of Christ and God" (Eph. 5:3–4). To God, the body is very important. It is the *body*, not the human spirit, that is called the dwelling-place of the Holy Spirit. It is our "mortal bodies" to which God will give life one day (Rom. 8:11). Paul even says, "I appeal to you therefore, brothers, by the mercies of God, to present your *bodies* as a living sacrifice, holy and acceptable to God, which is your spiritual worship" (12:1). Sexual immorality affects the body more than anything. Don't think that God does not care because it is "only" the body. He created it just as much as he created our soul, and he wishes to redeem it just as much as he wishes to redeem our souls! So, "may the God of peace himself sanctify you completely, and may your whole spirit and soul *and body* be kept blameless at the coming of our Lord Jesus Christ" (1 Thess. 5:23).

✢　✢　✢

DAY 311 – THE ADULTEROUS MIND
(Lord's Day 41, Q&A 109, part 2)

A. That is why God forbids all unchaste actions, looks, talk, thoughts, or desires, and whatever may incite someone to them.

With the Sixth Commandment, we have seen that hatred and murder are punished in different ways, but that both are equal proofs of humanity's fundamental sinfulness. Hatred and vindictiveness are sufficient to make a person eligible for eternal condemnation. Some sins are far worse than some other sins—but even the smallest sins make people sinners, and thus bring them under the wrath of God.

It is the same with the Seventh Commandment. We clearly distinguish between rape—which is always punished, if the evildoer is caught—and adultery, which is usually *not* tried in lawsuits because it is thought to belong to people's own responsibility. But many people do morally condemn adultery, and such people will always consider adultery to be far worse than "unchaste looks, talk, thoughts, or desires." Rightly so: sinning is worse than desiring to sin. Yet, even "unchaste looks" are enough to make one a sinner, and eligible for eternal condemnation. Desiring to sin is just as sinful as actual sinning.

Jesus said about this subject, "You have heard that it was said, 'You shall not commit adultery.' But I say to you that everyone who looks at a woman with lustful intent has already committed adultery with her in his heart. If your right eye causes you to sin [by wrongly looking at a woman], tear it out and throw it away. For it is better that you lose one of your members than that your whole body be thrown into hell" (Matt. 5:27–29). The word "but" does not mean that Jesus criticized the Seventh Commandment; he only wished to bring out its true depth: at bottom, adultery in a person's heart is just as sinful as the act of adultery—not in a civil court, nor in church discipline, but certainly before God's tribunal.

Of course, tearing your eye out must not be taken literally: after two wrong looks, you would have no eyes left! What it does say is: try to avoid any occasion in which you might look at other people in an unchaste way! Job said, "I made a covenant with my eyes not to let them lust after any girl" (Job 31:1 CJB). Avoid any occasions in which you might easily fall!

✧ ✧ ✧

DAY 312 – THE EIGHTH COMMANDMENT

(Lord's Day 42, Q&A 110, part 1)

Q. What does God forbid in the eighth commandment?

A. God forbids not only outright theft and robbery, punishable by law. But in God's sight theft also includes all scheming and swindling in order to get our neighbor's goods for ourselves, whether by force or means that appear legitimate, such as inaccurate measurements of weight, size, or volume; fraudulent merchandising; counterfeit money; excessive interest; or any other means forbidden by God.

In the Eighth Commandment, God forbids actual theft and robbery, as well as the various indirect forms of theft, summed up by the Catechism (biblical examples: e.g., Exod. 22:1; Deut. 25:13–16; Ps. 15:5; Prov. 11:1; Isa. 33:15; Ezek. 45:9–12; Micah 6:9–11; Luke 3:14; 6:35). There is one special case of theft that the Catechism does *not* mention, and that is the theft of *people*, as forbidden in Exodus 21:16 ("Whoever steals a man and sells him, and anyone found in possession of him, shall be put to death"). John mentions the "bodies" and "souls" of humans as belonging to the merchandise of "Babylon" (Rev. 18:13). Some expositors have presumed that the Eighth Commandment refers especially to this kind of theft.

In connection with this, it is remarkable that the six types of sinners mentioned in 1 Corinthians 5:11 seem to correspond precisely with the sinners whom Deuteronomy says had to be put away from Israel (cf. 1 Cor. 5:13) (in Deuteronomy this took place through stoning, in Corinth through excommunication). If this is correct, the "swindlers" (or "robbers") in Paul's enumeration correspond with Deuteronomy 24:7, "If a man is found stealing one of his brothers of the people of Israel, and if he treats him as a slave or sells him, then that thief shall die. So you shall purge evil from your midst."

Now look again at the Sixth through the Tenth Commandments. What they seem to say, in close mutual relationship, is this: do not sin against your neighbor by taking his *life* (the Sixth), or by taking his *wife* (the Seventh), or by taking his *freedom* (the Eighth), or by taking his *name* (or *reputation*) (the Ninth), or by taking (or at least desiring) his *possessions* (the Tenth Commandment). In the positive, New Testament sense, this becomes: "You shall love your neighbor so much that you protect his life, (the good name of) his wife, his freedom, his reputation, and his possessions. You shall love your neighbor as yourself, so that you will never value your own life, reputation, freedom, and possessions higher than your neighbor's."

❖   ✦   ❖

DAY 313 – GREED

(Lord's Day 42, Q&A 110, part 2)

A. In addition God forbids all greed and pointless squandering of his gifts.

For the third time, we find an important rule: the Bible condemns not only sinful *acts*, but also the sinful motives and desires from which they sprout. That is, not only murder as such, but also the hatred and vindictiveness that may lead to murder (Sixth Commandment). Not only sexual sins as such are condemned, but also the lust that may lead to adultery (Seventh Commandment). Not only theft is wrong, but also the covetousness that may lead to theft (Eighth Commandment). In fact, this covetousness is addressed in the Tenth Commandment: "You shall not covet your neighbor's house . . . your neighbor's wife . . . or anything that is your neighbor's."

Again we notice an interesting difference here: all societies condemn theft—but no civil government will ever sue you for covetousness. However, to God, greed is just as much a sin as actual theft. Jesus said, "Take care, and be on your guard against all covetousness, for one's life does not consist in the abundance of his possessions" (Luke 12:15). Covetousness is even called a form of idolatry (Eph. 5:5; Col. 3:5), because it implies setting your heart on things other than God. Not only the thieves but also the greedy will not inherit the Kingdom of God (1 Cor. 6:10). God condemns actual sin, but also the desire to sin.

Even if the Eighth Commandment refers especially to theft of people, the motive behind it is greed: the love of money that can be earned with trafficking in human beings. Paul says, "[T]he love of money is a root of all kinds of evils. It is through this craving that some have wandered away from the faith and pierced themselves with many pangs" (1 Tim. 6:10). Some translations even say that the love of money "is *the* root of *all* evil" (KJV, BRG, GNV, etc.)! Indeed, even in much hatred and vindictiveness (Sixth), in prostitution (Seventh), in theft and human trafficking (Eighth Commandment), the love of money plays a major role. And you know, you "cannot serve God and money" (Luke 16:13). Even to elders and pastors it had to be said, "[S]hepherd the flock of God . . . not for shameful gain, but eagerly" (1 Pet. 5:2).

✣   ✣   ✣

DAY 314 – SHARING

(Lord's Day 42, Q&A iii, part i)

Q. What does God require of you in this commandment?
A. That I do whatever I can for my neighbor's good, . . . and that I
work faithfully so that I may share with those in need.

Here again, we see how an originally negative commandment—"You shall not . . ."—is turned into a positive commandment. Thus, "You shall not steal" becomes this: "You shall love your neighbor so much that you do not only *respect* his possessions and his freedom, but you shall eagerly *protect* his possessions and freedom; yes, you shall *share* with him your own possessions if he is poor and needy." Already the prophet Isaiah described this true spiritual attitude: "Is it not to share your bread with the hungry and bring the homeless poor into your house; when you see the naked, to cover him, and not to hide yourself from your own flesh?" (Isa. 58:7).

In the New Testament, Paul says, "Let the thief no longer steal, but rather let him labor, doing honest work with his own hands, so that he may have something to share with anyone in need" (Eph. 4:28). "[L]et us not grow weary of doing good, for in due season we will reap, if we do not give up. So then, as we have opportunity, let us do good to everyone, and especially to those who are of the household of faith" (Gal. 6:9–10). "As for the rich in this present age, charge them not . . . to set their hopes on the uncertainty of riches, but on God, who richly provides us with everything to enjoy. They are to do good, to be rich in good works, to be generous and ready to share, thus storing up treasure for themselves as a good foundation for the future, so that they may take hold of that which is truly life" (1 Tim. 6:17–19).

John says, "[I]f anyone has the world's goods and sees his brother in need, yet closes his heart against him, how does God's love abide in him?" (1 John 3:17). And James says, "If a brother or sister is poorly clothed and lacking in daily food, and one of you says to them, 'Go in peace, be warmed and filled,' without giving them the things needed for the body, what good is that?" (2:15–16). The original commandment was: "You shall *not take*." The newer version is: "You shall *give!*" "Each one must give as he has decided in his heart, not reluctantly or under compulsion, for God loves a cheerful giver" (2 Cor. 9:7).

✤   ✤   ✤

DAY 315 – THE GOLDEN RULE
(Lord's Day 42, Q&A 111, part 2)

A. . . . that I treat others as I would like them to treat me.

In the midst of the Catechism's answer, we find this precious phrase: "I treat others as I would like them to treat me." This phrase reminds us immediately of Jesus' own words: "[W]hatever you wish that others would do to you, do also to them, for this is the Law and the Prophets" (Matt. 7:12). Jesus summarizes here "the Law and the Prophets," that is, the entire Old Testament (as far as neighbor–neighbor relationships are concerned), in this one sentence, which is often referred to as the Golden Rule: "Whatever you wish that others would do to you, do also to them."

Actually, this Rule is much older than the Sermon of the Mount, although it was usually known in its negative form only (sometimes called the Silver Rule). An ancient Jewish source says, "[W]hat you hate, do not do to any one" (Tobit 4:15 RSV). Just before the time of Jesus, rabbi Hillel said, according to the Talmud (possibly because of the word in Tobit): "What is hateful to you, do not to your neighbor: that is the whole Torah, while the rest is the commentary thereof; go and learn it."

The difference between Jewish tradition and Jesus is quite conspicuous. The book of Tobit and Hillel still moved in the negative sphere of the "You shall *not* . . . ." Do not do to others what you yourself dislike. But Jesus, as with so many other commandments, moves to the positive side: "Do to others what you would like others to do to *you*." The correspondence with Hillel is that both said that this was the core of the Tanakh, as far as mutual human relationships were concerned (the vertical relationship with God is a somewhat different matter).

In fact, the Golden Rule is nothing but a variation of Leviticus 19:18, "[Y]ou shall love your neighbor as yourself." Roughly speaking, there are two different motives for doing to others what we would like others to do to us: either legalism or love. That is, you are benevolent to your neighbor because you *have to* (perhaps against your own desires), or you do so because you *wish to*—because you love the neighbor with the love with which God has loved *you*!

✦ ✦ ✦

DAY 316 – THE NINTH COMMANDMENT
(Lord's Day 43, Q&A 112, part 1)

Q. What is the aim of the ninth commandment?
A. That I never give false testimony against anyone, twist no one's words, nor gossip or slander, nor join in condemning anyone rashly or without a hearing. Rather, in court and everywhere else, I should avoid lying and deceit of every kind; these are the very devices the devil uses, and they would call down on me God's intense wrath.

Again, this is a commandment that stands for a whole category of commandments, all of which have to do with telling the truth (cf. Prov. 12:22; Rev. 21:8). Bearing false witness against your neighbor (cf. Prov. 19:5) is just one example of twisting the truth. Other examples are gossip and slander (cf. Lev. 19:16; Ps. 15:3; 101:5; 140:11; etc.). Slanderous speech is quite a common vice (cf. Matt. 15:19; Rom. 1:29–30; 2 Cor. 12:20; Eph. 4:31; Col. 3:8; 1 Tim. 3:11; 2 Tim. 3:3; 1 Pet. 2:1); it is a form of judging others in an untruthful way (cf. Matt. 7:1). The problem with slander is twofold. First, the slanderer easily passes on falsehoods about his neighbor. Second, even if what he is telling others is true he has to wonder whether *he* is the person who, or *this* is the situation in which he, should pass these things on to others.

When it is said among Christians that he or she lives "in sin," we can almost be sure that sexual immorality is meant. This is strange because sexual immorality is just one of many vices. Why do we hear of cases of church discipline in which the Seventh Commandment is involved, and so few cases involving greed (Eighth) or slander (Ninth Commandment)? Why do we give little heed to the Catechism's strong language: "these are the very devices the devil uses"? Jesus said of the devil, "He was a murderer from the beginning, and does not stand in the truth, because there is no truth in him. When he lies, he speaks out of his own character, for he is a liar and the father of lies" (John 8:44). Lies, deceit, gossip, slander are from the devil!

Of course, we have to nuance matters here. Even the Bible mentions "white lies" without condemning them (Josh. 2:4–5; 2 Sam. 17:20). Or to take a modern example: if you would tell a hypochondriac the full therapeutic truth, you will probably worsen his condition instead of improving it. But apart from such exceptions, if we make a habit of lying we come under "God's intense wrath"! "Outside are the dogs and sorcerers and the sexually immoral and murderers and idolaters, and everyone who loves and practices falsehood" (Rev. 22:15).

✤   ✤   ✤

DAY 317 – LOVING THE TRUTH

(Lord's Day 43, Q&A 112, part 2)

A. I should love the truth, speak it candidly, and openly acknowledge it.

You remember that a negative commandment ("You shall not . . .") always turns into a positive commandment in the New Testament, thus manifesting its true, divinely intended depth. It is the same with the Ninth Commandment, which in fact turns out to mean: "You shall love your neighbor so much that you not only do not lie to him, but you serve him with the truth, in his best interest." As Paul says, true love "does not rejoice [as gossipers and slanderers do] at wrongdoing, but rejoices with the truth" (1 Cor. 13:6). And elsewhere he says, "Therefore, having put away falsehood, let each one of you speak the truth with his neighbor, for we are members one of another" (Eph. 4:25).

This "truth" refers both to "the Christian truth" in a general (doctrinal) way, but also with telling the truth in a very practical way. Not only *speak* truthful things, but *be* truthful, honest, transparent, straightforward: "Whoever speaks the truth gives honest evidence, but a false witness utters deceit" (Prov. 12:17).

In his exhortations to Timothy, the apostle Paul referred him to "Christ Jesus, who in his testimony before Pontius Pilate made the good confession" (1 Tim. 6:13). This is, among other things, what Jesus confessed to Pilate: "You say that I am a king. For this purpose I was born and for this purpose I have come into the world—to *bear witness to the truth*. Everyone who is of the truth listens to my voice" (John 18:37; cf. 8:40, 45). Pilate tried to weaken this statement by retorting, "What is truth?" (v. 38), but Jesus' statement stood firmly. On another occasion he said about the liars and himself, "The one who speaks on his own authority seeks his own glory; but the one who seeks the glory of him who sent him is true, and in him there is no falsehood" (7:18). He was "full of truth" (1:14). No human could ever say what he said, "I *am* the way, and the truth, and the life" (14:6). If we serve others with the truth, this basically means that we bear witness to Jesus himself. You love your neighbor so much that you serve him with the truth in the best possible way: with Jesus!

✣   ✣   ✣

DAY 318 – GUARDING THE NEIGHBOR'S REPUTATION
(Lord's Day 43, Q&A 112, part 3)

A. And I should do what I can to guard and advance my neighbor's good name.

Here the Catechism touches upon a very special aspect of the Ninth Commandment: guarding and advancing your neighbor's reputation. The Sixth Commandment protects the neighbor's *life*, the Seventh protects the neighbor's *marriage*, the Eighth protects the neighbor's *freedom*, the Ninth Commandment protects the neighbor's *name*. You shall love your neighbor so much that you respect and honor his life, his marriage, his freedom, and his reputation. "You shall love your neighbor as yourself" (Lev. 19:18) thus means: you shall value your neighbor's life, marriage, freedom, and reputation at least as highly as your own. As Peter said, "[A]ll of you, have unity of mind, sympathy, brotherly love, a tender heart, and a humble mind. Do not repay evil for evil or reviling for reviling, but on the contrary, *bless*, for to this you were called, that you may obtain a blessing" (1 Pet. 3:8–9). You are called to *bless*, and be a blessing to, your neighbor.

Of course, we all have the responsibility to guard our own names ourselves. Paul speaks of widows "having a reputation for good works: if she has brought up children, has shown hospitality, has washed the feet of the saints, has cared for the afflicted, and has devoted herself to every good work" (1 Tim. 5:10). What is your or my reputation? For what good things are we known to others? How can we expect others to guard and advance our good name if we do not first guard it ourselves? Solomon says, "A good name is to be chosen rather than great riches, and favor is better than silver or gold" (Prov. 22:1), and "A good name is better than precious ointment" (Eccl. 7:1; cf. Song 1:3).

We need brothers and sisters who come to the defense of a brother or sister whose reputation is in jeopardy for false reasons. Such a brother was Barnabas, who took Saul of Tarsus "and brought him to the apostles and declared to them how on the road he had seen the Lord, who spoke to him, and how at Damascus he had preached boldly in the name of Jesus" (Acts 9:27). No wonder Barnabas was called a "son of encouragement" (4:36)!

✵   ✵   ✵

DAY 319 – THE TENTH COMMANDMENT
(Lord's Day 44, Q&A 113, part 1)

Q. What is the aim of the tenth commandment?
A. That not even the slightest desire or thought contrary to any one of God's commandments should ever arise in our hearts.

The Tenth Commandment occupies a special place among the Ten insofar as it explicitly addresses the person's inner motives: "You shall not *covet* your neighbor's house; you shall not *covet* your neighbor's wife, or male or female slave, or ox, or donkey, or anything that belongs to your neighbor." In some sense, it works like a kind of summary: You shall not take your neighbor's life, you shall not even *covet* it. You shall not take your neighbor's wife, you shall not even *covet* her. You shall not take your neighbor's freedom, you shall not even *covet* it (i.e., covet to possess him as a slave). You shall not ruin your neighbor's name, you shall not even *covet* doing so. Apparently, the Catechism accepts this broad application: "[N]ot even the slightest desire or thought contrary to *any* one of God's commandments should ever arise in our hearts."

Here again, the negative commandment ("You shall not . . .") can be turned into a positive commandment: "You shall love your neighbor so much that you earnestly *desire* to do him good, to seek the best for him." It is difficult to assess desires. Earthly tribunals do not generally judge desires because they cannot; they can only judge actual deeds. It does reckon with motives, for instance, by distinguishing between (intentional) murder and (unintentional) manslaughter. But it can judge intentionality only on the basis of (outward) facts. It cannot do what God alone can do: judge the heart (cf. Ps. 7:9; Jer. 17:9–10; Mark 7:21; 1 Cor. 4:5; Rev. 2:23).

This is a very important point. Let us imagine that, seen from the outside, you perfectly fulfill the first nine commandments. You have never killed, committed adultery, stolen, or given false testimony. Congratulations. But then, at the end, comes the Tenth Commandment. In what you did, were you driven by jealousy or by benevolence? Were you driven by covetousness or love? "Do nothing from selfish ambition or conceit, but in humility count others more significant than yourselves. Let each of you look not only to his own interests, but also to the interests of others" (Phil. 2:3–4).

✴   ✴   ✴

DAY 320 – HATING SIN
(Lord's Day 44, Q&A 113, part 2)

A. Rather, with all our hearts we should always hate sin.

One form of legalism is that you fulfill the law because you have to, whereas in fact you *love* to do what this very law forbids. Now and then you *long* to see some nasty person dead. Now and then you *long* to commit adultery (when seeing a gorgeous woman whose appearance sets you on fire). Or you *long* to deprive your neighbor of (part of) his freedom, for instance, the freedom of speech. In other words, you may behave rather decently, whereas you sometimes *love* to behave very *indecently*. You want to keep God's law—for instance, out of fear for eternal condemnation, or simply out of fear for your pastor, elders, parents, spouse—so you avoid sinning as much as you can. But that does not mean you *hate* sin. You keep the law (more or less), but you still *covet* to do otherwise. This is what the Tenth Commandment is all about. It lays bare your real motives. You love sinning, although you avoid it because you are a legalist. You have never learned to *hate* sin.

Perhaps you were not even aware of your secret coveting—it is the prohibition that reveals it! Paul writes, "[I]f it had not been for the law, I would not have known sin. For I would not have known what it is to covet if the law had not said, 'You shall not covet.' But sin, seizing an opportunity through the commandment, produced in me all kinds of covetousness. For apart from the law, sin lies dead. I was once alive apart from the law, but when the commandment came, sin came alive and I died. The very commandment that promised life proved to be death to me" (Rom. 7:7–10). Sin may be fast asleep in you, until the law comes and brings it to light. There is hatred, or lust, or greed in your heart, but you did not realize it. Then comes the law that says, "Do not hate! Do not lust! Do not covet!" And you suddenly become aware that all these things are in your heart. It is good that the law does this because, if you are born again, you can now begin *hating* these very things you have discovered at the bottom of your heart. And Romans 8 shows you that you can do this only in the power of the Holy Spirit who dwells in you!

✦　　✦　　✦

DAY 321 – TAKING PLEASURE IN WHAT IS RIGHT
(Lord's Day 44, Q&A 113, part 3)

A. Rather, with all our hearts we should always . . . take pleasure in whatever is right.

To be sure, we need a lot of grace to learn to hate sin. This hating can be done only in a power that you do not have of yourself, even as a believer. It is the power of the Holy Spirit who dwells in every true believer. Through the Spirit, you not only begin to hate sin but you "take pleasure in whatever is right." Hating sin is the parallel of loving God and loving his commandments: "By this we know that we love the children of God, when we love God and obey his commandments. For this is the love of God, that we keep his commandments. And his commandments are not burdensome" (1 John 5:2–3). That is, they are not "burdensome" for the true believer, for he is filled with the Holy Spirit (Eph. 5:18) and with the love of God (Rom. 5:5).

Righteous is he whose "delight is in the law of the LORD" (Ps. 1:2). "[T]he precepts of the LORD are right, rejoicing the heart. . . . More to be desired are they than gold, even much fine gold" (19:8, 10). "I will delight in your statutes. . . . Lead me in the path of your commandments, for I delight in it . . . I find my delight in your commandments, which I love . . . I delight in your law . . . Oh how I love your law!" (119:16, 35, 47 [cf. 143], 70 [cf. 77, 92, 174], 97 [cf. 159]). A lovely word: "delight." You can delight in God's law only if you delight in the God of this law, and in what his commandments demand of you. We should not only strive for what is right, we should *love* what is right because we love the righteous God.

Justification is being made just (righteous). The righteous not only *do* what is right, they *love* what is right. Such a person is first and foremost righteous on the inside, and then also on the outside. "O LORD, who shall sojourn in your tent? Who shall dwell on your holy hill? He who walks blamelessly and does what is right and speaks truth *in his heart*" (Ps. 15:1–2). David walked before God "in faithfulness, in righteousness, and in uprightness of *heart*" (1 Kings 3:6). These are those whom the Lord longs for: not only the outwardly righteous but the "upright of *heart*" (Job 33:3; Ps. 7:10; 11:2; 32:11; 36:10; 64:10; 78:72; 94:15; 97:11; 119:7; 125:4).

✦   ✦   ✦

DAY 322 – PERFECT OBEDIENCE?
(Lord's Day 44, Q&A 114, part 1)

Q. But can those converted to God obey these commandments perfectly?
A. No. In this life even the holiest have only a small beginning of this obedience.

The first part of the Catechism's answer is quite somber and discouraging. Why should we try to "strive for . . . the holiness without which no one will see the Lord" (Heb. 12:14), if the maximum we may hope to reach in this striving is "only a small beginning of this obedience"? To explain this, let us first emphasize the distinction between our *positional* holiness—you *are* holy by faith in Christ—and our *practical* holiness, that is, the practical realization of our positional holiness. In our positional holiness, there is no distinction between the "less holy" and the "holiest." Of each believer, young or mature, carnal or spiritual, it can be said in principle: "[Y]ou *were* washed, you *were* sanctified, you *were* justified in the name of the Lord Jesus Christ and by the Spirit of our God" (1 Cor. 6:11). Believers are "called saints" (Rom. 1:7 DLNT, YLT; cf. 1 Cor. 1:2), or if you wish, "called to be saints"—not called to *become* saints. Paul never confuses our positional and our practical sanctification.

Yet, he is fully aware of the need for practical sanctification as well: "[P]resent your members as slaves to righteousness leading to sanctification . . . now that you have been set free from sin and have become slaves of God, the fruit you get leads to sanctification and its end, eternal life" (Rom. 6:19, 22). "[B]eloved, let us cleanse ourselves from every defilement of body and spirit, bringing holiness to completion in the fear of God" (2 Cor. 7:1). "[T]his is the will of God, your sanctification [or, holiness]" (1 Thess. 4:3–4, 7). "[M]ay the God of peace himself sanctify you completely, and may your whole spirit and soul and body be kept blameless at the coming of our Lord Jesus Christ" (5:23). Also in the sentence, "God chose you as the firstfruits to be saved, through sanctification by the Spirit and belief in the truth" (2 Thess. 2:13), Paul speaks not only of positional but also of practical sanctification on our way to perfect salvation.

In brief: become (practically) what you are (positionally). Or to put it even more strongly: *be what you are!*

✦ ✦ ✦

DAY 323 – BEGINNING TO OBEY

(Lord's Day 44, Q&A 114, part 2)

A. Nevertheless, with all seriousness of purpose, [the saints] do begin to live according to all, not only some, of God's commandments.

Yesterday we saw: You *are* holy, so *live* holy! "As obedient children, do not be conformed to the passions of your former ignorance, but as he who called you is holy, you also be holy in all your conduct, since it is written, 'You shall be holy, for I am holy'" (1 Pet. 1:14–16; cf. Lev. 11:44–45; etc.). Don't say, It's no use trying to live as a holy person, for "even the holiest have only a small beginning of this obedience." No, striving for holiness (cf. Heb. 12:14) is a divine command! And if God says, "You *shall* [i.e., must] be holy," he will also give you the strength of his Spirit to "begin to live according to all . . . of God's commandments."

Don't be discouraged if, here on earth, you will never fully reach this goal. In itself this is true because the sinful nature is still in you (cf. Rom. 7:14–15; 1 John 1:8). And yet you strive, you pursue, "with all seriousness of purpose," as the Catechism says, *as if* complete holiness on earth were possible. The very least you can do is to avoid "the counsel of the wicked," "the way of sinners," and "the seat of scoffers," and instead find your delight in, and find ample time for meditating on, God's Word (Ps. 1:1–2). *Feed* on the right food! *Fill* your time with the right meditations, yes, be filled with the Holy Spirit (Eph. 5:18)! Don't stop at "Wretched man that I am! Who will deliver me from this body of death?" but move on to "Thanks be to God through Jesus Christ our Lord!" (Rom. 7:24–25).

Both realistic and encouraging is this statement by Paul: "Not that I have already obtained this or am already perfect, but I press on to make it my own, because Christ Jesus has made me his own. Brothers, I do not consider that I have made it my own. But one thing I do: forgetting what lies behind and straining forward to what lies ahead, I press on toward the goal for the prize of the upward call of God in Christ Jesus" (Phil. 3:12–14). It is as if he says: Here on earth I can never reach it, but I press on *as if* I can reach it because such pressing will at least take me ever closer to the goal, day by day!

✦   ✦   ✦

DAY 324 – POINTEDLY PREACHED COMMANDMENTS
(Lord's Day 44, Q&A 115, part 1)

Q. Since no one in this life can obey the Ten Commandments perfectly, why does God want them preached so pointedly?
A. First, so that the longer we live the more we may come to know our sinfulness and the more eagerly look to Christ for forgiveness of sins and righteousness.

In certain circles, people require of a person a very profound knowledge of his own sinfulness before they will acknowledge him as truly converted. However, the biblical reality is quite different. On the one hand, one could hardly imagine a regenerate person without *some* awareness of sinfulness. On the other hand, a *deep* awareness of sinfulness is not a *prerequisite* for the assurance of salvation but a *consequence* of it, if at least the Holy Spirit is allowed to work in that person's heart and life.

A good illustration of this is Ezekiel 36, where the future restoration of God's people is described. First we read: "I will sprinkle clean water on you, and you shall be clean from all your uncleannesses. . . . And I will give you a new heart, and a new spirit I will put within you. And I will remove the heart of stone from your flesh and give you a heart of flesh" (vv. 25–26). This is what the New Testament calls rebirth or regeneration. Then it says, "And I will put my Spirit within you, and cause you to walk in my statutes and be careful to obey my rules" (v. 27). When the regenerate comes to the assurance of faith, God seals this faith with the Holy Spirit (Eph. 1:13; cf. 4:30). Only subsequently it is said, "Then you will remember your evil ways, and your deeds that were not good, and you will loathe yourselves for your iniquities and your abominations" (Ezek. 16:31; cf. 20:43).

If we look at this in terms of the chronological order of Paul's epistles, we see a remarkable progress. First, he wrote, "I am the least of the *apostles*, unworthy to be called an apostle, because I persecuted the church of God" (1 Cor. 15:9). Later he wrote, "I am the very least of all the *saints*" (Eph. 3:8). Finally he wrote, "Christ Jesus came into the world to save *sinners*, of whom I am the foremost" (1 Tim. 1:15). Apparently, the older he got, the more aware he was of the seriousness of what he had done before his conversion. However, this awareness never made him doubt his salvation. It did not *depress* him because he knew he was forgiven. It only brought him to more thanksgiving and worship!

✦   ✦   ✦

DAY 325 – NEVER STOP STRIVING!
(Lord's Day 44, Q&A 115, part 2)

A. Second, so that we may never stop striving, and never stop pray-ing to God for the grace of the Holy Spirit, to be renewed more and more after God's image, until after this life we reach our goal: perfec-tion.

Christian life is a life of "striving" and "pursuing": striving in prayers (Rom. 15:30), in building up others (1 Cor. 14:12), striving for the faith of the gospel (Phil. 1:27), striving to reach the end of our "wilderness jour-ney" (Heb. 4:11), striving for peace and holiness (Heb. 12:14). It is a life of pursuing "what makes for peace and for mutual upbuilding" (Rom. 14:19; cf. 1 Pet. 3:11), pursuing love (1 Cor. 14:1), righteousness, godliness, faith, love, steadfastness, gentleness (1 Tim. 6:11; cf. 2 Tim. 2:22). One might almost say: never a moment of rest—and yet a wonderful rest for one's conscience because of God's forgiveness, and a rest for our souls by learn-ing from Jesus, for he is gentle and lowly in heart (Matt. 11:28–29). It is a life of "praying without ceasing" (1 Thess. 5:17; cf. Luke 18:1; Rom. 12:12; Col. 4:2) to express one's dependence upon the "grace of the Holy Spirit." It is a life of the constant renewal "of your mind, that by testing you may discern what is the will of God, what is good and acceptable and perfect" (Rom. 12:2; cf. 2 Cor. 4:16; Eph. 4:23).

The goal of all spiritual maturation is this: the image of Christ, re-produced in us. We "have put on the new self, which is being renewed in knowledge after the image of its creator" (Col. 3:10). "And we all, with un-veiled face, beholding the glory of the Lord, are being transformed into the same image from one degree of glory to another" (2 Cor. 3:18; cf. Gal. 4:19).

This is the first goal, to be reached on earth: spiritual maturation. The second goal is to be reached in eternity: we are "predestined to be conformed to the image of his Son" (Rom. 8:29). "[W]e know that when he appears we shall be like him" (1 John 3:2). "Not that I have already obtained this or am already perfect, but I press on to make it my own, because Christ Jesus has made me his own. . . . [F]orgetting what lies behind and straining forward to what lies ahead, I press on toward the goal for the prize of the upward call of God in Christ Jesus" (Phil. 3:12–14). What a future—an important part of which is to be realized already now!

❖   ❖   ❖

DAY 326 – WHY PRAYER?
(Lord's Day 45, Q&A 116, part 1)

Q. Why do Christians need to pray?
A. Because prayer is the most important part of the thankfulness
God requires of us. . . .

We remember that the Catechism is divided into three parts. The third part, on gratitude, is again divided into three parts: the introduction, the Ten Commandments, and now the third part. This deals with prayer in general, and with the Lord's Prayer in particular. It underscores the enormous importance of prayer in the Christian life. The Catechism begins by asking: "Why do Christians need to pray?" One might expect that the answer will tie in with the original meaning of the verb "to pray" (from Latin *precare*, "to ask earnestly, to beg"). When you pray, you ask God to do, to give, to further, or to prevent something. A prayer is a request, a petition.

However, the Catechism takes the word in its much wider meaning, including *everything* that a person may say to God. In this case, not our requests come first, but our utterances of thankfulness. (Remember that this section on prayer belongs to the part on gratitude!) Before *asking* from God, you *bring* him your thanks and your praises. The book of Psalms is full of this. And Paul repeatedly emphasizes the importance of thanksgiving: "[B]e filled with the Spirit, addressing one another in psalms and hymns and spiritual songs, singing and making melody to the Lord with your heart, giving thanks always and for everything to God the Father in the name of our Lord Jesus Christ" (Eph. 5:18–20). "[W]hatever you do, in word or deed, do everything in the name of the Lord Jesus, giving thanks to God the Father through him" (Col. 3:17). "Pray without ceasing, give thanks in all circumstances; for this is the will of God in Christ Jesus for you" (1 Thess. 5:17–18).

Whatever your urgent needs may be, never forget to thank! "[D]o not be anxious about anything, but in everything by prayer and supplication *with thanksgiving* let your requests be made known to God" (Phil. 4:6). Look at the direct effect: "And the peace of God, which surpasses all understanding, will guard your hearts and your minds in Christ Jesus" (v. 7). In spite of great disappointment (humanly speaking), Jesus could say, " I thank you, Father" (Matt. 11:25)!

✦　✦　✦

DAY 327 – ASKING AND GIVING

(Lord's Day 45, Q&A 116, part 2)

A. And also because God gives his grace and Holy Spirit only to those who pray continually and groan inwardly, asking God for these gifts and thanking God for them.

After mentioning thanksgiving, the Catechism comes to our actual requests (praying in the narrower sense). Right away, it mentions the most important things that we could ask for: God's grace and God's Holy Spirit. Instead of asking for so many specific things (food and drink, good health, safekeeping, prosperity and success, and many other material blessings, as well as many spiritual blessings), we may replace them by one single term: grace. It is not only poor sinners who need redemptive grace; believers also need God's continual grace. This is why so many epistles start with wishing God's grace to believers. Since, even as believers, we deserve nothing, all our blessings depend on God's grace: "Give ear, O LORD, to my prayer; listen to my *plea for grace* [or, mercy]" (Ps. 86:6).

Grace and the Holy Spirit are clearly linked; on one occasion, the Spirit is even called the "Spirit of grace" (Heb. 10:29); compare the "Spirit of grace and of prayer" in Zechariah 12:10 (if we follow, e.g., the GNV, JUB). Although, since we have come to faith, the *person* of the Spirit dwells in us, we can always ask for more of (the *power* of) the Spirit: "If you then, who are evil, know how to give good gifts to your children, how much more will the heavenly Father give the Holy Spirit to those who ask him!" (Luke 11:13). The Father loves to give us more of his Spirit all the time (cf. Eph. 5:18).

The Catechism also seems to allude to Romans 8: "Likewise the Spirit helps us in our weakness. For we do not know what to pray for as we ought, but the Spirit himself intercedes for us with groanings too deep for words" (v. 26). Here, it is the Spirit himself who prays within and for us; it is *our* groanings in and through which the Spirit addresses the Father. Sometimes our prayers are not much more than "groanings" because we do not know what to say (cf. Acts 7:34; Rom. 8:23; 2 Cor. 5:2, 4). The Spirit, however, knows our deepest needs and desires, and brings them to God for us—or, to say the same with different words, it is *we* praying to God "in the Spirit" (Eph. 6:18; Jude 1:20).

✣　✣　✣

DAY 328 – CAN GOD CHANGE HIS MIND?
(Lord's Day 45, Q&A 116, part 3)

A. And also because God gives his grace and Holy Spirit only to those who pray continually and groan inwardly, asking God for these gifts and thanking God for them.

There is a peculiar element in the Catechism's answer that we should not overlook. God gives his blessings "only to those who pray continually." Here, a direct causal link is seen between our prayers and God's answers. Some people feel that God's sovereignty implies that he cannot make himself dependent on what humans ask. If God would depend on humans, in whatever small way, they argue, this would ruin his sovereignty. They overlook the fact that, apparently, God has *sovereignly* decided to involve human actions and decisions as well as prayers in his ways with the world: "Ask, and it will be given to you" (Matt. 7:7; cf. John 16:24; Ps. 145:19). "[W]hatever you ask in prayer, you will receive, if you have faith" (21:22). "Whatever you ask in my name, this I will do, that the Father may be glorified in the Son" (John 14:13). "You do not have, because you do not ask. You ask and do not receive, because you ask wrongly" (James 4:2–3). "[W]hatever we ask we receive from him, because we keep his commandments and do what pleases him" (1 John 3:22). "[I]f we ask anything according to his will he hears us" (5:14–15).

Some say that prayer is important because it changes *us*. They forget to wonder whether prayer might also change the mind of *God*. Take this clear example: "And the Lord said to Moses, '. . . let me alone, that my wrath may burn hot against them and I may consume them. . . .' But Moses implored the Lord his God. . . . And the Lord relented from the disaster that he had spoken of bringing on his people" (Exod. 32:9–14). Or this: "Jonah . . . called out, 'Yet forty days, and Nineveh shall be overthrown!' And the people of Nineveh . . . called for a fast and put on sackcloth. . . . 'Let everyone turn from his evil way and from the violence that is in his hands. Who knows? God may turn and relent and turn from his fierce anger, so that we may not perish.' When God saw what they did, how they turned from their evil way, God relented of the disaster that he had said he would do to them, and he did not do it" (Jonah 3:4–10). You see: Dare to ask! God answers prayers, and he does it with love!

✦　✦　✦

DAY 329 – PLEASING PRAYERS
(Lord's Day 45, Q&A 117, part 1)

Q. What is the kind of prayer that pleases God and that he listens to?
A. First, we must pray from the heart to no other than the one true God, revealed to us in his Word, asking for everything God has commanded us to ask for.

Whenever we pray, we do so out of the needs of our lives, usually in words that spring naturally from our hearts. However, this does not mean that it does not matter how we approach God. First, as the Catechism emphasizes, there cannot be any room for other gods in our hearts when we address the "one true God, revealed to us in his Word." That would be like telling your wife Sarah (or Abigail) how you love her, while having at the same time a Hagar (or a Bathsheba) in your heart. God is entitled to all your devotion, all your undivided love.

Second, what we may ask of God is determined not only by our own need, but also by what God is pleased to hear from us; otherwise he might not listen to our supplications. Is our prayer in the name of Jesus (John 16:24), that is, is it a prayer that he could have prayed himself? Is it a prayer "according to his will" (1 John 5:14), that is, the *kind* of prayer that God loves to hear? Or is it only a prayer of self-interest? Perhaps even a sinful prayer—like Simon the Magician's request (Acts 8:19)?

You see, on the one hand we are encouraged: "[I]n *everything* by prayer and supplication with thanksgiving let your requests be made known to God" (Phil. 4:6; cf. Ps. 62:8). So don't feel restricted in any way, as long as you can present your requests to God with a good conscience. On the other hand, there are things that *God* commands us to ask for; you might be so full of your own needs that you might forget *them*. For instance, pray constantly for the well-being of God's people, especially for God's servants (Rom. 1:10; 15:30; 2 Cor. 13:7–9; Eph. 6:18–19; Phil. 1:4, 9, 19; Col. 1:9; 4:3, 12; 1 Thess. 1:2; 5:25; 2 Thess. 1:11; 3:1; 3 John 1:2). Pray for the rulers of this world (1 Tim. 2:1–3). Pray about your food, your health, your marriage (1 Tim. 4:5; James 5:15–16; 1 Pet. 3:7). Pray for your persecutors and abusers (Matt. 5:44; Luke 6:28). Pray without ceasing. And do so always in the spirit of thanksgiving, praise, and worship (Eph. 5:20; Col. 3:16–17; 1 Thess. 5:17–18)! This is very pleasing to God (cf. John 4:23–24).

✦ ✦ ✦

DAY 330 – HUMBLE PRAYERS

(Lord's Day 45, Q&A 117, part 2)

A. Second, we must fully recognize our need and misery, so that we humble ourselves in God's majestic presence.

When we pray to God, we come in a humble attitude. We do so for at least two reasons. First, we come as small creatures to our majestic Creator. Second, we come as those who once had fallen into sin. Even though we may have been redeemed by faith, we still sin. And if it were only for our sinful nature, it would be enough to humble ourselves before God. As he says himself, "[T]his is the one to whom I will look: he who is humble and contrite in spirit and trembles at my word" (Isa. 66:2; cf. 57:15; Ps. 34:18).

Look at the difference between Job and Abraham. The former said, "I despise myself, and *repent* in dust and ashes" (Job 42:6). But Abraham said, "I have undertaken to speak to the Lord, I who *am* but dust and ashes" (Gen. 18:27). You see the difference? Abraham had nothing specific to repent of; yet, in the presence of the Lord, he realized how little he was: nothing but dust and ashes, compared to God's majesty.

Jesus could say of himself that he was "humble" (Matt. 11:29 CEB, CJB, GNT; etc.)—but he was never "humbled," nor did he ever have to "humble" himself because of sin or weakness. He "humbled" himself only "by becoming obedient to the point of death" (Phil. 2:8). We, however, always do humble ourselves when we come into "God's majestic presence": "Humble yourselves before the Lord, and he will exalt you" (James 4:10; cf. 1 Pet. 5:6). "Whoever exalts himself will be humbled, and whoever humbles himself will be exalted" (Matt. 23:12). You humble yourself before God when you have sins to confess—and even when you have nothing specific to confess, you humble yourself before God anyway.

To be sure, God is your Father; you have been brought near to his heart. You are his child and heir. That's great! Enjoy it. And yet, in eternity he will forever remain the majestic Creator God, and you will forever remain that small creature. Sure, as a child you come in love, intimacy, and confidence to your Father; nothing can take that away. And at the same time, you come as a slave of God to your Master (Rev. 22:3). The one metaphor is just as true as the other!

✣   ✣   ✣

DAY 331 – ANSWERED PRAYERS

(Lord's Day 45, Q&A 117, part 3)

A. Third, we must rest on this unshakable foundation: even though we do not deserve it, God will surely listen to our prayer because of Christ our Lord. That is what God promised us in his Word.

Roman Catholics sometimes use this argument to explain why they pray to Mary: She will pass their prayers on to her Son, and "he cannot refuse his mother anything." We read nothing of this in Scripture. Yet, I like the expression, but then applied to the Son of God and his Father: the Father cannot refuse his Son anything. "God will surely listen to our prayer because of Christ our Lord," says the Catechism. Jesus is interceding for us (Rom. 8:34). "[H]e is able to save to the uttermost those who draw near to God through him, since he always lives to make intercession for them" (Heb. 7:25). "[I]f anyone does sin, we have an advocate with the Father, Jesus Christ the righteous" (1 John 2:1).

Therefore, I firmly believe, for instance, that there is no request in the prayer of John 17 that the Father did not grant his Son. Some have argued that the prayer about unity (vv. 21–23) was not answered. Untrue. All genuine believers have received eternal life (v. 3), and, if they are spiritual enough, they will experience the unity of *life*, even if on the *organizational* level there is so much strife, rivalry, and dissension (cf. Gal. 5:20). There is certainly the side of our responsibility: "I therefore, a prisoner for the Lord, urge you to walk in a manner worthy of the calling to which you have been called, . . . eager to maintain the unity of the Spirit in the bond of peace" (Eph. 4:1–3). But on God's side the unity of the Body of Christ is fully guaranteed.

It was at the special request of the Son that the Father gave us the greatest post-Easter gift of all: the Holy Spirit (John 14:16–17; cf. v. 26). In addition to this, we have this promise of Jesus: "Truly, truly, I say to you, whatever you ask of the Father in my name, he will give it to you. Until now you have asked nothing in my name. Ask, and you will receive, that your joy may be full" (John 16:23–24). What a great promise! "[T]hrough [Christ] we both [i.e., Jewish and Gentile believers] have access in one Spirit to the Father" (Eph. 2:18). What a liberty and boldness this gives us when praying to God!

✳ ✳ ✳

DAY 332 – WHAT PRAYER?

(Lord's Day 45, Q&A 118, part 1)

Q. What did God command us to pray for?
A. Everything we need, spiritually and physically.

Our prayers to God are in view of our needs. If we are honest, we will admit that we usually spend more time praying for our physical (material) than for our spiritual needs. If we are asked what our physical needs are, our answer comes readily: we pray for our daily food, good health, our safekeeping at home and on the road, our social relationships, prosperity and success in our daily affairs (school, job, business), both for ourselves and for our beloved ones. Even if we pray for church affairs, it is often primarily for physical needs: the pastor's good health, the state of the church building, the success of the church bazaar, good weather for the Sunday school outing. . . .

If we are asked what our spiritual needs are, we might have more difficulty in coming up with a quick answer. This is sad, because actually we should be careful not to spend too much time on our physical needs: "[G]odliness with contentment is great gain, for we brought nothing into the world, and we cannot take anything out of the world. But if we have food and clothing, with these we will be content" (1 Tim. 6:6–8). So it's better to concentrate on your spiritual needs, such as: "[T]each us to number our days that we may get a heart of wisdom" (Ps. 90:12; cf. 1 Kings 3:9). Or, "Keep back your servant also from presumptuous sins; let them not have dominion over me! Then I shall be blameless, and innocent of great transgression" (Ps. 19:13). Or, "Search me, O God, and know my heart! Try me and know my thoughts! And see if there be any grievous way in me, and lead me in the way everlasting!" (139:23–24).

Or even better, Paul prays "that the God of our Lord Jesus Christ, the Father of glory, may give you the Spirit of wisdom and of revelation in the knowledge of him, having the eyes of your hearts enlightened, that you may know what is the hope to which he has called you, what are the riches of his glorious inheritance in the saints, and what is the immeasurable greatness of his power toward us who believe" (Eph. 1:17–19). What an immensely greater perspective than food, health, and prosperity!

✦   ✦   ✦

DAY 333 – THE PRAYER CHRIST TAUGHT US
(Lord's Day 45, Q&A 118, part 2)

Q. What did God command us to pray for?
A. Everything we need, spiritually and physically, as embraced in the prayer Christ our Lord himself taught us.

In the rest of its answer, the Catechism claims that our spiritual and physical needs are well summarized in "the prayer Christ our Lord himself taught us." This latter point is not mentioned in Matthew's Gospel, although it is *Matthew's* version of the Lord's Prayer that we always pray. Rather, it is Luke who tells us about Jesus teaching his disciples: "Now Jesus was praying in a certain place, and when he finished, one of his disciples said to him, 'Lord, teach us to pray, as John taught his disciples.' And he said to them, 'When you pray, say . . .'" (then follows Luke's version of what we call the Lord's prayer; Luke 11:1–3). Jesus may have prayed for hours (cf. Mark 1:35), but he summarized it all in a prayer of one minute.

Our spiritual needs are more important, and deserve more prayer time, than our physical needs. This comes to light clearly in the Lord's Prayer—I would venture to say even more clearly than the Catechism suggests. This prayer consists of six petitions, only one of which is concerned with our physical needs: "Give us this day our daily bread." The last two petitions could be viewed as a description of (some of) our spiritual needs: forgiveness and spiritual safekeeping.

But then, what about the first three petitions? Do they concern our spiritual or our physical needs? Actually, neither group of needs. They are occupied with *God's* interests. As long as we speak of needs, the prayers are about us. But the first three petitions of the Lord's Prayer are about God: *his* name, *his* Kingdom, *his* will. And yet, in a sense this does involve our needs as well: May your name be hallowed (or, given its special place) *through me*, in my life. May your Kingdom be practically realized *through me*, in my life, every day a bit more. May your will be accomplished *through me*, in my life, every day anew. Thus, my deepest needs correspond with God's interests: the prayer expresses my deep desire that my words and actions may further *God's* cause in this world. I look away from myself, and focus upon God. This is what profound prayer is all about: God is the primary content of it!

✢   ✢   ✢

DAY 334 – THE LORD'S PRAYER
(Lord's Day 45, Q&A 119, part 1)

Q. *What is this prayer?*
A. *Our Father in heaven, hallowed be your name. Your kingdom come, your will be done on earth as it is in heaven. Give us this day our daily bread, and forgive us our debts, as we also have forgiven our debtors. And lead us not into temptation, but deliver us from evil [or, the evil one].*

It is important to notice that we have two different versions of the Lord's Prayer in the New Testament, whereas we invariably recite the Matthew version (which I have quoted in the Catechism's answer from the ESV). For comparison, let me quote here the Luke version: "Father, hallowed be your name. Your kingdom come. Give us each day our daily bread, and forgive us our sins, for we ourselves forgive everyone who is indebted to us. And lead us not into temptation" (Luke 11:2–4). This version is a bit shorter than the well-known Matthew version; it does not contain the phrases "your will be done, on earth as it is in heaven" and ". . . but deliver us from evil," and there are a few other differences.

Because of the existence of two versions, one may wonder whether it was ever Jesus' intention to teach his disciples—let alone all of the Christian world— a formula prayer, which they would have to learn by heart. Today it is recited by millions of Christians, often without giving it much thought. If this should be *the* Christian formula prayer, we would certainly have to wonder about the things that are *missing* in this pre-Easter prayer: the great redemptive acts of Good Friday, Easter, Ascension Day, and Pentecost, and all the praise and worship that is linked with these events. Moreover, we should not forget that this is a pre-Easter prayer for *beginners*: young, immature disciples. In Matthew's Gospel, the Sermon on the Mount stands at the beginning of Jesus' ministry. We post-Pentecost Christians, especially if we are mature Christians, have so much more to pray and praise about (cf. the great prayers in the epistles, such as Eph. 1:15–23; 3:14–21; Col. 1:9–14).

And yet, even the most mature disciples have to return to the basics time and again: the honor of God's name, the progress of God's Kingdom in this world, our physical needs, sin and forgiveness, being kept by God in an evil world. We never become so "spiritual" that we do not need these basic prayers anymore. If we would think otherwise, this would just prove that we are actually more haughty than spiritual.

✦   ✦   ✦

DAY 335 – WHAT IS DUE TO GOD

(Lord's Day 45, Q&A 119, part 2)

A. Our Father in heaven, hallowed be your name. Your kingdom come, your will be done, on earth as it is in heaven.

The Lord's Prayer is divided into six petitions. In the first three, a central word is "your," which occurs three times. In the last three petitions, a central notion involves "we" and "us," plus "our" (which is literally "of us"), a notion that occurs eight times ("Give *us* this day *our* daily bread, and forgive *us our* debts, as *we* also have forgiven *our* debtors. And lead *us* not into temptation, but deliver *us* from evil"). These eleven pronouns constitute, as it were, the backbone of the Lord's Prayer. First, the spotlight is on "you" (i.e., God); second, the spotlight is on us. And, of course, this is the proper order. God's cause in the world is first, then *our* needs and circumstances in this same world.

The first three petitions presuppose an imperfect world. This is a world in which God's name is *not* self-evidently hallowed as it is in heaven, in which his rule is *not* automatically acknowledged everywhere as it is in heaven, and in which his will is *not* done by all persons as it is in heaven. This latter phrase, "on earth as it is in heaven," could be attached to all three petitions: "May your name be hallowed on earth as it is in heaven; may your rule become universal on earth as it is in heaven; may your will be done, on earth just as much as in heaven." In our mind, we may still add another phrase: "May your name be hallowed *through me*, in my life, within my sphere of influence. May your kingdom be practically realized *through me*, in my life, within my sphere of influence. May your will be accomplished *through me*, in my life, within my sphere of influence."

This is essential. The first three petitions are not some vague, nonbinding wish concerning God's interests in the world, one that does not necessarily involve us personally. It is just the opposite: the persons speaking to God present *themselves* as willing instruments, through whom, together with many other willing instruments, God realizes his cause in this world. Here we are, our Father in heaven, take us, prepare us, use us, deploy us! As the prophet once said, "Here I am! Send me" (Isa. 6:8).

✳ ✳ ✳

DAY 336 – OUR OWN NEEDS

(Lord's Day 45, Q&A 119, part 3)

A. Give us this day our daily bread, and forgive us our debts, as we also have forgiven our debtors. And lead us not into temptation, but deliver us from evil [or, the evil one].

The first part of the Lord's Prayer is about God and his interests, his cause in this world. The second part is about us: about our daily physical needs, our sins and the need of forgiveness, and the evil world we live in and God's safekeeping therein. If we have put God's interests first, there is nothing wrong with then bringing our own needs before him. We are even *encouraged* to do so: "[D]o not be anxious about anything, but in everything by prayer and supplication with thanksgiving let your requests be made known to God" (Phil. 4:6). And do so with the conviction that God not only hears our requests, but also loves to grant them to us, if this is appropriate.

Please notice this remarkable saying of Jesus: "Pray that your flight may not be in winter or on a Sabbath" (Matt. 24:20). This clearly implies that prayers can even influence the ways of God—if not, what use would such a prayer be? If our prayers can affect even the time of the great tribulation (v. 21), and the concomitant time of the Lord's second coming (vv. 27, 30), then God is certainly able to "give us this day our daily bread." We do know about hungry Christians in certain countries; yet, we pray that they may cling to this promise: "Who among us can dwell with the consuming fire? . . . He who walks righteously and speaks uprightly, . . . his bread will be given him; his water will be sure" (Isa. 33:14–16).

By the way, what would be more difficult for God: to give us our daily bread, or to forgive us our debts? If I had a thousand enemies, I might find it easier to forgive them all than to feed them all daily. However, with God it is different. It is enough that he is our Creator in order to supply us with what we need (cf. Ps. 104:24–28). But in order to forgive us he had to become our Savior God through the redemptive work of Jesus Christ. And it will be through this same work that God will one day rid this world of sin and Satan, and thus of all seductive temptations. That will be the glorious day when his Kingdom will finally have come in splendor and majesty!

✤   ✤   ✤

DAY 337 – THE ADDED WORDS
(Lord's Day 45, Q&A 119, part 4)

A. For yours is the kingdom and the power and the glory, forever. Amen.

The Catechism quotes the Lord's Prayer from Matthew 6, where older Bible translations (the KJV) have in verse 13 this doxology: "For yours is the kingdom and the power and the glory, forever. Amen." Other translations, such as the NASB, include the words between brackets, still other translations, such as the ESV, leave them out, or mention them in a footnote. The Catechism edition of the Christian Reformed Church in North America tells us in a footnote: "Earlier and better manuscripts of Matthew 6 omit the words 'For the kingdom and . . . Amen.'" We may add here that Protestants, as far as I know, always recite these words at the end of the Lord's Prayer, whereas Roman Catholics usually stop with the words "deliver us from evil."

The point is that, indeed, verse 13b is lacking in all the older manuscripts of the New Testament. We may assume, first, that the Lord's Prayer began to be used in the Christian liturgy at an early stage. Second, the custom arose of ending the prayer with a liturgical doxology, whose designer we do not know. Third, one of the scribes, when copying Matthew's Gospel, put this doxology in the margin of Matthew 6. Fourth, a later scribe thought that this was an error, and placed the words within the text of Matthew 6. This is a rather plausible explanation of what might have happened.

Whatever may be the explanation, at any rate there is, of course, nothing wrong with the doxology as such, whether it was part of the inspired text or not. On the contrary, it is a worthy and beautiful closure of the prayer. While the prayer as such contains petitions only—that is *asking* of God—the doxology brings in a note of praise and worship; that is *giving* to God. We proclaim that the Kingdom is God's: "The kingdom of the world has become the kingdom of our Lord and of his Christ, and he shall reign forever and ever" (Rev. 11:15). The "power" is the power of this Kingdom, for it will "come with power" (Mark 9:1; cf. 1 Cor. 4:20; Rev. 12:10). "Yours, O LORD, is the greatness and the power and the glory. . . . Yours is the kingdom, O LORD" (1 Chron. 29:11).

✦　✦　✦

DAY 338 – "OUR FATHER"
(Lord's Day 46, Q&A 120, part 1)

Q. Why did Christ command us to call God "our Father"?
A. To awaken in us at the very beginning of our prayer what should be basic to our prayer— a childlike reverence and trust that through Christ God has become our Father.

We should never forget at what early stage the Lord Jesus taught this prayer to his disciples. Were they really aware of the fact that "through Christ" God had become their Father? It is only in John 20, after his death and resurrection, that Jesus explicitly says that his Father is now also our Father: "I am ascending to my Father and your Father, to my God and your God" (v. 17). At the time Jesus taught this prayer to his disciples, they were long accustomed to calling God *Avinu Malkeinu*, "Our Father, our King"; at least we know from the Talmud that Rabbi Akiva († AD 135) prayed this.

In recent times, people have pointed repeatedly to the great similarities between the Lord's Prayer and certain Jewish prayers. One such prayer includes the phrase "Our God in heaven, hallow your name, and establish your kingdom forever, and rule over us for ever and ever. Amen." The expressions "Hallowed be your name" and "Lead us not into sin" are found in several other Jewish prayers. There is hardly any element of the Lord's Prayer that cannot be found in the Old Testament (cf. 1 Chron. 29:10–18; Ps. 119:134; Prov. 30:8) or the deuterocanonical books. The Old Testament also knows God as "our Father" (Isa. 63:15–16; 64:8). So, in this respect there was nothing new for the disciples.

Yet, we do not stop here. When *we* say the Lord's Prayer, we are saying it as post-Easter Christians. We are those who know that God is our Father not simply because he created his people (Deut. 32:6; Mal. 2:10). He is our Father because *his Son has become our life* (1 John 5:11–12), so that the eternal Father of the eternal Son has now become *our* Father as well. This is way beyond anything that was ever revealed to Israel. The Jew, as part of the chosen people, could call God his Father from his early youth. *We* call God "our Father" since our regeneration and faith, and thus our reception of eternal life (John 3:16; 17:3). *We* know God as Father not because of our birth but because of our rebirth. We say the Lord's Prayer not as members of a natural, ethnic people, but as members of a supernatural, spiritual people.

❖   ❖   ❖

DAY 339 – ASKING IN FAITH
(Lord's Day 46, Q&A 120, part 2)

A. . . . and that just as our parents do not refuse us the things of this life, even less will God our Father refuse to give us what we ask in faith.

The expression "Father" for God is a metaphor. The Bible uses the image of an earthly, human father to give us an idea of the heavenly, divine Father. He is our Father because he "fathered" us (cf. John 1:13; James 1:18; 1 Pet. 1:3; 1 John 5:1), but he is also our Father because he cares about us and looks after us: "[W]hich one of you, if his son asks him for bread, will give him a stone? Or if he asks for a fish, will give him a serpent? If you then, who are evil, know how to give good gifts to your children, how much more will your Father who is in heaven give good things to those who ask him!"(Matt. 7:9–11; cf. Luke 11:11–13). In general, even *evil* people know how to be good to their children. How much more will God the Father know how to be good to us! "Every good gift and every perfect gift is from above, coming down from the Father of lights" (James 1:17)—and every good gift is evidence that God cares about us and looks after us.

The Catechism speaks not only of God's goodness but also of our responsibility. God will not refuse the good things to us, but *we* have to ask for them in faith. As Jesus said, "[W]hatever you ask in prayer, you will receive, if you have faith"(Matt. 21:22). Let the believer "ask in faith, with no doubting, for the one who doubts is like a wave of the sea that is driven and tossed by the wind" (James 1:6). God's gifts are not just sovereign proofs of his own goodness, they are also responses to *our* confidence in him. James speaks of the "prayer of faith" in connection with sickness and healing (5:15), but this is a good expression for what *all* our prayers should be: prayers of confidence in God. It is God who blesses us, but the Bible also says that it is *faith* that procures the blessings (cf. Matt. 15:28; Mark 5:34; Luke 7:50; Acts 3:16). God's goodness is counterbalanced by our faith. From the perspective of sovereign grace, the blessings are due to God. From the viewpoint of human responsibility, the blessings are due to our confidence in him. Don't play them off against each other; the one is as true as the other!

✤ ✤ ✤

DAY 340 – "IN HEAVEN"
(Lord's Day 46, Q&A 121, part 1)

Q. Why the words "in heaven"?
A. These words teach us not to think of God's heavenly majesty as something earthly.

Psalm 115 says, "The heavens are the LORD's heavens, but the earth he has given to the children of man" (v. 16). This suggests that "heaven" is a name for God's dwelling-place. To be sure, king Solomon said, "[W]ill God indeed dwell on the earth [viz., in the newly built temple]? Behold, heaven and the highest heaven [lit., heavens and the heavens of heavens] cannot contain you; how much less this house that I have built!" (1 Kings 8:27). But three verses later he said to God, ". . . listen in heaven your dwelling place" (cf. v. 39, 43, 49). There is no contradiction: the fact is simply that God says himself, "Do I not fill heaven and earth?" (Jer. 23:24). He is everywhere (Ps. 139:1–10).

We have to be careful with the term "heaven," though. First, in the expression "heaven(s) and earth" (Gen. 1:1; 2:1; 14:19, 22; Exod. 20:11; 2 Kings 19:15; Ps. 69:34; 2 Pet. 3:7; etc.) we have no reference to God's dwelling-place at all, but to the entirety of the visible universe. Second, "heaven" or "heavens" is often nothing but a reference to what we call the "sky" or "skies," the place where we find the birds, as well as the clouds and the stars (e.g., Gen. 1:9, 14–17, 20, 26–30; Deut. 28:23; Job 35:5; Ps. 18:13). This is the heaven of which God could say to Abraham, "Look toward heaven" (Gen. 15:5).

In the New Testament, we find the same double meaning. If Paul says that Jesus "ascended far above all the heavens" (Eph. 4:10), we think of the skies: he ascended beyond the clouds and stars. But when Mark says that Jesus "was taken up into heaven and sat down at the right hand of God" (Mark 16:19; cf. Acts 7:56; Heb. 8:1; 1 Pet. 3:22), we think of God's dwelling-place *above* the skies. On the one hand, there is no corner of the earth where we cannot find God. On the other hand, his majesty is beyond the skies. When we address "our Father in heaven," we realize that we address someone who is as close as a Father can be, and at the same time far beyond anything that is purely earthly. Pray to God always in the awareness of both his nearness and his loftiness!

✣   ✣   ✣

DAY 341 – EXPECTING FROM GOD
(Lord's Day 46, Q&A 121, part 2)

A. . . . and to expect everything needed for body and soul from God's almighty power.

The argument of the Catechism is that the addition "in heaven" creates a certain distance that makes us more aware of our own insignificance and "God's almighty power." God's greatness is as far beyond my smallness as heaven is beyond the earth. "O Lord, what is man that you regard him, or the son of man that you think of him? Man is like a breath; his days are like a passing shadow. Bow your heavens, O Lord, and come down! Touch the mountains so that they smoke! . . . Stretch out your hand from on high" (Ps. 144:3–7).

The greater that God is in my eyes, the more I will expect from him "everything needed for body and soul." The smaller I make him in my own thinking—as if he would be as limited as we are—the more I will wonder whether God can really do this or that for me. Sometimes such an attitude is sheer unbelief, as in the case of the Israelites, who "tested the Lord by saying, 'Is the Lord among us or not?'" (Exod. 17:7).

We have to *trust* both God's greatness and his love. If God were only great, he would be *able* to give us so much blessing, but he would probably hardly care to do so. If God were only love, he would *desire* to give us so much blessing, but he would hardly be able to do so. But God is both great and loving. As Jesus said, "[I]f God so clothes the grass of the field, which today is alive and tomorrow is thrown into the oven, will he not much more clothe you, O you of little faith? Therefore do not be anxious, saying, 'What shall we eat?' or 'What shall we drink?' or 'What shall we wear?' For the Gentiles seek after all these things, and your heavenly Father knows that you need them all. But seek first the kingdom of God and his righteousness, and all these things will be added to you" (Matt. 6:30–34).

Paul says, "What then shall we say to these things? If God is for us, who can be against us? He who did not spare his own Son but gave him up for us all, how will he not also with him graciously give us all things?" (Rom. 8:31–32). God is always greater than our needs; he "is able to do far more abundantly than all that we ask or think" (Eph. 3:20).

✤ ✤ ✤

DAY 342 – "HALLOWED BE YOUR NAME"
(Lord's Day 47, Q&A 122, part 1)

Q. What does the first petition mean?
A. "Hallowed be your name" means: Help us to truly know you,
to honor, glorify, and praise you for all your works and for all that
shines forth from them: your almighty power, wisdom, kindness, jus-
tice, mercy, and truth.

In Greek, "to hallow" is the same as "to sanctify" or "to make holy." In the case of God's name, it does not mean, of course, that we can *add* anything to God's holiness, just as glorifying and magnifying God do not mean adding to his glory or his greatness. Rather, it means bringing to light the holiness, honor, glory, and greatness that his *name* already possesses. This is the same as the glory of his *being*; in the Bible, God's "name" is always the expression of his glorious being. We do manifest it in praising and worshiping God. This is identical with proclaiming his "power, wisdom, kindness, justice, mercy, and truth," etc., as we observe them in his works. These are the works of his creation and his providence, as well as his works of redemption and consummation. When observing his work, we always find reason to praise and worship God.

By "hallowing" (sanctifying) God's name we sanctify God himself, that is, we proclaim his holiness. God told Israel, "[Y]ou shall not profane my holy name, that I may be sanctified among the people of Israel" (Lev. 22:32). And concerning restored Israel he says, "[T]hey will sanctify my name; they will sanctify the Holy One of Jacob and will stand in awe of the God of Israel" (Isa. 29:23). God says to them, "I will vindicate the holiness of my great name, which has been profaned among the nations, and which you have profaned among them. And the nations will know that I am the LORD, . . . when through you I vindicate my holiness before their eyes" (Ezek. 36:23).

In each of the first three petitions, believers must realize that they themselves are involved. It is not a vague, passive prayer, but in fact they are saying: "Hallowed be your name *through us,* in and through our lives." Whereas so many people drag your name through the mud, let *our* lives, our thoughts, our words, our actions, always manifest the holiness and greatness of your name! One day, during the Messianic Kingdom, your name will be hallowed among all the nations worldwide—let it today be hallowed in and through us in the midst of a still wicked and rebellious world!

✦　　✦　　✦

DAY 343 – NO BLASPHEMY

(Lord's Day 47, Q&A 122, part 2)

A. And it means, Help us to direct all our living—what we think, say, and do— so that your name will never be blasphemed because of us but always honored and praised.

Blasphemy is the opposite of hallowing God's name. It is speaking evil of God, slandering his name, speaking ill of who he is and what he does, insulting him, offending him. This subject was already discussed in the Catechism when it dealt with the Third Commandment (Lord's Days 36–37). Even cursing, perjury, unnecessary oaths, and even sharing in such horrible sins by being silent bystanders, make us guilty of blasphemy. It is black and white in the Catechism, and rightly so: we are either hallowing God's name, or blaspheming it. We are either honoring and praising it, or we are profaning it. Our acts are either Spirit-inspired or flesh-inspired (cf, Gal. 5:16–18). We are either acting and speaking "in the name of the Lord Jesus, giving thanks to God the Father through him" (Col. 3:17), or we are dishonoring his name.

It is important to realize that, strictly speaking, there is no grey area in our lives, where our words and acts are more or less neutral: neither honoring nor dishonoring the Lord. No, such an area does not exist. Paul says, "[W]hoever has doubts is condemned if he eats, because the eating is not from faith. For whatever does not proceed from faith is sin" (Rom. 14:23). In a wider sense he says, Whoever has doubts in what he thinks, speaks, or does is condemned, because his thinking, speaking, and doing are not from faith. For whatever does not proceed from faith is sin. If you are not sure that what you think, speak, or do is "hallowing God's name"—is for the glory and honor of this name—watch yourself that you do not land in blasphemy!

You see what a serious petition this is. We are surrounded by people who are profaning God's name all the time, willingly or inadvertently. It is our calling to be islands in the world where God's name is hallowed, not just by our worship and our testimony, but also in the smallest things we speak or do. As always, Jesus himself is our great example: "I always do the things that are pleasing to [the Father]" (John 8:29). "I glorified you [i.e., the Father] on earth, having accomplished the work that you gave me to do" (17:4).

✦　　✦　　✦

DAY 344 – "YOUR KINGDOM COME"

(LORD'S DAY 48, Q&A 123, PART 1)

Q. What does the second petition mean?
A. "Your kingdom come" means: Rule us by your Word and Spirit in such a way that more and more we submit to you.

The Kingdom of God has a general meaning (God's universal rule from the world's beginning to its end), and a particular meaning: the rule of the glorified Son of Man over God's world. The Kingdom in the latter sense has again two meanings. First, it is the Kingdom in the "present age," which manifests itself at all places where Christians acknowledge Christ's Lordship in their personal and collective lives. Second, it is the Kingdom in the "age to come" (Luke 18:30; Eph. 1:21; Heb. 6:5), when the Son of Man will rule the "world to come" (Dan. 7:13–14; Matt. 13:41–43; 16:27–28; 24:27–30; Heb. 2:5–8).

The petition "Your kingdom come" can be taken either way. It might be taken in the latter sense, in which case it would imply the prayer that the day of Christ's coming again, and thus the establishment of his Kingdom, may arrive soon (cf. 1 Cor. 16:22; 2 Pet. 3:12; Rev. 22:20). However, it is more likely that the former meaning of Christ's Kingdom is intended, as also the Catechism takes it. "Your kingdom come" thus means: Let your rule—"by your Word and Spirit"—be manifested more and more in the present world, first, in believers' lives, second, in the lives of all those you are still going to add.

Of course, when Jesus was on this earth, this petition had to be addressed to God the Father, just as, for instance, in Matthew 6:33, "[S]eek first the kingdom of God and his righteousness, and all these things will be added to you." However, today this petition has acquired an entirely new meaning: Let the Lordship and rule of the glorified *Christ* become more and more visible in our lives, and in all those who are still added to his Kingdom as his disciples (cf. Matt. 28:18–20). Christ rules us through his Word and Spirit: "[I]f it is by the Spirit of God that I cast out demons, then the kingdom of God has come upon you" (Matt. 12:28). "[T]he kingdom of God is . . . a matter of . . . righteousness and peace and joy in the Holy Spirit" (Rom. 14:17). "[T]he kingdom of God does not consist in talk but in power [of the Spirit]" (1 Cor. 4:20). Let *this* Kingdom truly break through!

✤ ✤ ✤

DAY 345 – KINGDOM AND CHURCH
(Lord's Day 48, Q&A 123, part 2)

A. Preserve your church and make it grow.

If we take the church in the sense of the "holy congregation and gathering of true Christian believers" (Belgic Confession, Art. 27), then the Kingdom of God is wider than the church. If the church contains all true Christian believers, the Kingdom includes all Christian *confessors*, all those who acknowledge the name and the rule of Christ, whether wholeheartedly or only outwardly. This is why in the Kingdom parables in Matthew's Gospel we often find good and bad together: the wheat and the weeds (13:24–30, 36–43), the good and the bad fishes (vv. 47–50), the wise and the foolish virgins (25:1–13), the good and the wicked servants (vv. 14–30). They are all included in the Kingdom, and thus distinguished from those who are outside the Kingdom (the non-Christian world). But only the wheat, the good fishes, the wise virgins, and the good servants represent the true church of God. However, to make things more complicated, sometimes the word "church" in the New Testament does have the wider meaning of the whole Christian confession (see especially Rev. 2 and 3).

If we pray, "Your kingdom come," this also implies the petition that the truly valuable component of this Kingdom—Christ's own body and bride, his church—will prosper. Where God's Kingdom manifests itself more and more in this world—today, one third of the world's population is registered as Christian!—may especially the true church manifest itself within this Kingdom. The "true church" is not one out of many denominations, although some do claim to be the "true church." No, it is the totality of all "true Christian believers," in whatever denominations they may be found. May this church be preserved (in the sense of Matt. 16:18, "the gates of Hades shall not prevail against it"), and may it grow, not only in number but especially in spiritual depth: "[W]e are to grow up in every way into him who is the head, into Christ" (Eph. 4:15). Christ is "the Head, from whom the whole body, nourished and knit together through its joints and ligaments, grows with a growth that is from God" (Col. 2:19).

DAY 346 – THE DEVIL'S WORK

(Lord's Day 48, Q&A 123, part 3)

A. Destroy the devil's work; destroy every force which revolts against you and every conspiracy against your holy Word.

In the "age to come," the Kingdom of God and of his Christ will have no rival anymore. All the dark powers will be subdued forever. However, this is not yet the case in the Kingdom as it manifests itself during the "present age." On the contrary, there is a continual conflict going on between two kingdoms, as was explained by Jesus: "[I]f Satan casts out Satan, he is divided against himself. How then will his kingdom stand? . . . But if it is by the Spirit of God that I cast out demons, then the kingdom of God has come upon you" (Matt. 12:26–28). The kingdom of Satan is opposed to the Kingdom of God, as represented by Jesus, whose Spirit power was stronger than Satan's power. The foundation for the ultimate victory was laid on the cross (cf. Heb. 2:14; 1 John 3:8), but that victory will be gained only at Jesus' second coming.

Believers are clearly involved in this ongoing battle: "[W]e do not wrestle against flesh and blood, but against the rulers, against the authorities, against the cosmic powers over this present darkness, against the spiritual forces of evil in the heavenly places" (Eph. 6:12). The spiritual "young men" have already gained their victories in this battle (1 John 2:13–14), but none of them, or us, is able to gain the final victory that would definitively destroy Satan's kingdom. This ultimate victory is reserved for him who "will soon crush Satan under your feet" (Rom. 16:20).

When we pray, "Your kingdom come," we are praying for the furtherance of God's Kingdom in the "present age." Every time a demon is driven out (as Jesus said), or, through the gospel, a person turns "from the power of Satan to God" (Acts 26:18; cf. Col. 1:12–13), the kingdom of Satan has been driven back a step, and the Kingdom of God has taken a step forward. We earnestly pray for this as if the Kingdom's progress depended on God alone. And at the same time we each fulfill our ministry in the Kingdom of God as faithfully as we can, as if its furtherance entirely depended on us. This is what we pray: "Your Kingdom come *through us*—with your indispensible help—every day a bit further!"

✤　✤　✤

DAY 347 – THE KINGDOM'S FINAL FORM
(Lord's Day 48, Q&A 123, part 4)

A. Do this until your kingdom fully comes, when you will be all in all.

The Catechism knows of the Kingdom of God as a present spiritual reality, but it also knows that only one day, somewhere in the future, God's Kingdom will "fully come." This is the day when Jesus Christ will return. This great event is announced at the "seventh trumpet": "The kingdom of the world has become the kingdom of our Lord and of his Christ, and he shall reign forever and ever" (Rev. 11:15), and: "Now the salvation and the power and the kingdom of our God and the authority of his Christ have come" (12:10). Today, God's Kingdom is visible only to those who wish to, and are able to, see it due to rebirth and the Spirit's enlightenment (cf. John 3:3, 5). In the coming day, the Kingdom will be visible to all; nobody will be able to deny the rule of Christ anymore: "God has highly exalted him and bestowed on him the name that is above every name, so that at the name of Jesus every knee should bow, in heaven and on earth and under the earth, and every tongue confess that Jesus Christ is Lord, to the glory of God the Father" (Phil. 2:9–11). Imagine the day when all Jesus' adversaries—Annas and Caiaphas, Pilate and Herod—will finally bow their knees to him!

This is the ultimate meaning of the prayer, "Your kingdom come." One day, God's Kingdom will arrive in full glory and splendor, in power and majesty. "Then will appear in heaven the sign of the Son of Man, and then all the tribes of the earth will mourn, and they will see the Son of Man coming on the clouds of heaven with power and great glory" (Matt. 24:30). And ultimately "comes the end, when he delivers the kingdom to God the Father after destroying every rule and every authority and power. For he must reign until he has put all his enemies under his feet. The last enemy to be destroyed is death. For 'God has put all things in subjection under his feet.' . . . When all things are subjected to him, then the Son himself will also be subjected to him who put all things in subjection under him, that God may be all in all" (1 Cor. 15:24–28). With these last words, the Catechism's answer ends.

✳   ✳   ✳

DAY 348 – "YOUR WILL BE DONE"
(Lord's Day 49, Q&A 124, part 1)

Q. What does the third petition mean?
A. "Your will be done, on earth as it is in heaven" means: Help us
and all people to reject our own wills and to obey your will without
any back talk.

On Day 88 we made a distinction between the "irresistible" and the "resistible" will of God. Paul says, "[W]ho can resist his will?" (Rom. 9:19). This is the will of God's counsel, of which the LORD says, "My counsel shall stand, and I will accomplish all my purpose" (Isa. 46:10). Paul speaks of God "who works all things according to the counsel of his will" (Eph. 1:11). There is no way this will of God could ultimately be resisted. This is the will by which God realizes his plans, whatever his creatures may undertake. But there is also that other will; for instance, Paul says that God our Savior "wants all people to be saved" (1 Tim. 2:4 NIV); yet, we know that not all people *will* be saved. This is the "resistible" will of God. Jesus said, "How often I have wanted to gather your people just as a hen gathers her chicks under her wings. But you didn't want that" (Luke 13:34 CEB). *He* wanted, but they did *not* want; they resisted his will.

In the present Q&A we may in fact think of both types of God's will. First, there is the longing of believers that, one day, all God's counsels and promises will be fulfilled in Christ, at his coming and in the Messianic Kingdom. "Make haste, my beloved!" (Song 8:14). Let that day soon come when the entire universe will be subdued to your will as heaven is, and always was, submitted to it.

However, it seems more obvious to think of God's resistible will. We pray: Lord, your will may be resisted by the evil powers of darkness as well as by disobedient people. But let your will prevail over all these adversaries—human, angelic, demonic—by the power of your Spirit. Here we are, Lord; we desire to be at your disposal. Use us, Lord, as instruments through which today your will is realized a bit further in this world. Help us to submit our own wills to your will "without any back talk," so that we obey you (cf. Rom. 12:1–2; Col. 1:9–11; Heb. 13:20–21), so that your plans may be furthered here on earth. Not our will, but yours, be done (cf. Luke 22:42). Not the evil powers' will, but yours, be done! And use *us* to this end, Lord!

✳ ✳ ✳

DAY 349 – "YOUR WILL ALONE IS GOOD"
(Lord's Day 49, Q&A 124, part 2)

A. Your will alone is good. Help us one and all to carry out the work we are called to.

God created us with many qualities, such as intelligence, feeling, and a will. This ability to want is not like the will in animals, which is entirely determined by their instincts. No, we humans can think about what we are wanting, we can consider the advantages and disadvantages thereof. We can make free and deliberate decisions, varying from how we will dress today to where we are going to live and work. God *respects* this will to a certain extent; he never wishes to turn us into robots (cf. Apollos in 1 Cor. 16:12). Therefore, it would be terrible to say that the believer's will has to be "broken," as has been said sometimes. If the will is broken, what is left *is* a robot. It is the same in education: the will of the child must not be "broken" but *bent* under (i.e., trained to comply with) the will of the parents. Similarly, the will of the believer must be bent under the will of God, so that the two merge as it were: "[M]ay the God of peace . . . *equip* you with everything good that you may do *his will*, working in us that which is pleasing in his sight, through Jesus Christ" (Heb. 13:20–21).

The human will may be very strong, and often it should be, especially in leading personalities. Yet, believers ought to do not what they *want* but what they are *called to* by God. Their will is not ruled out, but is brought in line with the will of God. The development of this interplay of God's will and the believer's will is a vital aspect of spiritual maturity. Paul says, "[B]e *transformed* by the renewal of your mind, that by testing you may discern what is the *will of God*, what is good and acceptable and perfect" (Rom. 12:1–2). And elsewhere, "[W]e have not ceased to pray for you, asking that you may be filled with the knowledge of *his will* in all spiritual wisdom and understanding, so as to walk in a manner worthy of the Lord, fully pleasing to him, bearing fruit in every good work and *increasing* in the knowledge of God" (Col. 1:9). "Transformation" and "increase" are two terms for this growing in the knowledge of the will of God and this learning to comply with this will.

❖   ❖   ❖

DAY 350 – AS THE ANGELS IN HEAVEN
(Lord's Day 49, Q&A 124, part 3)

A. Help us . . . to carry out the work we are called to, as willingly and faithfully as the angels in heaven.

If the Lord's Prayer says that God's will is done in heaven, it is natural to think of the angels in heaven, "the mighty ones who do his word, obeying the voice of his word"; they are "his hosts, his ministers, who do his will" (Ps. 103:20–21). There is perfect obedience in heaven—apart from the fall of Satan, about which the Bible does not tell us anything with certainty, though (perhaps there are hints—no more than that—in Job 15:15; Isa. 14:12–15; Ezek. 28:13–15; 1 Tim. 3:6; by the way, Rev. 12:7–12 is taken by many to refer to an event still to come).

Actually, we do not know very much about angels. The word "angel" comes from a Greek word that, just like the corresponding Hebrew word, means "messenger." Angels are heavenly messengers from God to people. They were created by God through his Son: "[I]n [Christ] all things were created, in heaven and on earth, visible and invisible, whether thrones or dominions or rulers or authorities" (Col. 1:16), the last four nouns referring to angelic powers, which are now subjected to the glorified Man Jesus Christ (cf. Eph. 1:20–21; 6:12; 1 Pet. 3:21–22).

Angels have the position of *servants*. They are sometimes called "sons of God" (Job 1:6; 2:1; 38:7; perhaps Gen. 6:2–4; Deut. 32:8), but, according to Hebrew idiom, this does not have to mean anything more than "belonging to the divine world." As Hebrews 1 says, "[T]o which of the angels has he ever said, 'Sit at my right hand until I make your enemies a footstool for your feet' [Ps. 110:1]? Are they not all *ministering* spirits sent out to *serve* for the sake of those who are to inherit salvation?" (vv. 13-14). Even though some of them are "thrones or dominions or rulers or authorities," their basic position is that of servants of God. As such they are always subject to, and submit to, the commands of God, and as such they are an example for humanity. One day, all creatures in this world will do God's will, just like the angels in heaven. But the believer prays that, already now, God's will may be done more and more among humans, by the conversion of sinners, and by the training of believers.

✢ ✢ ✢

DAY 351 – "OUR DAILY BREAD"

(Lord's Day 50, Q&A 125, part 1)

Q. What does the fourth petition mean?
A. "Give us this day our daily bread" means: Do take care of all our physical needs so that we come to know that you are the only source of everything good.

The expression "our daily bread" means the bread that we need for today (CEB, CJB, ERV, etc.). We are not asking for some guarantee that we will *always* have enough food, or even that we will have food next week; we are happy to receive today what we need (cf. Matt. 6:34, "Therefore do not be anxious about tomorrow, for tomorrow will be anxious for itself. Sufficient for the day is its own trouble"). This attitude is one of utter dependence: every day again we need the Lord's provisions; on no day do we take these for granted, every day we thank him anew: "[E]verything created by God is good, and nothing is to be rejected if it is received with thanksgiving, for it is made holy by the word of God and prayer" (1 Tim. 4:4–5).

Of course, our daily bread is just part of our daily physical needs, but certainly a vital one. As Paul says, "[W]e brought nothing into the world, and we cannot take anything out of the world. But if we have food and clothing, with these we will be content" (1 Tim. 6:7–8). God says about the righteous, "[H]is bread will be given him; his water will be sure" (Isa. 33:16). Jesus always looked after his disciples, and could say to them, "[D]id you lack anything?" They answered, "Nothing" (Luke 22:35).

By receiving from God what we daily need we will "come to know" him more and more as "the only source of everything good." Even *all* creatures look to God "to give them their food in due season. When you give it to them, they gather it up; when you open your hand, they are filled with good things" (Ps. 104:27–28; cf. 145:15–16). Even concerning the heathen, who do not know God, it is said, "[H]e did good by giving you rains from heaven and fruitful seasons, satisfying your hearts with food and gladness" (Acts 14:17). All the more do believers know that "[e]very good gift and every perfect gift is from above, coming down from the Father of lights with whom there is no variation or shadow due to change" (James 1:17). It is just as important to thank God every day for our daily bread as it is to thank him daily for the redemption he wrought in Christ!

✦   ✦   ✦

DAY 352 – NO GOOD WITHOUT BLESSING
(Lord's Day 50, Q&A 125, part 2)

A. . . . and that neither our work and worry nor your gifts can do us any good without your blessing.

There is an interesting difference between a Christian and a Jewish prayer before a meal. It is quite common to hear a Christian pray something like this: "Heavenly Father, bless this food. . . ." A Jew, however, will not ask God to bless the food but will bless *God*, the giver: "Blessed are you, Lord our God, King of the world. . . ." He may argue that God has already promised to bless his bread and his water (Exod. 23:25); he accepts them from God's hand as already having been blessed. The only thing remaining is for him to bless (praise) God.

We read of Jesus: "[T]aking the five loaves and the two fish, he looked up to heaven and said a blessing" (Matt. 14:19). Many translations suggest that Jesus blessed the loaves and the fish, or asked a blessing (TLB); only a few translate properly: "Jesus said a blessing," that is, a *b'rakhah* (CJB), in which *God* is blessed, not the food (see Day 245 above). This idea of praising God is better preserved in the English expression "to say grace." Here "grace" has the ancient meaning of "thanks(giving)," so the phrase "to say grace" means "to give thanks." You thank God for the food, or even better: you praise the Giver of the food.

Yet, what would our meals be without God's blessing? Psalm 127 says, "Unless the LORD builds the house, those who build it labor in vain. Unless the LORD watches over the city, the watchman stays awake in vain. It is in vain that you rise up early and go late to rest, eating the bread of anxious toil; for he gives to his beloved sleep [or, gives it to his beloved while they sleep]" (vv. 1–2). Please note that God's blessing never means that he himself undertakes to do what *we* have to, and can, do ourselves. It is *builders* who build houses—but under God's blessing. It is *watchmen* watching over the city—but under God's blessing. It is farmers, millers, and bakers who prepare the bread—but under God's blessing. "The sluggard does not plow in the autumn; he will seek at harvest and have nothing" (Prov. 20:4). "If anyone is not willing to work, let him not eat" (2 Thess. 3:10). *We* necessarily do the work—but *God* gives his indispensible blessing to it.

✤ ✤ ✤

DAY 353 – TRUST IN GOD ALONE
(Lord's Day 50, Q&A 125, part 3)

A. And so help us to give up our trust in creatures and trust in you alone.

God, the giver of the food, is the great source of *all* our blessings. Moses said to the people, God "fed you with manna . . . that he might make you know that man does not live by bread alone, but man lives by every word that comes from the mouth of the Lord" (Deut. 8:3; cf. Matt. 4:4). God gives us bread so that we become aware of all the other things with which he blesses us—his Word in particular. "Every good gift and every perfect gift is from above, coming down from the Father of lights" (James 1:17).

God may certainly make use of our own labors, and those of other creatures. We are not just to sit back, lazy, as if God has to do all the work. *We* do the work. But *blessing* comes only from him. That is, only through him, our labors become useful and fruitful. Only through him, our food becomes profitable to our bodies. In general, God does not do for us what we could do ourselves, and for which he has given us so many capabilities. But *God* gives his indispensible blessing to it, so that our work becomes useful, profitable, fruitful.

So we see, God's blessing does not exclude our labors. Similarly, our trust in God alone does not exclude our trust in other people. How could we possibly live if there were no mutual trust in marriages, in families, in churches, at work? It might even point to some mental disorder if we would literally trust no other people. If overseers must hold firm to the "trustworthy" word (1 Tim. 3:1; Titus 1:9), it means they themselves must be people who can be trusted. However, this is not what the Catechism is talking about. It points out that we will *always* become disappointed in people, but never in God. "It is better to take refuge in the Lord than to trust in princes" (Ps. 118:9). "Put not your trust in princes, in a son of man, in whom there is no salvation" (146:3). But of God it is said, "Trust in him at all times, O people; pour out your heart before him; God is a refuge for us" (62:8). "Cursed is the man who trusts in man. . . . Blessed is the man who trusts in the Lord" (Jer. 17:5, 7). In the end, people will always fail you—but God will never fail you.

❖   ❖   ❖

DAY 354 – "FORGIVE US OUR DEBTS"

(Lord's Day 51, Q&A 126, part 1)

Q. What does the fifth petition mean?
A. "Forgive us our debts, as we also have forgiven our debtors"
means: Because of Christ's blood, do not hold against us . . . any of
the sins we do.

We have to remember that the Lord's Prayer is a collective prayer; it starts with *"Our* Father," and it says, "Forgive *us our* debts." I mention this because, when we pray individually to God, we do not simply ask for forgiveness. That would be too cheap; we would thus get away with our sins too easily. The Bible encourages us to *confess* our sins, and then the Lord *will* forgive them: "If we confess our sins, he is faithful and just to forgive us our sins and to cleanse us from all unrighteousness" (1 John 1:9). When, as a boy, I asked my Dad to forgive me, he would invariably answer: *"What* do I have to forgive 'me'?" This forced me to put my trespasses into words!

This is confession. This is what we should do one toward the other ("confess your sins to one another," James 5:16), and this is what we should do toward God. It was the same under the Law of Moses: the trespasser "realizes his guilt in any of these and confesses the sin he has committed" (Lev. 5:5; cf. 16:21; 26:40; Num. 5:7). David said, "I acknowledged my sin to you, and I did not cover my iniquity; I said, 'I will confess my transgressions to the Lord,' and you forgave the iniquity of my sin" (Ps. 32:5). "I confess my iniquity; I am sorry for my sin" (38:18). Don't say, But I cannot possibly remember all my sins! Or I am not always aware *that* certain actions are sins! Okay, in that case you can pray, "Who can discern his errors? Declare me innocent from hidden faults" (Ps. 19:12).

The reason why we may with certainty expect the Father to forgive us our debts is because of his Son's blood: "[T]he blood of Jesus his Son cleanses us from all sin" (1 John 1:7). On the one hand, John encourages us *not* to sin. We have received a new life, and we have the Holy Spirit dwelling in us; we have no excuse for sin. We have been freed from the power of sin (cf. Rom. 6:7, 18, 22). On the other hand, "[I]f anyone does sin, we have an advocate with the Father, Jesus Christ the righteous. He is the propitiation for our sins" (1 John 2:1–2). The blood of Jesus, our advocate, is constantly pleading for us before the Father!

✦　　✦　　✦

DAY 355 – "POOR SINNERS"
(Lord's Day 51, Q&A 126, part 2)

A. . . . poor sinners that we are . . . the evil that constantly clings to us.

Can a true Christian still be called a sinner? From the *positional* viewpoint, the answer is No. As Paul says, "God shows his love for us in that while we *were* still sinners, Christ died for us" (Rom. 5:8). Apparently, now we are no longer sinners. That is, we may still sin, but we are not in the power of sin anymore (cf. 6:7, 18, 22). But from a *practical* viewpoint, if a believer falls into sin, and cannot even help himself out, he *is* called a sinner: "My brothers, if anyone among you wanders from the truth and someone brings him back, let him know that whoever brings back a *sinner* from his wandering will save his soul from death and will cover a multitude of sins" (James 5:19–20).

This is the continual tension we must live with: no longer sinners, and yet—sometimes sinners again. It is the tension that John describes: "No one born of God makes a practice of sinning . . . he cannot keep on sinning because he has been born of God" (1 John 3:9; cf. 5:18). But also: "If we say we have no sin, we deceive ourselves, and the truth is not in us" (1:8). James says, "[T]he one who looks into the perfect law, the law of liberty, and perseveres, being . . . a doer who acts, he will be blessed in his doing" (1:25). But also: "[W]e all stumble in many ways" (3:2).

Paul says, "There is therefore now no condemnation for those who are in Christ Jesus. For the law of the Spirit of life has set you free in Christ Jesus from the law of sin and death" (Rom. 8:1–2). But a few verses earlier (describing the believer who does not live by the power of the Holy Spirit): "So I find it to be a law that when I want to do right, evil lies close at hand. For I delight in the law of God, in my inner being, but I see in my members another law waging war against the law of my mind and making me captive to the law of sin that dwells in my members. Wretched man that I am! Who will deliver me from this body of death? Thanks be to God through Jesus Christ our Lord! So then, I myself serve the law of God with my mind, but with my flesh I serve the law of sin" (7:21–25). This is the tension we must live with!

✢   ✢   ✢

DAY 356 – DETERMINED TO FORGIVE
(Lord's Day 51, Q&A 126, part 3)

A. Forgive us just as we are fully determined . . . to forgive our neighbors.

It is of great interest that the Lord's Prayer makes God's forgiveness dependent on our preparedness to forgive each other. To enjoy the assurance of our Father's forgiveness, there are at least these three conditions (apart from contrition, confession, and faith in Christ). First, we have to believingly *accept* this forgiveness from God on account of the work of Christ.

Second, we have to forgive *ourselves*. Some people want to be "holier" than God in that they have difficulty accepting his forgiveness, given the gravity of their sins. We encourage them by showing to them that God forgave even the "foremost" of all sinners (1 Tim. 1:15). Jesus prayed for his worst enemies: "Father, forgive them, for they know not what they do" (Luke 23:34). It is said of the great sins of Israel that God casts them "into the depths of the sea" (Micah 7:19), and: "I will forgive their iniquity, and I will remember their sin no more" (Jer. 31:34). So what person would wish to be wiser than God by claiming that his or her sins are too great to be forgiven?

The third condition is that we forgive our neighbors. If we refuse to do that, why would God forgive *us*? The parable of the unforgiving servant ends as follows: "So also my heavenly Father will do to every one of you [viz., punish you forever], if you do not forgive your brother from your heart" (Matt. 18:35). That is, you should not just forgive your neighbor reluctantly, with bad grace, but wholeheartedly. This is possible only if we begin to realize that *our numerous* sins toward God are infinitely graver than our *neighbor's few* sins toward us. I think too few Christians truly realize how strongly God condemns an unforgiving attitude! "Be kind to one another, tenderhearted, forgiving one another, *as God in Christ forgave you*" (Eph. 4:32). "Put on then, as God's chosen ones, holy and beloved, compassionate hearts, kindness, humility, meekness, and patience, bearing with one another and, if one has a complaint against another, forgiving each other; *as the Lord has forgiven you*, so you also must forgive" (Col. 3:12–13).

✢ ✢ ✢

DAY 357 – EVIDENCE OF GOD'S GRACE
(Lord's Day 51, Q&A 126, part 4)

A. Forgive us just as we are fully determined, as evidence of your grace in us, to forgive our neighbors.

You could mention hardly any blessing that God gives his children that they are not supposed to pass on to others. God forgave us, so we forgive others what they have done to us. God redeemed us, so we "redeem" others who have gotten into some spiritual bondage toward us by their misdoings. God grants us love, grace, mercy, righteousness, peace, joy, patience, meekness; we (by the power of the Holy Spirit) grant others love, grace, mercy, righteousness, peace, joy, patience, meekness. God does not "have to" forgive us; if he does so, he does it wholeheartedly, not reluctantly or grudgingly. It is the same with us. We do not forgive others the wrongs they have done against us because some "law" forces us to do so. We do not forgive reluctantly or grudgingly, because such forgiveness is no true biblical forgiveness.

I remember a Christian sister saying to someone in a sharp tone: "I forgive you, but I will never forget what you did!" This is not forgiving wholeheartedly. True forgiveness involves forgetting; not in the literal sense, of course, but in the sense of never holding it against the other person anymore. This is what God means when he says, "I will forgive their iniquity, and I will remember their sin no more" (Jer. 31:34; cf. Heb. 8:12; 10:17).

This attitude of forgiveness may also involve *allowing* others to forgive *us*, even if we are hardly conscious of any sins toward those others: "[I]f you are offering your gift at the altar and there remember that your brother has something *against you* [not the other way around!], leave your gift there before the altar and go. First be reconciled to your brother, and then come and offer your gift. Come to terms quickly with your accuser while you are going with him to court, lest your accuser hand you over to the judge, and the judge to the guard, and you be put in prison. Truly, I say to you, you will never get out until you have paid the last penny" (Matt. 5:23–26). You go to your brother not only to forgive *him*, but also to find out what he may have against *you*, so that you can make a confession (if necessary), and he can forgive you!

✥   ✥   ✥

DAY 358 – "NO TEMPTATION"

(LORD'S DAY 52, Q&A 127, PART 1)

Q. What does the sixth petition mean?
A. "And lead us not into temptation, but deliver us from evil"
means: By ourselves we are too weak to hold our own even for a mo-
ment.

I have quoted the ESV in the Catechism, while the CRC version of 2011 says, "And do not bring us to the time of trial, but rescue us from the evil one." Some translations avoid the word "temptation" because it seems to suggest that God *might* allow some seduction to sin; why else ask him not to do so? But James says, "Let no one say when he is tempted, 'I am being tempted by God,' for God cannot be tempted with evil, and he himself tempts no one. But each person is tempted when he is lured and enticed by his own desire" (1:13–14).

The problem is that "temptation" is an ambiguous term. In the same chapter, James says, "Count it all joy, my brothers, when you meet trials of various kinds, for you know that the testing of your faith produces steadfastness. . . . Blessed is the man who remains steadfast under trial, for when he has stood the test he will receive the crown of life, which God has promised to those who love him" (vv. 2–3, 12). In Greek, the word for "trial" is the same as that for "temptation"! What James apparently means is that God never tempts us with evil, but that he does tempt us in the sense of allowing trials to test our faith. This is also the meaning in Genesis 22:1, "After these things God tested Abraham [or "put Abraham to the test]," where other translations have "tempted" (KJV).

It is clear that the Lord's Prayer does not intend that we pray for God to avert all trials for us, and will never put our faith to the test. That would be a wrong prayer because such trials, necessary for our education, will definitely come. But we do pray that the trials will never develop to the point where we would be seduced to sin. This is why Jesus told his disciples in Gethsemane, "Watch and pray that you may not enter into temptation. The spirit indeed is willing, but the flesh is weak" (Matt. 26:41). This is what Paul refers to: "No temptation has overtaken you that is not common to man. God is faithful, and he will not let you be tempted beyond your ability, but with the temptation he will also provide the way of escape, that you may be able to endure it" (1 Cor. 10:13).

✦   ✦   ✦

DAY 359 – "OUR SWORN ENEMIES"
(Lord's Day 52, Q&A 127, part 2)

A. And our sworn enemies—the devil, the world, and our own flesh—never stop attacking us.

The spiritual battle of believers is both a defensive and an offensive spiritual battle. It is defensive insofar as "the devil, the world, and our own flesh never stop attacking us." This defensive battle is described often. Concerning the devil: "Put on the whole armor of God, that you may be able to stand against the schemes of the *devil*. For we do not wrestle against flesh and blood, but against the rulers, against the authorities, against the cosmic powers over this present darkness, against the spiritual forces of evil in the heavenly places" (Eph. 6:11–12). Concerning the world: "If the *world* hates you, know that it has hated me before it hated you. . . . I chose you out of the world, therefore the world hates you" (John 15:18–19). Concerning our own flesh: "I see in my members another law waging war against the law of my mind and making me captive to the law of sin that dwells in my members" (Rom. 7:23). "[T]he desires of the *flesh* are against the Spirit, and the desires of the Spirit are against the flesh, for these are opposed to each other, to keep you from doing the things you want to do" (Gal. 5:17).

However, let us never forget that we are not just defending ourselves; in the power of the Spirit there is also an *offensive* spiritual battle. For instance, believers must be "standing firm in one spirit, with one mind *striving* side by side for the faith of the gospel, and not frightened in anything by your opponents. . . . For it has been granted to you that for the sake of Christ you should not only believe in him but also suffer for his sake, engaged in the same *conflict* that you saw I had and now hear that I still have" (Phil. 1:27–30). Or this: "[Christ] we proclaim, warning everyone and teaching everyone with all wisdom, that we may present everyone mature in Christ. For this I *toil, struggling* with all his energy that he powerfully works within me. For I want you to know how great a *struggle* I have for you and for those at Laodicea and for all who have not seen me face to face, that their hearts may be encouraged" (Col. 1:28–2:2).

✠   ✠   ✠

DAY 360 – OVERCOMING IN STRUGGLE
(Lord's Day 52, Q&A 127, part 3)

A. And so, Lord, uphold us and make us strong with the strength of your Holy Spirit, so that we may not go down to defeat in this spiritual struggle.

The "strength of God's Holy Spirit" is the secret of our spiritual battle. The answer to this word: "I see in my members a . . . law waging war against the law of my mind and making me captive to the law of sin that dwells in my members. Wretched man that I am! Who will deliver me from this body of death?" (Rom. 7:23–24), is this: "Thanks be to God through Jesus Christ our Lord! . . . There is therefore now no condemnation for those who are in Christ Jesus. For the law of the *Spirit of life* has set you free in Christ Jesus from the law of sin and death" (Rom. 7:25—8:2).

The "young men" in faith have had their individual victories over the "evil one" (1 John 2:13–14)—that is the devil—and in the Spirit's power they will also be able to prevail over that other danger, the "world": "Do not love the world or the things in the world . . . [A]ll that is in the world—the desires of the flesh and the desires of the eyes and pride of life—is not from the Father but is from the world. And the world is passing away along with its desires, but whoever does the will of God abides forever" (vv. 15–17).

Paul says it this way: "[W]alk by the Spirit, and you will not gratify the desires of the flesh. For the desires of the flesh are against the Spirit, and the desires of the Spirit are against the flesh, for these are opposed to each other, to keep you from doing the things you want to do. But if you are led by the Spirit, you are not under the law. . . . [T]he fruit of the Spirit is love, joy, peace, patience, kindness, goodness, faithfulness, gentleness, self-control; against such things there is no law. And those who belong to Christ Jesus have crucified the flesh with its passions and desires" (Gal. 5:16–24).

This makes clear what the prayer is essentially about: we need no *passive* redemption from evil, but we need the *active* strength of the Holy Spirit to combat it! If you do not have enough of such strength, remember Jesus' promise (Luke 11:13): "If you then, who are evil, know how to give good gifts to your children, how much more will the heavenly Father give the Holy Spirit to those who ask him!"

✦   ✦   ✦

DAY 361 – THE COMPLETE VICTORY
(Lord's Day 52, Q&A 127, part 4)

A. . . . so that we may not go down to defeat in this spiritual struggle, but may firmly resist our enemies until we finally win the complete victory.

*I*n principle, the victory over sin, death, the devil, and world was already gained on the cross of Calvary, when, first, "the body of sin" was "brought to nothing" (Rom. 6:6). Second, Christ "abolished death" (2 Tim. 1:10). Third, he destroyed "the one who has the power of death, that is, the devil" (Heb. 2:14); and, fourth, on the way to the cross he said, "I have overcome the world" (John 16:33). But this was "in principle." In practice, sin, death, the devil, and world seem as powerful as ever. However, it is like a chicken whose head has been cut off. It may still run around for a while, but soon it will fall down. Two thousand years may seem a long period, but for God they are not: "a thousand years in your sight are but as yesterday when it is past" (Ps.90:4); "with the Lord one day is as a thousand years, and a thousand years as one day" (2 Pet. 3:8).

"After two days he will revive us; on the third day he will raise us up, that we may live before him" (Hos. 6:2). Sin, death, the devil, and world may have been running around for two "days" with their heads cut off, but when Jesus will appear, they will finally have to surrender. As to sin: "[W]e are waiting for new heavens and a new earth in which righteousness dwells" (2 Pet. 3:13); sin will have been taken away from the cosmos (John 1:29). As to death: "Death and Hades were thrown into the lake of fire" (Rev. 20:14), as will happen to the devil as well (v. 10). And as to the world: "[T]he world is passing away along with its desires" (1 John 2:17).

The believers are involved in the final victory; as the Catechism says, we "firmly resist our enemies until *we* finally win the complete victory." Paul says, "The God of peace will soon crush Satan under your feet" (Rom. 16:20). And John says, "Then I saw heaven opened, and behold, a white horse! The one sitting on it is called Faithful and True, and in righteousness he judges and makes war. . . . And the armies of heaven, arrayed in fine linen, white and pure, were following him on white horses" (Rev. 19:11–14, assuming that these are believers, not angels).

✤   ✤   ✤

DAY 362 – THE PRAYER'S CONCLUSION
(Lord's Day 52, Q&A 128, part 1)

Q. What does your conclusion to this prayer mean?
A. "For yours is the kingdom and the power and the glory, forever"
means: We have made all these petitions of you because, as our all-powerful king, you are both willing and able to give us all that is
good.

The concluding words of the Lord's Prayer are lacking in modern editions of the Greek New Testament; very probably they have been added to later manuscripts for liturgical reasons, after early Christians had been accustomed to saying the Lord's Prayer in church (see Day 337). If this is correct, it is quite worthwhile to maintain them for precisely these reasons. At the end of the prayer, it is highly fitting to bring to God a word of praise and worship by celebrating him as the all-powerful and all-glorious King of the universe. This is the way numerous Jewish prayers begin: "Blessed are you, our Lord God, King of the universe. . . ." It underscores the fact that both Jews and Christians direct their prayers to a God who is not only willing but also able to answer them and give believers "all that is good," as the Catechism says.

These closing words strongly remind us of king David's prayer: "Blessed are you, O LORD, the God of Israel *our father*, forever and ever. Yours, O LORD, is the greatness and the *power* and the *glory* and the victory and the majesty, for all that is *in the heavens* and *in the earth* is yours. *Yours is the kingdom*, O LORD, and you are exalted as head above all. Both riches and honor come from you, and you rule over all. In your hand are power and might, and in your hand it is to make great and to give strength to all. And now we thank you, our God, and praise your glorious *name*" (1 Chron. 29:10–13; cf. Ps. 145:11; Dan. 2:37). I have italicized all the words in this prayer that we also find in the Lord's Prayer.

Prophetically speaking, David uttered these words in view of the great kingdom of his son, king Solomon, David and Solomon together constituting a wonderful double-type of Christ, the great King of kings. Every time we say, "Yours is the kingdom," we think of the glorious Kingdom of the Father (cf. Matt. 13:43; 25:34; 26:29), "in the dispensation of the fullness of the times," in which he will "gather together in one all things in Christ, both which are in heaven and which are on earth" (Eph. 1:10 NKJV). What a day will that be!

※   ※   ※

DAY 363 – TO GOD ALL PRAISE
(Lord's Day 52, Q&A 128, part 2)

A. . . . *and because your holy name, and not we ourselves, should receive all the praise, forever.*

The Westminster Larger Catechism begins with this: "Man's chief and highest end is to glorify God, and fully to enjoy him forever." These words strikingly correspond with Q&A 6 of the Roman Catholic Baltimore Catechism: "God made me to know Him, to love Him, and to serve Him in this world, and to be happy with Him for ever in heaven."

Whatever we are going to do in the coming eternity, two things will be certain: we will eternally glorify, praise, and worship God, and we will "enjoy" him forever, "be happy with him for ever in heaven." We may add that believers can experience this already now: enjoy God in the intimacy of our relationship with him (1 John 1:3–4). This is even a prerequisite for true worship. How could we expect a person to enthusiastically praise and worship God if he were not "happy" with him? Why would two lovers say sweet things to each other if they were not happy with each other? True praise presupposes communion, fellowship, relationship, intimacy, love. The Lord's Prayer may have a collective character ("our," "us"), but it is also a very intimate prayer.

This praise is even mutual. To be sure, as the Catechism indicates, we ourselves do not deserve any praise; all worship is due to God. Yet, the Lord tells his faithful: "Well done, good and faithful servant" (Matt. 25:21, 23; cf. Luke 19:17). There is mutual appreciation. Our praise is a token of our love for God; but how could this love be maintained if we were not convinced of his love for *us*? In the Song of Solomon, the praises of the bride regarding the bridegroom are counter-balanced by *his* praises regarding *her*. True praise can never be extorted from someone; it must be the spontaneous utterance of appreciation, admiration, if not love. We are to him "a lily among brambles" (Song 2:2), he is to us as "an apple tree among the trees of the forest" (v. 3). Christ's Bride is *everything* to him, as our Bridegroom is everything to *us*. In the everlasting language of love, we will keep praising each other, speaking to each other about the other's beauty and magnificence. How glorious that will be!

✤   ✤   ✤

DAY 364 – THE CLOSING AMEN

(LORD'S DAY 52, Q&A 129, PART I)

Q. What does that little word "Amen" express?
A. "Amen" means: This shall truly and surely be!

The word "Amen" is one of a few Hebrew words found in the Greek New Testament; others are Hallelujah, Hosanna, Mammon, Sabbath, Sabaoth. "Amen" is related to the Hebrew word for "truth" and involves a kind of confirmation, such as "It is true," or "It shall truly be." We find it at the end of prayers (like the Lord's Prayer; also cf. Rom. 15:33; Gal. 6:18) or doxologies (1 Chron. 16:36; Neh. 8:6; etc.; Rom. 1:25; 9:5; 11:36; Gal. 1:5; etc.), or certain exclamations (Deut. 27:15–26; Neh. 5:13; etc.). We say "Amen" to the prayers of others if we can agree with them (1 Cor. 14:16), thus saying as it were, "So it is!" or "So it may be!" We say "Amen" to the promises of God (2 Cor. 1:20), thus expressing our firm expectation that they will be truly fulfilled. Knowing God means knowing that what he says will come true.

There are many things in our lives that are very uncertain. We might not even know for sure what God wants, or will do, in certain circumstances. That is, we might not be sure of God's "ways" with us or with the world—but we can be very sure of his "counsels." We might not be sure *how* he will accomplish them, but we are sure *that* he will fulfill "his purpose, which he set forth in Christ as a plan for the fullness of time, to unite all things in him, things in heaven and things on earth" (Eph. 1:9–10). We might not be certain about all the details, but we *are* certain that one day he "delivers the kingdom to God the Father after destroying every rule and every authority and power. For he must reign until he has put all his enemies under his feet. . . . For 'God has put all things in subjection under his feet.' . . . When all things are subjected to him, then the Son himself will also be subjected to him who put all things in subjection under him, that God may be all in all" (1 Cor. 15:24–28).

Christians are not sure about their itineraries; but they can be sure about their destination: the Kingdom of God. He is "declaring the end from the beginning and from ancient times things not yet done, saying, 'My counsel shall stand, and I will accomplish all my purpose'" (Isa. 46:10).

✢   ✢   ✢

DAY 365 – GOD ANSWERS PRAYERS!

(Lord's Day 52, Q&A 129, part 2)

A. It is even more sure that God listens to my prayer than that I really desire what I pray for.

What a great statement to end the Heidelberg Catechism with! Not only can I be sure of God, but I can even be surer of him than I can be of myself. He knows me, as well as my desires and motives, better than I know myself. I have often asked Christian adolescents about who knew them best: they themselves, or their Moms. Roughly half of them were of the opinion that Mom knew them better than they knew themselves. Of course, ten years later this would have changed drastically. But with believers it remains always this: God knows (understands, sees through) them better than they do themselves.

This is one of the great things about the tribunal of Christ (cf. Rom. 14:10; 2 Cor. 5:10): "Now I know in part; then I shall know fully, even as I have been fully known" (1 Cor. 13:12). One day we will reign with Christ. But how will we be able to do this as long as we do not see all things the way he sees them, know all things the way he knows them? And how will this be possible as long as we do not know ourselves the way he knows us? This is one reason why God's tribunal is so precious to us.

Today it is still different. We "know in part," including knowing ourselves. We pray in the awareness that God knows better what is at the bottom of our hearts than we know ourselves. With Peter we say to the Lord: "Lord, you know everything; you know that I love you" (John 21:17). Even if we do not always properly show this love, the Lord sees it is there. With David we pray, "Search me, O God, and know my heart! Try me and know my thoughts! And see if there be any grievous way in me, and lead me in the way everlasting!" (Ps. 139:23–24; cf. Deut. 8:2; 1 Chron. 29:17). And Solomon said, "[Y]ou, you only, know the hearts of the children of mankind" (2 Chron. 6:30; cf. 32:31). God "knows the secrets of the heart" (Ps. 44:21; cf. Jer. 12:3; Acts 1:24; 15:8; Rev. 2:23).

Thus the Catechism ends with a note of intimacy. God knows us, and yet he loves us. He will know and love us forever, and we will know and love him. This is our prospect: everlasting understanding, everlasting intimacy, everlasting love!

INDEX OF SCRIPTURE PASSAGES

Proverbs 11:1	312	Isaiah 64:6	200
Proverbs 12:17	317	Jeremiah 2:2	282
Proverbs 12:22	316	Jeremiah 4:1-2	292
Proverbs 19:5	316	Jeremiah 5:24	81
Proverbs 20:4	81, 352	Jeremiah 12:3	365
Proverbs 20:20	300	Jeremiah 13:23	25
Proverbs 21:1	80, 88	Jeremiah 16:7	233, 245
Proverbs 22:1	318	Jeremiah 17:5, 7	283, 353
Proverbs 22:2	81	Jeremiah 17:9	16, 305,
Proverbs 23:20-21	308		319
Proverbs 23:22	300	Jeremiah 17:10	306
Proverbs 23:25	302	Jeremiah 20	84
Proverbs 23:26	12	Jeremiah 23:24	80, 149,
Proverbs 25:21	163, 303		340
Proverbs 28:13	8, 266	Jeremiah 31:31-34	171, 178,
Proverbs 29:24	291		227, 273,
Proverbs 30:8	338		308, 356,
			357
		Jeremiah 32:19	306
Ecclesiastes 3:13	195		
Ecclesiastes 5:19	195		
Ecclesiastes 7:1	318	Ezekiel 18:20	22, 40
Ecclesiastes 7:20	179, 189	Ezekiel 18:31	56
Ecclesiastes 9:10	275	Ezekiel 20:18-19	277
Ecclesiastes 9:11	83	Ezekiel 22:30	44
Ecclesiastes 10:11	21	Ezekiel 28:13-15	350
		Ezekiel 33:11	56
		Ezekiel 36:23	342
Song of Solomon 1:3	318	Ezekiel 36:26-27	60, 324
Song of Solomon 2:2	363	Ezekiel 41:22	238, 248
Song of Solomon 2:3-5	242	Ezekiel 44:16	238, 248
Song of Solomon 5:10	284	Ezekiel 45:9-12	312
Song of Solomon 5:16	284		
Song of Solomon 7:8	242	Daniel 2:37	362
Song of Solomon 7:10	61	Daniel 4:26	254, 292
Song of Solomon 8:14	348	Daniel 5:23	80, 88
		Daniel 6:10	188
		Daniel 7:13	150, 344
Isaiah 9:6-7	55, 75	Daniel 9:4	273
Isaiah 14:9	183	Daniel 12:1-2	4, 130,
Isaiah 14:13-14	27		172, 185
Isaiah 45:14-15, 21	70		
Isaiah 53	53, 213	Hosea 6:2	361
Isaiah 58:7	314	Hosea 9:7	94
Isaiah 61:10	193	Hosea 13:14	129
Isaiah 64:4	187	Hosea 14:2	263

1 Timothy 2:14	28	Titus 3:3	16
1 Timothy 3:1	353	Titus 3:4-6	74
1 Timothy 3:6	27, 350	Titus 3:5	167, 206, 214, 222, 240
1 Timothy 3:11	316		
1 Timothy 3:13-17	297	Titus 3:7	189, 191
1 Timothy 3:16	67	Titus 3:10	248
1 Timothy 4:4-5	154, 329, 351	Titus 3:14	276
1 Timothy 4:13	298		
1 Timothy 5:10	318		
1 Timothy 5:17	297	Hebrews 1:1-2	55
1 Timothy 6:6-8	77, 154, 332, 351	Hebrews 1:2	39, 76
1 Timothy 6:10	313	Hebrews 1:3	143
1 Timothy 6:11	265, 325	Hebrews 1:6	103
1 Timothy 6:12	4, 101	Hebrews 1:13	161
1 Timothy 6:13	317	Hebrews 1:17	100
1 Timothy 6:16	126	Hebrews 2:4	166
1 Timothy 6:17-19	314	Hebrews 2:5-8	102, 155, 158, 190, 344
1 Timothy 6:18	276		
		Hebrews 2:8	96
		Hebrews 2:14	2, 45, 49, 107, 111, 113, 126, 346, 361
2 Timothy 1:10	2, 129, 138, 361		
2 Timothy 2:2	297		
2 Timothy 2:11	128	Hebrews 2:15	119
2 Timothy 2:12	102, 155	Hebrews 2:16-17	113
2 Timothy 2:19-20	257	Hebrews 2:17	54, 95, 139
2 Timothy 2:21	273, 276	Hebrews 2:18	113, 151
2 Timothy 2:22	265, 325	Hebrews 4:2	58
2 Timothy 2:24-26	261	Hebrews 4:11	325
2 Timothy 3:3	316	Hebrews 4:15	45, 95, 113, 137, 151
2 Timothy 3:5	258, 259		
2 Timothy 4:1	145, 162	Hebrews 4:16	59
2 Timothy 4:8	45, 162, 202	Hebrews 5:6, 10	95, 294
		Hebrews 5:7	137
		Hebrews 5:8	194
Titus 1:1-2	172	Hebrews 6:1	24, 199, 220, 274
Titus 1:5-11	251	Hebrews 6:4	223, 258
Titus 1:9	353	Hebrews 6:5	190, 344
Titus 2:4	309	Hebrews 6:13-14	294
Titus 2:7	276	Hebrews 6:20	95
Titus 2:11	56	Hebrews 7:11, 17	95
Titus 2:12	154	Hebrews 7:25	95, 144, 331
Titus 2:13-14	42, 46, 49, 63, 70, 74, 108, 109, 170, 181, 199, 202	Hebrews 7:26	113, 114
		Hebrews 7:27	246
		Hebrews 8	171
		Hebrews 8:1-2	144, 340
Titus 3:1	273, 276, 301, 304	Hebrews 8:6	44

CPSIA information can be obtained
at www.ICGtesting.com
Printed in the USA
FFOW04n2228010216
20907FF